The Purcell Compendium

The Boydell Composer Compendium Series

The aim of the Composer Compendium series is to provide up-to-date reference works on major composers and their music that can both provide instant information and act as a gateway to further reading. The authors are all leading authorities on the composers in question who have been given the remit not only to assemble and present already existing data but also, where appropriate, to make personal interpretations, to introduce new facts and arguments and to shed light on the many discourses surrounding the chosen musicians from their lifetime up to the present day.

The core of each volume is a dictionary section with entries for people, institutions and places connected with the composer; musical, analytical and historical terminology of particular relevance to them; significant events in the reception history of their music; the genres in which they composed; individual compositions or groups of compositions – in short, anyone and anything judged to be pertinent. Entries in the dictionary section are carefully cross-referenced to each other and also to a very comprehensive bibliography section at the end of the volume. Between the dictionary and the bibliography there is a work list based on the latest information, and the volume is prefaced by a concise biography of the composer. Numerous music examples and illustrations are included. By means of this simple formula, the series aims to provide handbooks of wide and durable interest responding to the needs of scholars, performers and music-lovers alike.

Michael Talbot
Series editor

Proposals are welcomed and should be sent in the first instance to the publisher at the address below. All submissions will receive prompt and informed consideration.

Boydell & Brewer, PO Box 9, Woodbridge, Suffolk, IP12 3DF
email: editorial@boydell.co.uk

Previous volumes in this series:

The Vivaldi Compendium, Michael Talbot, 2011
(Also available in paperback)
The Rameau Compendium, Graham Sadler, 2014
(Also available in paperback)
The Janáček Compendium, Nigel Simeone, 2019
The Telemann Compendium, Steven Zohn, 2020

The Purcell Compendium

Peter Holman and Bryan White

THE BOYDELL PRESS

© Peter Holman and Bryan White 2025

All Rights Reserved. Except as permitted under current legislation no part of this work may be photocopied, stored in a retrieval system, published, performed in public, adapted, broadcast, transmitted, recorded or reproduced in any form or by any means, without the prior permission of the copyright owner

The right of Peter Holman and Bryan White to be identified as the authors of this work has been asserted in accordance with sections 77 and 78 of the Copyright, Designs and Patents Act 1988

First published 2025
The Boydell Press, Woodbridge

ISBN 978 1 83765 268 6

The Boydell Press is an imprint of Boydell & Brewer Ltd
PO Box 9, Woodbridge, Suffolk IP12 3DF, UK
and of Boydell & Brewer Inc.
668 Mt Hope Avenue, Rochester, NY 14620-2731, USA
website: www.boydellandbrewer.com

Our Authorised Representative for product safety in the EU is
Easy Access System Europe - Mustamäe tee 50, 10621 Tallinn, Estonia,
gpsr.requests@easproject.com

A CIP catalogue record for this book is available
from the British Library

The publisher has no responsibility for the continued existence or accuracy of URLs for external or third-party internet websites referred to in this book, and does not guarantee that any content on such websites is, or will remain, accurate or appropriate

For Olive and Thelma

Contents

viii   List of Illustrations

x   List of Music Examples

xi   Introduction

1   Biography

15   Dictionary

207   Works

245   Bibliography

Illustrations

1. First page of the last will and testament of Henry Purcell, 21 November 1695, with his signature in the lower right-hand corner, GB-Tna, PROB 1/8; reproduced by the permission of the National Archives, London.   14

2. Letitia Cross, engraved by John Smith after a painting by Thomas Hill (*c.*1700); © The Trustees of the British Museum.   51

3. Henry Purcell, *The Vocal and Instrumental Musick of the Prophetess, or the History of Dioclesian* (1691), p. 3, Second Music; © Google Books.   59

4. Thomas D'Urfey, anonymous engraving after a painting by Gerard van der Gucht; © Yale Library Digital Collections.   66

5. Annabella Howard, engraved by John Smith after a painting by Godfrey Kneller (1697); courtesy of the Lewis Walpole Library; © Yale Library Digital Collections.   92

6. Arabella Hunt, engraved by John Smith after a painting by Godfrey Kneller (1706); courtesy of the Lewis Walpole Library; © Yale Library Digital Collections.   93

7. An example of 'Double Descant' in Purcell's 'The Art of Descant' from Playford's *Introduction to the Skill of Musick* (1697). The passage is by Carlo Ambrogio Lonati, wrongly attributed by Purcell to Lelio Colista; reproduced with the permission of Special Collections, Leeds University Library.   108

8. Roger North, engraved by George Vertue (1740) after a painting by Peter Lely; © National Portrait Gallery, London.   119

9. John Dryden, *An Ode, on the Death of Mr. Henry Purcell* (1696); reproduced with the permission of Special Collections, Leeds University Library.   125

10. Henry Purcell, bass part of the Pavan in F minor in the composer's hand, US-NHb, Osborn MS 515, f. 9r; © Yale Library Digital Collections.   131

11. John Playford, engraved by David Loggan (1680); © National Portrait Gallery, London.   141

12. Henry Purcell, engraved by Robert White (1683); © National Portrait Gallery, London.   143

13. The interior of St Bride's Church showing the organ case made by Renatus Harris (1694) in the west gallery, *Round London: An Album of Pictures from Photographs of the Chief Places of Interest in and Round London* (1896).   158

14. Saul, the ghost of Samuel and the Witch of Endor, engraved by William Faithorne, from Joseph Glanvill, *Saducismus Triumphatus* (1682); Boston Public Library; © Internet Archive Books.   160

15. View of Whitehall Palace from above the River Thames, drawn by Leonard Knyff (*c*.1695); © The Trustees of the British Museum.   199

The authors and publisher are grateful to all the institutions and individuals listed for permission to reproduce the materials in which they hold copyright. Every effort has been made to trace the copyright holders; apologies are offered for any omission, and the publisher will be pleased to add any necessary acknowledgement in subsequent editions.

Music Examples

1. Trio Sonata in C major Z795, bb. 1–7.   33

2. Three Parts upon a Ground Z731A, b. 18.   60

3. Purcell's keyboard setting of 'La Furstemberg'.   77

4. The solo bass part of 'They that go down to the sea in ships' Z57, bb. 40–8.   81

5. Jig from *The Gordion Knot Unty'd* Z597/5, with 'Lilliburlero' in the bass.   106

6. Purcell's version of 'There's not a swain on the plain'.   114

7. (a) Chaconne from *The Gordion Knot Unty'd* Z597/6, bb. 31–40, compared with (b) the bass part of the version in Osborn MS 515.   154

8. The bass and continuo parts of the Largo from Trio Sonata in E minor Z796/4, bb. 11–14.   155

9. Purcell's keyboard setting of J.B. Lully, 'Scocca pur tutti tuoi strali', bb. 1–5.   175

10. 'From rosy bowers' Z578/9, bb. 1–14.   203

Introduction

A compendium or encyclopedia devoted to a single composer is the ultimate accolade from the scholarly community. After the complete works, the biographies, the critical and source studies and the scholarly conferences, a single volume consisting mainly of dictionary-style entries relating to various aspects of the life, works and reputation is a convenient way of summarising the accumulated scholarship devoted to a great composer. In Henry Purcell's case, this volume appears 30 years after the tercentenary of the composer's death in 1995, so it is a good moment to take stock. 1995 produced a spate of new Purcell biographies, none of them detailed and authoritative enough to replace Franklin B. Zimmerman's classic but ageing *ZimPur* – to use the bibliographic code explained below. Our brief *Biography* is intended only as a stopgap: there is an urgent need for a new full-length treatment, taking account of recent archival work and source studies, and in particular deploying a more sophisticated understanding than in the past of Purcell's milieu and his relationships with his family, colleagues and patrons. However, readers will notice that we frequently cite chapters from the two volumes of scholarly essays produced for the tercentenary, *PurStu* and *PMHP*, the latter the proceedings of a conference held at New College, Oxford in 1994.

A few years later, in 2000, Robert Shay and Robert Thompson revolutionised our knowledge of Purcell's manuscripts with *ShaMan*, work subsequently built upon by Rebecca Herissone in *HerCre*; in her invaluable online appendix *HerCat*; and in a series of ground-breaking articles, notably *HerFow* of 2006. Another anniversary, the 350th of Purcell's birth in 2009, failed to produce much of note, though chapters in Herissone's *ARCHP* of 2012 are frequently cited here, as is Alan Howard's *HowArt* of 2020, the most important recent contribution to our understanding of Purcell's approach to composition. Our aim is not to be comprehensive in the *Bibliography* (that would require a volume much larger than this one), but to reflect the best current Purcell scholarship in all its diversity.

In deciding what to include in our *Dictionary*, the bulk of this compendium, we have found room for individual entries for all of Purcell's odes and the major stage works, though we have had to be selective for smaller pieces, singling them out for their quality; for their historical significance; or sometimes (as with the Toccata in A major and 'When Night her purple veil') because their authorship is open to question. However, the list of *Works* includes only those we consider genuine, or at least plausibly attributed to Henry Purcell. We have also covered the range of Purcell's output with entries surveying the various genres he contributed to; with those explaining the titles and terms he used (or used today by Purcell scholars); and with those devoted to the instruments he wrote for. Furthermore, there are individual entries for important performance-practice issues (including Ornamentation, Pitch, Temperament and Tempo); those devoted to the most important primary manuscript and printed sources of Purcell's music; and those describing the institutions he worked for and the buildings he worked in.

Crucial strands of the *Dictionary* are those allocated to people associated with Purcell. We include a selection of entries devoted to earlier composers known or thought to have influenced him (Monteverdi and Orlando Gibbons, for example); his composer colleagues (such as John Blow and Giovanni Battista Draghi); the most prominent of his fellow performers, particularly his solo singers and dancers (e.g. Jemmy Bowen, John Gostling and Josias Priest); the most important copyists, publishers and instrument makers associated with him (e.g. John Walter, John and Henry Playford and Bernard Smith); his patrons and employers (from Charles II and his family to Christopher Rich); those whose words he set (Abraham Cowley, John Dryden, Dr John Patrick and Nahum Tate, for example); his pupils and followers (such as Jeremiah Clarke, William Croft and John Weldon); and those at the time who wrote about him or his milieu (such as Thomas Brown, Thomas Mace, Peter Motteux and Roger North).

We have also included a strand devoted to the individuals and institutions responsible for maintaining (or sometimes altering) and then rediscovering his legacy. This is in part a response to Herissone's observation (*ARCHP*, 303) that books on Purcell usually 'stop more or less dead in 1695', which begins her ground-breaking survey of Purcell reception. We have followed her lead by including entries on some of the later composers who have responded to Purcell's music, from Thomas Arne and William Boyce to Peter Maxwell Davies and Michael Nyman; on some of those who collected and edited him, from Edward Finch to the original Purcell Society; and on the institutions and significant individuals who performed his music over the centuries after his death, from the Academy of Ancient Music to Michael Tippett and Benjamin Britten – both of whom were also influenced by his music as composers. We have, however, resisted the temptation to fill the book with potted biographies of today's Purcell performers. These are readily available elsewhere, and the vagaries of time and fashion would soon have rendered our choices obsolete.

As already mentioned, most of the entries in the *Bibliography* are headed by a code consisting of the first three letters of the author's surname followed by three letters derived from a key word in the title (hence *BurHis* for Charles Burney's *General History of Music*), and the relevant ones are given in an alphabetical sequence at the end of each entry of the *Dictionary*. We have assumed that those interested in particular topics will also look at the relevant entries in *Oxford Music Online* and the online *Oxford Dictionary of National Biography*, and at the introductions and critical commentaries of the relevant volumes of *PS*, the Purcell Society's revised *Works of Henry Purcell*, frequently the best source of information about particular pieces and sources. However, references are sometimes given to particular *PS* volumes in the discussions of specific pieces and issues. Theses and dissertations play an increasingly important role in Purcell scholarship, and for the many now available online (and for other material freely available on the internet, such as digitised books available from Google Books and Internet Archive or editions of music at the IMSLP / Petrucci Music Library site) we have used the symbol <@>. This means that at the time of publication a digital copy could be found by entering key words of the title in a search engine, thus sidestepping the problems associated with unsightly and often lengthy web addresses; ephemeral websites with ever-changing URLs; and broken links.

Cross references in the *Dictionary* are indicated by the use of asterisks at their first mention in particular entries, or by references in bold at the end of entries.

Since the *Dictionary* will nearly always be used for quick reference to individual entries, we have allowed ourselves a certain amount of repetition between them, to make them easy to use and to avoid the reader having to flit constantly between different parts of the volume. Asterisks are not used in the *Biography*, since the names of persons, institutions and places mentioned are mostly the subject of individual *Dictionary* entries, and the list of *Works* also provides basic information about individual pieces. In the *Dictionary* and *Bibliography* the entries are listed in alphabetical order following the word-by-word system, though indefinite and definite articles are ignored in the ordering – making our lists rather different from Zimmerman's in *ZimCat*, which takes account of indefinite and definite articles in the ordering of titles. Quotations from primary sources are given without altering spelling, punctuation or capitalisation, though readers should be alert to the possibility that those taken from secondary sources might have been modernised.

In the list of *Works* we order the sections for the vocal works in alphabetical order by title for all genres except for category no. 6, 'Welcome songs and extended occasional works', which is ordered chronologically since the exact dates of their first performances are known in virtually every case. We have taken a programmatic approach to the ordering of the instrumental music. 'Consort music' (category no. 8) is divided into three by type: the fantasias are ordered by ascending number of parts and then by date where known; the contents of the two sets of trio sonatas are listed as they appear in the publications; and the miscellaneous pieces are also listed by ascending number of parts and then by date. Similarly, the keyboard music (category no. 9) is divided into domestic keyboard music and organ music, with the former subdivided into the three primary sources and then by the ordering in them; the organ music follows the ordering in *ZimCat*.

We have included the Z numbers of *ZimCat* in the *Dictionary* as well as the list of *Works* where they exist, since Zimmerman's invaluable catalogue is still in everyday use despite now being seriously out of date: a substantial number of pieces have been discovered since it was published, and subsequent scholarship has modified the dates of many pieces, particularly among the anthems, the domestic sacred music and the consort music. Space has prevented us from giving entries in the *Dictionary* to individual Purcell scholars working in modern times, though we have made an exception in Zimmerman's case, partly because of his pivotal role in the development of Purcell scholarship and partly as a centenary tribute: he was born in Wauneta, Kansas on 23 June 1923, and is still alive at the time of writing. It also enables our *Dictionary* to be a true A–Z: *Abdelazer* to Zimmerman.

A work of synthesis of this sort by definition owes an enormous amount to the work of others, so we must first thank the community of Purcell scholars and performers past and present, on whose shoulders we inevitably stand. In particular, we have benefitted greatly from the expertise, generously shared, of our colleagues on the Editorial Committee of the Purcell Society; and equally from our performing colleagues in Leeds Baroque and at the Suffolk Villages Festival. These two institutions have given us many opportunities in recent years to explore in performance a range of works by Purcell, his contemporaries and followers, enabling us to form judgements about pieces, genres and performance issues from the inside. We owe a particular debt of gratitude to those who read drafts of the *Dictionary* in whole or in part: Olive Baldwin and Thelma Wilson, Cheryll Duncan, Alan Howard, Alon Schab, Michael Talbot, Robert Thompson and Andrew Woolley. We have benefitted greatly from their advice and criticism: they provided information we otherwise would have missed, and on occasion saved us from serious error.

Thanks are also due to the institutions listed above in the list of illustrations for permission to reproduce the items detailed there; to Andrew Woolley and David J. Smith for providing us with extracts for our music examples from their forthcoming revision of *PS* 6 (begun by the late Christopher Hogwood); to Jonathan Wainwright for helping us process the examples; and to Michael Middeke, the commissioning editor at Boydell, and his staff for their invaluable advice, encouragement and help. We must also thank Michael Talbot, the series editor for the Boydell Composer Compendium Series, for suggesting the idea of a Purcell volume and for helping us to shape it at every stage of the project. Finally, our greatest debt is to Olive and Thelma, who patiently answered queries throughout the lengthy writing process, helping us greatly to develop our coverage of Purcell's singers and of the Restoration theatre. If this volume breaks new ground it is mostly in this area, and it is largely because of their unrivalled knowledge of the subject. We therefore dedicate it to them, with gratitude.

Peter Holman, Colchester
Bryan White, Wakefield
October 2024

Biography

Henry Purcell's early life is obscure. His birth date is unknown, though he was 24 in 1683 according to his portrait in *Sonnata's of III Parts*, and he was in his 37th year when he died on 21 November 1695. Thus he was born in 1659 or possibly late 1658. When the court musician John Hingeston made his will in 1683, he named Henry Purcell, son of Elizabeth, as his godson. This must be the Elizabeth named as relict in the probate of Henry Purcell, Gentleman of the Chapel Royal and Master of the Boys at Westminster Abbey, who died on 11 August 1664. Henry senior and Elizabeth had six children, of whom Henry junior was third, probably born in the house the couple shared in Great Almonry near the Abbey; Daniel, the youngest, may have been born after his father's death. Henry senior had sung in *The Siege of Rhodes*, the first English opera, in 1656, and received a place in the court Lutes and Voices in 1662.

After Henry's death Elizabeth moved, presumably with her children, from Great Almonry to a dwelling leased from Westminster Abbey in nearby Tothill Street. She must have benefitted from the support of her brother-in-law Thomas, a Gentleman of the Chapel Royal like his brother, as well as composer to the Twenty-Four Violins. No string music survives by him, and it was probably a sinecure: court posts were often allocated just because they fell vacant at a convenient moment. No document mentions Henry junior before 1673, the year his voice broke and he left the Chapel; boys were normally about eight when they joined. He had flourished under Henry Cooke, the Master of the Choristers; Cooke had spectacularly resurrected the Chapel choir at the Restoration, recruiting talented boys including John Blow, Pelham Humfrey and William Turner. In addition to singing and studying English and Latin, Purcell would have been taught the lute and theorbo, violin and keyboard, the last probably by Christopher Gibbons, a Chapel Royal organist and keyboard virtuoso. Cooke, a celebrated singer, was a poor composer, so Purcell's main composition teachers were probably Humfrey (who succeeded Cooke in July 1672) and Blow (who succeeded Humfrey two years later).

The Purcell family was well entrenched at the Restoration court, though the origins of that connection are mysterious. Thomas was a Groom of the Robes in addition to his posts as a musician; Thomas's son Charles was a scholarship boy at Westminster School; Henry's older brother Edward was a Gentleman Usher; and Daniel became a Chapel Royal chorister. Nevertheless, Henry's musical skills were quickly perceived as exceptional. On leaving the Chapel Royal he received £30 maintenance, intended to support him until a paid court post became available. In June 1673 he was made unpaid assistant to his godfather John Hingeston, keeper of the court's wind and keyboard instruments. This developed his knowledge of organ building and tuning; he was paid for tuning the Westminster Abbey organ between 1674 and 1678, and in later life he frequently advised on the construction of new organs in London's churches.

Purcell's composition studies, probably supervised by Blow, continued after he left the Chapel, and he was also evidently close to Matthew Locke (a court musician and apparently a family friend, but a Catholic and therefore not a member of the Chapel); Purcell marked Locke's death in 1677 with a heartfelt elegy. The boy's earliest compositions include the first version of settings of sentences from the Burial Service, perhaps written for Humfrey's funeral in 1674, and the Staircase Overture, probably dating from 1675. The earliest manuscripts in his hand date from this period. They include copies of his own compositions, as well as arrangements of works by Humfrey and Blow. Copying was an important part of his early work and training. He was paid £5 in 1676 'for pricking out two bookes of organ parts' for Westminster Abbey, and in early 1678 he began collecting Chapel Royal repertoire into GB-Cfm, MS 88, including many works by Blow (its first owner), alongside compositions by Thomas Tallis, William Byrd and Orlando Gibbons. Copying was also a way of studying composition: discussing ground basses in his composition treatise 'The Art of Descant' (1694), Purcell wrote: 'the best way ... is to score much, and chuse the best Authours'.

Purcell succeeded Locke in September 1677 as composer for the violins, his first paid court post – an appointment perhaps intended for him to write symphony anthems for the Chapel. By then, his symphony anthem 'My beloved spake' had been performed in Charles II's presence and six of his anthems had been copied into partbooks at Westminster Abbey. At the same time he undertook a sort of self-imposed compositional finishing school, writing sets of works in different genres to test his skills to their limits, particularly in the discipline of counterpoint. Many of them were copied into GB-Lbl, Add. MS 30930; at one end it has 16 English and Latin sacred part-songs composed mostly in 1679; at the other end, fantasias (some with dates in June and August 1680) and other contrapuntal consort music. By the end of 1680 he had also probably completed his monumental complete Service in B$^\flat$ Z230, featuring ten canons.

In September 1679 Purcell succeeded John Blow as organist at Westminster Abbey. With several court posts, Blow may just have been overworked, though Bruce Wood suggested he took the decision to enable his talented protégé to start a family: about this time Henry married Frances Peters. No marriage record survives, though their first child, Henry junior, was baptised on 9 July 1681. Frances was the daughter of the leather merchant John Baptista Pieters (d. 1675) and his wife Amy, who had moved to London from Ghent in the early 1660s. Pieters became an outwardly conforming Anglican on arrival, though he was baptised a Catholic and probably raised his children in that faith. The inventory made at Pieters's death shows that the family lived in Thames Street in the parish of All Hallows the Less and was well off; Henry junior's death, nine days after his baptism, was recorded at All Hallows, so the Purcells may initially have lived with Frances's mother.

By 1680 Purcell was expanding his activities beyond the court and Westminster Abbey. He provided music for Nathaniel Lee's *Theodosius*, staged at the Dorset Garden Theatre by the Duke's Company that spring or summer. John Downes, its prompter, recalled the play's success much later: 'being perfectly perform'd, with several Entertainments of Singing; Compos'd by the Famous Master, Mr. *Henry Purcell*, (being the first he e'er Compos'd for the Stage) ... the Court, especially the Ladies ... gave it great Encouragement'. Five songs were published with the play, albeit anonymously. The five songs John Playford had included in *Choice Ayres and Songs*, book 2 (1679), are thought to be Purcell's first published pieces; his growing reputation was recognised by the inclusion of nine songs, three from *Theodosius*, in *Choice Ayres and Songs*, book 3, dated 1681 but published in late December 1680.

Purcell's success with *Theodosius* was followed later in 1680 with a song for Nahum Tate's adaptation of Shakespeare's *King Richard the Second*, renamed *The Sicilian Usurper* in an unsuccessful attempt to hide the play's dangerous relevance to the Popish Plot. Nevertheless, his primary responsibilities remained at court, where in September 1680 he wrote a welcome song or ode for Charles II's return to London from Windsor. Hitherto, musical odes had been performed on New Year's Day and for the king's birthday; Blow composed music for both occasions in 1680. Marking the king's annual autumn return to Whitehall was an innovation, perhaps instituted to exploit Purcell's remarkable talents. He set the anonymous 'Welcome vicegerent of the mighty king', the first of eight welcome songs for Charles and James II. Additionally, in late May 1682 he wrote a welcome song, 'What shall be done in behalf of the man', to receive James, Duke of York after the duke's exile in Scotland during the Exclusion Crisis; and 'From hardy climes', celebrating the marriage of Princess Anne to George Prince of Denmark on 28 July 1683. He copied all of these into the largely autograph volume GB-Lbl, R.M. 20.h.8, in a sequence of secular music composed for performance at court; the odes are in chronological order, which helps date the smaller works copied between them. They include several substantial symphony songs, mostly composed in late 1682 and 1683.

Purcell was also busy in the Chapel Royal, becoming one of its three organists in the summer of 1682. He added symphony anthems to R.M. 20.h.8 by the common expedient of turning the volume over and copying from the back, entering 14 of them in whole or part between 1680 and Charles II's death in February 1685. Less is known of his work at Westminster Abbey, though he must have been involved with music there, and his Service in B^b was copied into the Abbey's partbooks in 1681. Around this time he began an important artistic partnership with the bass John Gostling. They were apparently introduced by Thomas Purcell, who in February 1679 wrote to Gostling in Canterbury: 'my sonne is Composing: wherein you will be chiefly consern'd'. Later that month Gostling joined the Chapel Royal and Henry was soon writing specifically for him, exploiting his extremely wide range, agility and interpretative abilities in anthems for the Chapel and in odes and songs for the Private Music. Their relationship lasted to the end of Purcell's life, and Gostling was later a significant collector and copyist of his music.

Sometime in 1682, Henry and Frances moved to Great St Anne's Street, Westminster, where their second son, John Baptista, was born. John Baptista was baptised on 9 August 1682, only a week after Purcell's uncle Thomas was buried in Westminster Abbey; the baby survived only a few months and was buried at the Abbey in turn on 17 October. Between these sad events Purcell wrote 'God bless Mr Henry Purcell September ye 10th 1682' on a flyleaf of GB-Cfm, MS 88. Scholars have wondered what this inscription signified. It was the day the king returned to Whitehall after the summer, and it might also have marked the moment Blow formally passed his scorebook of church music to Purcell, perhaps in recognition of his appointment as Chapel Royal organist. That day might even have been Henry's birthday. On 4 February 1683 Purcell took the sacrament in public at St Margaret's, Westminster 'according to the usage of the Church of England'. We do not know why he did this. Perhaps his marriage to a Catholic (if indeed Frances was one) aroused suspicion in the anti-Catholic temper of the times, or it might just have been a formality relating to his position at court.

Despite his court commitments, Purcell found time in 1683 to prepare for publication a set of 12 trio sonatas, some of which had been composed as early as 1679. *Sonnata's of III Parts* was published at his own expense, as were almost all single-composer collections at the time. It was financed at least in part by subscription: on 28 May he advertised in the *London Gazette* that the books were 'now completely finished, and shall be delivered to [subscribers] upon the 11th of June next'. Thomas Cross junior engraved the music, and Robert White the elaborate portrait appearing as the frontispiece to the violin 1 partbook. Purcell advertised himself as 'Composer in Ordinary to his most Sacred Majesty, and Organist of his Chappell Royall' on the title page, and dedicated the collection to the king, doubtless in gratitude for his court preferments and in hope of a gift of some sort – of which there is no evidence. Purcell's portrait, Cheryll Duncan has argued, with its full-bottomed wig, lace cravat and Roman cloak, presents him as a man of rank, while the coat of arms at the base of the enclosing roundel is that of the Purcells of Onslow in Shropshire; the star or mullet surmounting the shield identifies him as the third son, claiming the arms as an inheritance from his father (see p. 143). With this collection, the first set of sonatas published in England, Purcell announced himself as a composer equal to 'the most fam'd Italian Masters', and as a gentleman worthy of the respect of the cultural and social elite.

In November 1683 Purcell took a leading role in a new venture that widened the profile of the musical ode and its court performers. In celebration of St Cecilia's Day, 22 November, he set an ode by Christopher Fishburn, 'Welcome to all the pleasures', in praise of music and its patron saint in the manner of Charles II's welcome songs. No details of its performance are known, but the work was printed in the following year at the expense of the Musical Society, whose stewards were already planning a similar event for November 1684. This second Cecilian celebration was at Stationers' Hall, during which Blow's setting of John Oldham's ode was followed by a feast; it too was published by the Musical Society. These two were the only large-scale concerted odes to be published before the eighteenth century, and they helped establish St Cecilia's Day as a highpoint in London's musical calendar. Purcell and fellow court musicians apparently joined with prominent music lovers to institute the celebration, offering a public platform for ode performances and paid work for court musicians. Purcell also composed 'Laudate Ceciliam', 'A Latine song made upon St Cecilia ... made in ye year 1683', for three voices, two violins and continuo. He copied it into R.M. 20.h.8 – an indication it was written for the court; it was perhaps performed there before 'Welcome to all the pleasures' was given later the same day.

Purcell continued to flourish at court. On or shortly after 25 September, when the king returned from Winchester, his welcome song 'Fly, bold rebellion' was performed; it celebrated Charles's delivery from the Rye House Plot, foiled in March 1683. Court interest in musical theatrical entertainments was developing at this time, and it is likely that Blow's *Venus and Adonis* was performed in 1683, in Whitehall or at Windsor. That summer Charles sent the leading actor Thomas Betterton to Paris to bring a French opera production to London. When that proved impossible, Betterton recruited Louis Grabu, formerly Master of the King's Music, to set an English text in the French style. The result was Grabu's music for John Dryden's *Albion and Albanius*, eventually performed at Dorset Garden in June 1685. Scholars have argued that Purcell composed *Dido and Aeneas* around this time for a court performance because of its similarity to *Venus and Adonis*; its allegorical prelude (the music is lost) resembles the prologues of earlier court musical theatrical entertainments. However, no performance then is known, and *Dido* is first heard of in the summer of 1688, in association with Josias Priest's girls' school in Chelsea.

When John Hingeston died in December 1683 Purcell succeeded him as keeper of the wind and keyboard instruments at a salary of £60, which, combined with his posts of composer for the violins (approximately £30 and at least £16 for livery), Chapel Royal organist (£70), as well as £10 and an £8 housing allowance from Westminster Abbey, should have allowed Henry and Frances to live securely. However, Charles II was notorious for failing to pay the salaries of court musicians: Thomas Purcell's widow was owed over £220 for her late husband's court posts five years after his death. Purcell's assorted freelance activities, such as providing Playford with songs, seven of which appeared in *Choice Ayres and Songs*, book 5 (1684); his work for St Cecilia's Day; and the publication of *Sonnata's of III Parts*, would therefore have provided him with essential extra income. The collection must have been expensive to produce, though at least two impressions were made in 1683, suggesting a good demand and perhaps some profit. Some time in 1684 the Purcells moved from Great St Anne's Street to the nearby Bowling Alley East. This was not a significant improvement, to judge from the rates (a form of local taxation), which were the same on the two properties.

In 1684 Purcell was involved in the 'Battle of the Organs', the celebrated competition between Bernard 'Father' Smith and Renatus Harris to provide an instrument for the Temple Church. It involved alternating public recitals, with Blow and Purcell playing Smith's organ, and Giovanni Batista Draghi, organist of the queen's Catholic chapel, playing Harris's. Smith eventually won, and the public nature of the competition would have served to enhance Purcell's reputation. Meanwhile, he continued to produce material for the growing market for printed music. John Playford was in the process of handing his business over to his son Henry, who launched a new song series, *The Theater of Music*, with the court violinist Robert Carr. They dedicated the first book to Blow and Purcell (who provided five songs), thanking them for their work as editors. Meanwhile, Playford senior was preparing one of his last anthologies, *Catch that Catch Can*, which appeared in 1685 with 12 Purcell catches, several decidedly obscene.

If Purcell took time around New Year 1685 to reflect on his circumstances, he would surely have felt some pride in his achievements. At 26 he held prominent positions at court and at Westminster Abbey; his music was regularly published; he had made a promising start in the theatre; and he was playing a leading role in the new Cecilian celebrations. Charles II had overcome serious political challenges and was ascendant over his foes; court employees might therefore have hoped to receive regular and full payment of their salaries in future. This auspicious situation was thrown into doubt on 6 February, when Charles died unexpectedly. His deathbed conversion to Catholicism soon became public, and no state funeral was held. Purcell's intense eight-voice 'Hear my prayer, O Lord' may have been the opening of a funeral anthem, laid aside in favour of the extended solo song 'If pray'rs and tears', entitled 'Sighs for our late Sov'raign King Charles ye 2d'.

James II, the Exclusion Crisis behind him, was initially welcomed as king, and Purcell and his colleagues focussed their attention on 23 April 1685, the most musically elaborate coronation before that of George II in 1727. Nine anthems were performed, two by Purcell: the full anthem 'I was glad' was sung by the Abbey choir at the king and queen's entry at the west door, and the symphony anthem 'My heart is inditing' was performed after Mary of Modena's crowning by 'the whole *Consort* of *Voices* and *Instruments*' – the Chapel and Abbey choirs plus an enlarged Twenty-Four Violins. Purcell participated as a Chapel Royal bass, though as Abbey organist he also provided a small organ placed in a gallery with the Chapel Royal and had its main organ removed; for this he was paid £34. 12s., also taking into account unspecified 'services performed'.

James's interest in the court music did not match his brother's, though he set about modernising and streamlining its establishment, redressing the accumulated salary arrears. Purcell's post of composer to the violins was discontinued, but he was appointed to the new post of 'Harpsicall' at £40 per annum in the Private Music, as the combined court groups were now called. His post as keeper of the wind and keyboard instruments was also discontinued. However, tuning and maintenance was still required, and Purcell continued with this until June 1687, when he petitioned the king for over £20 in respect of work undertaken 'without any consideration'. He received £25 as a result, and a new post of organ tuner with a salary of £56 was created for him.

This episode was a symptom of the decline of music at court. Purcell continued to provide welcome songs; the first for James, 'Why are all the Muses mute?', performed in October 1685, was one of his finest large-scale works to date. But his composition of smaller-scale court works fell off markedly. In the last four months of Charles's life he copied four into R.M. 20.h.8, but throughout James's reign he added only seven more, including 'If pray'rs and tears'. By contrast, his contributions to printed song anthologies increased: 14 pieces appeared in *The Theater of Music*, books 2–4 (1685–7), and five more in the first two books of its sequel, *The Banquet of Musick* (1687–8). In 1688 Purcell and Playford developed a new publishing venture, *Harmonia sacra*, the first anthology of devotional song to be published in England; Purcell selected and edited its contents. Of his twelve contributions to the collection, he selected three from R.M. 20.h.8 and may have composed six specially.

More significant change came in the Chapel Royal. As a Catholic, James did not attend services there and created a Catholic chapel with a separate musical establishment. Without the king in attendance, the symphony anthem, a sonic representation of the monarch's presence, lost much of its importance, though examples continued to be performed when Princess Anne, James's younger daughter, attended the Chapel. Tensions between the Anglican establishment and the king grew, especially after his attempts to enforce the Declaration of Indulgence, first issued in 1687. By the summer of 1688, during the Trial of the Seven Bishops, the Chapel was effectively in open revolt. Blow composed two verse anthems with solo parts for Gostling with Psalm texts that seem intended to be understood as opposing James and his policies. As far as is known, Purcell did not oppose James directly, and composed a symphony anthem, 'Blessed are they that fear the Lord', for the thanksgiving for the queen's pregnancy on 15 January 1688; he contributed a smattering of other verse and symphony anthems during James's reign, though his work for the Chapel declined significantly after 1685.

With a slackening of his court activities, Purcell cultivated other musical opportunities. In September 1686 he tested Bernard Smith's new organ for St Katherine Cree and helped its vestry choose its organist. Later that year he petitioned the Dean of Exeter Cathedral for help in obtaining £27 'for half a year's teaching & boarding ... and for necessaries which I laid out' on behalf of 'Hodg' – perhaps Robert Hodge (d. 1709), later organist of Wells Cathedral and St Patrick's Cathedral, Dublin. Purcell returned to the theatre in 1688, supplying eight songs for Thomas D'Urfey's *A Fool's Preferment*, which probably opened in April. *Dido and Aeneas* was also probably performed that spring: Rowland Sherman, apprentice Levant merchant, mentioned in a letter a 'mask' Purcell had 'made for Preists [sic] Ball'. This must be a reference to *Dido*, showing that by the summer of 1688 Purcell had offered it to Josias Priest and his girls' school in Chelsea.

Other evidence shows that Purcell taught amateurs and played with them. Sherman visited him in the summer of 1688 to take his leave before embarking for Aleppo. Purcell apologised to him for failing to write down his 'rules' for continuo playing, otherwise unknown; they were probably similar to the surviving ones by Locke and Blow. Sherman also wrote from Aleppo to his merchant friend Philip Wheak to ask Purcell (by then 'Harry' to him) to copy out two sonatas with the bass figured and ornaments supplied in the violin parts; he would 'offer what seems best [...] in recompense for Mr Purcell's trouble and courtesy'. Sherman, with Wheak, had been a member of the 'brothers of the string', probably a section of the Musical Society, sponsor of the Cecilian celebrations. Purcell's engagement with the Society would have created opportunities to offer paid musical services to well-to-do merchant families, as well as courtiers and members of the nobility and gentry. The lawyer and writer Roger North, for instance, reported playing Purcell's trio sonatas with the composer and North's brother Francis, the Lord Keeper.

In his personal life, Purcell suffered the loss of two children during James's reign: Thomas, whose date of birth is unknown, and Henry, baptised on 9 June 1687; they were buried in the Abbey respectively in August 1686 and on 23 September 1687. Frances, his first daughter and the first child to survive into adulthood, was baptised on 30 May 1688. Less than two weeks later James Francis Edward was born to James II and Mary, supplanting the king's Protestant daughters, Mary and Anne, in the line of succession. The prospect of a Catholic succession, compounded with the Trial of the Seven Bishops, spurred leading figures of the English nobility and clergy to invite William of Orange and his wife Mary, James's daughter, to replace James II as joint monarchs – initiating the train of events commonly called the Glorious Revolution.

The coronation of William and Mary on 11 April 1689 was less elaborate than in 1685, and Purcell provided only one new work, the symphony anthem 'Praise the Lord, O Jerusalem'. He once again arranged for an organ to be erected in the Abbey, at a cost of £32, for which he was not reimbursed for well over a year. Furthermore, in the weeks following the coronation, he was ordered by the Dean and Chapter to repay 'money as was received by him for places in the Organ loft'. It was customary for the Abbey organist to arrange for temporary seating for paying spectators at coronations, as Purcell must have done in 1685. However, this led to a misunderstanding: on this occasion the Dean and Chapter demanded all the proceeds, so Purcell turned over £78. 4s. 6d., £35 of which was eventually returned as a gift.

William and Mary's reign was not an auspicious one for music at court. William, whose taste was seemingly limited to martial music, was preoccupied with his annual campaigns: musical entertainments were not a priority. Mary, by contrast, enjoyed music, and so her birthday on 30 April was celebrated with odes supplied by Purcell; they replaced the annual welcome songs. The six he wrote for her, beginning with 'Now does the glorious day appear' in 1689, are among his finest large-scale works. It seems that he was also assigned royal commissions related to Princess Anne, if the fragment of 'The noise of foreign wars' marking the birth of her son the Duke of Gloucester in July 1689 is indeed his work. Purcell's last ode, 'Who can from joy refrain?', marked the duke's sixth birthday.

Otherwise, the significance of the Private Music waned. Only the first two of Mary's birthday odes were copied into R.M. 20.h.8, neither in Purcell's hand; the second, 'Arise, my muse', is incomplete and is the last work entered into the volume – which contains no court songs from the new reign. In May 1690 William and Mary reduced the court musical establishment, disbanding the 'vocall part' of the Private Music, which abolished Purcell's post as harpsichord accompanist, though he retained his post as organ tuner. However, Hawkins's anecdote about an informal entertainment for Mary, in which Purcell accompanied Arabella Hunt and Gostling, suggests he was still involved in private music-making at court. William and Mary, in line with their Calvinist proclivities, banned instruments in the Chapel apart from the organ, effectively bringing the symphony anthem genre to an end. Purcell retained his post as organist, focussing primarily on organ-accompanied verse anthems for special occasions.

With court duties curtailed, Purcell turned elsewhere. He continued to provide music for printed collections, including *The Banquet of Music*, book 3 and the keyboard anthology *Musick's Handmaid*, part 2, both advertised in May 1689. He served as the latter's editor and arranger and contributed at least 14 independent pieces and a suite, his first published keyboard compositions. Purcell also found new occasions for the composition of odes. Cecilian celebrations were suspended in 1688 during the Glorious Revolution and in the following year, though other organisations commissioned celebratory works. On 5 August 1689 his 'Celestial music did the gods inspire' was performed at Lewis Maidwell's school; and on 27 March 1690 his extravagant setting of Thomas D'Urfey's 'Of old when heroes thought it base' (The Yorkshire Feast Song) was performed at Merchant Taylors' Hall for the Feast of the Gentlemen of Yorkshire.

However, the theatre now became the focus of Purcell's activities. He composed music for the sacrifice scene in Charles Davenant's *Circe*, probably for a revival in 1689–90. By early 1690 he must have been working with Thomas Betterton on the dramatic opera *The Prophetess, or the History of Dioclesian*, which opened at Dorset Garden in late May 1690. It was the first new dramatic opera since the 1670s; *Albion and Albanius* had drained the United Company's funds in 1685. *Dioclesian* was also the longest and most elaborate score Purcell had yet composed, and Downes recalled that 'it gratify'd the Expectation of Court and City; and got the Author great Reputation'. More commissions flowed in: by the end of the year he had composed music for at least three more plays, notably for Dryden's *Amphitryon* in October. Dryden's preface to the published text praised Purcell fulsomely as 'equal with the best abroad', and his songs were included in it. He moved quickly to capitalise on his ascendancy in the theatre by printing the music to *Dioclesian* by subscription; it appeared in March 1691. He doubtless intended to match *Albion and Albanius*, published in full score in 1687, as well as Lully's operas, mostly issued by Ballard in sumptuous editions soon after their productions. However, he remarked in an 'Advertisement' at the end of the score that its length had swelled 'beyond my expectation', and found 'too late, [that] the Subscription-money will scarcely amount to the Expense of compleating this Edition'.

Two lawsuits discovered by Cheryll Duncan suggest that Purcell was under financial pressure in the early 1690s. In June 1691 he sued for a *cognovit actionem* against his sister-in-law Amy Howlett over a £40 loan he had made to her. His reasons for doing so are unclear, but it may have been an attempt to secure the loan in law, or perhaps to create a mortgage for his property in Bowling Alley East. Some time in 1691 Henry and Frances left this property, which was then occupied by Frances's mother; she was subsequently joined by Amy, her widowed daughter, the *cognovit* perhaps securing a mortgage for her. The Purcells had baptised a son, Edward, in September 1689, and Henry lost his Private Music post in May 1690. With the disappointing return on the publication of *Dioclesian*, he was perhaps unwilling to make a loan to his sister-in-law without legal security. A second lawsuit, taken out by the Covent Garden linen draper Mordant Cracherode against Frances Purcell in 1698, shows that Henry became indebted to him in June 1692. Cracherode sued for a debt of £100, though the original sum was probably less than a third of that amount; he served an exclusive clientele, so he may have provided Purcell with fashionable clothing, in keeping with the composer's social aspirations and the prominence his theatrical success brought.

In May 1691 Betterton brought Dryden's dramatic opera *King Arthur* (written in 1684 but unperformed then) to the Dorset Garden stage, with Purcell's wonderfully varied and elaborate music. According to Downes, 'Excellently Adorn'd with Scenes and Machines', 'The Play and Musick pleas'd the Court and City, and being well perform'd, twas very Gainful to the Company'. Purcell contributed songs to several other plays during the year, and in November began teaching a young gentlewoman, Rhoda Cartwright. Lessons continued irregularly until June 1693, bringing him £18 in all. Rhoda married Henry Cavendish, second son of the 1st Duke of Devonshire, and Frances Purcell dedicated to her the set of trio sonatas she published in 1697.

In 1692 another substantial theatrical commission beckoned: music for the dramatic opera *The Fairy Queen*, mounted by the United Company at Dorset Garden. It was Purcell's most elaborate and extensive work, and the evidence of the theatre score suggests that he worked feverishly on it until its première, on 2 May 1692. According to Downes, 'the Court and Town were wonderfully satisfy'd', but because of the extravagant production 'the Company got very little by it'. Stung by the difficulties of publishing the music to *Dioclesian*, Purcell instead issued a selection of songs from *The Fairy Queen*, produced more quickly, cheaply and profitably than a complete score. More theatrical music followed, including that for Dryden and Lee's *Oedipus*, perhaps revived in June 1692. Purcell was soon hard at work on a second Cecilian ode, a setting of Nicholas Brady's 'Hail, bright Cecilia', his longest and most elaborate ode, equivalent in ambition to *The Fairy Queen*. Peter Motteux reported that it was 'perform'd twice with universal applause' on 22 November 1692. Weeks later an unhappier occasion arose when Purcell and members of the Chapel Royal performed an anthem at the funeral of the actor and playwright William Mountfort on 13 December 1692, who had been stabbed to death in the Strand. Purcell had written songs for him in D'Urfey's *The Fool's Preferment*.

Doubtless because of the great expense of *The Fairy Queen*, the United Company did not produce a new dramatic opera in 1693, relying on revivals of *The Fairy Queen* in February and *Dioclesian* in May, the latter with two new songs. Purcell composed songs, duets, dialogues and theatre airs for seven or eight other plays over the year. In the summer *Harmonia sacra*, book 2 was published, with eight works by Purcell, the majority probably composed specifically for the anthology. That spring he took on John Weldon, another pupil training for the music profession and then a chorister at Eton. Weldon's lessons, for which Purcell received biannual payments of £5 with some expenses, continued for a year.

Early in 1694 Purcell began teaching Diana Howard, granddaughter of the prominent courtier Sir Robert Howard. His contact with the Howards predated his teaching of Diana, since several songs in the Gresham autograph may have been written for Annabella, Sir Robert's fourth wife, whom he married on 26 February. She had previously been a maid of honour to Princess Anne, and Robert Thompson has linked the manuscript to Anne's circle. Annabella would later pay for Purcell's memorial tablet in Westminster Abbey, and Frances Purcell dedicated *Orpheus Britannicus*, book 1 to her, noting that Purcell had been her teacher. He had other pupils in the last years of his life: he evidently copied his portion of the Purcell-Draghi Manuscript, GB-Lbl, MS Mus. 1, in 1693–4 for one or more unidentified pupils, while according to Hawkins he taught Katherine Shore, sister of the trumpeter John Shore, 'to sing and play on the harpsichord'.

On 10 December 1693 the Purcells baptised their last child, Mary-Peters. Around this time they took a dwelling on the newly built Marsham Street, running south from Westminster. Henry was then completing another commission, a setting of Tate's 'Great parent, hail', for the centenary of the founding of Trinity College, Dublin; it was performed there on 9 January 1694. Meanwhile, his theatre work continued unabated. In January he provided a song for Dryden's short-lived *Love Triumphant*; in February, two songs for Southerne's *The Fatal Marriage*; and in April, theatre airs and a song for Crowne's *The Married Beau*. At the end of April 'Come, ye sons of art away', Mary's last birthday ode, was performed, while in May and June he contributed a substantial amount of vocal music to D'Urfey's *Don Quixote*, Parts 1 and 2.

With the theatres soon to close for the summer, Purcell, with his Chapel Royal colleague Stephen Crespion, was given oversight of 'the amending & altering & new Makinge' of the organ at Westminster Abbey. Bernard Smith did the work, and Purcell must have participated in its planning and supervision, though he would not live to enjoy its benefits; Smith was only paid for completing the work on 28 November 1695. In 1694 Playford again sought Purcell's expertise in a publishing venture: the title page of the 12th edition of *An Introduction to the Skill of Musick*, begun by his father 40 years earlier, stated it was 'Corrected and Amended by Mr. Henry Purcell'. Purcell's contribution included replacing the out-of-date composition treatise by Christopher Simpson with his own 'Art of Descant: or, Composing Musick in Parts'.

In 1694 Purcell again provided music for St Cecilia's Day, this time the D major Te Deum and Jubilate for the morning service in St Bride's church before the feast. His elaborate settings, accompanied by trumpets, strings and continuo, made a strong case for instrumentally accompanied church music. They were repeated in the Chapel Royal in December as part of the extended thanksgiving for William's successful summer campaign, and Frances Purcell had them printed in 1697. They became the most performed of Purcell's large-scale works, playing a crucial role in his posthumous reputation. Purcell continued to be in demand in the theatre, his music appearing that autumn in Dryden's *Tyrannick Love* and Edward Ravenscroft's *Canterbury Guests*. However, the United Company soon descended into turmoil because Christopher Rich, its manager, tried to cut production costs and salaries, and then the theatres were closed following Queen Mary's unexpected death from smallpox on 28 December 1694; her elaborate funeral eventually took place on 5 March 1695. Purcell wrote a March and Canzona for four flat trumpets, the March accompanying the procession of the coffin to Westminster Abbey, and the Canzona played at the interment. As organist, he led the service, which included his setting of the funeral sentence 'Thou knowest, Lord, the secrets of our hearts' Z58C. He subsequently set two Latin elegies in her memory.

By the time the theatres reopened on 25 March, Betterton had organised a break-away company at Lincoln's Inn Fields. Purcell stayed behind at Drury Lane, in a company weakened by the loss of its most experienced actors and singers. It nevertheless pressed on with a dramatic opera adapted from Sir Robert Howard's *The Indian Queen*, with Purcell's music. It may have been performed in June, though the Act V masque, set by Daniel Purcell, was probably added after his brother's death. Henry had been working at a furious pace since 25 March, when his theatre airs and a song accompanied a revival of Behn's *Abdelazer*. In the months that followed he composed one song each for revivals of *The Tempest* and Dryden's *The Spanish Fryar*, as well as a substantial masque for *Timon of Athens*. Music for Shadwell's *The Libertine*, a song and two ample scenes (reusing the March from Mary's funeral music), were seemingly performed in July.

As soon as Drury Lane closed for the summer Purcell turned to setting the ode 'Who can from joy refrain?' for the Duke of Gloucester's sixth birthday on 24 July, and he was soon coping with the demands of the autumn theatre season. Dates for the performance of his theatre airs for D'Urfey's *The Virtuous Wife* and his songs for Thomas Scott's *The Mock Marriage* are not certain, but his music for *Bonduca* – theatre airs, three songs and an extended sacrifice scene – was ready for October. In the same month three songs and an overture appeared in Gould's *The Rival Sisters*, while a duet for Southerne's *Oroonoko* probably belongs to November.

Purcell probably fell ill in early November. His condition cannot initially have been life-threatening since he continued to compose. His song 'Sweeter than roses' may belong to this time, though it was not used until the following year, in *Pausanias*, a play probably by Richard Norton. 'From rosy bowers', for D'Urfey's *Don Quixote*, Part 3 which opened in December, was described as 'the last Song that Mr *Purcell* Sett, it being in his Sickness' when published in *Orpheus Britannicus*. His condition must have deteriorated suddenly on 21 November, the day before his friends and colleagues were due to gather at Stationers' Hall for the Cecilian feast. His will, witnessed by neighbours and his brother-in-law John Baptist Peters, bears that date and was clearly copied at speed. His signature, scrawled at the bottom of the document, is barely legible (see p. 14). He had died by the close of the day.

The cause of Purcell's death has never been established. Hawkins's well-known account, which he acknowledged as 'tradition' rather than fact, has Purcell contracting 'a disorder' after being locked out by his wife when he returned home late 'heated with wine from the tavern'. Given the frantic activity of his last months, overwork may have been a contributing factor. Notice of his death appeared in *The Flying Post* on the day of his funeral, 26 November, when it was reported that he would be 'interred in the Abbey, with all the Funeral Solemnity they are capable to perform for him'; the combined choirs of the Abbey and Chapel Royal performed 'Dirges composed by the Deceased for her late Majesty'.

Frances, left to care for Frances junior (seven), Edward (six) and Mary-Peters (almost two), was sole executrix of Henry's estate. She moved from Marsham Street to Dean's Yard, Westminster, where she was joined by Henry's mother Elizabeth (d. 1699), who had perhaps already been living with the family. She set about diligently printing her former husband's works in (for English music) an unprecedented series of memorial publications. In short order she issued *A Choice Collection of Lessons for the Harpsichord or Spinnet* (1696), *A Collection of Ayres, Compos'd for the Theatre, Ten Sonata's in Four Parts* and the Te Deum and Jubilate (all 1697), and the monumental song collection *Orpheus Britannicus* (1698), dedicating each to patrons she doubtless hoped would help support her family. *Orpheus Britannicus* was published by Playford, whose help must have been required to undertake such a large-scale and expensive project; Frances is not named in *Orpheus Britannicus*, book 2, published in 1702. In 1705 she moved to her brother John Baptist Peters's house in Richmond, where she died the following year. She was survived by Frances junior and Edward (no burial record survives for Mary-Peters, but she is not mentioned in her mother's will); she left Edward (who became an organist) 'all the books of music in general, the organ, the double spinnet, the single spinnet'. They had presumably been her husband's.

Purcell's death prompted an outpouring of poetic and musical memorials, notably Dryden's 'Mark how the lark and linnet sing', set by John Blow and printed by Playford in July 1696. They demonstrate the great esteem in which he was held, but unfortunately for modern historians they are largely hagiographic, offering little insight into his biography or character. Only those by Henry Hall, a boyhood friend in the Chapel Royal, provide a more personal portrait. His poem 'To the Memory of my Dear Friend' from *Orpheus Britannicus*, book 1, for instance, touches self-deprecatingly on their shared lessons with John Blow.

There are no other notable contemporary descriptions of Purcell's personality, only scattered comments by 'R.G.' (probably Richard Goodson senior), Anthony Aston, Thomas Tudway, Roger North and Rowland Sherman. They confirm that he revelled in pitting his skill against any and all competitors, in Sherman's words, 'refus[ing] to be outdone in climbing the ladder of talent'. However, what the historical record lacks is more than adequately repaid by the quality and quantity of his music, which continues to offer fulsome testimony to his skill. We hope what follows will contribute to its understanding and enjoyment.

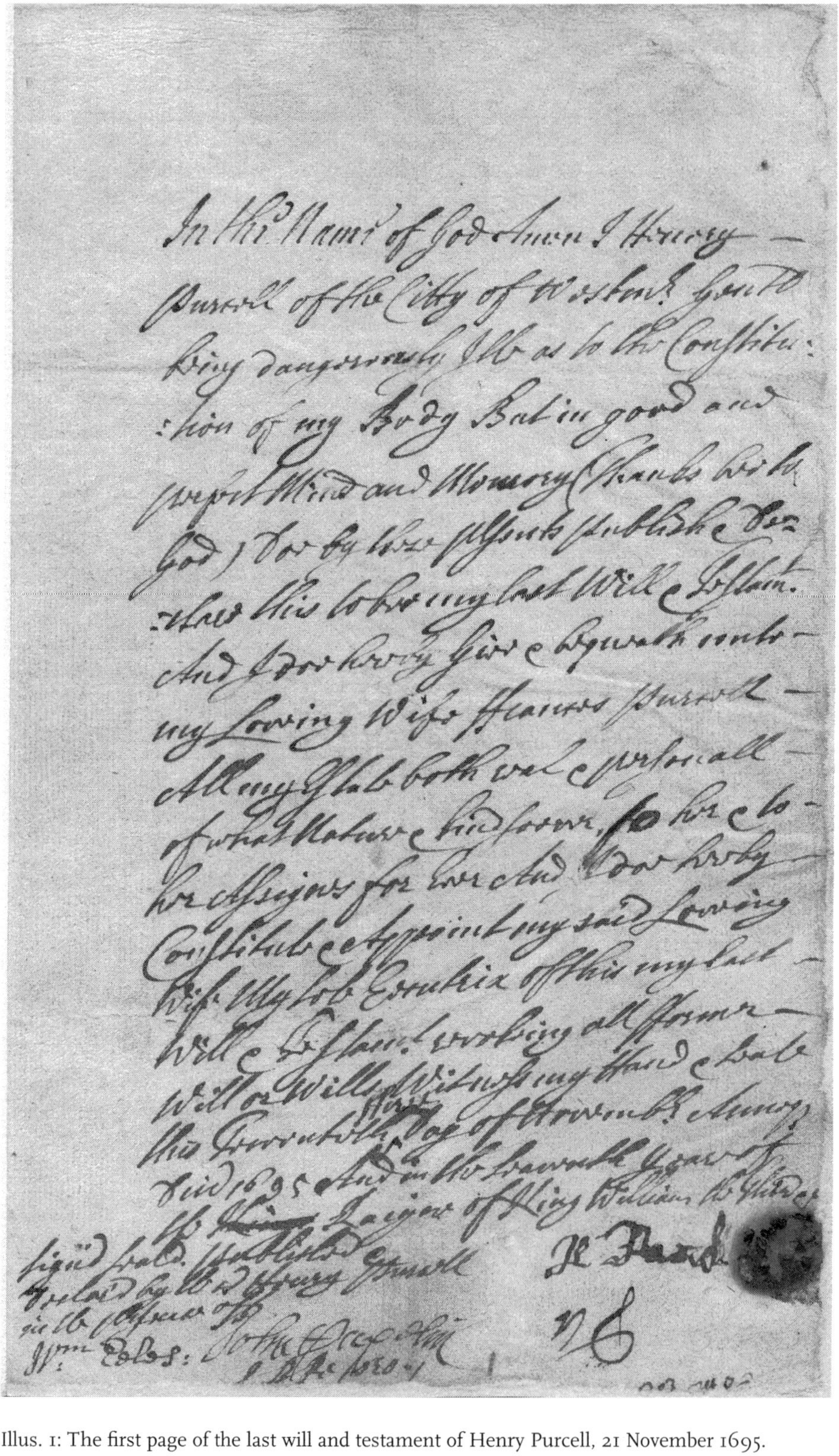
In the Name of God Amen I Henry
Purcell of the City of Westmr. Gentl
being dangerously Ill as to the Constitu:
:tion of my Body But in good and
perfect Mind and Memory (thanks be to
God) I doe by these presents publish & de=
:clare this to be my last Will & Testam:t
And I doe hereby Give & bequeath unto
my Loving Wife Frances Purcell
All my Estate both real & personall
of what Nature & kind soever, to her & to
her Assignes for ever And I doe hereby
Constitute & Appoint my said Loving
Wife My sole Executrix of this my last
Will & Testam:t revoking all former
Will or Wills Witness my Hand & Seale
this Twentyfirst Day of November Anno
Dni 1695 And in the Seaventh Year of
the Reigne of King William the Third &c

H Purcell

Sign'd Seal'd Published & Declared by the sd Henry Purcell in the presence of
Wm Eeles: John Chapelin
J Bartlett

Illus. 1: The first page of the last will and testament of Henry Purcell, 21 November 1695.

Dictionary

Abdelazer, or The Moor's Revenge Z570 Purcell wrote a song, 'Lucinda is bewitching fair', and theatre airs* for a revival of Aphra Behn's bloody tragedy set in fifteenth-century Spain. The play was produced at Drury Lane* probably on 25 March 1695, with Jemmy Bowen* singing the song on stage. The airs were printed in 1697 in *A Collection of Ayres** with the overture placed first and the other movements reordered, but an early manuscript (the violin book GB-Lbl, Add. MS 35043) preserves the order as played in the theatre – followed in *PS* 16. Benjamin Britten's* *Young Person's Guide to the Orchestra* (Variations and Fugue of a Theme of Purcell, Op. 34, 1945) made famous the Third Act Tune Z570/2, a rondeau* in hornpipe* rhythm. However, the First Act Tune Z570/8, another hornpipe, was more popular at the time: its tune, entitled 'The hole in the wall', was given a country dance* choreography and was printed in all editions of *The Dancing Master* from 1698. *BalSta, PlaDan, PriPur.*

Academy of Ancient Music The Academy was founded in 1726 as the Academy of Vocal Music by professional musicians including the composers J.C. Pepusch and Maurice Greene, with Bernard Gates (1686–1773) and Henry Needler (1685–1760) leading its singers and orchestra. The last two had Purcellian connections. As a Chapel Royal choirboy, Gates would have known Purcell, while Needler, an accountant, had been taught the violin by John Banister* junior and 'the principles of harmony' by 'Purcell' – presumably Daniel Purcell* or Henry's son Edward. Following the notorious quarrel in 1731 over Bononcini's plagiarism of a madrigal by Lotti, and the subsequent departure of Greene and others to found the rival Apollo Academy, its name was changed to the Academy of Ancient Music. Under the direction of Pepusch and his successor Benjamin Cooke it focussed on old music, including Purcell, though it was never exclusively antiquarian, performing much modern Italian concerted music.

The Academy's most ambitious Purcell performances were of *King Arthur** (1742, and in various forms up to 1796); the Te Deum and Jubilate in D major* (1768, 1772), presumably in William Boyce's* rewriting; and a modernised concert version of *Dido and Aeneas** (1774, 1785, 1787). By the 1780s it was being rapidly eclipsed by the Concerts of Ancient Music*. It responded by changing from a music club into a concert-giving organisation, though with mixed results. In 1786 it was castigated by 'The Ghost of Purcell' for neglecting the composer – an echo of Tom Brown's* famous letter purportedly from Purcell to John Blow* – and it finally gave up its own ghost in 1802. The name of the Academy was revived by Christopher Hogwood* in 1973. *See also* **Performance history from 1695**. *HarDid, HawHis, HigRec, JohAca, McVCat, RimBon, TimSte, TupEig, WebCla.*

Act tunes The four instrumental pieces played between the acts of Restoration plays, components of sets of theatre airs*. They were mostly cast in dance forms though they do not seem to have been danced. They ensured that the performance of plays was continuous (there were no intervals in the Restoration theatre), and they were thought to provide the necessary variety, as John Dryden* put it in 1668: 'A Scene of mirth mix'd with Tragedy has the same effect upon us which our musick has betwixt the Acts'. Vocal music occasionally replaced or supplemented act tunes, as with four of the songs Purcell wrote in 1680 for *Theodosius** – a practice that became more common after 1700. *HolThe, LamBal, PriThe.*

Air (Ayre) A word with multiple, overlapping meanings in Purcell's time. Around 1600 it mostly meant a lute-accompanied song, and this sense was still current in Purcell's day, as in John Playford's* series of *Choice Ayres, Songs and Dialogues*. By extension, as with *aria* in Italian, it was applied to instrumental pieces, particularly those in duple time with two repeated sections but without the specific characteristics of particular dances. In *PlaInt* Purcell used the word to mean melody, while Roger North's* essays show it was also a synonym for 'tune', and it was used loosely to mean the key of a piece. *MacMus, NorMus, StrDic.*

Aldrich, Henry The celebrated dean of Christ Church, Oxford* (1648–1710; dean from 1689) was something of a Renaissance man: an influential high churchman, mathematician, classical scholar, architect and accomplished composer. His active involvement in the Christ Church choir, choosing the boys and men, singing in services and organising weekly music meetings in his lodgings, was an inspiring model for raising standards in cathedral music. His music library, the main component of the Christ Church music collection, includes several important Purcell manuscripts, including Mus. 38, a score of the complete Service in B$^\flat$ Z230 copied by John Walter*; and Mus. 628, an anthology copied by John Blow* in the late 1670s that contains most of Purcell's early devotional part-songs. Aldrich was the dedicatee of *Harmonia Sacra**, book 2 (1693). *CCLMC, CheChu, HerCat, HolBat, ShaAnc, ShaMan, SpiCat, WaiPat.*

Almand The English name for the binary-form dance, called *allemande* in French and *allemanda* in Italian. Purcell treated it as a keyboard genre – there are no examples in his theatre airs* – and in his suites* almands are normally paired with corants*, occasionally giving the two genres matching melodic shapes and harmonic progressions. Standard features are short upbeats to each section and prevailing dotted rhythms. In Purcell's most elaborate examples, such as the Almand in D minor Z668/1, labelled 'Bell Barr'*, *style brisé** textures suggest contrapuntal part-writing through broken-chord patterns. *See also* **Rhythmic alteration**. *FerPur, HolPur.*

Amphitryon, or The Two Sosias Z572 Purcell wrote two songs, a dialogue, a dance and a set of theatre airs* for John Dryden's* witty and popular comedy after Plautus and Molière, first produced at Drury Lane* in October 1690. Dryden included the vocal pieces as a supplement to the published play text, remarking in the preface that in Purcell 'we have at length found an *English-man*, equal with the best abroad' – effectively repenting of having praised Louis Grabu* at the expense of English composers in his preface to *Albion and Albanius*. Dryden had been won over to Purcell by the great success of *Dioclesian**; *Amphitryon* was their first collaboration.

The two songs are both strophic with ritornellos* for two violins and continuo. 'Celia, that I once was blest' was sung by John Bowman* in Act

III, and 'For Iris I sigh' by Charlotte Butler* in a comic magic scene conjured by Mercury in Act IV. After Butler's song Purcell provided a delightful Dance for Tinkers, choreographed by Thomas Bray*, with a fast section evoking the hammering of pots and pans. It only survives in two parts, but there is a four-part reconstruction in PS 16. The scene ends with a fine pastoral dialogue*, 'Fair Iris and her swain', sung by Butler and Bowman – including what is probably the origin of the phrase 'kiss and tell'. The set of theatre airs, printed in concert order in *A Collection of Ayres**, is in the original theatre order in the 'Cambury Manuscript'* – followed in PS 16. The set is not especially memorable, though the Fourth Act Tune Z571/4 is a delightful example of the Scots idiom popular in Restoration London. *See also* **Scots (Scotch) songs and dances**. *LauCam, LS, PriPur, PriThe, RobBow.*

Anne, Princess and Queen The second surviving child of James, Duke of York and Anne Hyde, Princess Anne (1665–1714) married Prince George of Denmark in the chapel of St James's Palace on 28 July 1683, an event marked by Purcell's ode 'From hardy climes'*. As a Catholic, her father did not attend the Chapel Royal*, but after his accession as James II* in 1685 Anne's continued attendance there enabled Purcell to continue writing symphony anthems*, including 'Behold, I bring you glad tidings'* (1687) and 'O sing unto the Lord'* (1688). In the next reign Purcell was largely taken up with writing birthday odes for Anne's elder sister Queen Mary*, though he may have written 'The noise of foreign wars'*, marking the birth of her son, William Duke of Gloucester* on 24 July 1689. His last ode, 'Who can from joy refrain?'*, celebrated William's sixth birthday. Purcell's late song 'Lovely Albina's come ashore'* seems to be concerned with Anne's relationship with William III*.

Like most of the Stuarts, Anne was musical. She was taught the guitar* by Francesco Corbetta and a Mr Delawney; her guitar book, now at The Hague, contains 22 arrangements of songs and dances by Purcell. She was taught the harpsichord by G.B. Draghi*, and Frances Purcell dedicated *A Choice Collection** to her, mentioning that 'Your Highness's Generous Encouragem<en>t of my deceas'd Husband's Performances in Musick, together with the great Honour your Highness has don that Science, in your Choice of that Instrument, for which the following Compositions were made'. Her Charles Hayward spinet*, 'the loudest and perhaps the finest that ever was heard' (*HawHis*, ii. 718), was passed down to successive Masters of the Children of the Chapel Royal. Anne was taught singing by Arabella Hunt*, and included Annabella Howard* (née Dyve), a friend of Sarah Churchill, in her circle at Berkeley House in Piccadilly; she had rented it in 1692 from the Duke of Somerset* after her rift with William III and Mary. Robert Thompson has suggested that Purcell copied the Gresham autograph* for Howard. *HalPri, HolDra, HolHar, HunPat, MurOde, PagGui, SpiOde, ThoHow, WhiNoi, WinAnn.*

Anniversary celebrations The first Purcell anniversary event seems to have been on 30 January 1858, when the bicentenary of what was thought to be the composer's birth was marked by the Purcell Club* with a banquet and concert in a London tavern. In November 1895 the bicentenary of his death was marked by an exhibition of manuscripts, prints and portraits at the British Museum; a list is in *PurExh*. Events included: a commemorative service in

Westminster Abbey*; a production of *Dido and Aeneas** at the Lyceum Theatre; the first London performance of Hubert Parry's *Invocation to Music, an Ode (in Honour of Henry Purcell)*; and a performance of 'Hail, bright Cecilia'* by the Philharmonic Society conducted by Alexander Mackenzie. In 1959 the tercentenary of Purcell's birth and the bicentenary of Handel's death were marked by a Purcell-Handel Festival, which included another exhibition at the British Museum (see *PurHan*); another stage production of *Dido and Aeneas*, in the Great Hall at Hampton Court; the first production since the eighteenth century of the Restoration version of *The Tempest**, with the music thought today to be by John Weldon* attributed to Purcell; and a series of BBC broadcasts. The most lasting outcome was the collection of Purcell essays *HPEM*.

In 1995 the celebrations extended to English music as a whole with *Fairest Isle*, the year-long series of BBC Radio 3 programmes. The Purcell tercentenary concert on 21 November in Westminster Abbey featured the first London performance of 'Jehova, quam multi sunt hostes mei'* as orchestrated by Elgar. The events included the customary exhibition (see *ThoGlo*); conferences at the British Library and the Barbican in London; a production of *King Arthur** at Covent Garden conducted by William Christie; and the release of Tony Palmer's film *England, My England**. There was also an outpouring of new Purcell recordings and biographies, though of more lasting value were three volumes of scholarly essays, *PurStu*, *PC* and *PMHP*, the last being the proceedings of a 1993 Oxford conference. The public profile of the celebrations was raised by the fortuitous discovery in 1994 of the Purcell-Draghi Manuscript*. The 350th anniversary of Purcell's birth in 2009 was understandably a lower-key celebration, though it was marked by a notable production of *The Fairy Queen** at Glyndebourne, and (taking advantage of the Handel, Haydn and Mendelssohn anniversaries that year) a conference devoted to all four composers at New College, Oxford. *See also* **Stage history from 1695**. *BurCra*, *BurElg*, *BurRem*, *GroPur*, *HerRec*, *PinPhe*, *PurCom*, *RylTem*.

Anthem A setting of an English religious text, to be sung in the Anglican liturgy. Unlike liturgical texts such as the Magnificat, anthem texts* were freely chosen. Anthems had been sung in services since 1549, but they were not assigned a position in the liturgy until the 1662 *Book of Common Prayer*, where they are specified at morning and evening prayer after the third collect 'In Quires and Places where they sing'. Anthems were also sometimes performed during the communion service at the Chapel Royal* when the monarch was in attendance, at special thanksgiving services and at coronations. Purcell wrote examples of all the types of Restoration anthem. The full anthem employed the choir throughout, while the full-with-verse anthem interspersed passages for a smaller ensemble (the verse) between the choral sections, usually in the patterns F–V–F or F–V–F–V–F. Both types always had organ accompaniment, despite being full-voiced and often transmitted without a continuo* part. The verse anthem* with organ consisted largely of passages for a single voice or a small ensemble. Contrast was created by varying the vocal scoring between the verses, and by introducing the full choir, usually at the mid-point and the end of the work. In solo anthems all the verses were taken by a single virtuoso soloist. The symphony anthem*, the most glamorous type with its string symphonies* and ritornellos*, was essentially confined to the Chapel Royal during Charles

II's* reign. Purcell, like his contemporaries, favoured the various types of verse anthem because of the opportunities they provided for declamatory and virtuosic solo vocal writing. *See also* **Services**. *CheChu, HerOrg, HolPur, SpiCat, VanChu.*

Anthem texts 55 of Purcell's 70 anthems set texts from the Psalms in the translation made for the Great Bible of 1540 and adopted in the Psalter of the Book of Common Prayer. Of the remainder, five texts are taken from the Book of Common Prayer outside the Psalter, six from the Old Testament and two from the New Testament. In addition, two combine lines from Psalms and Isaiah, and these, both for coronations*, are the only texts for which the compilers are known: William Sancroft, Archbishop of Canterbury, and Henry Compton, Bishop of London, respectively compiled 'My heart is inditing'* and 'Praise the Lord, O Jerusalem'*. 15 anthems set 'discontinuous' texts in which intermediate verses are omitted or reordered, in some cases to create or strengthen an allusion to topical events. Even when texts are not discontinuous, a specific allusion may have been intended, as with 'Blessed are they that fear the Lord' Z5, a complete setting of Psalm 128 composed for the thanksgiving service for the pregnancy of James II's* wife Mary of Modena. The most artfully devised text is 'The way of God is an undefiled way' Z56, which consists of discontinuous verses from Psalm 18, skilfully selected to celebrate William III's* return from the summer campaign of 1694; they were reordered (perhaps by Purcell himself) to make them more conducive for musical setting. *RanCor, VanChu, SpiCat, WhiPol.*

'Arise, my muse' Z320 Purcell's 1690 ode for Queen Mary's* birthday, scored for pairs of trumpets*, oboes* and recorders* with Italianate five-part string writing, shows his increasingly sophisticated handling of the orchestra. The Italianate opening symphony*, inserted later into *King Arthur**, begins with an ostinato figure in the bass contrasted with fanfares in the upper parts (an idea much imitated by Daniel Purcell* and Jeremiah Clarke*, among others), and is remarkable for its independent writing for trumpets – probably doubled by oboes, though this is unclear in the sources. The ritornello* following the countertenor duet and chorus, 'Hail, gracious Gloriana', is a quintet for two trumpets, two oboes (now given independent parts) and continuo*, a scoring Purcell also used in *Dioclesian**, written soon after.

Thomas D'Urfey's* text, as printed in *Poems on Affairs of State*, iii (1698), shows that Purcell, perhaps pressed for time preparing *Dioclesian*, did not set the two final stanzas. However, it enabled him to end the ode with a dramatic masterstroke: he rearranged the text so that Eusebia (a personification of the Anglican Church), represented by a countertenor with two recorders, mourns the imminent departure of Caesar (William III*, about to start his campaign against James II* in Ireland). The bass soloist interrupts with 'But Glory cries, "Go on, illustrious man"', only for Eusebia to resume her mourning. Finally, the chorus enters to repeat the bass soloist's command, bringing the ode to an abrupt conclusion. *See also* **Odes**. *AdaPur, HolPur, MurOde, SpiOde, WooOde, WooPur.*

The Armstrong-Finch Manuscript This large oblong quarto scorebook* came to public attention in 1899 through Alfred Moffat's edition of Purcell's hitherto unknown Sonata in G minor Z780*. It was begun by the viola player and copyist William Armstrong (d.1717), though it is mostly in the hand of its owner, Edward Finch* (1663–1738). Armstrong and Finch worked together, producing a large anthology of solo sonatas variously for violin, recorder or flute. The reversed portion includes a four-part arrangement of the Adagio from the Golden Sonata* and Purcell's anthem 'O give thanks unto the Lord' Z33. Later owners included members of the Sharp family (Finch family friends), Thomas Taphouse (the owner in 1899), the botanist Ellen Willmott, and after her death in 1934 her brother-in-law Robert Berkeley and his descendants. The British Library purchased it at Sotheby's on 3 December 2019, allocating it the shelf-mark MS Mus. 1851. *DarCha, HolMan.*

Arne, Thomas Augustine As the most prominent and prolific English theatre composer of his time, Arne (1710–78) was involved in a number of revivals of plays and dramatic operas for which Purcell had written music. In 1740 he replaced Purcell's contributions to *The Libertine** and *Oedipus** with his own (lost) music for productions at Drury Lane*, a process he repeated at the Smock Alley Theatre in Dublin in 1744 with *Theodosius**. *Dioclesian** (Covent Garden, 1 February, 23 November 1758) was advertised as having 'several New Songs' by Arne, giving the impression that Purcell's music was largely retained. However, the published play-text for the November production shows that most of it was discarded, including the Act V masque*, replaced by 'The Sultan', a masque incongruously set in Ottoman Turkey.

Arne's most important involvement with Purcell came with David Garrick's adaptation of *King Arthur** (Drury Lane, 13 December 1770). He originally proposed replacing most if not all of Purcell's score, complaining to Garrick that, among other things, some of the solos had unsuitable ranges for his singers; the Act I sacrifice scene was a 'dull, tedious, antiquated suite of Chorus'; and that 'All the other Solo Songs of Purcell are infamously bad, – so very bad, that they are privately the objects of sneer and ridicule to the Musicians'. However, the printed score (1771) shows that Arne's contribution consisted mainly of numbers never set by Purcell, though he provided new settings of 'How blest are shepherds' and 'St George' as well as a new overture. He also made detailed changes to the original music, partly to take account of Garrick's cuts to the play and partly to bring it up to date. He later complained to Garrick that 'several other things that employed my utmost efforts' had been 'laid aside' in favour of Purcell's settings, which were 'cathedral, and not to the taste of a modern theatrical audience'. Nevertheless, Charles Dibdin (*DibSta*, v. 239) wrote that 'ARNE idolized PURCELL', and took pride in placing him 'in that conspicuous situation the brilliancy of his reputation demanded'. *See also* **Stage history from 1695**. *GilArn, GilGar, HarArt, HerRec, HigRec, LS.*

Augmentation *See* **Counterpoint**

Autographs In a seminal 2006 article (*HerFow*), Rebecca Herissone listed the 30-plus music manuscripts in Purcell's hand, dividing them into five types according to function. 'Fowle originalls' (Type A) are original copies, inelegantly written with composing corrections but nevertheless capable of being used by others to copy performance material and other scores. Most are of anthems, though the type also includes a few loose-leaf scores of odes, including 'Hail, bright Cecilia'*. Performance material (Type B) divides into loose-leaf parts apparently copied for a particular occasion, such as the part-autograph string parts for 'My song shall be alway'*; and bound partbooks intended for repeated use, such as the Chapel Royal* vocal bass book J-Tn, N5/10, into which Purcell copied the chorus part of his verse anthem 'Sing unto God' Z52. The Gresham autograph* is another type of performance manuscript, perhaps compiled for his own use to accompany singers.

Purcell's most compendious autographs are scorebooks* (Type C) containing file copies made for reference purposes; they were copied at both ends, each section collecting a particular genre. Transmission copies (Type D) are typically loose-leaf scores apparently made by Purcell for provincial colleagues. Among them are some separate copies of anthems now in the Flackton Collection*, and Purcell's copy of an anthem by Daniel Roseingrave*, probably made to be sent to the composer in Winchester*. The Purcell-Draghi Manuscript* is the only surviving autograph evidently copied for teaching purposes (Type E), for an unidentified keyboard pupil. The most recent autograph to come to light is a portion of a bass vocal part for 'I was glad' Z19; it was auctioned in 2003, and its current whereabouts are unknown (*WhiPre, ThoSou*, 35–6). *See also* **Copyists, Handwriting, Revisions, Stratigraphic Scores**. *BamBar, ForAut, ForOsb, HerCat, HerCre, HerOrg, HogMan, HolPur, HolRos, PriAut, PurGre, ShaAnc, ShaCol, ShaMan, SmiPer, ThoGlo, ThoFan, WooAut, WooKey, ZimCat, ZimHan*.

Ayliff, Mrs The singer and actress Mrs Ayliff (first name unknown; at the time the honorific 'Mrs' was not restricted to married women) sang in *The Fairy Queen** in 1692 and subsequently became Purcell's leading soprano, taking part in at least 20 of his works up to late 1694 including 'Celebrate this festival'* and 'Hail, bright Cecilia'*. Her performance of 'Ah me to many deaths decreed' Z586 led Peter Motteux* to comment: 'had you heard it sung by Mrs. *Ayliff* you would have own'd that there is no pleasure like that which good Notes, when so divinely sung, can create'. She joined Thomas Betterton's company* when the United Company* broke up in the spring of 1695 and was therefore no longer available to Purcell. She disappears from stage records in 1696. Almost nothing is known of her life, though the varied and demanding roles Purcell gave her moved Olive Baldwin and Thelma Wilson to describe her as 'the finest singer with whom Purcell worked in the theatre'. *BalSop, BalSta, WalSon*.

Babel, Charles The bassoonist and music copyist (d.1716), the father of the violinist, harpsichordist and composer William Babell (1688–1723), came from Évreux in Normandy, though nothing is known of his life until 1688–90, when he was a member of the Hanover court orchestra. He is next heard of at The Hague in 1696 and served William III* there in 1697–8. He probably came to England in 1698; became a naturalised British citizen in 1699; and settled in London, where he combined work as a music copyist with playing in theatre bands. 13 manuscripts in his hand are known, most of them anthologies of songs, consort music or keyboard music. They contain music from all over Europe, often organised by key into extended suites* containing pieces by several composers. Some manuscripts were probably commissioned by patrons, though his two keyboard anthologies were copied for his son. Pieces by Purcell are found in all the anthologies Babel copied at The Hague and in London, including the uniquely preserved trumpet part for Purcell's *Bonduca** overture; the only known consort version of the Cibell*; and some unique keyboard arrangements of songs and consort pieces. They are an important resource for Purcell scholarship, still not fully explored: some suites consisting of music largely by Purcell include anonymous pieces that may be by him. *BDECM, HerCat, HerMag, LasBab, WooBab, WooKey.*

Backfall *See* **Ornamentation**

Band The word used in Restoration England for a large group of instrumentalists, particularly the Twenty-Four Violins*, as when Roger North* (*NorMus*, 300) wrote that Charles II 'set up a band of 24 violins to play at his dinners'. Smaller groups were normally called consorts*, as with John Singleton's ten-man 'Private Consort', set up at court in 1660, though the two terms overlapped to some extent: in 1662 John Banister* formed the 'Select Band' at court, consisting of half the Twenty-Four Violins. *HolFid.*

Banister family John Banister senior (*c.*1624–79), the most prominent English violinist at Charles II's court, formed a 'select band' of twelve from the Twenty-Four Violins* in 1663, which in 1664 became the house band of the King's Company; he became an important theatre composer, contributing to at least ten productions up to 1670. He is best known for his role in developing public concerts, starting a series in 1672 at his house in Whitefriars. He also dabbled in music publishing, collaborating with the Chapel Royal* singer Thomas Lowe in *New Ayres and Dialogues* (1678), which included some early Purcell songs. Roger North* wrote that Banister 'had a good theatricall vein, and in composition had a lively style peculiar to himself' (*NorMus*, 352), and he was doubtless an important influence on the young Purcell, particularly for developing an English version of the French orchestral idiom. He wrote some effective theatrical songs, though his consort music (admittedly surviving mostly in poor sources) suggests he lacked the technique to write effective and error-free four-part harmony.

Banister's son John junior (1662–1736) inherited his father's court place as a violinist and also developed a successful freelance career promoting public concerts and playing in theatre orchestras. Father and son played wind instruments as a sideline: North also wrote that Banister senior 'did wonders upon a flageolett to a thro-base', while Banister junior was additionally a leading recorder* player, often playing duets with James Paisible*. He was a more accomplished composer than his father, though little of his music survives. Jeffery or Jafery Banister (*c.*1640–84), probably John senior's younger brother, a court violinist from 1662, is mainly remembered for running with James Hart a ladies' boarding school in Chelsea, a forerunner of Josias Priest's* school where *Dido and Aeneas** was performed. *BDECM, HolFid, LasRec, LocDra, PriPur, PriThe, SpiSon, TilCha, WolVio.*

Barnard, John Singing man (minor canon at St Paul's Cathedral* from 1637), music copyist and composer (b. c.1591). He was the compiler of *The First Book of Selected Church Musick*, published in ten partbooks in London on the eve of the Civil War in 1641. Purcell drew on it, probably in 1682, when compiling his anthology of church music at the back of what is now GB-Cfm, MU MS 88, scoring up pieces by William Byrd, Orlando Gibbons*, William Mundy and Nathaniel Giles from it. He may have done this partly for study purposes, but he also corrected mistakes, resolved problems with the underlay and sorted out inconsistent accidentals, suggesting he had performance in mind or at least the production of performing parts. See also **Autographs**. BamBar, CheChu, HolPur, KruPri, ShaAnc, ShaCol, ShaMan.

Bassoon The four-piece Baroque bassoon replaced the Renaissance-type curtal in England when it was imported from France around 1680. James Talbot* wrote that the sackbut or trombone was 'left off towards the latter end of K<ing> Ch<arles> 2d & gave place to the Fr<ench> Basson'. Purcell specified it only once, in *Dioclesian** Z627/2a (see Illus. 3, p. 59), where it acts as the bass to an oboe* consort, though its use can be assumed in similar circumstances. Bassoons are often used today in the solo passages of Purcell's concerted works, but during his lifetime they seem to have been confined to tutti sections. BaiTal, HayHau, HolFid, HolPur, OweObo.

Bass violin The original large bass member of the violin family*, called *basse de violon* in French and *violone* in Italian; few instruments have survived without being cut down to violoncello size. Writing in the 1720s, Roger North* (*NorMus*, 304) called it 'a very hard and harsh sounded base, and nothing so soft and sweet as now', and for this reason the bass viol* was generally preferred in Restoration England as a continuo instrument. The range and character of Purcell's orchestral bass parts suggests that he expected the original BB^b–F–c–g tuning, though he only occasionally exploited the bottom note. The change to the CC–G–d–a tuning apparently went hand-in-hand with the change to the more modern combination of violoncello and double bass in London orchestras around 1710. Confusingly, 'bass violin' continued in use, meaning a violoncello in a non-solo role. See also **Violin family**. HolFid, HolLif.

The Battle of the Organs The celebrated competition between the organ builders Bernard ('Father') Smith* and Renatus Harris* to provide an organ* for the Temple Church in London. The Inner and Middle Temple records provide much information about the protracted process (1683–6), which resulted in victory for Smith. Hawkins* (*HawHis*, ii. 691–2) and Burney* (*BurHis*, iii. 437–9), drawing seemingly on now-lost documents, state that the judging (overseen by the notoriously severe Judge Jeffreys) involved alternating public recitals, given by John Blow* and Purcell for Smith and G.B. Draghi* for Harris. BicOrg, DunSmi, FreSmi, KniBat, NorMus, ZimPur.

Beaumont and Fletcher The supposedly co-authored plays by the Jacobean dramatists Francis Beaumont (1584/5–1616) and John Fletcher (1579–1625), subsequently published in two folios (1647, 1679), were immensely popular on the Restoration stage. As with Shakespeare's plays*, Purcell and his contemporaries mostly set the words of later adapters. He contributed eight songs (including 'I'll sail upon the dog-star'*) to *A Fool's Preferment, or The Three Dukes of Dunstable* Z571, Thomas D'Urfey's* adaptation of *A Noble Gentleman* (Dorset Garden, ?April 1688). A three-part catch*, 'At the close of the evening' Z599, was sung in a revival of *The Knight of Malta* (?1690–1). In addition, *Dioclesian** (originally *The Prophetess*, 1622) and *Bonduca** (c.1613) were adapted for Purcell in 1690 and 1695 respectively. However, modern scholarship attributes the first of these plays to Fletcher and Anonymous; the second to Nathan Field, Philip Massinger and Fletcher; the third to Fletcher and Massinger; and the fourth to Fletcher alone. In addition, the duet 'There ne'er was so wretched a lover' and the mock-song* 'There's not a swain on the plain would be blest' Z587, were used in a revival, possibly in the winter of 1693–4 of Fletcher's *Rule a Wife and Have a Wife* (1624). *PriPur, PriIsl, PriThe, WalSon, ZimCat.*

'Behold, I bring you glad tidings' Z2 This symphony anthem* was first performed in the Chapel Royal* on Christmas Day 1687. Its virtuosic bass solo was written for John Gostling*, who recorded the date of the work in his scorebook, US-AUS, HRC 85. Its Italianate style, particularly in the opening bipartite symphony, seems to be Purcell's initial response to G.B. Draghi's* *Song for St Cecilia's Day, 1687*, performed at the Cecilian celebrations* the previous month. The anthem is noteworthy for its dramatic character, with the bass soloist portraying the angel announcing Christ's birth, and a trio of soloists and the choir representing the exchanges between the angels and shepherds. The effect would have been enhanced by the layout of the chapel at Whitehall*, where the soloists sang from a gallery, with the choir stationed in the choirstalls below. *SpiCat, HolPur, ZimGos.*

The Bell Anthem *See* **'Rejoice in the Lord alway'**

Bell Barr The title of Purcell's song 'I love and I must' Z382 in the Gresham autograph*, and a subtitle of the Almand* in D minor Z668/1 in *A Choice Collection**. It apparently refers to a hamlet in the parish of North Mymms south of Hatfield in Hertfordshire, where Sir Robert Howard* and his wife Annabella had a summer retreat from 1693 until his death in 1698. It was conveniently close to Holywell House in St Albans, owned by Annabella's close friend Sarah Churchill, Countess (later Duchess) of Marlborough. *HowMou, ThoHow, ThoSou.*

Bergmann, Walter German harpsichordist, editor and composer (1902–88). He came to England in 1939 and worked with Michael Tippett* at Morley College in south London from 1941, participating in its ground-breaking Purcell performances, including 'Hail, bright Cecilia'*. He had a particular interest in Purcell, collaborating with Tippett in an extensive series of practical editions of his vocal music (1947–66) for Schott & Co, including 'Come, ye sons of art, away'* as well as the odes on Purcell's death by John Blow* and Jeremiah Clarke*. He accompanied Alfred Deller* in some notable recordings*, including (in 1949) 'Music for a while'* and 'If music be the food of love'* Z379B. *ClaDel, ColMor, ColTip, MarBer, HarDel.*

Bess of Bedlam *See* 'From silent shades'

Betterton, Thomas Actor and manager (1635–1710), the dominant figure in the London theatre during Purcell's working life. In 1660 he initially joined the King's Company, but soon switched to William Davenant's Duke's Company, becoming its co-manager in 1668. He produced the company's series of dramatic operas* in the 1670s, beginning with *Macbeth* in 1673, basing this new genre on his experience of French theatrical practice during visits to Paris. In 1683 Charles II* sent Betterton back to Paris to invite Lully* and the Académie royale de musique to produce an opera in London, but when that proved impossible Louis Grabu* was recruited to set Dryden's* *Albion and Albanius* (1685). The United Company* sustained a significant loss on that production, and Betterton did not attempt any further substantial musical theatre works until 1690, when he turned to Purcell to set his adaptation of *Dioclesian** (1690), having apparently tried out the young composer in 1689–90 by commissioning him to set a scene from *Circe**; he may also have made the adaptation of *The Fairy Queen** (1692).

Betterton was paid £50 to adapt *The Indian Queen** in 1694, though the break-up of the United Company in the spring of 1695 prevented any further collaboration between the two men: Betterton took his company to the Lincoln's Inn Fields Theatre while Purcell remained at Drury Lane*. In 1700 he mounted the first public production of *Dido and Aeneas**, woven into Charles Gildon's* adaptation of Shakespeare's *Measure for Measure*; in 1704 it was reassembled to serve as an afterpiece to two plays. Gildon's biography (*GilBet*), published shortly after Betterton's death, is an important source of information about his acting style. *LS, MulDio, MulWor, PriPur, PriThe, SawRic.*

Bevin, Elway Master of the Choristers and organist of Bristol Cathedral (c.1554–1638). He was mainly remembered in Restoration England for the canons in his *Briefe and Short Instruction in the Art of Musicke* (1631). Purcell knew them: he recommended their 'wonderful variety' to 'the Younger Practitioners' (*PlaInt*, 114). *HerCrc, HerThe, HowArt.*

Biography The first account of Purcell's life, valuable for its anecdotes apparently handed down from the composer's circle, was published in 1776 by Sir John Hawkins* (*HawHis*, ii. 743–59). It was followed in 1789 by Charles Burney's* much longer, more balanced and thorough treatment (*BurHis*, iii. 483–511; see also *BurRee*). These were the main sources for subsequent dictionary entries and journal articles, though Vincent Novello's* 'Biographical Sketch of Henry Purcell', informed by his work as a Purcell editor, was effectively the first book devoted to the composer. The first formal book-length biography was *CumPur* (1881), by the singer, organist and collector W.H. Cummings, a founder of the Purcell Society* in 1876. It was followed by more than 20 such volumes in English, of which the most notable are Sir Jack Westrup's *WesPur* in the J.M. Dent series The Master Musicians (1937), subsequently revised five times and then reprinted with Curtis Price's introduction (1995); and Franklin Zimmerman's* *ZimPur* (1967; 2/1983), the most comprehensive to date. The most recent is Bruce Wood's short *WooPur* (2009). None of the five Purcell biographies published for the tercentenary in 1995 offered much new, and there is a pressing need for a new full-length treatment taking account of recent archival research and studies of the primary sources.

The Blessed Virgin's Expostulation Z196 'Tell me, some pitying angel', Purcell's remarkable extended devotional song with words by Nahum Tate*, was first published in *Harmonia Sacra**, book 2 (1693); it was perhaps composed specially for the publication. Tate's poem (subtitled '*When our Saviour (at Twelve Years of Age) had withdrawn himself*, &c. Luke 2. v. 42') is an astonishingly vivid depiction of a mind in turmoil, with a series of disconnected statements, commands and questions expressed in simple, direct language and aptly laid out in verse of shifting metre. Purcell responded to Tate's cantata-like alternation between action and reflection with an Italianate sequence of recitative-like declamatory passages and binary airs, using his full repertory of affective devices, most memorably with the cries of 'Gabriel!' set to repeated g''s over a sequence of increasingly clashing passacaglia*-like harmonies. The song is a wonderful example of how Purcell used idioms drawn from modern secular song (particularly mad songs*) to revitalise the devotional song* genre. *HolPur*.

Blow, John According to his epitaph in Westminster Abbey, the organist and composer John Blow (1649–1708) was 'Master to the famous Mr H. Purcell', probably meaning that as Master of the Children of the Chapel Royal he was Purcell's composition teacher. Blow certainly seems to have fostered Purcell's interest in counterpoint, witness the full anthem 'O Lord God of hosts'*, modelled on Blow's 'God is our hope and strength', or the Service in B$^\flat$ Z230 with its elaborate canons*, clearly indebted to those in Blow's Service in G. Blow also led the way in secular music. His Cowley* setting 'Awake, awake my lyre' (?1676) initiated the symphony song* genre, developed by Purcell in the 1680s; his court odes provided immediate models for Purcell's early odes, particularly in their airs constructed over running ground basses*; and his miniature opera *Venus and Adonis* (1683) inspired *Dido and Aeneas** on a number of levels, from its dramatic and musical planning to the style of its vocal and instrumental writing.

There is abundant evidence of a continuing close relationship between the two men, though Purcell increasingly took the lead in developing new genres and types of writing. In 1679 Blow relinquished the post of organist of Westminster Abbey in favour of his young colleague. They both demonstrated Bernard Smith's* instrument in the Battle of the Organs*, and they evidently worked together in planning their symphony anthems for the coronation* of James II* on 23 April 1685. Purcell's Te Deum and Jubilate in D major* (1694) was the immediate model for Blow's setting, performed on the same occasion the following year. After Purcell's death in November 1695 Blow led the mourners with his eloquent setting of John Dryden's* ode 'Mark how the lark and linnet sing'; and his song collection *Amphion Anglicus* (1700) was inspired by *Orpheus Britannicus**, book 1. Blow was an uneven composer (Charles Burney* catalogued his supposed technical lapses as 'Specimens of D^r. Blow's Crudities' in *BurHis*, iii. 449–52), though at his best he can stand comparison with Purcell. *See also* **Continuo**, **Italian Music**, **Odes on the death of Henry Purcell**. *AdaOde, BloMot, BloVen, BDECM, CBCR, CheChu, ShaMan, SpiSon, ThoOpe, WhiCec, WooEqu, WooPur, ZimPur*.

'Blow up the trumpet in Sion' Z10 This full-with-verse anthem (seven-part verse; eight-part chorus), among the finest of Purcell's early sacred works, was copied into the Westminster Abbey* partbooks by the autumn of 1677. Its austere text, from Joel 2, may have been selected to mark a specific occasion, such as the annual fast for the martyrdom of Charles I. Purcell's setting begins in the trumpet key of C major, but the text is a desolate plea for mercy, and after the opening fanfares it shifts to the minor, exploiting the penitential aspects of the verse with chromatic and angular part-writing. The verse soloists are deployed with a dramatic flair extraordinary for a composer in his teens, sometimes pitting high voices against low, and elsewhere gathering all the voices together in homophonic appeals for salvation. The seven-part verse writing was probably inspired by the verse passages in Matthew Locke's* 'Be thou exalted, Lord', a thanksgiving anthem from 1666. *AdaPur, HolPur, SpiCat, VanChu.*

Bonduca, or The British Heroine Z574 An anonymous adaptation of Fletcher's play about the struggles of the 'British heroine' (Boadicea or Boudica to us) against the Romans, produced at Drury Lane* in late October 1695; it was probably Purcell's last major theatre work. He provided a fine set of theatre airs* as well as vocal music for three scenes: a catch, 'Jack, thou'rt a toper', sung by three Roman soldiers in Act II; an extended temple scene in Act III, Scene 2, in which Druids pray for victory; and the song 'O lead me to some peaceful gloom' in Act V. This was sung by Bonduca's daughter Bonvica (Letitia Cross*) as she prepares for death; she was accompanied by 'Lucius *with a Lute*' – apparently a musician, also onstage. 'Britons, strike home!'*, which concludes the temple scene, was the most enduringly popular number, though the finest is 'O lead me to some peaceful gloom', an excellent example of the fashionable two-section song, with a declamatory passage balanced by a vocal minuet. The remorseless tread of the bass at the opening beautifully illustrates the girl's approaching fate. Curtis Price pointed out that the overture, for trumpet and strings, is unusual for the time in that it prefigures the tragedy's dénouement by plunging from C major into a wild chromatic close in C minor. *See also* **Beaumont and Fletcher, Musical Antiquarian Society.** *HolBat, HolPur, PriPur, RimBon.*

Bowen, Jemmy (James) The boy treble Jemmy Bowen was one of Purcell's leading theatre singers between Easter 1695 and the composer's death that November. Purcell gave him some technically and emotionally demanding music, including the roles of Cupid in the Masque from *Timon of Athens**; Quivera and the God of Dreams in *The Indian Queen**; and Genius in the 1695 revival of Nathaniel Lee's* *The Massacre of Paris*, singing the remarkable second setting of 'Thy genius, lo!' Z604B. He continued to sing at Drury Lane* after Purcell's death, notably taking the demanding role of a young shepherd in Jeremiah Clarke's* *Song on the Death of the Famous Mr Henry Purcell* (?January 1696). His voice evidently broke that summer, when he disappeared from the stage (he reappeared as an alto in 1698), so he was probably born around 1680 and was about 15 when he sang for Purcell. He is last heard of in December 1701, either because he died then or started another career.

The well-known anecdote told by the playwright Anthony Aston suggests that Purcell set great store by the young Bowen. It has the composer saying to his instrumentalists (who were trying to tell the boy how 'to grace and run a

Dictionary

27

Division in such a Place') 'O let him alone ... he will grace it more naturally than you, or I, can teach him'. Roger North* (NorCur, 237) wrote around 1700 that 'our gallants and yong ladies' only wanted to impersonate the Scottish countertenor John Abell, the castrato Sigismondo Fideli or 'Jemmy Bowen'. He is sometimes associated with the 'Rev. J. Bowen' who (according to ZimPur, 299) owned a copy of the 1706 Orpheus Britannicus*, book 1, writing a verse in Purcell's honour on a flyleaf. However, CCED does not list a clerical James Bowen from that period. BalSta, BurRem, BDA, HolPur, LS.

Bowman, John The singing actor with the longest working relationship with Purcell, at court and the theatre. There is conflicting evidence of his birth, though he was probably born around 1660, supposedly joining the Duke's Company aged seven, and would have been about 20 in 1680, when he created the role of the high priest Atticus in Theodosius*. He became a bass soloist in the Private Music* in 1684; he is named as a soloist in 'Sound the trumpet, beat the drum'*, 'Hail, bright Cecilia'*, 'Celebrate this festival'*, and the Te Deum and Jubilate in D major*. In the theatre he was evidently equally strong as a character actor and a singer. He created such demanding roles as Genius in The Massacre of Paris (October–November 1689), singing the first setting of 'Thy genius, lo!' Z604A; Grimbald and perhaps the Cold Genius in King Arthur* (part of his regular duet partnership with Charlotte Butler*); and Cardenio in Don Quixote*, Part 1, singing the great mad song* 'Let the dreadful engines' Z578/3. Bowman was no longer available to Purcell as a theatre singer after the break-up of the United Company* in 1695, though he continued as a prominent member of Thomas Betterton's* company and (apart from possible spells in Dublin) remained on the London stage until shortly before his death, on 23 March 1739. The music Purcell wrote for him shows that he was a baritone rather than a true bass, with the range $G–g'$. BalSta, BDECM, BurRem, BDA, HolPur, LowSta, RobBow, WalSon.

Boyce, William Boyce (1711–79), composer, organist and music editor, engaged with Purcell's music in several ways. In Cathedral Music, his pioneering anthology of English church music, he included five Purcell anthems in vol. 2 (1768), and four in vol. 3 (1773) with the complete Service in B$^\flat$ Z230; five of the anthems and the Service were first publications. In 1755 he produced a modernised version of the Te Deum and Jubilate in D major* for the Festival of the Sons of the Clergy at St Paul's Cathedral*. This was the version generally performed for the rest of the century, and Vincent Novello* published it in full score in 1829. Boyce lengthened Purcell's score by about a third, adding extended instrumental passages and repeating some of the vocal sections. He also added string parts to some of the solos and augmented the orchestra with oboes (doubling flutes), bassoons and timpani. Boyce's Cecilian ode 'See fam'd Apollo and the nine' (1739) shows that he knew 'Hail, bright Cecilia'*: he adapted Purcell's canon 3 in 1 at the end of 'Soul of the world' for the chorus 'Hail Harmony!'. HolBat, WhiCec, ZimCat.

Brady, Nicholas Irish clergyman and writer (1659–1726). He settled in London in 1691 as curate of St Catherine Cree, and his tragedy The Rape, or The Innocent Impostors was staged at Drury Lane* in May 1692 thanks to Thomas

Shadwell's* influence. Shadwell may also have recommended him as the poet for that year's Cecilian ode. The result, 'Hail, bright Cecilia'*, was set by Purcell and published by Peter Motteux* in *The Gentleman's Journal*. Brady's sermon for the 1697 Cecilian celebrations*, delivered in St Bride's, Fleet Street*, was published as *Church-Musick Vindicated*. He is mainly remembered for collaborating with Nahum Tate* on *A New Version of the Psalms of David* (1696), which ran to more than 300 editions over 150 years. ArkGen, LS, TemPar, WhiCec.

Bray, Thomas Dancer and dancing master. He was a member of the United Company* at the Drury Lane Theatre* by 1689, but defected with Thomas Betterton* to the Lincoln's Inn Theatre when the company broke up in 1695. He is best known for his *Country Dances* (1699), dedicated to the young Prince William, Duke of Gloucester*, who was his patron and probably his dance pupil. It comprises two parts: the first consists of pieces, including three by Purcell, with instructions for country dances*, while the second, entitled 'The Newest *French* Dances in Use', consists mainly of theatrical dances, including seven set to pieces by Purcell. These choreographies are not included, though Bray attributed some of them to Josias Priest* and claimed others for himself, including dances for *Dioclesian** and *Amphitryon** (both 1690). He included bass parts for the dance tunes and printed accurate musical texts, so he was presumably a competent musician as well as a dancer. *See also* **Country dances**, **Dance**. LS, SemDan.

Bressan, Peter Oboist and wind-instrument maker (1663–1731), born Pierre Jaillard at Bourg-en-Bresse in eastern France; he called himself Peter Bressan (from his native town) after settling in England around 1688. He established his home and workshop in Duchy House, Somerset House Yard, becoming the leading maker in London of the new French oboe* and recorder*; he subsequently mainly made recorders for the amateur market. A number of Bressan's instruments were measured by James Talbot*, and his surviving recorders have helped scholars establish the pitch* used for Purcell's secular music. BDECM, HayHau, HayPit.

'Britons, strike home!' Z574/16 The simple but highly effective minuet* song from the Druidic temple ceremony in *Bonduca**, scored for tenor solo, choir and orchestra including trumpet. It became enduringly popular as a patriotic song alongside Arne's* 'Rule, Britannia!', Handel's* 'See, the conqu'ring hero comes!' and Boyce's* 'Heart of oak are our ships'; its title subsequently became a loyal and political catchphrase. It was supposedly played during the Battle of Dettingen (1743) and at many later battles and victory celebrations, including (inappropriately, given its setting) naval battles, notably on board HMS *Tonnant* during the Battle of Trafalgar, and most memorably during the pageant of model boats that ends Sheridan's comedy *The Critic*. HigRec, HolPur, RimBon, VanBri, WinRed, ZimPur.

Britten, Benjamin Britten (1913–76) engaged with Purcell's music in three main ways: as a performer, as an arranger and editor and as a composer. As a pianist and duo-partner with the tenor Peter Pears (1910–86), Britten included Purcell's songs in recitals with his piano 'realisations' of the continuo* parts, starting in

1939 with 'Hark! the echoing air' Z629/48b from *The Fairy Queen**. Some of these versions, including the Golden Sonata* and selections from *Harmonia Sacra** and *Orpheus Britannicus**, were published by Boosey & Hawkes from 1946. Later publications included *Dido and Aeneas** (1950–1; published 1960), and a 'masque' fashioned from *The Fairy Queen* (1967; published 1970), both 'edited and realised' with Imogen Holst; and an edition of 'When Night her purple veil'* (1965; published 1977). Britten's version of *The Fairy Queen* has been described (*BurDeb*, 160) as 'totally illogical in dramatic terms', so it was perhaps for the best that his proposal in 1944 to reorchestrate the work was rejected by Covent Garden.

Britten's best-known work inspired by Purcell is *The Young Person's Guide to the Orchestra* (Variations and Fugue on a Theme of Henry Purcell), Op. 34, based on the Hornpipe Z570/2 from *Abdelazer**. It was commissioned in 1945 for the Crown Film Unit as a film score and was first performed as a concert piece the following year. The *Holy Sonnets of John Donne*, Op. 35 (1945) and *Canticle I: My beloved is mine*, Op. 40 (1947) were in part responses to Purcell. Britten wrote in 1945: 'I had never realised, before I met Purcell's music, that words could be set with such ingenuity, with such colour'. He also began to engage with Purcell's consort music in the 1940s. He used Purcellian ground-bass* techniques in the finale (entitled 'Chacony') of his String Quartet no. 2 (1945). In 1946 he played the viola in a recording of the Fantasia upon One Note*, and in 1947–8 produced his orchestral version of Purcell's Chacony*. He wrote a number of pieces entitled 'Passacaglia'*, notably the fine orchestral work extracted from *Peter Grimes* (1945); the concluding song, 'Death, be not proud', of the *Holy Sonnets*; and the eloquent finale of String Quartet no. 3 (1975). Purcell also influenced the conception of such works as the W.H. Auden setting *Hymn to St Cecilia*, Op. 27 (1941–2) and *Rejoice in the Lamb*, Op. 30 (1943). *BurGall*, *BurRem*, *ColTip*, *GreArt*, *HerRec*.

Broadside ballads Topical verses cheaply printed on large sheets from the sixteenth to the nineteenth centuries and sold at fairs and around the streets. More than 20 tunes by Purcell were used for them, including theatre songs with extra verses added, such as 'Ah! cruel bloody fate' Z606/9 from *Theodosius**; 'If love's a sweet passion'*; and ''Twas within a furlong of Edinboro' town'*. Ballads were also set as mock-songs* to dances from *A Collection of Ayres**, such as Enfield Common using the Hornpipe Z572/7 from *Amphitryon**, or The Evening Ramble using the Jig Z629/6 from *The Fairy Queen**. The latter was used in the 1690s for a number of political ballads. *LamBal*, *LebTra*, *SimBal*.

Brown, Thomas (Tom) Satirical writer (1662–1704), who contributed a poem '*To his unknown Friend Mr*. Henry Purcell' to *Harmonia Sacra**, book 2 (1693), praising his word-setting: 'For where the Author's scanty Words have fail'd, | Your happier Graces, *Purcell*, have prevail'd'. In *Letters from the Dead to the Living*, part 2 (1703) he included one from Purcell to John Blow* describing life in the 'Infernal Territory', infested with 'innumerable Crouds of Poets and Musicians'; it offers satirical glimpses of Nicholas Staggins*, Thomas Farmer* and Robert Smith*, among others. Blow's supposed reply casts an equally satirical eye on musical life in London's churches and theatres. *ArkGen*, *BurRem*, *HigRec*, *LucSha*, *ZimPur*.

Bull, John Purcell copied out a score of an ingenious ten-part canon* (8 in 4 with the *cantus firmus* and a free bass) on the plainsong 'Miserere mei, Domine' by this Elizabethan composer and keyboard virtuoso (1562/3–1628). He copied it into a manuscript (formerly owned by Thurston Dart* and now untraceable (though a photocopy is at GB-Lbl, MUS RP 3774), that also includes fantasias by John Coprario and Orlando Gibbons*, a dialogue by Nicholas Lanier and three madrigals by Monteverdi*. Purcell copied the canon around 1679–81, the time he was subjecting himself to an intensive programme of study devoted to mastering formal counterpoint*. *DarBul, HerCre, ShaMan.*

Burial Service The Anglican Burial Service contains seven funeral sentences appropriate for musical setting. Three are sung at the beginning of the service, three at the graveside and the last as 'earth is cast upon the body'. Purcell set the graveside sentences, 'Man that is born of a woman' Z27, 'In the midst of life' Z17A&B and 'Thou knowest Lord' Z58A&B, in the 1670s. His copies of the second and third of these, in GB-Lbl, Add. MS 30931, were perhaps composed as early as 1672. 'Man that is born of a woman' was almost certainly composed at the same time.

Purcell composed the sentences in full-with-verse style for four-part choir and organ, probably for Westminster Abbey*; the choir might have stood inside the door leading from the nave to the cloisters, where bodies were buried. Purcell's sentences may have been designed to complement those of Henry Cooke*, which lacked the graveside settings. Potential occasions for which they were composed or used include the funerals of Cooke (1672), Pelham Humfrey* (1674) and Christopher Gibbons* (1676); all were buried in the Abbey cloisters. Purcell's revisions* of the sentences in the later 1670s, which increased their contrapuntal character and refined their word-setting, may have originated in subsequent performances. He revised the first two sentences again when he copied them into his scorebook* GB-Cfm, MU MS 88 sometime between 1679 and 1681, leaving a page blank, presumably for the third sentence. In 1694 Purcell made an unrelated setting of 'Thou knowest Lord' Z58C* for the funeral of Mary II*. *ForFun, HerCre, HerRev, HolPur, HowCre, ManRev, ShaAnc, ShaFun, ShaMan, VanChu, WooFun.*

Burney, Charles The composer and music historian Charles Burney (1726–1814) had a conflicted relationship with Purcell's music. In 1789 he published by far the best-researched and most comprehensive account of the composer to date (*BurHis*, iii. 483–511), followed by his entry for Purcell in *BurRee*, published in 1814. Modern writers on Purcell tend to refer to Hawkins's* *HawHis* rather than Burney, mainly because of Hawkins's apparently first-hand anecdotes about the composer and his circle. However, Burney, though younger than Hawkins and writing later, had the better Purcellian connections. He wrote that his father, the violinist and dancing master James Macburney, 'was nineteen years of age when Purcell died, remembered his person very well, and the effect his anthems had on himself and the public at the time that many of them were first heard' (*BurHis*, iii. 479). Another connection was with the clergyman George Lluellen*, who as a child had known Purcell, became an enthusiast for his music and may have taught the young Burney in Shropshire.

Burney's discussion of Purcell was far in advance of its time in that it was based on a wide knowledge of his music, acquired by studying a variety of printed and manuscript collections, including the autograph* GB-Lbl, R.M. 20.h.8, which Philip Hayes* gave to George III in 1781. He ranked Purcell with Shakespeare, Milton, John Locke and Newton (*BurHis*, iii. 485), and likened him to Haydn in a letter (*BurLet*, 391–4). However, he saw musical history in determinedly evolutionary terms, exclaiming: 'Unluckily for Purcell! he built his fame with such perishable materials, that his worth and works are daily diminishing' (*BurHis*, iii. 485), and he wrote off ground basses*, including Purcell's, as a 'Gothic' practice, 'an unworthy employment for men possessed of such genius and original resources' (*BurHis*, iii. 494). He also criticised Purcell's dissonances*, particularly in the Service in B$^\flat$ Z230, which he suggested cathedral organists should 'scruple not to change for better harmony' (*BurHis*, iii. 482). He used the slightly disreputable tactic of blaming John Blow* (*BurHis*, iii. 447–53) rather than Purcell for features of the Restoration musical idiom, many of which they shared. *HerHay, LucSha*.

Busby, Thomas This composer and writer (1754–1838) inserted some sheets reproducing 'FAC SIMILES OF CELEBRATED COMPOSERS' into his three-volume *Concert Room and Orchestra Anecdotes* (1825). They were seemingly printed by lithograph from tracings of manuscripts mostly in the library of the composer William Shield. Among them is an extract from the lost autograph score of Purcell's 'Come, ye sons of art, away'*, showing that the familiar version of the ode, edited from a score copied by Robert Pindar* in 1765, gives the work in a rescored, modernised version. *BroFac, HerPin*.

Butler, Charlotte A popular and lively actress and singer, Charlotte Butler was a member of the Duke's Company apparently from 1674. She sang in the court masque *Calisto* in 1675 though no theatre roles for her are known until 1680, when she played an ingénue in Thomas Otway's *The Orphan*; she was perhaps born about 1660. She was also an accomplished dancer. She appeared in *Amphitryon*, Dioclesian*, King Arthur** and *The Fairy Queen**, in the last singing Spring in the Act IV Masque of the Four Seasons. Butler is best known for her roles in *King Arthur* as Philidel and as Cupid in the Frost Scene*, with John Bowman* as Grimbald and (probably) the Cold Genius. Roger North* (*NorMus*, 217–18) recalled her memorable performance of Cupid's first solo, 'a *recitativo* of calling towards the place where Genius was to rise', in which she turned her back on the audience, hiding the contortions of her face (necessary 'to sound well') from 'her gallants'. She left London for Dublin at the end of the 1692 season and is last heard of at the city's Smock Alley Theatre in the late spring of 1693. *BalSop, BalSta, BurRem, BDA, HolPur, LowSta, SavGen, WalSon*.

The 'Cambury Manuscript' The portmanteau nickname given by Margaret Laurie to two surviving portions of a manuscript, now separated as GB-Cfm, MU MS 659 (formerly 683) and GB-Ob, Tenbury MS 785. It mostly contains music by Purcell from plays produced in the 1690–1 season, principally *Amphitryon*, Distress'd Innocence** and *The Gordian Knot Unty'd**. It is an early source (copied in the early 1690s), preserving the theatre airs* in their original performance order and offering better texts than *A Collection of Ayres**;

it is used as the primary source for them in *PS* 16 and 20. *HerCat, LauCam, ShaMan, SchAyr.*

Canaries Purcell used this vigorous triple-time dance supposedly from the Canary Islands (*canario* in Italian, *canarie* or *canaries* in French) in *Dioclesian**, Act V Z627/34. A keyboard piece ZT677 is also entitled 'Canary' but is actually a setting of the Third Act Tune Z630/18 from *The Indian Queen**, a beautiful piece in rondeau* form that demands a moderate tempo; it may just have been confused with Z627/34. *See also* **Dance**.

Canon A special type of counterpoint* in which two or more voices use the same melodic material, the first followed at a fixed interval and distance by one or more following voices. Purcell was particularly attracted to the technique. He copied an ingenious ten-part canon by John Bull*, and recommended Elway Bevin's* collection of them (1631), calling the genre 'the noblest sort of Fugeing' (*PlaInt*, 114). He introduced canons and canonic passages into several of his larger works as well as writing some standalone examples. Purcell's catches* are simple unison canons, and some of the separate sacred canons are not much more complex than them, though this group of pieces (neglected by modern performers) also includes the eloquent double canon (4 in 2) 'Miserere mei' Z109; 'Gloria Patri et Filio' Z105, an inversion canon (4 in 1 'per arsin et thesin'); and the ingenious 'Alleluia' Z101, a double retrograde canon (4 in 2 'recte et retro'), in which pairs of voices share the same music, one singer reading forwards, the other backwards.

Canons were traditionally introduced into the doxologies ('Glory be to the Father' sections) of services*; Purcell included ten canons in his Service in B$^\flat$ Z230, emulating the ones in John Blow's* Service in G major. In his Te Deum and Jubilate in D major* he included a canon 4 in 1 at 'O go your way' in the Jubilate and worked in several freely canonic passages, including the 'ever world without end' passage in the Te Deum, with its fourfold augmentation in the bass. Notable canons in Purcell's instrumental music include the four in Three Parts upon a Ground*, one using inversion, another retrograde motion; the opening of the Sonata in C major Z795, with its simultaneous double and fourfold augmentation (Ex. 1); the peerless chaconne* 'Two in One upon a Ground' (in C minor for two recorders and bass in *Dioclesian** Z627/16 but also existing as a separate piece in A minor for violins); and the 'Dance for the Followers of Night' from *The Fairy Queen**, Act II Z629/15, a 4 in 2 canon modelled on the concluding movement from Matthew Locke's* theatre airs* for *The Tempest** (1674). *HerCre, HerThe, HolCom, HolPur, HowArt, TilTec.*

Ex. 1: Trio Sonata in C major Z795, bb. 1–7 (continuo part omitted).

Canterbury Eighteenth-century Canterbury was an important centre for collecting and performing Purcell. His music was regularly included in its music society's St Cecilia's Day concerts, started around 1725 or earlier. Daniel Henstridge*, the cathedral organist and an important collector of Purcell's sacred music, copied a keyboard part for 'Welcome to all the pleasures'* before 1719, the year his failing sight forced him to pass his duties to William Raylton (1688–1757). Raylton made some important copies of Purcell, including a complete set of parts for 'Hail, bright Cecilia'* (GB-Ob, Tenbury MS 1309, once thought to be in Henstridge's hand), probably for the use of the society, and anthems taken from now-lost sources owned by John Gostling*, a Canterbury minor canon as well as a member of the Chapel Royal*. Gostling's son William (1696–1777), also a Canterbury minor canon, inherited the collection, adding copies by Henstridge and others. When he died his friend Sir John Hawkins* drew up the sale catalogue of the collection; William was probably the source of the anecdotes about his father and Purcell in *HawHis*. The Canterbury bookseller and collector William Flackton, a former cathedral chorister, assembled his own collection of Purcell manuscripts (now known as the Flackton Collection*), drawn in part from those collected and copied by Henstridge and Raylton. *See also* **Cecilian Celebrations**. *ForCan, HerHay, ShaMan, SpiCat, WhiCec*.

Cantoris *See* **Choir**

Canzona The name originally given to the late sixteenth-century Italian instrumental genre modelled on the French chanson, though Purcell mostly followed later Roman practice in using it as the label for the main contrapuntal section of a trio sonata*, often following an initial Adagio in full harmony. The contrapuntal second sections in the symphonies* and overtures* of Purcell's concerted vocal works are also often labelled 'canzona' today, though the only labels apparently deriving from the composer are for those in the Symphony to 'Hail, bright Cecilia'*; the Symphony or Sonata in *The Fairy Queen**, Act IV Z629/27b; and the Trumpet Overture in *The Indian Queen**, Act III Z630/16b. The Canzona Z860/2 for four flat trumpets*, written for Queen Mary's* funeral, is a standalone piece in two repeated sections, oddly similar in form and style to the sixteenth-century type. *See also* **March and Canzona**. *HowArt, TilTec*.

Carr, John London bookseller and music publisher who established a shop at the Middle Temple around 1672. He collaborated with his near-neighbour John Playford* in selling a number of music publications, including Purcell's *Sonnata's of III Parts** (1683) and the scores of 'Welcome to all the pleasures'* (1684) and *Dioclesian** (1691). In 1687 he published the first collection using John Heptinstall's* 'new tied note', aptly entitled *Vinculum societatis*. His son Robert Carr, a court viol player, briefly went into business with Henry Playford*. *BDECM, CarPub, DaySon, HerPla, HumPub, KruPri, MPP*.

Cartwright, Rhoda *See* **Rhoda Cavendish**

Catch A simple type of unison canon* popular in Restoration England, for three or four voices, occasionally with a continuo part. The phrases are separated by cadences, so the first voice completes a defined statement before the second joins in, the voices occasionally combining to reveal a *double entendre*. Purcell's catches have a reputation for indecency (Michael Nyman's* *PurCat* was the first modern edition with unbowdlerised texts), though they more often deal with the pleasures of the bottle (as in 'Come, come, let us drink' Z245 or 'Drink on till night be spent' Z248), and there are many that demonstrate the composer's loyalty ('God save our sov'reign Charles' Z250), or reflect politics and the news ('Since the duke is return'd, we'll damn all the Whigs' Z271 and 'Is Charleroy's siege come too?' Z257).

Purcell's 60-odd catches were written and published – principally in John Playford's* *Catch that Catch Can* (1685) and *The Second Book of the Pleasant Musical Companion* (1686) – for the all-male milieu of the tavern, sometimes organised into formal catch clubs. However, many of them are hard to sing, with fast-moving, angular lines ranging across nearly two octaves, and may have been written for off-duty professional singers. They continued to be republished and copied in the eighteenth century, and some of them were in the repertory of the Noblemen and Gentlemen's Catch Club, founded in 1761 at the Thatched House Tavern, St James's Street in London. *ChaMee, HarPla, HigRec, HolPur, MunPla, RobCat, SpiSoc, TupEig, WalPol.*

Cavendish, Rhoda Between October 1691 and June 1693 Purcell was 'Spinnet Master' to Rhoda (1674–1730), daughter of William Cartwright of Aynho in Northamptonshire. The lessons presumably took place at Cartwright's London house at Barn Elms, across the Thames from Fulham. Purcell was replaced by a Mr Delawney, presumably the Delawny who had been Princess Anne's* guitar* teacher in 1682. Rhoda married Lord Henry Cavendish in 1696, and in 1697 Frances Purcell dedicated *Ten Sonata's in Four Parts** to her, mentioning that her husband had admired her skill in music. *BurCav, HunPat, PagGui.*

Cazzati, Maurizio Purcell copied 'Crucior in hac flamma', a dialogue for two voices and continuo, into his scorebook GB-Lbl, R.M. 20.h.8, apparently not knowing it was by Maurizio Cazzati, from *Tributo di sacri concerti*, Op. 23 (Bologna, 1660). Cazzati (1616–78), at the time *maestro di cappella* at San Petronio in Bologna, was an influential composer of sonatas, some of which circulated in Restoration England, so he may have been one of the 'most fam'd Italian Masters' Purcell mentioned as models for his *Sonnata's of III Parts**. It has also been suggested that the pioneering trumpet sonatas in Cazzati's *Sonate*, Op. 35 (Bologna, 1665) provided Purcell with models for his Sonata in D major Z850*. *HolPur, ShaMan, SmiTru, TilTec.*

Cecilian celebrations 22 November, the feast day of St Cecilia, the patron saint of music, was first formally celebrated in England in 1683 with Purcell's 'Welcome to all the pleasures'*. The ode was published in the following year with a dedication to the Gentlemen of the Musical Society (also known as the Gentlemen Lovers of Musick), which from 1684 to 1700 organised a feast and musical performance at Stationers' Hall* on St Cecilia's Day – or the following Monday when it fell on a Sunday. An elaborate musical setting of a new poem in praise of music and St Cecilia was commissioned each year by the Society from the most eminent poets and composers of the day, and was performed by court musicians, sometimes supplemented with theatre singers. The feast was overseen by stewards, originally four but eventually rising to eight, two of whom were always professional musicians. William III's* invasion put paid to the 1688 celebrations, and they did not recommence until 1690. Purcell's setting of Nicholas Brady's* 'Hail, bright Cecilia'* (1692) represents the pinnacle of the series, but other notable contributions include G.B. Draghi's* setting of Dryden* (1687); four odes by John Blow*; and John Eccles's* setting of Congreve* (1701) – which remained unperformed when the celebrations collapsed in that year.

Peter Motteux* described the celebrations in *The Gentleman's Journal*, insisting that they were not Catholic in nature but devoted solely to the celebration of music. He also described instrumental music performed while those attending were dining. Tickets for the feast (extant for 1696) were expensive, at 10s apiece. From 1693 a service was held at St Bride's* (but at St Paul's Cathedral* in 1698) before the feast, at which a sermon was preached defending the use of instrumental music in the church. Purcell composed his orchestrally accompanied Te Deum and Jubilate in D major* for this service in 1694; it was repeated in 1697 (the year his widow published it) and was the model for canticle settings by John Blow and William Turner*, performed in the intervening years. Cecilian odes were repeated in later years at York Buildings* several weeks after the feast as benefits for the musician stewards. 'Hail, bright Cecilia' was also performed there in January 1694 for Prince Louis William, Margrave of Baden-Baden. Cecilian celebrations began to be established outside London from the 1690s, often as vehicles for performances of Purcell's Cecilian odes and the Te Deum and Jubilate. *See also* **Canterbury**, **Ferrar family**. *WhiCec.*

'**Celebrate this festival**' **Z321** Purcell's setting of Nahum Tate's* verses for Mary II's* 1693 birthday is the longest of his court odes. An early score includes the names of 12 soloists, with trebles unusually prominent: Mrs Ayliff* sang the melismatic arioso 'Let sullen Discord smile' and the theatre-style song 'Kindly treat Maria's day', while an unnamed boy sang ''Tis sacred' with trumpet* obbligato; they both sang the ground-bass* duet 'Britain now thy cares beguile'. Purcell borrowed the first two sections of the symphony from 'Hail, bright Cecilia'*, transposing them from D major to C major, removing the kettle-drums* and replacing the second trumpet with an oboe*. Striking instrumental effects include the trumpet part in the florid solo bass *da capo* air 'While for a righteous cause' (sung by Leonard Woodson), taken in the middle section from C major to A minor and D minor; and the passages in 'Return, fond Muse!' for two treble recorders and viola (or perhaps bass recorder; see *PS* 24) that gently alternate with the solo countertenor (Anthony Robert) and continuo. The fine ground-bass air 'Crown the altar' for countertenor (John Howell) also exists in the keyboard transcription ZD222. *See also* **Odes**. *AdaPur, HolPur, MurOde, SpiOde, WooOde, WooPur.*

'**Celestial music did the gods inspire**' **Z322** In GB-Lbl, R.M. 20.h.8 Purcell entitled this work: 'A Song that was perform'd at M$^{r.}$ Maidwells a schoolmaster on the 5th of August 1689 y^e words by one of his scholars'; the young author of these surprisingly accomplished verses in praise of music is unidentified. The Rev. Lewis Maidwell (*c.*1650–1716) ran a school from his house in King

Street, Westminster; his connection with Purcell probably came through their common friend Nahum Tate*. Though modest in scale, it is an attractive work, continuing the bold approach to string writing in 'Sound the trumpet, beat the drum'*: solos for countertenor and bass are accompanied by four-part strings, as are the choruses, which are extended with ritornellos*. 'Her charming strains', a particularly fine countertenor* solo with two recorders* over a modulating ground bass*, draws on a similar movement in G.B. Draghi's* *Song for St Cecilia's Day, 1687*. If Purcell composed 'The noise of foreign wars'*, performed on 24 July, it would explain why he saved time by borrowing the symphony for 'Celestial music' from his coronation anthem 'My heart is inditing'*. Surprisingly for an occasional work written for a London school, a set of parts belonged to Stamford's music club, where it was perhaps performed on St Cecilia's Day in the 1690s. *See also* **Ferrar Family, Odes**. HolPur, WhiCec, WhiNoi, WhiFer, WooOde.

Chaconne (*chacona, ciaccona, chacony*) A standard major-mode triple-time chord sequence and/or ostinato bass, said to have originated in the New World. By 1632, when Monteverdi* published his famous duet 'Zefiro torna', it had achieved its classic form as a catchy four-bar cadential phrase involving offbeat chord changes. After 1650 the chaconne began to converge with the more restrained minor-mode passacaglia*, with which it was sometimes paired and contrasted. It was elaborated and refined (often in England without the offbeat chord changes), and with modulations to minor keys; correspondingly, the passacaglia began to be transposed in whole or part into the major, taking on some chaconne-like characteristics in the process. Purcell wrote three true chaconnes: 'Triumph, victorious love' Z527/38 in the Act V masque from *Dioclesian**; the 'Chacone' at the end of the ode 'Who can from joy refrain?'*; and the song 'She loves and she confesses too'*. However, like most later composers, Purcell sometimes forgot (or chose to disregard) the traditional distinction between the two archetypes. Thus his Chacony in G minor Z730* and the Chaconne in D minor Z597/6 in *The Gordian Knot Unty'd** are essentially passacaglias. *See also* **Dance, Ground**. HolPur, SchChu, SchGro, SchLul, SilFre, SilPas, TylGui.

Chacony in G minor Z730 This matchless set of 18 variations on an eight-bar ground bass* is Purcell's best-known consort piece today; it was first published for string quartet by Hannah Bryant in 1925 and was popularised by Benjamin Britten's* string orchestra arrangement (1947–8; published 1965). We do not know why and when Purcell wrote it, except that he copied it around 1680 into his autograph scorebook GB-Lbl, Add. MS 30930; the markedly different shades of ink indicate that he entered the outer parts first, though there is no sign that he was composing as he copied. Its nobly restrained idiom, eschewing the extravagant virtuosity and elaborate counterpoint of Three Parts upon a Ground*, together with its four-part, two-treble scoring, suggests that it was composed for the Twenty-Four Violins*; it could conceivably have accompanied dancing at court.

The ground, consisting of the descending fourth of the passacaglia* balanced by a cadence (but cunningly inflected with an F$^\sharp$ and a B$^\natural$), migrates to the upper parts, incorporating transitory modulations to B$^\flat$ major, D minor and

C minor. The use of paired events – two modulatory passages, two with the bass running in quavers, two with the bass silent and so on – recalls the paired *couplets* of French chaconnes and passacaglias, and in general the work seems to belong to the tradition deriving from the examples in Lully's theatre works, first taken up in England by Robert Smith*. *See also* **Chaconne (***chacona, ciaccona, chacony***)**. *HolPur, SchCha, SchGro, ShaMan*.

Chants Purcell's name is associated with a number of Anglican chants, the harmonised melodic formulas used to accommodate non-metrical texts such as the Psalms and the Canticles by matching speech rhythms to a variable number of repeated notes. *ZimCat* lists six examples, Z120–5 (with nine more as ZD30–8), though there is little or no evidence that Purcell wrote any of them. Some of them may be by other members of his family, others just attributed to him through wishful thinking. *See also* **Hymn tunes**. *TemPar, WilCha*.

Chapel Royal The name given to the institution that provided the monarch and the court with daily choral services, as well as the buildings it sang in – principally the small chapel at Whitehall* in Purcell's time. It also accompanied Charles II* to Windsor* for most summers between 1671 and 1683, but sang in a chapel inside the Castle, not in St George's Chapel. Purcell joined the Chapel as a choirboy in the 1660s, at which time it consisted of the subdean, 12 boys and 32 gentlemen (12 priests and 20 laymen), three of whom were its organists; Purcell became a gentleman and an organist in 1682. The whole choir sang on Sundays and holidays with their eves, but otherwise the men attended according to a roster, half one month, the other half the next, which allowed some of them also to sing at St Paul's Cathedral*, Westminster Abbey* and St George's Chapel, Windsor*. Purcell, organist of Westminster Abbey from 1679, was one of these pluralists, which means that it is unclear in many cases for which institution his church music was composed. However, apart from coronations*, symphony anthems* were only performed in the chapel at Whitehall, so it follows that Purcell wrote his contributions to this genre for it rather than Westminster Abbey. *BurCha, CBCR, DexQui, HolFid, ShaSuc, SpiCat*.

Charles II King Charles II (1630–85) came to the English throne when his father was executed on 30 January 1649, though his reign effectively began at the Restoration* in May 1660 when he returned to London from exile; he was crowned in Westminster Abbey* on 23 April 1661. Like other Stuarts, he was 'a professed lover of musick', as Roger North* put it (*NorMus*, 350), playing the guitar* and exercising his taste in favour of the modern French and Italian music he would have encountered while in exile in France and the Netherlands. His taste can readily be heard in the symphony anthems* and court secular music Purcell wrote during his reign. North added that Charles had a fondness for the minuet-like 'step tripla' in songs; 'could not bear any musick to which he could not keep the time'; had 'an utter detestation of Fancys' or fantasias*, and 'could not forbear whetting his witt upon the subject of the Fancy-musick' – doubtless making him unsympathetic to the contrapuntal *Sonnata's of III Parts**, which Purcell dedicated to him. The eloquent extended elegy 'If pray'rs and tears' Z380 (subtitled 'Sighs for our late sovereign King Charles the

Second') was presumably written soon after the king's death on 6 February 1685. *See also* **Restoration**, **Whitehall**. *BurRem, HolFid, PagGui, ZimPur*.

A Choice Collection The first of the memorial volumes of Purcell's music, published in July 1696 by his widow Frances and sold by Henry Playford*; there was a second edition (1697), now lost, and a third (1699). *A Choice Collection of Lessons for the Harpsichord or Spinnet*, to give it its full title, was dedicated to 'the Princess of Denmark' (later Queen Anne*), and was engraved, none too accurately, by Thomas Cross*. It contains eight suites*, presumably taken from a lost autograph manuscript, followed by five (six in 1699) arrangements of consort pieces. The 1699 edition included 'Instructions for beginers' (dealing with the rudiments of notation) and 'Rules for Graces', attributed to 'ye late famous Mr H Purcell' by John Walsh* in *The Harpsicord Master* (1697). *CarPub, HarPla, HerThe, HigRec, HogCor, JohOrn, WooKey, ZimCat*.

Choir Nearly all of Purcell's church music was written for two leading Anglican choral institutions, the Chapel Royal* and the choir of Westminster Abbey*. The Chapel choir consisted of 12 boys and 32 gentlemen, though the full complement of singers was only used on special occasions. Some of its singers were also members of the Abbey choir, which makes it difficult to estimate the effective strength of the latter: it consisted of ten boys and 18 men on paper but only 16 were listed in the procession for the 1685 coronation* (*SanCor*, 70), seven of whom were replaced with deputies since they processed with the Chapel choir. Then as now, choirs in collegiate foundations were divided into two, placed in facing *decani* and *cantoris* stalls (*decani* and *sub-decani* in the Chapel Royal), respectively on the south and north sides of the quire (choir in its spatial sense); the two sides alternated phrases in some types of music. This meant that the Abbey choir would have consisted of a maximum of 5-3-3-3 on each side, while the full Chapel Royal sang four-part music with about 6-5-5-5 on each side, with one of the gentlemen at the organ. However, in verse anthems* and symphony anthems* the groups of soloists were apparently placed in the organ gallery at Whitehall*; the layout of Purcell's scores suggests that they did not automatically double the choir in full sections.

Less is known about the size and composition of the choirs that sang in Purcell's secular music. Some of his early court odes* and 'Welcome to all the pleasures'*, scored just with strings and continuo, might have been sung by quite small groups, though the later odes use a full Baroque orchestra* and presumably required the complete Chapel Royal choir plus the solo singers of the Private Music*. Indications in the scores of G.B. Draghi's* *Song for St Cecilia's Day, 1687* suggest there were 25-30 voices; no fewer than 13 solo singers are listed in the autograph score of 'Hail, bright Cecilia'*. Female soloists sang in some odes, and they may have doubled the boys in choral sections, as they did in later secular concerted music.

There are indications that the vocal groups in Purcell's dramatic operas* were also substantial. In *King Arthur** the Act I sacrifice scene has the stage direction 'The rest of the stage is fill'd with Priests and Singers', while Act II has double-choir writing for groups of spirits led by Philidel and Grimbald, and 'Come follow me' needs four solo treble voices in Philidel's group, making at least eight trebles if the two groups were of equal size. Boys, including Jemmy

Bowen*, were used as soloists in Purcell's theatre works, so they may also have sung the treble chorus parts alongside female members of the company. Purcell's choral 'countertenor'* parts seem to have been sung by high tenors rather than falsettists, as shown by the alto chorus part of *Dido and Aeneas**, which goes down to d. See also **Chorus**, **Singers**. *BurCha, CBCR, DexQui, HolBat, HolFid, HolPur, MorVoi, ParPer, RECM, RosPer, SpiCat, WhiCec.*

Chorus Like his contemporaries, Purcell used the word 'chorus' in church music and concerted secular music to indicate the entry of the choir* after a verse* or solo section, though it was also used in domestic music without implying the entrance of a complete group of additional singers. He wrote a number of songs in which a bass voice enters for a concluding section, often marked 'Chorus', as with his elegies for Matthew Locke*, John Playford* and Thomas Farmer*, and he also used the word in a purely descriptive sense just to indicate a tutti passage, as in the final section of Saul and the Witch of Endor*.

Cibell An English instrumental genre inspired by the 'Descente de Cybelle', the solo with chorus 'Vous devez vous animer d'une ardeur nouvelle' at the end of Act I of Lully's* opera *Atys* (1676). It circulated in England in an instrumental transcription, and Purcell imitated its gavotte-like rhythms and solo bass passages in his Cibell for trumpet, strings and continuo, better known in its keyboard transcription, 'Trumpet Tune called the Cibell' ZT678. Cibells by Gottfried Finger*, Jeremiah Clarke*, Robert King and others mostly divide into those in the minor that imitate Lully's original and those in the major that use the trumpet* idiom of Purcell's piece. *DarCib, WooKey.*

***Circe* Z575** Charles Davenant's tragedy was first performed in 1677 with music by John Banister*. Purcell reset the temple scene in Act I, Scene 4 for a revival, probably in 1689–90; Margaret Laurie (*PS* 16) suggested that Thomas Betterton* commissioned it to test the composer's capacity to set *Dioclesian**. Iphigenia, Priestess of Diana on the island of Tauris, has attracted the love of King Thoas and Prince Ithacus; the situation leads Queen Circe to summon spirits to foretell the future. Purcell's setting consists of a sequence of solos and choruses sung by priests, of which the most memorable are the ground-bass* air and chorus 'The air with music gently wound' Z575/2b, in which a priest extols the sweet smells and sounds of the ceremony; and 'Pluto, arise!' Z575/6, the recitative at the end of the scene for a bass priest accompanied by four-part strings. This powerful movement is preceded by the eloquent and sombre Magicians' Dance Z575/5, which Purcell reused in a revised and transposed version as the Slow Air Z603/2 in *The Married Beau**. *AdaPur, HolPur, LS, PriPur.*

Clarke, Jeremiah (Jeremy) Organist and composer (c.1674–1707), a prominent Purcell follower. He may have been a member of a family, including musicians, working at Windsor and Eton*, and was a choirboy in the Chapel Royal* from at least April 1685 (when he sang in James II's* coronation) to 1691. The following year he became organist of Winchester College, where he apparently wrote his first major work, the *Song on the Assumption*, a setting of Richard Crashaw's poem. He returned to London in the winter of 1695–6 to help Daniel Purcell* at Drury Lane* in the wake of Henry's death, and perhaps also to assist John Blow* at St Paul's Cathedral*; he was certainly organist there by 1699. His striking *Song on the Death of the Famous Mr Henry Purcell*, 'Come, come along with a dance and a song', was performed, probably early in 1696, 'upon ye Stage in Druery Lane' according to William Croft's* annotation on London A's* score, in GB-Lbl, Add. MS 30934. A highlight is the spine-chilling orchestral 'Mr Purcell's Farewell'.

Clarke developed a light, attractive idiom, combining tuneful melodies, witty counterpoint and bold writing for voices and instruments. He sometimes imitated particular Purcell pieces, writing several fine Cibells*, including one in the Purcell *Song*. His full anthem for Queen Anne's* coronation (1702) pays graceful tribute to Purcell's setting of the same text, 'Praise the Lord, O Jerusalem'*, as well as 'My heart is inditing'*. Two Clarke pieces were misattributed to Purcell in later times: the so-called Trumpet Voluntary* is really his Prince of Denmark's March; the Trumpet Tune in D major ZS124 is the Second Act Tune from *The Island Princess* (1699). *See also* **Farewell, Odes on the Death of Henry Purcell, Scotch tune**. *BDECM, CudVol, DexQui, HolCla, HowOde, LowSta, MurOde, PriIsl, PriThe, RanCor, ShaSuc, SpiPau, SpiRes, TayCla, WhiCla, ZimCat.*

Closterman, John German-born artist (1660–1711), who came to London probably in 1680 and developed a successful practice as a portrait painter. Among his sitters were John Dryden*, Christopher Wren and Charles Seymour, Duke of Somerset*. His head-and-shoulders chalk drawing of Purcell, done in 1695 (National Portrait Gallery, NPG 4994), is the finest portrait* of the composer and was the model for a number of later images. *HolPor, RogClo, ZimPur.*

'Cold and raw' Purcell used this ballad tune, supposedly a Scots song and also called 'Stingo, or Oil of Barley', as the bass line to the solo 'May her blest example chase' and the succeeding ritornello* in his ode 'Love's goddess sure was blind'* (1692). Hawkins* (*HawHis*, ii. 564) recounted a charming anecdote supposedly explaining the circumstances. Arabella Hunt* and John Gostling* were entertaining Queen Mary* one afternoon with 'several compositions by Purcell, who accompanied them on the harpsichord'. But the queen, 'beginning to grow tired', asked Hunt to sing 'Cold and raw' to her own lute accompaniment. Purcell was 'not a little nettled at the queen's preference of a vulgar ballad to his music', and 'seeing her majesty delighted with this tune, he determined that she should hear it upon another occasion'. He applied the same unusual stratagem, apparently also conveying coded messages, to 'Hey, boys, up go we'* and 'Lilliburlero'*. *DayDur, HerCre, HolPur, SimBal.*

Cold Genius By far Purcell's most memorable stage personification, the Cold Genius was devised by John Dryden* for the Frost Scene* in *King Arthur*, Act III. Dryden conceived a bizarre and suitably fantastic conceit: that the villainous Osmond might seduce the virtuous Emmeline by showing her a vision of a frozen country, warmed by Cupid enchanting the Cold Genius and his wretched subjects. Purcell used typically daring chromatic harmonies to transform Dryden's picturesque cipher into a genuinely awe-inspiring figure, given a talented singer-actor (probably John Bowman*) and a relatively brisk tempo for his solo. Purcell borrowed its striking repeated-note shivering effect from Lully*. No wonder the poet Thomas Gray, who saw *King Arthur* in 1735, thought it 'the finest song in the play'. *See also* **Tempo**. *BurRem, HigRec, HolPur, LucSha, PriPur.*

Colista, Lelio Roman lutenist and composer (1629–80), known in Restoration England for a set of trio sonatas* that circulated widely in manuscript attributed to him, though about half of them are actually by the Milanese violinist Carlo Ambrogio Lonati* – including the one Purcell quoted from in *PlaInt* (see Illus. 7, p. 108). *AllSon, HolPur, TilTec.*

A Collection of Ayres The second of the memorial volumes of Purcell's music, entitled in full *A Collection of Ayres, Compos'd for the Theatre, and upon other Occasions* (*AT* for short), was published in the summer of 1697 by his widow Frances; it was sold by Henry Playford* and two other London booksellers. She dedicated it to Charles Seymour, Duke of Somerset*, the dedicatee of *Dioclesian**, and it was printed by John Heptinstall*. It consists of 13 sets of theatre airs* printed in four partbooks (two violins, viola and bass); there is no continuo book or any figuring in the bass part. Nine sets come from ordinary plays; four were selected from the dramatic operas* *Dioclesian**, *King Arthur**, *The Fairy Queen** and *The Indian Queen**; it is unclear what, if any, the 'other Occasions' were.

AT had a troubled gestation. Subscriptions were called for in April 1696, more than a year before publication, but even so there are signs of haste. The editor – perhaps Daniel Purcell* – mostly excluded movements with essential wind parts, but several with missing trumpets crept in, notably *The Fairy Queen* overture Z629/3, printed in a mangled form. *AT* is not an accurate source: an errata sheet enabling the parts 'to be Mended with a Pen' was printed in December 1697, but many errors were not spotted and were unfortunately repeated in Roger's* engraved reprint. The extent of the problem was only revealed in the relevant revised volumes of *PS*, whose editors showed that the early manuscript scores are usually more reliable and often preserve sets in their original theatre order. Nevertheless, *AT*'s editor showed skill and discrimination in the selection and ordering process, and the large-scale sets for the dramatic operas (which include some song tunes*) deserve to be published and used today. *See also* **The 'Cambury Manuscript'**, **Theatre airs**, **Editions, from 1695**. *BurRem, CarPub, HarPla, HerThe, HigRec, HolPur, SchAyr, ZimCat.*

'Come, ye sons of art, away' Z323 The last of Purcell's odes for Queen Mary's* birthday, 30 April 1694, setting anonymous verses probably by Nahum Tate*. In the only surviving complete score, copied in 1765 by Robert Pindar*, the orchestra consists of pairs of oboes, recorders and trumpets, kettledrums, strings and continuo. This manuscript was the basis of all editions, performances and recordings until Rebecca Herissone, using a fragment of the lost autograph score published in facsimile by Thomas Busby* in 1825, demonstrated that Pindar must have modernised the scoring, word-setting and other details, as he had in his copies of several other Purcell odes. Her reconstruction of the original version, published by Stainer & Bell (2010), simplifies the scoring, omitting the second trumpet and the kettledrums. Uncertainty extends to the opening D major symphony, which is the same as the first three sections of the four-section C major symphony in Act II of *The Indian Queen**. Purcell may have added the final section when he reused it in the theatre or Pindar may have removed it when he made his arrangement. Alternatively, it is possible that Purcell's original symphony has not survived, since Pindar found substitutes for instrumental movements in his copies of other Purcell odes.

The ode is of the highest musical quality throughout. It uses a tautly structured plan in which a series of solo and choral minuets alternate with three ground basses*. Contrasted with them is the declamatory treble solo 'Bid the virtues', effectively a duet between the soloist and an obbligato oboe. The first of the ground-bass movements, the memorable countertenor* duet 'Sound the trumpet', has become one of the most widely performed of Purcell's vocal works. The original audience would also have been struck by the poet's pun on the surname of the Shore* family of court trumpeters: 'Sound the trumpet, till around | You make the list'ning shores rebound' – a joke compounded by Purcell not including trumpets in this movement. *AdaPur, BroFac, HerPin, HolPur, MurOde, TalPin, WooOde.*

Concerts of Ancient Music A concert organisation, also called the Ancient or Antient Concerts, devoted to putting on professional concerts of old music; it gave subscription seasons in London from 1776 to 1848. Its programmes were chosen by its musical director Joah Bates (1741–99), and by a rota drawn from its aristocratic directors. These initially included Purcell enthusiasts such as John Montagu, 4th Earl of Sandwich (1718–92), Sir Watkins Williams-Wynn (1749–89) and Richard, Viscount Fitzwilliam (1745–1816); the last two evidently drew on Purcell manuscripts in their private libraries. Works by the composer performed at the eighteenth-century Ancient Concerts included extracts from *King Arthur**, *Bonduca**, *The Indian Queen** and the music for *The Tempest** (then thought to be by Purcell rather than John Weldon*); the Te Deum in D major*; and the ode 'Celebrate this festival'*. The organisation also seems to have inspired its soloists to sing Purcell in other London concerts and in provincial festivals. *HolBat, McVCat, TupEig, WebCla.*

Congreve, William Poet and dramatist (1670–1729), the leading young playwright working for the United Company* in its last years, when Purcell was composing for it. Their collaboration probably started with a song, 'Tell me no more I am deceiv'd' Z601/3, that Congreve contributed to Act V, Scene 1 of Thomas Southerne's* comedy *The Maid's Last Prayer*, first produced at Drury Lane* in February or March 1693. A week or two later Purcell wrote a set of theatre airs* and two songs for *The Old Batchelor**, Congreve's first play; and then a set of airs and two songs for *The Double Dealer**, produced in November that year.

When the United Company broke up early in 1695 Congreve joined Thomas Betterton's* company, and so Gottfried Finger* and John Eccles* wrote music for his next comedy, *Love for Love*, produced at the Lincoln's Inn Fields Theatre on 30 April that year. However, Purcell continued to set Congreve's verses as separate songs, the last apparently being 'Ah! what pains, what racking thoughts' Z354, left incomplete in the Gresham autograph*. Curtis Price (*PriPur*, 182) pointed out that the songs in Congreve's early comedies are 'not quite in touch with the drama', as if he was 'unconvinced of the wisdom of mixing the two media'. We can only regret that Purcell never worked with him on a large-scale theatrical project, as Eccles did with the opera *Semele*. LS, PriThe, ZimCat.

Consort The seventeenth-century English word (derived from the Italian *concerto*) for sets of instruments intended to be played together, for the groups that used them, or for ensemble music in general. The 1696 edition of Edward Phillips's *New World of English Words* defined it as 'a piece of Musick consisting of three or more parts, which is either Instrumental or Vocal' (*StrDic*), while Matthew Locke* used it for a number of his instrumental collections, including his *Little Consort of Three Parts* (1656) and 'The Broken Consort' – the latter apparently written in 1661 for a court ensemble of the same name with violins, bass viols, lutes and keyboard instruments. The word was sometimes applied to large ensembles, as when Francis Sandford* (*SanCor*, 101) wrote that 'My heart is inditing'* was performed 'by the whole *Consort* of *Voices* and *Instruments*' during the coronation of James II* and Mary of Modena in Westminster Abbey* on 23 April 1685. HolFid, MacMus, NorMus.

Continuo Keyboard players and lutenists accompanied most types of ensemble music in England from the early seventeenth century, but they differed in the types of music they read from and the styles of accompaniment they provided. Organists were taught to accompany polyphonic music from score, largely doubling the vocal or instrumental lines, with the music often written in stratigraphic scores* across an opening. Alternatively, two-stave organ* parts were produced because, Roger North* explained (*NorMus*, 351), 'the old masters ... formed the organ part express; because the holding out the sound required exact concord, else the consort would suffer; or perhaps the organists had not then the skill as since, for now they desire onely figures'. English organists did not generally use figured bass until after the Restoration; Matthew Locke's *Melothesia* (1673) includes the first surviving English continuo treatise (*ArnAcc*, i. 154–63). Lutenists, usually playing the theorbo for accompanying, mostly abandoned written-out tablature parts around 1620 in favour of unfigured or partly figured basses, a practice expounded by Thomas Mace* (*MacMus*, 216–30).

Purcell would have been taught the various types of accompaniment as a child in the Chapel Royal*, probably using the theorbo as well as keyboard instruments; John Blow* presumably taught him using his own manuscript continuo treatise (*ArnAcc*, i. 163–72). By then, harpsichords* and spinets* were beginning to be used to accompany song (hitherto the preserve of lute*-family instruments) and consort music (hitherto largely accompanied using chamber organs). As an adult Purcell would have directed his odes and theatre music from the harpsichord (two instruments were probably used in dramatic operas*, following French and Italian practice), but he still specified an organ as the first choice for his trio sonatas*, and probably preferred one in his other early consort music and domestic sacred vocal music. The musical sources, including stratigraphic scores and written-out organ parts, suggest that Blow and Purcell accompanied full-voiced church music largely by doubling the vocal lines. The absence of a continuo line in some Purcell autographs* does not indicate unaccompanied performance, and it is also likely that he followed tradition by accompanying his fantasias* from score using a chamber organ.

The style of continuo realisation in Purcell has been a matter of conjecture and controversy in modern times, with a florid style of accompaniment demonstrated in the middle of the twentieth century in recordings by leading players such as Benjamin Britten* (piano) and Thurston Dart* and Walter Bergmann* (harpsichord); it was embodied in contemporary editions, including those of the Purcell Society*. In recent years a better knowledge of seventeenth-century continuo treatises and written-out organ parts has prompted the use of a more straightforward style of realisation, providing the outline harmonies rather than following the voice around in solo vocal music, though players today are still reluctant to use doubling in full-voiced vocal music.

The surviving written-out parts (such as Locke's for his anthem 'How doth the city sit solitary' (ed. in *HerOrg*, 122–31) suggest that the best Restoration organists used a bold and dissonant style of harmonisation; this is also suggested by the examples in Blow's continuo treatise. Writing about Locke, North stated (*NorMus*, 348) that the Italian singers in Catherine of Braganza's Catholic chapel 'did not approve of his manner of play, but must be attended by more polite hands'; the solution was for G.B. Draghi* to play 'the great organ' and for Locke to use 'a small chamber organ' to perform 'the same services' – evidence in England for the use of two organs for continuo, a practice common in Italy. The figuring in *Orpheus Britannicus** and other posthumous Purcell editions should not be assumed to derive from the composer. *See also* **Dissonance**. *GoeHar, HerOrg, HolOrg, HolPur, JonSon, ParPer, SayLut, SpeChi, SprLut.*

Cooke, Henry Bass singer, lutenist and composer (*c*.1615–72). He became Master of the Children of the Chapel Royal* in 1660 after service in the Royalist army in the Civil War (hence his honorific title of Captain Cooke) and worked as a singing teacher in Commonwealth London. His duties in the Chapel included recruiting, feeding, clothing and educating a prodigiously talented group of children, including John Blow*, Pelham Humfrey*, William Turner*, Thomas Tudway* and Purcell. Cooke was also responsible for their musical instruction, presumably teaching singing and theorbo accompaniment himself. He was the leading English exponent of the older Italian style of ornamented singing, set out in directions (derived from Caccini) for 'Singing after the *Italian* manner', printed in the 1664 edition of *An Introduction to the Skill of Musick** by John Playford*, who stated they were as used by Cooke, 'that Orpheus of our time'. On 13 February 1667 Samuel Pepys* remarked on Cooke's 'strange mastery' of making 'extraordinary surprizing closes, that are mighty pretty' (*PepDia*, viii. 59).

Cooke's own music is poor, with short-winded phrases, inept part-writing and aimless harmonies, so his influence would have been more as a performer and remarkable choir trainer than as a composer. He died on 13 July 1672 and was buried in Westminster Abbey; Bruce Wood suggested that the young Purcell composed the first version of his Funeral Sentences Z17A, 58A for this ceremony. They complement Cooke's own setting of four of the sentences to make a complete Burial Service*, and are related to them in key and scoring. *See* also **Ornamentation**. *BDECM, CBCR, CheChu, HerThe, HolPur, RosPer, SpiCat, WooFun, ZimPur.*

Copyists Purcell's music mostly survives in manuscripts copied by a wide circle of colleagues, followers and admirers. They do not seem to have been independent full-time copyists (a profession developing in Italy at the time), though London A*, apparently working partly as Purcell's assistant and partly for the Drury Lane Theatre*, was perhaps the closest English equivalent. Most early Purcell copyists, such as Edward Braddock and William Tucker* at the Chapel Royal* and Westminster Abbey* and Stephen Bing at St Paul's and Westminster Abbey, were singers who provided scores and parts for their institutions. The same is also true of some provincial singers and organists: Daniel Henstridge* at Rochester and Canterbury*; Richard Goodson* senior and Francis Withy* at Oxford*; William Isaack* and John Walter* at Windsor*; John Reading* at Winchester*; and James Hawkins* at Ely. They were also part of an ever-widening circle of Purcell admirers who built up their own collections of his music partly to study and preserve it. His fellow composers and performers, including John Blow*, William Croft* and John Gostling*, also contributed to this process. Purcell later became the subject of historical enquiry and memorial, beginning with Thomas Tudway*, who copied a large-scale historical anthology of English church music for Edward, Lord Harley; he was followed by Philip Hayes* and the Chapel Royal singer Thomas Barrow (d.1789), among others. However, editions of Purcell eventually made large-scale copying of the scores of his music unnecessary. *See also* **Autographs, Editions, from 1695, Reception**. *BoyBin, HerCat, HerCre, ShaMan, ThoGlo, ThoMan, ThoSou.*

Corant The English name for the triple-time binary-form dance, called *courante* in French and *corrente* in Italian. Purcell treated it as a keyboard genre (there are no examples in his theatre airs*), and in his suites* he followed continental and English practice by pairing them with almands*, occasionally giving the two genres matching melodic shapes and harmonic progressions. Standard corant features are upbeats to each section; prevailing dotted rhythms; *pas de courante* hemiolas at cadences; and *style brisé** textures. *FerPur, HolPur.*

Corelli, Arcangelo Purcell does not seem to have been much influenced by his great Italian contemporary. The 'most fam'd Italian Masters' he mentioned as models for his *Sonnata's of III Parts** generally seem to have been born in the 1620s or 30s (Legrenzi*, Colista* and Vitali*, for instance) rather than the next generation, led by Corelli (1653–1713). Corelli's trio sonatas began to circulate in manuscript in England in the 1680s and all 48 (Opp. 1–4) were readily available in Antwerp and Amsterdam reprints by the middle of the 1690s. Roger North* (*NorMus*, 310–11) wrote that 'Corelly's first consort … cleared the ground of all other sorts of musick whatsoever', and the English vogue for Corelli probably reduced the potential sales of Purcell's two sets of trio sonatas; significantly, 'The Golden Sonata'*, one of the latest and most Corellian of them, was the only one reprinted in the eighteenth century. Alan Howard has argued that Purcell modelled the canzona* in the Sonata while the Sun Rises from *The Fairy*

Queen* Z629/27b on Corelli's early Sinfonia in D major WoO 4 for trumpet, two violins and continuo.

As near contemporaries, leaders of musical life in their respective countries and prominent trio sonata* composers, Corelli and Purcell were inevitably linked. They were both extolled as reincarnations of Orpheus: Corelli as 'the new Orpheus of our times' ('nuovo Orfeo de' nostri giorni'), Purcell posthumously and more modestly as 'Orpheus Britannicus'. They were also linked by anecdotes. Joseph Addison, writing to William Congreve* (*ConLet*, 202–4) from Paris in August 1699, had been told that 'Corelli has a very mean opinion of Harry Purcell's works'. Redressing the balance, Charles Dibdin (*DibTou*, i. 190) told the delightful but improbable story that Corelli had visited England 'on purpose to see PURCELL', but hearing of his death on reaching Rochester, returned to Italy without visiting London, exclaiming '"There can be nothing worthy [of] my curiosity since PURCELL is dead"'. *AllCor, CunSon, HigRec, HogTri, HolPur, HowArt, KanCor, KanTri, TilTec.*

Coridon and Mopsa The famous rustic dialogue 'Now the maids and the men' comes from the masque put on by Titania to charm Bottom in *The Fairy Queen**, Act III Z629/22. It was sung by the countertenor John Pate* as the coy Mopsa ('*in Woman's habit*' according to Thomas Cross's* single-sheet edition) and the baritone John Reading* as her suitor Coridon. However, Mopsa was allocated to Mrs Ayliff* in *Orpheus Britannicus**, book 1, either because she took the role in the original 1692 production (with Pate replacing her for the 1693 revival), or perhaps because she subsequently sang the part in concert. A complication is that there are two versions: in G major in Purcell's part-autograph score of the opera (with a prelude for two solo violins and continuo), and in F major in the printed sources and the Gresham autograph*. *BalSta, BurFai, HerCro, PriPur, WooFai.*

Coronations Purcell participated in two coronations at Westminster Abbey*, for James II* and Mary of Modena on 23 April 1685 and William III* and Mary II* on 11 April 1689. We know a good deal about the 1685 coronation from Francis Sandford's* book *SanCor*, published in 1687. It shows that Purcell (listed among the Chapel Royal* basses) contributed two works: 'I was glad'*, a five-part full anthem performed in procession by the Abbey choir at the beginning of the service; and the symphony anthem* 'My heart is inditing'*, placed after the queen's crowning near the end. This was performed by the combined Chapel Royal and Westminster Abbey choirs with an enlarged Twenty-Four Violins*; one of Sandford's plates shows John Blow* beating time. The coronation also included Blow's symphony anthem 'God spake sometime in visions', written for the king's crowning. Blow and Purcell evidently planned these magnificent works together, using the same unusual eight-part vocal scoring. As keeper of the court keyboard instruments, Purcell also provided a small organ, placed in a gallery with the Chapel Royal.

Much less is known about the 1689 coronation, though there were probably similar numbers of singers and instrumentalists, and once again Purcell provided an organ. 'I was glad' does not seem to have been used in 1689 – the text specified then differs considerably from the one he set in 1685 – but he did contribute a new symphony anthem, 'Praise the Lord, O Jerusalem'*, sung after the joint crowning of William and Mary. No more music by Purcell was heard until George V's coronation (22 June 1911), when 'Let my prayer come up' (Frederick Bridge's contrafactum of 'Ego cubui et dormivi' from 'Jehova, quam multi sunt hostes mei'*) was sung as the Introit. 'Hear my prayer, O Lord'* was sung during the Homage in George VI's coronation (12 May 1937). *BurCha, HolBat, HolFid, HolPur, RanCor, RanGla, RanPig, WooCor, ZimPur.*

Counterpoint Purcell greatly valued this traditional compositional practice, which organised the relationship between two or more independent musical lines; he attained a technical mastery unmatched among post-Civil War English composers. An early preoccupation with perfecting his contrapuntal technique (he perhaps felt that his Chapel Royal* upbringing had been deficient in this respect) is apparent in the serial revisions to his early funeral sentences*, and in the 16 fantasias* composed in the summer of 1680. These systematically explore the techniques of combining a short musical subject (or 'point') with itself across multiple parts.

Purcell called the process 'fugeing' in his treatise *The Art of Descant* (included in *PlaInt*), where he codified its different techniques, providing musical examples for each. They proceed in a hierarchy: simple 'fuge', demonstrating tonal answers; '*Imitation* or *reports*', a 'diminutive sort of Fugeing' in which a few notes in the treble are repeated or 'answered' in another part; '*Double Fuge*', the working of two different points at once; '*Per Arsin & Thesin*', working a point with its inversion; '*Per Augmentation*', a proportional lengthening of the notes of a point; '*Recte & Retro*', working a point forward and backwards; '*Double Descant*', invertible counterpoint; and '*Canon*'*, the 'noblest sort of Fugeing'.

Purcell described all of these as 'fugeing', though they reflect two distinct contrapuntal traditions. Those relating to manipulations of a point derive from pre-Civil War English models, while '*Double Descant*' was rooted in the counterpoint of mid-century Italian trio sonatas* (and was also related to the catch*). In this latter type, two or more lines enter successively and are subsequently combined, rotating through the different parts, so that each line can form the bass – i.e. each is invertible. Purcell honed his skills in '*Double Descant*' in the canzona* movements of his trio sonatas*, some of which are permutation fugues.

Purcell's commitment to sophisticated contrapuntal technique has parallels in other arts, in which artifice was a means of heightening or perfecting the representation of nature; John Dryden* articulated this in his critical essays on drama and poetry. When Purcell applied his contrapuntal practice to vocal works, sometimes borrowing techniques from much earlier consort music, 'fugeing' often interacted with, or embodied, the text being set, suggesting a highly self-conscious engagement with the expressive potential of counterpoint. *See also* **Burial Service**. *AdaPur, GoeHar, HerRev, HerThe, HowArt, HowSin, TalFug.*

Countertenor The highest adult male voice type, usually (though not exclusively) notated in the C3 clef. It is roughly equivalent to the French *haute-contre* and is best described as high tenor; the modern tradition that Purcell wrote his solo 'countertenor' parts for falsettists only goes back to Alfred Deller* and Michael Tippett*. Purcell sometimes wrote for the same singer in C3 and C4 clefs, suggesting he intended no fundamental difference in vocal production between them. He twice used C2 for the distinctive high vocal range of John Howell (c.1670–1708): in the duet 'Hark each tree' from 'Hail, bright Cecilia'* (labelled 'High Contra tenor for Mr Howel') and the solo 'Crown the altar' from 'Celebrate this Festival'*. The upper part of 'Sound the trumpet' from 'Come, ye sons of art, away* (up to e'') may also have been composed for him. The use of 'feigned' (i.e. falsetto) voices was often associated with a treble tessitura. John Evelyn* (*EveDia*, iv. 270) described John Abell (1653–after 1716) as 'the famous Trebble', suggesting that Abell incorporated falsetto into his technique, though Giacomo (Jakob) Greber described him as a tenor (*BalCou*, 14). Pitch* must be considered when evaluating the range and tessitura of 'countertenor' parts: secular music was at least a tone lower than the Chapel Royal* organ*. High countertenor voices were recognised as rare, a point confirmed by Burney* (*BurHis*, iii. 460) when he described William Turner's* voice as 'settling to that pitch; a circumstance which so seldom happens, *naturally*, that if it be cultivated, the possessor is sure of employment'. *See also* **Alexander Damascene, John Freeman, William Mountfort, John Pate**. *BalDel, BalSta, DexQui, MorVoi, ParPer, RosPur.*

Country dances A measure of Purcell's posthumous fame was the many pieces by him used as country dances in *The Dancing Master* (1651–c.1728), started by John Playford* and continued by Henry Playford and others; simple dance instructions were printed with the tunes. They include (using the numbering in *PlaDan*): 343 'Siege of Limerick' (*Dioclesian** Z627/4); 345 'Tythe pig' (*King Arthur** Z628/37); 366 'St Martin's Lane' (*The Virtuous Wife** Z611/9, also known as 'La Furstemberg'*); 377 'The hole in the wall' (*Abdelazer** Z570/8); and 392 'Westminster Hall' (*Bonduca** Z574/7). In addition, the dancing master Thomas Bray* fitted dance instructions to three Purcell pieces in the first part of his *Country Dances* (1699): no. 2, 'The Duke of Gloucester's March' (*The Indian Queen* Z630/1b); no. 13, 'Short and sweet' (*The Gordian Knot Unty'd** Z597/5); and no. 18, 'The Scotch Measure' (*Amphitryon** Z572/4). *See also* **Dance**. *SemFur.*

Cowley, Abraham This poet and dramatist (1618–67) appealed greatly to serious-minded Restoration composers because he retained the lofty tone and extravagant images of the metaphysical poets, but developed a simple, bold and informal style, suitable for setting to music. He was evidently Purcell's favourite poet: there are 16 Cowley settings among his non-theatre songs, more than any other except Anonymous. A number are from Cowley's collection *The Mistress* (1647), and several (including 'If ever I more riches did desire'*) are multi-sectional symphony songs*, their model being John Blow's* Cowley setting 'Awake, awake my lyre'. *HolPur, SavScu.*

Croft, William Composer and organist (1678–1727), one of Purcell's most prominent followers. He was a Chapel Royal chorister, a pupil and protégé of John Blow*. In 1700 he became organist of St Anne's, Soho in London and returned to the Chapel Royal; he succeeded Blow in 1708 as its 'Master of the Children and Composer' as well as organist of Westminster Abbey, though he was also active as a theatre composer for a few years after 1700. Croft was initially strongly influenced by Purcell, sometimes imitating particular pieces.

Striking examples are the Symphony to his ode 'The heavenly warlike goddess now disarmed' (?1697) (ed. in *CroOde*), with antiphonal exchanges between trumpets and strings derived from the opening of 'Hail, bright Cecilia'*, and the overture to his theatre airs* for *Courtship A-la-Mode* (1700) (ed. in *HolThe*), which starts with a passage inspired by the Prelude in *The Fairy Queen* Z629/1a. Croft's keyboard Ground in C minor uses Purcell's idiosyncratic *style brisé** harmonisation of the ground, which caused it to be misattributed and catalogued as ZD221. He collected manuscripts of Purcell's music, and included the 1695 setting of 'Thou knowest, Lord' Z58C* in his own complete Burial Service*, for reasons, he wrote when publishing it in *Musica Sacra*, i (1724), 'obvious to every Artist'. *See also* **The Golden Sonata**. *BDECM, CBCR, LowSta, ShaMan, SpiCat, WhiCec, ZimCat.*

Cross, Letitia This actress, singer and dancer was probably only 13 when she started to take stage roles for Purcell in the spring of 1695, following the break-up of the United Company*. Nevertheless, she quickly became his leading soprano, giving first performances of such memorable songs as 'I attempt from Love's sickness to fly' from *The Indian Queen** Z630/17h; 'O lead me to some peaceful gloom' from *Bonduca** Z574/17; and the great mad song 'From rosy bowers'*. Purcell evidently thought she had great histrionic and musical potential. After his death she went on to create the role of Hoyden in Vanbrugh's *The Relapse* (November 1696), and after some years away from the stage (she was Peter the Great's mistress while he was in London in 1698), she created the role of Dorisbe in Thomas Clayton's Italianate opera *Arsinoe* (1704). She continued to perform in London until 1732, dying in 1737. *BalBir, BalSop, BalSta, BDA, LowSta, WinSoc.*

Cross, Thomas Engraver, printer, publisher and music seller, the probable son of the engraver Thomas Cross senior. He established in London cheap music printing from engraved copper plates, hitherto a luxury, low-volume process. Unlike traditional typesetting, still used by the Playfords*, the Carrs* and others, it enabled him to imitate music handwriting (apparently using John Playford's hand as a model) and to run off extra copies as required from the plates. He began in 1683 with *Sonnata's of III Parts**, elegantly engraved for Purcell, and produced other instrumental collections, including *A Choice Collection**. However, in the 1690s he mainly engraved and published single-sheet songs, including many from Purcell's theatre works. They were often sold in anthologies or were bound for collectors by booksellers. Cross had the field to himself until 1695, when John Walsh* imitated and quickly outcompeted him. Cross claimed his song-sheets were 'exactly engrav'd', and in 1700 Henry Hall* gave him a backhanded compliment: 'at the Shops we daily dangling view / False Concord, by *Tom Cross* Engraven true'. His single-sheet editions provide important information about Purcell's singers and performance practice. *See also* **Printing and Publishing**. *CarPub, DaySon, HerCro, HerPla, HigRec, HumPub, HunPri, KruPri, MPP, SmiWal, ThoSou, WalSon, WooKey.*

Cross-relations *See* **Dissonance**

Illus. 2: Letitia Cross.

'Crown the year' Z335/3 The memorable ground-bass* air from Purcell's 1687 ode 'Sound the trumpet, beat the drum'*. It is in B minor as a countertenor* solo in the ode (the key of the fine keyboard arrangement with *style brisé** harmonisations of the ground, probably made by the composer), though in *Orpheus Britannicus**, book 2 it is in G minor as a treble/tenor solo – which relates it to a group of G minor grounds inspired by Lully's 'Scocca pur'*. *WooSco.*

Curtain tune An early-Restoration term for the piece played in the theatre after the spoken prologue as the curtain was raised. Some sets of theatre airs*, notably Matthew Locke's* for *The Tempest** (1674), include pieces so named, though after about 1680 composers generally preferred the word 'overture'* (from the French *ouverture*) as Lully's* type became popular in England. Purcell's Curtain Tune in *Timon of Athens** Z632/20 is a late use of the term, probably applied in error. *HolThe, PriPur, PriThe.*

Da capo aria Purcell used some elements of da capo arias in two of his most Italianate theatrical airs, 'Ye gentle spirits of the air' Z629/21 and 'Thus the gloomy world' Z629/43, both in *The Fairy Queen**. They use the A–B–A pattern, with the B section setting a contrasted portion of text and changing to a different time signature and tempo. Some of Purcell's late ground-bass* airs, such as 'Wondrous machine' Z328/8 from 'Hail, bright Cecilia'* and 'Music for a while' Z583/2 from *Oedipus** resemble da capo arias in that the return to the tonic coincides with a return to the opening words and music. Purcell was credited with full-blown da capo airs when the music for *The Tempest** was thought to be by him; it was probably written by John Weldon* in the first decade of the eighteenth century – at a time when Italian operas and cantatas featuring them were becoming familiar in England. *HolPur, PriPur.*

Damascene, Alexander French-born Protestant countertenor* and composer (d.1719), presumably trained as an *haute-contre*. He settled in London around 1680 and sang at court from 1689. He succeeded Purcell as a member of the Chapel Royal* in 1695 and remained in the Chapel for the rest of his life, also singing a solo in at least one court ode by John Eccles*. He sang in five Purcell odes and the Te Deum and Jubilate in D major*, taking among other solos 'But ah, I see Eusibia drown'd in tears' in 'Arise, my muse'*, 'The airy violin' in 'Hail, bright Cecilia'*, and 'Strike the viol' in 'Come, ye sons of art, away'*. 'Monsieur Damasen' taught Mary Verney in 1691, and was described by her grandfather Sir Ralph Verney as 'the best singing master in England' (*ThoPri*, 204). *BalCou, BDECM, MurOde, WhiCec.*

Dance Purcell engaged with dance and dance music in various ways. He wrote examples of current or obsolete social dances throughout his career. He started with pavans* as a teenager, and moved on to the longstanding components of the keyboard suite*, the almand*, corant*, saraband* and jig*, as well as more recent French imports such as the minuet* (*menuet*) and borry (*bourée*). Purcell often labelled dances in sets of theatre airs* not by their proper titles but according to function ('First Music'*, 'Act Tune'* and so on), or with the catch-all label 'air'*.

Virtually all functional social dances would have fitted standard choreographies, and those current ones would have been taught to the upper classes from childhood by dancing masters, mostly at dancing schools. However, in the theatre (and apparently during some court odes) dancing masters devised special choreographies to fit each piece. Purcell's first-known theatrical dances, for *Dido and Aeneas**, were presumably devised and taught by the dancing master Josias Priest*, who ran the boarding school in Chelsea where the opera was staged; 17 are called for in its libretto. One of them, The Witches' Dance Z626/34a, is a fine late example of the antimasque dance from the court masque, in which the bizarre capers of rustic, comic or sinister characters were accompanied by equally bizarre changes of rhythmic and melodic direction. Purcell would also have collaborated with a court dancing master, perhaps the French immigrant Jeremy Gohori or Gohory (d.1703), in his ode 'Sound the trumpet, beat the drum'* (1687), which includes the Chaconne Z335/7 later used in *King Arthur** Z628/1a. Such ground-bass* pieces (there is another chaconne* in 'Who can from joy refrain?'* Z342/7) were ideal vehicles for the talents of a dance troupe, their episodic construction providing obvious opportunities for mixing solos and ensembles.

In the public theatres dancing was routinely accompanied by onstage fiddlers, who apparently provided their own music, though the scores of Purcell's dramatic operas* show that his brief also included writing stage dances. Josias Priest collaborated with him in *Dioclesian**, *King Arthur*, *The Fairy Queen** and *The Indian Queen**, while Thomas Bray* claimed to have devised choreographies for *Amphitryon** and *Dioclesian**, though these may not have been for the original productions. The stage dances in Purcell's dramatic operas include examples of the antimasque type (Dance of Furies, *Dioclesian* Z627/14; Monkeys' Dance, *The Fairy Queen* Z629/46) and chaconnes ('Triumph, victorious Love', *Dioclesian* Z627/38; Dance for a Chinese Man and Woman, *The Fairy Queen* Z629/51), although he also used the ordinary patterns of social dances, such as the minuet-like Country Dance Z627/25; the Paspe* Z627/29; and the Canaries* Z627/34, all in *Dioclesian*. See also **Country dances**. *BalHon, BDECM, GofGoh, HolPur, MulDio, PriFid, PriThe, SemDan, SemFur, ThoDan, ThoIsa, ThoOpe, WalAct, WeaDan, ZimCat.*

The Dancing Master See **Country dances**

Dart, Robert (Bob) Thurston The harpsichordist and musicologist Thurston Dart (1921–71) combined research and performance in equal measure in a ferociously productive and tragically short career, much of it devoted to Purcell. After service in the RAF in World War II and study in Brussels with Charles van den Borren (a former student of Arnold Dolmetsch*), he was appointed assistant lecturer in the Cambridge music faculty in 1947, followed by university lecturer (1952) and professor (1962); he left Cambridge in 1964 to create a new music faculty at King's College, London. As a harpsichordist he combined a solo career with work as a continuo player and musical director, particularly with the Jacobean Ensemble and the Philomusica of London. His editorial and publishing commitments included: secretary to Musica Britannica; a director and eventually chairman of Stainer & Bell*; and member of the editorial committee of the Purcell Society*.

Dart's contribution to Purcell scholarship began with *DarCib*, on the Cibell* (1952), followed by *PurGro*, the first edition of Three Parts upon a Ground* (1953). The 1959 Purcell anniversary celebrations* produced *DarHar* and *DarCha*, on Purcell's harpsichord and consort music respectively, the latter a taster for his complete edition, *PS* 31 (1959), which included his reconstruction of the lost bass viol part of the Sonata in G minor Z780*. Dart's Purcell recordings were perhaps more influential than his scholarly work. Notable solo LPs included the *Complete Works for Harpsichord and Clavichord* (1956) and organ pieces on historic English organs (1958; CD reissue 1994). Ensemble recordings included the first complete recording of the trio sonatas* with the Jacobean Ensemble (1956, 1957) and a memorable contribution as continuo player to Anthony Lewis's recording of *Dido and Aeneas** (1961). See also **John Bull**, **March and Canzona**, **Recordings**. *DarInt, DarMus, MorDar, PerDar.*

Davies, Peter Maxwell Davies (1934–2016) wrote in a programme note for his Fantasia and Two Pavans after Henry Purcell WoO 95 (1968): 'I have long been fascinated by Purcell's music, but utterly bored by well-meaning "authentic" performances ... I am sure that many people will consider my Purcell realizations wholly immoral'. His 'realization' of the Fantasia (actually Three Parts upon a Ground*) is relatively straightforward, arranged to imitate the shrill sound of a chamber organ 'with its brazen twelfth stop', though he transformed two of Purcell's three-part pavans* into foxtrots, 'sparked off' by recordings from the 1920s and 30s in his collection as played on a pre-electric horn gramophone. His Purcell pieces were written for his group The Fires of London, and were 'very much preparatory studies for a large orchestral work, *St Thomas Wake*'. BurRem.

Decani *See* **Choir**

Declamatory vocal writing *See* **Songs**

Deller, Alfred The first falsettist to achieve prominence as a soloist since the eighteenth century, Alfred George Deller (1912–79) was a lay clerk at Canterbury Cathedral in 1944 when Michael Tippett* came to the city for the first performance of his motet 'Plebs angelica'. Deller sang 'Music for a while'* for him on that occasion, whereupon (the composer wrote) 'the centuries rolled back' and he 'recognised absolutely that this was the voice for which Purcell had written'. Tippett immediately began to use Deller as a soloist at Morley College and elsewhere; Deller made his London debut on 31 December 1944 singing ''Tis Nature's voice'* from 'Hail, bright Cecilia'*, and subsequently took part in Tippett's complete performances of that ode, as well as 'Come, ye sons of art, away'* and other Purcell works. He made many notable Purcell recordings*, some with Walter Bergmann* as accompanist. His finest achievement as a conductor was the first recording of the Act V masque and other music from *Dioclesian** (1965). BalDel, ClaDel, ColMor, ColTip, HarDel, MarBer, PurCon.

Devotional songs and part-songs Thomas Mace*, Samuel Pepys* and Roger North* wrote about a tradition of domestic sacred music in seventeenth-century England, a genre to which Purcell made an important but neglected contribution. Antecedents include William and Henry Lawes's* *Choice Psalmes* (1648) for three voices and continuo, and Richard Dering's Latin motets. The latter, along with a collection of two-voice English anthems with continuo by composers such as Benjamin Rogers, Christopher Gibbons* and Matthew Locke*, were published by John Playford* as *Cantica Sacra* (1662, 1674). Locke's metrical psalm settings, Latin motets by Italian composers and John Blow*, and anthems by Locke, Pelham Humfrey* and Blow were also significant influences.

Purcell copied 16 of his domestic sacred works into his scorebook* GB-Lbl, Add. MS 30930. The majority are three or four-voice metrical psalms, nine with words by Dr John Patrick*. Four (one incomplete) are Latin motets, notably 'Jehova quam multi sunt hostes mei'*. They were probably all composed in 1678–9, about the same time as the fantasias* and other consort music copied at the other end of the same volume. Purcell used both genres to assimilate and develop the musical techniques of his predecessors and older contemporaries.

None of these works were published; they circulated in manuscripts mostly connected with cathedrals or private music meetings in Oxford*.

Purcell shared with his predecessors a liking for gloomy, penitential texts, which provided ideal subject matter for angular melodic lines and tense counterpoint. The four-part settings, mostly for tr tr ct b or tr tr t b with continuo, share many characteristics with his verse anthems*, but the full-voiced sections are more soloistic, and are compulsively focussed on dissonant and chromatic part-writing, taken to extremes in 'Lord, I can suffer' Z136 at the words 'Pity my languishing estate; | And those perplexities I feel'. The three-part pieces, set for ct/t t b with continuo, explore surprisingly varied textures (perhaps influenced by continental motets), including the upper voices pitted against the bass, homophonic declamation, three-part counterpoint and extended passages for single voices. Two other three-part works, 'Oh that my grief was throughly weigh'd'* ZD42 and the incomplete 'O happy man' Z139, are probably genuine despite not being in Add. MS 30930.

Purcell's contribution to devotional solo song began with 'Sleep, Adam, sleep' Z195, perhaps as early as 1677. More ambitious works followed around 1683, with 'Let the night perish' Z191, Jeremy Taylor's verse paraphrase of Job: 3. It, along with 'With sick and famish'd eyes' Z200 (George Herbert*), 'Awake, and with attention hear' Z181 (Abraham Cowley*) and 'Begin the song' Z183, were copied into GB-Lbl, R.M. 20.h.8, the last incomplete there. As with the secular songs*, symphony songs* and court odes* in the scorebook, they were doubtless sung by the skilled soloists of the court Private Music*. 'Awake, and with attention hear', a lengthy multi-sectional bass solo, is an only partially successful essay in the Italian style, as typified by Carissimi's 'Lucifer, coelestis', which was published (in a corrupt version) in *Harmonia Sacra**, book 2. Purcell made little distinction in compositional style between devotional and serious secular poetry, witness his Cowley settings, though scholars and performers have traditionally treated them as separate genres, to the detriment of the former. He apparently stopped setting devotional part-songs after about 1680, though he continued to write superb devotional solo songs and duets (and the dramatic dialogue* Saul and the Witch of Endor*), collecting them in *Harmonia Sacra*. See also **Italian music**, **'Now that the sun hath veiled his light'**, **'Since God so tender a regard'**, **'Tell me, some pitying angel'**. *AdaPur, ForDom, HolPur, HowSin, SmaEnd*.

Dialogues A special type of declamatory song popular from Jacobean times, the dialogue typically dramatises a brief exchange between two characters from the Bible, classical myth, allegory or just Arcadian fantasy. The genre was obsolete in England when Purcell was a boy; he must have been virtually the last composer to set such well-worn subjects as Orpheus and Charon: 'Haste, haste gentle Charon' Z490 (1682–3); Horace and Lydia: 'While you for me alone had charms' Z524 (?spring 1683); Love and Despair: 'Hence, fond deceiver!' Z492 (autumn 1687); and Thyrsis and Daphne: 'Why, my Daphne, why complaining?' Z525 (1690). Purcell's standalone dialogues contain some fine music, though they are (along with his duets for treble, bass and continuo) among his least-known works, overshadowed by his mature theatrical dialogues such as 'Hark, my Damilcar' Z613/1 (for a revival of John Dryden's* play *Tyrannic Love* in

1694); 'You say 'tis love' (*King Arthur** Z628/35), or, in a comic vein, Coridon and Mopsa*. *See also* **Songs**. *DaySon, HolPur, RohPoe, SpiSon, ZimCat.*

Dido and Aeneas Z626 We do not know why or when Purcell composed this small-scale, all-sung operatic masque. The earliest source is an undated printed libretto prepared for a performance at Josias Priest's* boarding school for girls in Chelsea. A letter from Rowland Sherman* that describes *Dido* as 'the mask he made for Preists [sic] Ball' implies that its music had been composed by July 1688. Its Prologue (included in the Chelsea libretto; the music is lost) resembles the prologues of French operas praising Louis XIV, raising the possibility that the opera was conceived as an allegorical panegyric to Charles II* or James II*, to be performed at court. John Blow's* *Venus and Adonis*, the close model for *Dido*, was certainly written and performed for the king in 1683, at Whitehall* or at Windsor*, and was repeated at Priest's school the following year. However, Sherman's statement that Purcell had 'made' *Dido* for Priest implies that for some reason his opera did not achieve a court production, and that its première was indeed at Chelsea, albeit a little earlier than 1689, the date long accepted by Purcell scholars.

Nahum Tate's* libretto draws on the Dido legend as related in Virgil's *Aeneid*, Ovid's *Epistles* and his own play, *Brutus of Alba* (1678), though condensed and reimagined as an opera. Tate's innovation was to replace the classical gods, who traditionally separate the lovers, with witches, whose motivation is wholly malicious and enigmatic. His verse, skilfully varied in metre and rhyme in a tightly controlled and fast-moving plot, has been routinely derided, but it gave Purcell what he needed for a compelling musical drama. Numerous attempts have been made to discern specific allegorical schemes; those relating to William III* and Mary II* have now been superseded by the discovery of Sherman's letter and its 1688 date. We find attempts to identify Aeneas with Charles II or James II unconvincing.

The earliest surviving scores of the opera were copied in the last quarter of the eighteenth century. Three sources, J-WAkt, Nanki N-4/41 (the earliest, copied before 1774), GB-Ob, Tenbury MS 1266 and GB-KNt, MR 2-5.3 (copied by Philip Hayes*), all seem to descend from a source used at the Lincoln's Inn Fields Theatre in 1700 and 1704 that is no longer extant. Several other sources that descend from Nanki N-4/41 are related to performances at the Academy of Ancient Music* in 1774; subsequent performances took place there in 1785 and 1787. No source contains all the music needed to set the Chelsea libretto, which calls for 17 dances: the Prologue is missing, as are a chorus and dance closing Act II, Scene 2 and several of the dances. However, 'A Dance Gittars Chacony' and 'Gitter Ground a Dance' were probably improvised or supplied by the guitarist, and some of the other dances might have been performed to instrumental repeats of vocal sections.

The sources disagree over the gender of the singer who played the Sorceress. Witches were traditionally portrayed by men, a convention that continued after actresses appeared on the public stage in the 1660s; the Sorceress's vocal line, and its relationship to the four-part string accompaniment, makes most sense at the lower octave. A bass singer was certainly used at the Lincoln's Inn Fields Theatre in 1700, when *Dido* was broken up and reordered for use between the acts of Charles Gildon's* adaptation of Shakespeare's* *Measure for Measure*. The play text for this production, which includes the opera and an altered version of its prologue, is a significant independent source of the work. In 1704 *Dido* was reassembled, perhaps with the prologue cut, to serve as an afterpiece to two different plays; Curtis Price plausibly argued that the missing music was discarded at that point.

The deserved popularity of *Dido* can be explained by a combination of a tight, focussed libretto with an immaculate musical structure, meticulous vocal declamation, memorable melodies and the emotional insight of Dido's arias. The succession of short movements, often linked by proportional tempo* relationships, drive the drama swiftly and inexorably forward, throwing into sharp relief the extended ground-bass* airs at the beginning ('Ah, Belinda') and end ('When I am laid in earth', Dido's Lament*), through which Dido's character is vividly illuminated. Dance* is crucial to the opera's musical dramaturgy, punctuating scenes and creating contrasts with vocal movements; offering visual realisations of the opera's intense emotions; and creating diverting spectacle. The intimate musical forces – soloists, chorus and four-part strings – apparently included a guitar*, contributing the two guitar grounds and probably playing in the continuo* group.

The opera made little impact in Purcell's lifetime, and only three movements were published before 1841 (when it was published by the Musical Antiquarian Society*): 'Ah, Belinda' in *Orpheus Britannicus**, book 1, and 'Fear no danger' and 'Come away, fellow sailors' in single-sheet editions related to its performance in 1700. *Dido*'s popularity from the late nineteenth century, caused in part by the resonance of its imperial themes in a classical setting and by the modern dominance of all-sung opera, has obscured Purcell's achievement as a composer of dramatic operas*, the mainstream in his lifetime. *See also* **Key Characteristics**, **Political Allegory**, **Recordings**, **Thomas D'Urfey**. *AdaPur, BalHon, BloVen, HarDid, HelPre, HolPur, PinDeu, PinWhi, PriPur, PurDid, WalAct, WhiAle, WhiShe, WooDid, WooPur.*

Dido's Ghost An opera by Errollyn Wallen (b.1958) to a libretto by Wesley Stace, first performed by the Dunedin Consort in 2021. It tells the story of Dido's sister Anna: she is taken to Aeneas's court after being washed up on the shore of Troia Nova in Italy. The opera includes a complete performance of *Dido and Aeneas** in flashback, ordered by Aeneas's jealous wife Lavinia, with Anna as Dido. The ghost of Dido appears to Aeneas offering to lift her curse on the Trojan race if he allows Anna to escape. He agrees but, appropriating his former lover's lament, is left broken by this encounter with the past.

Dido's Lament Z626/38 'When I am laid in earth', the sublime air sung by the queen of Carthage at the climax of *Dido and Aeneas**, is Purcell's best-known ground-bass* air. It is founded on 11 unvaried statements of a chromatic five-bar form of the passacaglia* bass, long associated with love and death in Italian music; it is in G minor, Purcell's 'death key'. The vocal line is memorable for its subtle relationship with the inexorable bass, sometimes coinciding with its cadences, sometimes soaring independent of it, and for its haunting mixture of suave melody and the declamatory cries of 'Remember me!'. Also essential to the effect is the rich four-part string accompaniment (unusual in Purcell's England for the accompaniment of treble voices), which provides acerbic dissonance in weeping appoggiaturas. In the extraordinary concluding ritornello* the bass is transferred to the upper parts in counterpoint with itself. *See also* **Key associations**. *AdaPur, HolPur, PriPur*.

Diminution *See* **Counterpoint**

Dioclesian Z627 When *The Prophetess, or The History of Dioclesian* opened at Dorset Garden* in late May 1690, it was the first large-scale musical production attempted by the United Company* since 1685, when it sustained financial loss mounting *Albion and Albanius* by John Dryden* and Louis Grabu*. Purcell's music was on a grand scale, employing a full Baroque orchestra* in a London theatre for the first time. Thomas Betterton* adapted *The Prophetess* (1622) by Philip Massinger and John Fletcher into a dramatic opera*, concentrating the most extended musical passages in Acts II and V. In Act II Delphia conjures a long series of symphonies, solos and choruses to celebrate the Roman soldier Diocles's victory over Aper. The significance of dance and scenic display emerges when, in response to Diocles's acceptance of Aurelia as his bride, Delphia summons 'a dreadful Monster'. It 'moves slowly forward' to mysterious 'Soft music', after which 'They who made the Monster separate in an instant, and fall into a Figure, ready to begin a Dance of the Furies'. Its music is full of the rushing scales characteristic of Lully's* demonic dances, which Grabu imitated in his music for *Valentinian* (1684) and in *Albion and Albanius*. The 'Soft music' returns in Act IV, accompanying a vision of Aurelia's tomb, which becomes transformed into a dance of butterflies.

    The climactic spectacle is the Act V Masque of Cupid and Bacchus, in which five entries of dancers and singers were deployed on four stacked tiers of an extravagant machine, filling the entire stage. This machine, the scheme for the masque and the text of the final chorus were informed by Betterton's knowledge of Lully's *Le Triomphe de l'Amour*, staged at the Paris Opéra in 1681. Highlights during about 40 minutes of continuous music are the sensuous treble duet 'Oh, the sweet delights of love'; the prelude to 'Behold, O mightiest of gods', deploying the strings and a four-part oboe* band in antiphonal exchanges; and the culminating 'Triumph, victorious Love', modelled on the massive Act II chaconne* in *Albion and Albanius*. The last uses the standard chaconne bass and explores kaleidoscopic antiphonal exchanges between soloists, choir, trumpets, oboe band, strings and continuo. John Downes* wrote that Purcell's music 'gratify'd the Expectation of Court and City; and got the Author great Reputation'.

    Purcell's decision to publish the music in full score by subscription was in part a response to Grabu's publication of *Albion and Albanius* (1687), and beyond it to Ballard's scores of Lully's operas. He had to employ two printers for the publication, which finally appeared in March 1691. It seems not to have been a financial success – his subsequent dramatic operas were not published in full – though it established his reputation as the leading English theatrical composer. *Dioclesian* was popular at the time, but modern critics have judged it the least successful of Purcell's dramatic operas, and the byzantine and undramatic plot has militated against staged modern revivals. *See also* **Political Allegory**. *HamDry, HerPla, HerScr, HolPur, LamBal, MulDio, MulWor, PriPur, SchDio, ThoCha, TupFri, WalDra, WhiStu, WooPur*.

Illus. 3: *Dioclesian*, Second Music.

Dissonance Purcell's music is renowned for the richness of its harmony, and that richness was produced by the judicious mixture of concord and discord; Nathaniel Giles (*HerThe*, 154–5) wrote in 1622 that mixing them produces 'a more delightfull and pleasing sound unto the eare'. Purcell would have been taught, as John Blow* put it in his manuscript continuo treatise (*ArnAcc*, 163–72), that 'Discords must be prepared by Concords, & resolv'd into Concords'. Nevertheless, his older contemporaries, including Christopher Gibbons*, Matthew Locke* and Blow, frequently broke the rules, peppering their music with unprepared dissonances, including false or cross-relations, particularly in the 'English cadence', which typically produced a clash between the simultaneous sharpened and flattened versions of the seventh degree of the scale (Ex. 2).

Ex. 2: Three Parts upon a Ground Z731A, b. 18.

Blow included false relations in three specimen examples of cadences in his treatise; many of the irregular dissonances in his music were collected by Charles Burney* as 'Specimens of D^r. Blow's Crudities' (*BurHis*, iii. 449–52).

Purcell brought an exceptionally discriminating ear to this tradition, never straying over the line into unwarranted harshness, and he was attuned to new types of dissonances principally brought to England in Italian vocal and instrumental music. In 1694 (*PlaInt*, 131–2) he wrote about two discords 'mightily in use among the *Italian* Masters': 'the *Sharp Seventh*', the #7–4–2 chord, 'you will find frequently in Recitative Songs', and 'a *Flat Seventh* [diminished chord] used commonly at a Close or Cadence'. Purcell included many daring dissonant passages at approaches to cadences, such as the increasingly clashing descending harmonies in "'Tis Nature's voice'* at the word 'charms' – a late example of the *cadentia duriscula* favoured by Italian composers and described by Christoph Bernhard. *GoeHar*, *HerThe*, *NorMus*.

Distress'd Innocence, or The Princess of Persia Z577 Purcell contributed a set of theatre airs* to this tragedy by Elkanah Settle (with contributions by William Mountfort*), first performed at Drury Lane* in October or November 1690. It was published in *A Collection of Ayres** with the overture placed first, though it is preserved in the original theatre order (followed in *PS* 16) in the 'Cambury Manuscript'*. There are two versions of the viola part (both ed. in *PS* 16): the one in the manuscript is generally superior; the published one was probably devised after Purcell's death because the original part was not available. The set is not one of Purcell's finest, though it is of interest in that, as Curtis Price suggested, the Second Act Tune, a plangent and eloquent slow air, apparently represents the fate of the wrongfully accused and deposed general Hormidas, while the running bass of the Third Act Tune depicts 'the violent storm raging during the interval'. *LauCam, LS, PriThe, SchAyr*.

Divisions Purcell grew up with the English tradition of divisions on ground basses*, originally for bass viol but later mostly for violin, as collected by John Playford* in *The Division-Violin* from 1684. We do not have any sets of divisions for solo instruments by Purcell apart from the keyboard Ground in Gamut Z645, though he drew on the tradition in several consort pieces, notably the great G minor ground Z807, no. 6 of *Ten Sonata's in Four Parts**, and Three Parts upon a Ground*. The latter uses a ground borrowed from Christopher Simpson* (whose *Division-Violist* is a detailed treatise on improvising and composing divisions), and both include running passages in semiquavers (the word 'divisions' implies dividing long notes into short ones), either canonic* or freely canonic in the manner of John Jenkins*.

Dolmetsch, Arnold (Eugène) A multi-instrumentalist and instrument maker of French origin (1858–1940). He was effectively the father of the later British early music movement, particularly for promoting the use of old instruments (he restored, made and played the harpsichord, clavichord, lute, viols and recorders), and his enthusiasm for sixteenth- and seventeenth-century English composers, including Purcell. After studying the violin in Brussels and at the newly founded Royal College of Music (1883–5), Dolmetsch taught at Dulwich College, where he introduced his pupils to Purcell; they played pieces from *The Fairy Queen** in a London concert on 10 June 1890. He provided illustrations on 21 November that year for a lecture on English music by Frederick Bridge, including two Purcell trio sonatas*. He regularly included the composer in his own concerts (including the Fantasia upon One Note* in 1895), in London and at the Haslemere Festival, founded in 1925. In 1892 he published a collection of arrangements for violin and piano of pieces from *Dioclesian**, *King Arthur** and *The Fairy Queen*. In 1897 he and his wife Elodie played the continuo* on two harpsichords for Hans Richter's Birmingham performance of *King Arthur*. *See also* **Performance history from 1695**, **Recordings**, **George Bernard Shaw**. *CamDol, DolInt, HofGam, HolHar, HolLif, ShaMus*.

Don Quixote Z578 The three plays by Thomas D'Urfey* after Cervantes, *The Comical History of Don Quixote*, were performed at Dorset Garden* in May or June 1694 (Part 1), June 1694 (Part 2) and early December 1695 (Part 3). They were effectively dramatic operas* on the cheap, an imperative for the United Company* after the great expense of *The Fairy Queen** in 1692. They featured a good deal of music and dance but did not require costly scenic effects or large casts: there is no chorus and some of the important characters were taken by singing actors, including Anne Bracegirdle (Marcella), John Bowman* (Cardenio) and Letitia Cross* (Altisidora in Part 3). This reduced the need for a double cast of actors and singers, and facilitated an unusual integration of the music into the action. The first two plays were enormously successful, though the third was a failure. D'Urfey complained in the preface to the play text that its 'Songish part' had suffered from lack of rehearsal and its dances had lacked 'some good Performers'.

Purcell shared the composition of the vocal music in Parts 1 and 2 with John Eccles*, while the songs were provided in Part 3 by a consortium, including Raphael Courteville and Thomas Morgan*, Purcell only contributing 'From rosy bowers'* (by then Eccles was a member of Thomas Betterton's* rival company); *PriDon* collects facsimiles of the surviving music. Purcell's 'Let the dreadful engines' Z578/3 and 'From rosy bowers'* Z578/9 are justly famous mad songs*, while 'With this sacred charming wand' Z578/4 is a fine conjuring scene, sung by Montesmo (Cardenio in disguise) and two accomplices in Part 1, Act V, Scene 2 to entice Don Quixote and Sancho Panza into captivity. Equally remarkable are some of Eccles's songs, including the duet dirge 'Sleep poor youth, sleep in peace' in Part 1, accompanied by three recorders and continuo, and the mad song 'I burn, I burn', sung by Bracegirdle as Marcella in Part 2. *BalMad, DayDur, HolPur, LS, PriPur, PriThe, RobMad, SpiSon, WinHow, ZimCat.*

Dorset Garden Theatre The theatre in Dorset Garden at Whitefriars on the Thames was opened by the Duke's Company in 1671. It was better equipped with stage machinery than the Drury Lane Theatre*, but was more expensive to run, so the United Company* tended to reserve it for spectacular productions, including Purcell's dramatic operas*. It had a music room above the proscenium arch, though an orchestra pit in front of the stage must have been used for the large orchestras Purcell wrote for in *Dioclesian**, *King Arthur** and *The Fairy Queen**. The Act V masque in *Dioclesian* shows that its machinery could fill the theatre 'from the Frontispiece of the Stage to the farther end of the House', and could be deployed in four tiers, with dancers and singers on each level. Dorset Garden was used less frequently after Purcell's death and was demolished in 1709. *See also* **Christopher Rich**. *BurBan, LS, MulDio, MulWor, PriThe.*

The Double Dealer Z592 William Congreve's* famous comedy was first performed at Drury Lane* in November 1693. Purcell provided a set of theatre airs* and a large-scale bipartite song, 'Cynthia frowns when e'er I woo her', sung by Mrs Ayliff* in Act II accompanied by onstage musicians. The original order of movements of the airs is not known since the primary source is *A Collection of Ayres**. Notable in a fine set are the large-scale overture in F major, with its complex and brilliant fugue and its striking turn into F minor for the concluding Adagio, and the A minor Air Z592/4 with its biting dissonances. The Minuet or Slow Air in D minor Z592/6 was a dry run for the more sophisticated C-minor one in *Bonduca** Z574/4. *LS, PriPur, PriThe.*

Double organ The term in Restoration England for a two-manual organ*. Purcell's Voluntary for Double Organ in D minor Z719 has indications for 'Great Organ', and 'Chair Organ', using stops on the Great for florid solos accompanied by the Chair. It also exists in a single-organ version, Z718. *BicOrg, CoxOrg.*

Downes, John Initially an actor, Downes (d.?1712) became the prompter* of the Duke's Company in the 1660s, a role he continued with the United Company* from 1682, and with Betterton's* company after the split of 1695. He retired in 1706 and subsequently published *Roscius Anglicanus, or An Historical Review of the Stage* (1708; ed. DowRos), the first comprehensive book on the subject. Downes was interested in music (his son was an aspiring musician), and he included a few interesting nuggets of information about Purcell's works, such as that the production of *The Fairy Queen** was so expensive 'the Company got very little by it'. As prompter, Downes would have had a crucial role in the production of Purcell's dramatic operas* and other theatre works until the break-up of the United Company. BDA, HolBat.

Draghi, Giovanni Battista Nothing is known for sure of the Italian keyboard player and composer (d.1708) before Samuel Pepys* (*PepDia*, viii. 54–7) encountered him in London on 12 February 1667, though Hawkins* (*HawHis*, ii. 717) suggested he was the brother of the singer and opera composer Antonio Draghi (1634/5–1700), who came from Rimini. Giovanni Battista settled in London, becoming organist of Queen Catherine of Braganza's Catholic chapel at Somerset House in 1673, then of James II's* Catholic chapel at Whitehall* in 1686. He demonstrated Renatus Harris's* organ in the Battle of the Organs* and was active as a harpsichord teacher; his pupils included Princess (later Queen) Anne* and, presumably, the unidentified owner or owners of the Purcell-Draghi Manuscript*. He was also active in the theatre, contributing lost orchestral music to the dramatic operas* *The Tempest** (1674) and *Psyche* (1675). He also contributed songs for plays put on by the Duke's Company and then the United Company* in the 1680s, including the beautiful Italianate recitative and ground-bass* air 'Where art thou, God of Dreams', for the anonymous play *Romulus and Hersilia* (1682).

It is unfortunate that only one large-scale work by Draghi survives, the great setting of John Dryden's* *Song for St Cecilia's Day*, 1687, 'From harmony, from heav'nly harmony' (ed. DraCec). Its effect on his English contemporaries is clear from the five surviving early scores, one copied by John Blow*. The ode's influence can be clearly heard in the music Purcell and Blow wrote over the next few years, notably in its use of Italianate five-part string writing with two violins and two violas, taken up by Purcell in 'Now does the glorious day appear'* and 'Arise, my muse'*, and in its use of obbligato trumpets*, first imitated by Purcell in three works composed in the spring of 1690. Purcell also responded to Draghi's virtuosic Italianate solo vocal writing and massive choruses (the first chorus, for instance, was clearly the inspiration for the equivalent movement in 'Hail, bright Cecilia'*), and throughout Draghi showed English composers how to combine voices and instruments in sophisticated and novel ways. His keyboard music (ed. DraHar and WooPer) uses the Restoration idiom familiar from the suites of Blow and Purcell, with elaborate *style brisé* almands* and corants* contrasted with simpler tune-and-bass pieces; it is not inferior to them in quality. His Sonata in G minor for two violins and bass (ed. in HolTri) is closer to Locke* than Purcell, and was perhaps written about 1670. BDECM, DixIta, HogMan, HoldFid, HolPur, HolDra, LebAlb, MabIta, PriAut, WhiCec, WinAnn.

Dramatic opera The term devised by John Dryden* for plays with elaborate musical scenes, costume and dance, often in the form of self-contained all-sung masques*. The genre, also called semi-opera* or English opera, began with the Shakespeare* adaptations put on by Thomas Betterton's* Duke's Company: *Macbeth* (1673) and Thomas Shadwell's* version of *The Tempest* (1674), followed by Shadwell's *Psyche* (1675). Betterton developed the genre in a series of spectacular productions with Purcell's music in the 1690s: *Dioclesian* (1690), his adaptation of *The Prophetess* by Fletcher and Massinger; *King Arthur* (1691), Dryden's play 'in blank verse, adorn'd with Scenes, Machines, Songs and Dances' (his definition of the genre), originally written in 1684 but not produced at the time; and *The Fairy Queen* (1692), a Shakespearean adaptation also probably by Betterton. The great expense of *The Fairy Queen*, with its threefold cast of actors, singers and dancers, brought the series to a halt, though Thomas D'Urfey's* *Don Quixote* plays (1694–5) can be thought of as dramatic operas on the cheap, as can *The Indian Queen* (1695–6). The most notable later dramatic opera was *The Island Princess* (1699), with music mainly by Daniel Purcell*, Jeremiah Clarke* and Richard Leveridge*, the most popular English operatic work before *The Beggar's Opera*. Italian opera along with new and restrictive theatre patents put paid to new dramatic operas around 1710, and the modern assumption that all-sung opera is inherently superior to it has largely prevented successful stage revivals of Purcell's masterpieces. BurBan, BurDeb, HolPur, LucExo, PriIsl, PriPur, PriThe, ThoOpe, WalDra.

Drury Lane Theatre Purcell wrote much of his theatre music for the Theatre Royal, Drury Lane in Covent Garden, opened in 1674. The United Company* mostly used it for ordinary spoken plays, relying on the better-equipped Dorset Garden Theatre* for spectacular productions requiring stage machinery, including Purcell's dramatic operas*. The string consorts that played theatre airs* for ordinary spoken plays at Drury Lane may have been placed in a music room located in a box near the stage, leaving dances and songs to be accompanied on stage or in the wings, though some dramatic operas and Italian operas were subsequently performed there, implying the presence of an orchestra pit. The 1674 theatre was demolished in 1791; the present building is the fourth on the site. *See also* **Christopher Rich**. HolThe, LS, PriThe, SawRic.

Dryden, John Poet, playwright and critic (1631–1700), the leading Restoration writer. He was Poet Laureate from 1667 until the Glorious Revolution*, when, as a Catholic convert, he was replaced by Thomas Shadwell*. He made crucial contributions to musical life, including the two finest odes for the annual Cecilian celebrations* at Stationers' Hall*: *A Song on St Cecilia's Day, 1687* (ed. DraCec), set by G.B. Draghi*, and *Alexander's Feast*, set by Jeremiah Clarke* in 1697. He collaborated with Louis Grabu* on the all-sung opera *Albion and Albanius*, staged in 1685. In his preface to its printed libretto, the most significant critical essay on opera written in seventeenth-century England, he placed Grabu above 'any man who shall pretend to be his rival upon our stage'. He was late to appreciate Purcell's talent, but the success of *Dioclesian* in May 1690, for which he provided a satirical prologue (banned after the initial performance), led to their first collaboration, *Amphitryon*, produced that October. In the preface to its printed text he acknowledged Purcell as 'equal with the best abroad', and in 1691 he was the ghost writer for the composer's preface to the printed score of *Dioclesian*.

The same year Purcell composed the music for Dryden's dramatic opera* *King Arthur*, originally written as a companion piece to *Albion and Albanius* but not staged at that time. It too had been intended to flatter Charles II*, but Dryden claimed to have altered it to suit the new political circumstances, although the extent of the revision is unclear. Purcell provided songs for Dryden's *Aureng-Zebe*, *Cleomenes*, *The Indian Emperor* and *Tyrannic Love* over the next few years, as well as for *Love Triumphant* and *The Spanish Friar*, setting words not by the playwright. More significant was his music for a revival of *Oedipus** (?1692), by Dryden and Nathaniel Lee*, and for *The Indian Queen** (a play by Sir Robert Howard* to which Dryden made a minor and unspecified contribution), converted into a dramatic opera in 1695. Dryden's 'Mark how the lark and linnet sing', set by John Blow*, was the finest of the odes marking Purcell's death. *See also* **Odes on the death of Henry Purcell**. *AdaPoe*, *HamDry*, *LucExo*, *PinDou*, *ShaArt*, *WhiCec*, *WhiLos*, *WinArt*.

D'Urfey, Thomas Poet, dramatist and singer (c.1653–1723). He came to London from his native Devon in the 1670s, and pursued a career in the theatre and at court, despite a pronounced stutter which reportedly disappeared when he swore or sang. Purcell was a long-standing colleague, writing music for eight of his plays. He started with an extended storm song Z589/1 for *Sir Barnaby Whigg*, produced by the King's Company in (probably) June 1681. D'Urfey had a role in developing the mad song* genre, with 'I'll sail upon the dog star'* in *A Fool's Preferment, or The Three Dukes of Dunstable* (spring 1688), and 'Behold the man' Z608/1, a 'Dialogue between a Mad Man & a Mad Woman' in *The Richmond Heiress* (May 1693). Their most notable collaboration was the three *Don Quixote** plays (1694, 1695), Part 3 of which includes 'From rosy bowers'*, Purcell's last song. D'Urfey also wrote an epilogue for a production of *Dido and Aeneas** at Josias Priest's* Chelsea boarding school, where he worked as a singing teacher in the summer of 1689.

D'Urfey provided the verses for two odes Purcell wrote in 1690: 'Arise, my muse'* and the Yorkshire Feast Song*. He was also a notable exponent of the mock-song*, many examples of which were published in the six-volume collection of ballads and popular songs *Pills to Purge Melancholy**. A number are based on songs and dances by Purcell, including 'When first Amintas sued for a kiss' Z430, apparently D'Urfey's adaptation of a Scots jig by Purcell. The stuttering, scurvy poet in Act I of *The Fairy Queen** has been seen as a rather unkind portrait of D'Urfey, though the idea (put forward in *WooFai* and *PS* 12) that he played the part himself in the 1693 production seems unlikely. Elkanah Settle, a 'thick-sculd-poetaster' in Roger North's* opinion (*NorMus*, 306), was another stuttering poet. *See also* **'Hey, boys, up go we'**, **Scots (Scotch) songs and dances**, **"T'was within a furlong of Edinboro' town'**, ***The Virtuous Wife***. *BDA*, *DayDon*, *LS*, *PriDon*, *PriPur*, *PriThe*, *RobMad*, *SavScu*, *SpiSon*, *WhiAle*.

Eccles (Eagles), John The violinist and composer John Eccles (1670–1735), labelled John II in *HolEcc*, came from a family of professional string players, active over at least six generations from the sixteenth to the eighteenth centuries in Hertfordshire, Guildford and London. They include the violinist Henry II

Illus. 4: Thomas D'Urfey.

(1646–1711) and the bass violin player Solomon II (1649–1710), John's father and uncle respectively and both court musicians; and the violinists Henry III (b. c.1680) and Thomas II (b. c.1685). According to Hawkins*, these were John II's younger brothers, though they were probably his adopted younger cousins, perhaps taken in by Henry II after the death of their unidentified father.

John Eccles was Purcell's colleague in the United Company* from 1690 or soon after, collaborating directly with him in Thomas D'Urfey's* *Don Quixote* plays Parts 1 and 2 (1694), though in the spring of 1695 he joined Thomas Betterton's* breakaway company at the Lincoln's Inn Fields Theatre. He was the leading composer of theatre music around 1700, contributing music to about 80 productions and often collaborating with William Congreve*, the librettist of his remarkable all-sung Italianate opera *Semele* (?1707, but not performed). In 1700 he succeeded Nicholas Staggins* as Master of the Music at court, and was apparently active until late in life leading orchestras for state occasions and also directing his odes. Despite being a violinist, John Eccles was at his best in vocal music, particularly the striking mad songs* he wrote for Anne Bracegirdle. So far as is known, he wrote no sacred music and only a few non-theatrical instrumental pieces. *BalBir, BDECM, HolEcc, LowSta, MurOde, PriPur*.

Editions, from 1695 After Purcell's death his music was initially disseminated in print mainly through the 'memorial' publications initiated by his widow Frances and issued by Henry Playford*: *A Choice Collection** (1696) of keyboard music; *A Collection of Ayres**, his collected theatre airs*; *Ten Sonata's in Four Parts**; the Te Deum and Jubilate in D major* (all 1697); and the various editions of *Orpheus Britannicus** (from 1698). John Walsh* reissued or reprinted the Te Deum, *A Choice Collection* and selections from *Orpheus Britannicus* as well as separate editions of songs and the Golden Sonata*; he also included some of the catches* in anthologies.

A break with the continuous publishing tradition, and the beginning of editing Purcell as a historical monument, came with William Boyce's* *Cathedral Music*, which included several hitherto unpublished works in vols. 2 and 3 (1768, 1773). The first attempt at a collected edition, proposed by Benjamin Goodison* in 1788, only achieved nine volumes. Vincent Novello's* near-complete edition of *Purcell's Sacred Music* (1828–32) paved the way for four Purcell volumes in the Musical Antiquarian Society's* publications, and then for the Purcell Society* edition, inaugurated in 1876. The Society stopped publication in 1928, leaving a substantial amount of Purcell's music unpublished, including some odes* and symphony songs* as well as much of the consort music, a gap filled in the case of the fantasias* by *PurWar* (1927) and *PurJus* (1930, 1935). The revived Purcell Society completed the edition in the 1950s and 60s, and began revising it in the 1970s, a process now nearing completion. *HarPla, HerRec, HigRec, HogCor, HumPub, JonPub, KinGoo, MPP, PalNov, SmiWal, ZimCat*.

England, My England Directed by Tony Palmer with a script by John Osborne completed by Charles Wood, this film was first broadcast on Christmas Day 1995. It pursues parallel storylines in London, one set during Purcell's lifetime, the other in the 1960s tracing the development of a play about the composer's life. Several actors appear in both strands: Simon Callow is Charles II* and the modern actor/playwright, while Lucy Speed is Nell Gwyn and the actor/playwright's girlfriend. Michael Ball plays the adult Henry Purcell. Apart from two pieces (William Walton's 'The Symphony of the Air', which underscores scenes from the Great Fire of London, and the Finale of Britten's* *A Young Person's Guide to the Orchestra*, used at the end), all the music is by Purcell. The extensive score, ranging from the duet 'Upon a quiet conscience' to the Frost Scene* from *King Arthur**, was recorded by John Eliot Gardiner, the Monteverdi Choir and the English Baroque Soloists. Rather than offering a historically accurate depiction of Purcell's life, the film presents the England of his day as a mirror of the present, and the composer's music as an antidote to disenchantment and mediocrity. *CloEng*.

English cadence *See* **Dissonance**

Eton College *See* **Windsor and Eton**

An Evening Hymn *See* **'Now that the sun hath veil'd his light'**

'Fairest isle' **Z628/38** This memorable minuet song, sung by Venus in the Act V masque of *King Arthur**, is perhaps Purcell's most popular song; it was used for the title of BBC Radio 3's celebration of British music during the Purcell Tercentenary in 1995. However, it was not as popular at the time as 'If love's a sweet passion'*, despite having words by John Dryden* and a tune that perfectly matches them. Singers were perhaps deterred by its unusually high tessitura in the original key, B$^\flat$ major; it was copied in G major with some interesting ornaments in a keyboard manuscript, GB-Lbl, Add. MS 40139. It is also uncertain whether the eighth note of the melody should be A natural or flat; whether Purcell intended the setting in *A Collection of Ayres**, labelled 'Song Tune'*, to serve as a prelude and ritornello* to the song, as in most performances of *King Arthur* today; or whether this consort version was made by the composer – it has some unconvincing part-writing. *See also* **Anniversary celebrations**, **Rhythmic alteration**. *HerCat, PriPur, SchAyr, WooKey, ZimCat.*

The Fairy Queen **Z629** Purcell's most elaborate dramatic opera*, an adaptation of Shakespeare's* *A Midsummer Night's Dream*, was first performed at Dorset Garden* on 2 May 1692. The anonymous adapter of the play (ed. in full in *PS* 12), probably Thomas Betterton*, cut and rearranged scenes, provided new texts for masques at the end of each act, and devised spectacular scenic transformations; Josias Priest* devised the dances. The opera was revived in February 1693, but the loss of the theatre score in or shortly after 1695 rendered complete performances impossible. The manuscript re-emerged at the beginning of the twentieth century in the library of the Royal Academy of Music.

No single source preserves all the music. The theatre score, GB-Lam, MS 3, is the most complete. A part-autograph, it shows that Purcell worked in haste, sometimes sketching outer parts for movements that other copyists completed. Discrepancies between this score and the printed 1692 wordbook reveal that significant changes were made, including the introduction of the Act I Scene of the Drunken Poet. Neither the overture nor 'When I have often heard' appear in the theatre score; the latter was published around May 1692 in Purcell's *Some Select Songs ... in the Fairy Queen*. This print names five singers who must have participated in the original performances: Mrs. Ayliff*, Charlotte Butler*, Mary Dyer (soon to be Hodgson*), John Freeman* and John Pate*. A revised wordbook printed for the 1693 revival advertised new additions, though probably only The Plaint* was added then.

Purcell's score is wonderfully varied. The Drunken Poet scene, in comic opera mode, evokes a mischievous fairy world with quicksilver shifts between solos, duets and choruses. The Masque of Sleep (Act II), inspired in text and music by a similar scene in Lully's* *Le Triomphe de l'Amour*, and the Masque of the Four Seasons (Act IV), are both centred on a series of four solos contrasting in mood and instrumentation. Notable in this rich mix is the treble solo 'See, even Night herself', in which muted violins and viola without bass weave ethereal counterpoint around the voice; and the striking bass solo, 'Next, Winter comes slowly', where chilly chromatic fugal entries in the four-part string accompaniment draw in the singer, who concludes the song with a line plunging dramatically from e' to A. Other outstanding movements include 'Ye gentle spirits of the air' (Act III), effectively an Italianate da capo aria*; and 'Thus the gloomy world' (Act V), a da capo aria over two modulating ground basses*, in which a sprightly, duple-time outer section accompanied by obbligato trumpet* is contrasted sharply with a meditative middle section accompanied by two violins.

The instrumental movements are equally rich in quality and invention, ranging from the mysterious Dance of the Followers of Night (Act II), a four-part double canon*, to the Act IV 'Sonata' for the rising sun, a five-section Italianate symphony for two trumpets, kettledrums* and strings, which begins with a drum solo. *The Fairy Queen* is Purcell's greatest theatrical achievement, but it has been badly served by modern stage productions, particularly by ill-conceived attempts to combine Purcell's music with Shakespeare's original play rather than the 1692 play text. *See also* **Benjamin Britten**, *A Collection of Ayres*, 'If love's a sweet passion', **Stage history from 1695**. *AdaPur*, *BurDeb*, *BurFai*, *BurGal*, *BurRem*, *DowRos*, *HerCre*, *HowArt*, *HolPur*, *NorMus*, *PriPur*, *SavFai*, *SquFai*, *TupTri*, *WalDra*, *WooFai*, *WooPur*.

False relation *See* **Dissonance**

Fantasias Purcell entered 16 fantasias into his autograph* scorebook*, GB-Lbl, Add. MS 30930: three in three parts Z732–4; nine in four parts Z735–43 (dated between 10 June and 31 August 1680); the first section of a tenth four-part piece (24 February 1683); the five-part Fantasia upon One Note* Z745; and two In Nomines*, in six parts Z746 and seven parts Z747. The undated pieces seem also to have been written around 1680 or a little later. His plan was never completed, to judge from the headings 'Here Begineth ye 5 Part Fantazies' and 'Here Begineth ye 6, 7, & 8 part Fantazia's'.

Purcell's fantasias are cornerstones of the modern viol repertory, though it is uncertain whether Purcell would have wanted, or been able, to assemble a complete consort* with three sizes of viol, and there is not much evidence that they circulated beyond the composer's immediate circle; only one, an early version of Z733, exists in a set of parts, in GB-Lbl, Add. MS 31435. Roger North* thought that Matthew Locke* had written the last viol consort music (*NorMus*, 349), and it may be that Purcell wrote his own contributions to the English fantasia tradition partly as composition exercises in connection with an intensive programme of self-education in formal counterpoint*.

Purcell's immediate models for his three- and four-part fantasias were the classics of these two genres: Orlando Gibbons's* *Fantazias of III. Parts* and Locke's *Consort of Four Parts* (he apparently owned the latter's autograph score, GB-Lbl, Add. MS 17801, which includes them), though he did not place them at the head of suites, as Locke did, and he was much more interested than him in arcane formal counterpoint. Inversion is found in most of the four-part fantasias, and it is combined with augmentation* in the opening section of Z739 (19/22 June 1680); with single and double augmentation in the opening section of Z735 (10 June 1680); and with single, double and triple augmentation in an astonishing passage at the end of Z743 (31 August 1680).

Purcell's fantasias seem to have been virtually unknown until Arnold Dolmetsch* performed Z745 and an unidentified three-part work in 1895, though the composer Joseph Gibbs had made a keyboard reduction of Z732 and Z734 around 1730, and the singer Thomas Barrow (d.1789) copied out most of them from the autograph. They were eventually published in 1927 (*PurWar*), 1930 and 1935 (*PurJus*). The first complete recording*, for Archiv in 1954, was made by a viol consort led by August Wenzinger. Twentieth-century composers were mostly attracted to Z745, though George Benjamin and Colin Matthews made versions of Z738 and Z744 for *A Purcell Garland*, performed at the Aldeburgh Festival in 1995. *See also* **Viol (viola da gamba)**. *BoaClo, HerHay, HolGib, HolLif, HolPur, HowArt, HowPoe, SchCon, ShaMan, ThoFan*.

Fantasia upon One Note Z745 Purcell headed a page of his autograph scorebook*, GB-Lbl, Add. MS 30930, 'Here Begineth ye 5 Part: Fantasias', though we have only one by him, Z745 in F major. It features a single middle C, repeated throughout in the second tenor part. This conceit, together with its bright scoring using two equal treble parts and its brilliant writing after a dramatic plunge into F minor in the middle, has made it Purcell's most popular fantasia*. It has been recorded many times, on violins as well as viols*, and inspired some twentieth-century responses from Elliott Carter, Oliver Knussen and Steve Martland, among others. The 1946 recording by the Zorian String Quartet has a guest appearance by Benjamin Britten*, using a viola to play the middle C.

Farewell The conventional name for a short instrumental piece marking the departure or death of a notable individual, often included in sets of theatre airs*. They were typically eloquent slow triple-time movements modelled on sarabands* or French-style minuets*, as with Purcell's 'Sefauchi's Farewell' Z656, marking the departure of the castrato Siface* from London in 1687. Purcell's unexpected early death produced three farewells, also conforming to the type: by Jeremiah Clarke* (a remarkable orchestral movement in his *Song on the Death of the Famous Mr Henry Purcell*), Gottfried Finger* (the first movement of a four-movement suite) and Thomas Morgan*; those by Clarke and Finger are edited in *HowOde*. *See also* **Odes on the death of Henry Purcell**. *HolThe, PriThe, TayCla*.

Farmer, Thomas Purcell's fine extended song 'Young Thyrsis' fate ye hills and groves deplore' Z473 commemorates the death in 1688 of this violinist and composer, a member of the Twenty-Four Violins* from 1671 and an instrumentalist in James II's* Catholic chapel. He was also a theatre composer, writing music for at least ten plays put on by the Duke's Company from 1672 to 1683. He is often identified with a Thomas Farmer born in 1615, though the description of him as 'young Thyrsis' and his career profile suggests he was actually that person's son, baptised on 26 January 1651. He was a reasonably competent but unenterprising composer, so Purcell (and his anonymous poet) were presumably paying tribute to him mostly as a performer. *See also* **Rondeau (Round O), Nahum (Nathaniel) Tate**. *BDECM, LeeCat, ODNB, PriThe*.

Ferrar family With the help of his brother John (c.1588–1657), Nicholas Ferrar (1593–1637) established a high Anglican religious community at Little Gidding near Stamford in the 1620s. Music played an important educational and devotional role, one that passed down to John's grandsons: the clergyman Thomas (1663–1739), the grocer Basil (1667–1718) and the lawyer Edward (1671–1730). Basil played a significant part in a music club active in Stamford in the 1690s, in which Thomas, rector of Little Gidding, also participated. In 1696 the club celebrated St Cecilia's Day with a performance of 'Welcome to all the Pleasures'*, the movements of which were interlaced with movements from Corelli's* trio sonatas Opp. 2 and 4. The Ferrars also had access to a set of parts for 'Celestial Music'*, perhaps copied for performance by the club. Edward, who lived in Huntingdon, collected and copied solo bass viol* music, including Purcell pieces arranged for the instrument. The Ferrar family music collection is now divided between Magdalene College and the Fitzwilliam Museum in Cambridge. *See also* **Cecilian celebrations**. *HerMag, HolCon, WhiCec, WhiFer.*

Figured bass *See* **Continuo**

Filmer collection The music manuscripts assembled for members of the Filmer family of East Sutton in Kent were acquired by Yale University in 1946. The collection (listed in *ForFil*) consists of 37 manuscripts (US-NH, Filmer MSS 1–37), ranging in date from the late sixteenth to the early eighteenth centuries, more than half of which apparently date from Purcell's lifetime. A number include Restoration theatre airs*, seemingly connecting them with the playwright and lawyer Edward Filmer (1651/2–1703), and six contain pieces by Purcell, some of which remain to be investigated in detail. They may have been acquired for the Filmers by the composer and organist Francis Forcer*, also a theatre musician. The most important is MS 8, a bass partbook which includes the five-part Overture in G minor Z772 with five otherwise unknown dances. MS 15, a collection of 14 keyboard pieces, was started in 1678 by Forcer for Amy Filmer (b.1657), Edward's sister. It includes an arrangement of 'Ah! cruel bloody fate' Z606/9 from Purcell's music for *Theodosius**. *See also* **Suite**. *HerCat, HolFid, HolThe, ShaBas, ShaMan, WolVio, WooKey.*

Finch, Edward The Honourable and Reverend Edward Finch (1663–1738), a son of Heneage Finch, 1st Earl of Nottingham, was ordained in 1695 after Cambridge, the Inner Temple and a brief political career, becoming a prebendary at York Minster* in 1704. Music was his chief recreation, as a recorder and flute player, prolific copyist and reasonably fluent amateur composer, notably of a set of violin sonatas started in the 1680s. Finch copied them with his other compositions and much other English and continental music into three large scorebooks*, including the Armstrong-Finch Manuscript* and GB-Gu, MS Euing R.d.39, the latter including 'Some of Harry Purcel's Rules for Composition' taken from *PlaInt*. His other manuscripts are mostly in Durham University Library.

Finch apparently knew Purcell. The Armstrong-Finch Manuscript includes his copy of the Sonata in G minor Z780*; as well as the Adagio of the Golden Sonata* arranged in four parts; and a Gloria Patri by Thomas Roseingrave that was added to the Evening Service* in G minor Z231, now thought to be by Daniel Purcell*. Purcell's influence can be heard in Finch's own music: in a sonata entitled 'On the Bells' he alluded to the famous prelude to 'Rejoice in the Lord alway'* (suggesting that he had access to its original symphony anthem* version), and placed a country dance, 'The Hempdresser', in the bass of a subsequent passage, imitating Purcell's use of this unusual device with the tunes 'Hey, boys, up go we'*, 'Cold and raw'* and 'Lilliburlero'*. *GriMin, HolMan, PikRej, SimBal.*

Finger, Gottfried (Godfrey) This versatile and prolific Moravian composer (*c.*1655–1730) came to London from his native Olomouc, possibly in 1685 via Munich with August Kühnel, a fellow bass viol* virtuoso. He seems also to have played the baryton, bass violin* or violoncello, lute* and trumpet*. After service in James II's* Catholic chapel (1687–8) he embarked on a successful freelance career, composing and publishing instrumental solos and consort sonatas, writing vocal music and theatre airs* for the stage, and promoting public concerts at York Buildings*. He visited France and Italy between spring 1697 and early 1699, and left England permanently in 1701 after coming last in the competition to set Congreve's* masque *The Judgment of Paris*. He worked subsequently in Breslau, Innsbruck, Neuburg an der Donau, Mannheim and elsewhere. Finger apparently introduced Purcell and his English contemporaries to the colourful central-European modes of combining trumpets and woodwind with strings, often using double- or triple-choir effects. More specifically, his Sonata in C for trumpet, oboe, violin and continuo (*RawFin*, RI202) seems to have inspired the Act V Symphony in *King Arthur** Z628/33. His Op. 1, nos. 1–3 (1688), for violin, obbligato bass viol and continuo, would have provided obvious models for Purcell's Sonata in G minor Z780*. *See also* **Flat trumpet**, **Odes on the death of Henry Purcell**. *BDECM, CunSon, HolFin, HolLif, HolPur, HolThe, HowOde, LeeCat, LowSta, PriThe.*

First and Second Music The sequence of movements played in Restoration plays before the curtain tune* or overture*, fulfilling a function akin to the warning bells in the modern theatre. We can see from *Dioclesian**, *The Fairy Queen**, *The Indian Queen** and some sets of theatre airs* for which the original theatre order is known, that Purcell often used the sequence of two pairs of pieces, each consisting of duple- and triple-time airs and sometimes contrasting minor and major keys. *HolThe, PriThe.*

Flackton Collection The Canterbury* bookseller, collector and composer William Flackton (1709–98) assembled the collection of music manuscripts now bound as GB-Lbl, Add. MSS 30931–3, the first two entitled 'Anthems Ancient and Modern', the third consisting largely of services*. The contents, including separate autographs of seven Purcell anthems, were apparently collected by Canterbury Cathedral musicians, including Daniel Henstridge* and John Gostling*. A fourth Flackton volume, GB-Lbl, Add MS 30934, is a collection of odes, including the autograph of 'Who can from joy refrain?'*. Philip Hayes* borrowed some of these manuscripts in the 1780s while compiling his own Purcell collection. *See also* **Autographs**. *ForCan, HerCat, HerCre, HerHay, ShaMan, ShaSuc, SpiCat, ThoSou, ZimCat.*

Flat trumpet The English Restoration term for a trumpet* playing in 'flat' or minor keys. Purcell seems to have written his March and Canzona*, performed at Queen Mary's* funeral on 5 March 1695 (and subsequently used in *The Libertine**), for the instrument described by James Talbot*: a slide instrument with a range C to c'''; it was probably invented by a member of the Shore family*. Roger North* (*NorCur*, 119) wrote about another device used by 'Mr. Shoar' 'to adapt his trumpet to consort': 'an imperceptible lengthening or shortning the tube, by the help of a screw or worme', so that 'his exotick notes fall all into use'. The Shores probably used it to play the non-harmonic notes that Purcell, Jeremiah Clarke* and others sometimes included in their trumpet parts, though another way of coping with these 'exotick notes' was to double trumpets with oboes, as specified in an early set of parts for 'Hail, bright Cecilia'*.

Furthermore, a method of playing in minor keys using notes available on the ordinary natural trumpet was developed in central Europe and was used in England by Gottfried Finger*. His Sonata in C for trumpet, violin and continuo RI171 (ed. *FinSon*) uses the trumpet in a C minor section. In 'While for a righteous cause' Z321/12 from 'Celebrate this festival'*, Purcell takes a C trumpet into A minor and D minor. This might also have been the technique Finger used in 'some flat Tunes' he provided for trumpets to play during the 1691 Cecilian celebrations*, according to Peter Motteux*. In Finger's lost Ode on the Death of Mr. Henry Purcell, James Talbot's* text states that a solo verse about 'the Warlike Trumpet' was accompanied by 'Flat Trumpet' alternating with 'Sharp Trumpet'. *See also* **Odes on the death of Henry Purcell**. *BaiTal, DowExo, HolCla, HowOde, PinTru, RawFin, RycTru, SteTru, WebTru, WhiCec, ZimPur.*

Fletcher, John *See* **Beaumont and Fletcher**

Flute When Purcell and his colleagues specified 'flute' (from the French *flûte*, normally understood at the time as *flûte douce*) they always meant the end-blown recorder* rather than the transverse flute, and nearly always the treble or alto instrument in F. The Baroque flute only began to be used in England shortly after 1700; the Renaissance transverse flute was obsolete by the 1680s, at least in art music. *LasRec.*

'Fly, bold rebellion' Z324 Purcell's third welcome song* for Charles II* sets an anonymous poem that refers to the Rye House Plot, an unsuccessful plan to assassinate the king and the Duke of York (the future James II*) on their return from Newmarket in March 1683. The description of traitors 'to Avernus by Justice thrown down', in a solo verse exploiting the striking low register of the singer John Gostling*, suggests it was written after the trial and execution of a leading conspirator, William, Lord Russell, on 21 July. The ode therefore probably marked Charles's return from Winchester on 25 September. It was Purcell's finest ode to date, notable for a creative engagement with the text and more varied musical styles than before, including sophisticated counterpoint* in five- and seven-part verse sections. Purcell drew heavily on John Blow's* odes, especially the 1683 New Year ode 'Dread Sir, Father Janus', but he consistently achieved more convincing musical results. Highlights are the countertenor* ground-bass* air 'Be welcome then, great sir', and the charming high-voice trio 'But Heaven has now dispell'd those fears'. However, for the first time in Purcell's odes, the overall conception matches the quality of the best individual sections. *See also* **Odes**. *AdaOde, AdaPur, HolPur, SpiOde, WooEqu, WooOde, WooPur*.

Forcer, Francis An organist and composer from Durham who settled in London in 1669, Forcer (1649–1705) was a prominent London church organist and theatre composer on the fringes of Purcell's circle. He was not a court musician, though he played the small organ Purcell installed in Westminster Abbey* for James II's* coronation* in 1685. He also worked for the Filmer family of East Sutton in Kent, teaching Amy Filmer in 1678 and perhaps obtaining manuscripts of theatre airs* and other consort music for them, including an otherwise unknown Suite in G minor by Purcell. Forcer was a composer of limited technique, at his best in light songs, dances and keyboard music. His extended five-part Ground in B$^\flat$, copied (probably by a member of the Isaack family*) with Purcell's fantasias in US-NYp, Drexel MS 5061, is over-ambitious. *See also* **Filmer Collection, Suite**. *ForFil, HolBat, HolThe, PriThe, RanCor, ShaMan, SpiSon, WooKey, WooPer*.

Forefall *See* **Ornamentation**

Freeman, John A high tenor or countertenor* (1666–1736), one of Purcell's leading theatre soloists, starting in 1690 with *Dioclesian**, in which he sang 'Let the soldiers rejoice', 'Sound, Fame, thy brazen trumpet' and 'Let monarchs fight'. Other notable roles included Secrecy in *The Fairy Queen** ('One charming night' Z629/13), Saint George in *Don Quixote**, Part 2 ('Genius of England' Z578/7) and an Indian Boy in the Prologue to *The Indian Queen** (Z630/4). He was also a concert singer, taking part in 'Hail, bright Cecilia'* and 'Who can from joy refrain?'* as well as Jeremiah Clarke's* *Song on the Death of the Famous Mr Henry Purcell*. He joined the Chapel Royal* and St Paul's* choirs in 1700 and 1702 respectively. He was still singing in 1727, when Handel listed him as the leader of the countertenors for his coronation anthem 'The king shall rejoice'. *BalCou, BalDel, BalSta, BDA, BDECM, CBCR, CHE*.

'From hardy climes' Z325 This ode, the first of three Purcell composed in 1683, celebrated the marriage on 28 July of Prince George of Denmark* to Princess (later Queen) Anne*. According to the anonymous poet, George had left the 'toils of war' for Britain's 'beniger Isle', where, joined with Anne, from his 'great loins' a race of 'Kings and Queens of Christendom' would come. In the event, Prince William, Duke of Gloucester*, their only child to survive infancy, died at the age of eleven. Purcell drew productively on precedents set by John Blow's* 1683 New Year ode 'Dread Sir, Father Janus'. Examples are in the compound-time second section of the opening symphony; and in the following paired declamatory and triple-time airs for John Gostling*. Blow's ode also provided the model for the ground bass* of 'The sparrow and the gentle dove', a fine tenor solo with a string ritornello*, in which arpeggiated quavers create a dialogue suggesting separate interlocking lines. Purcell explored the possibilities of this device in the two odes he composed later that year. *See also* **Odes**. *AdaOde, AdaPur, HolPur, WinAnn, WooEqu, WooOde*.

'**From rosy bowers**' Z578/9 This great mad song*, said in *Orpheus Britannicus**, book 1 to have been 'the last Song that Mr. Purcell Sett, it being in his Sickness', was originally sung by Letitia Cross* as Altisidora in Act V, Scene 1 of Thomas D'Urfey's* *Don Quixote**, Part 3. It was first performed in December 1695, a few weeks after Purcell's death. Altisidora pretends she is in love with Don Quixote and that his loyalty to Dulcinea has driven her mad. *Don Quixote*, Part 3 was a failure because (D'Urfey complained) its vocal music had suffered from a lack of rehearsal. This is not surprising: Cross was perhaps as young as 13 at the time, and Purcell's complex and psychologically acute setting would have needed a good deal of rehearsal, apparently undertaken immediately after the composer's death.

As in 'From silent shades'*, dance-like airs interrupt the declamatory passages, though D'Urfey mapped out a more coherent five-section cantata-like plan for Purcell, heading it in the play text 'In Five Movements' and specifying 1: 'Love', 3: 'Melancholy', 4: 'Passion' and 5: 'Frenzy', rather like the states classified in Burton's *Anatomy of Melancholy*. D'Urfey subsequently characterised them in *Pills to Purge Melancholy** as 'Sullenly mad', 'mirthfully mad' (a faux-naïf gavotte), 'Melancholy madnes', 'Fantastically mad' (a jig*-like passage) and 'Stark mad' (the concluding declamatory passage leading to deranged bursts of brilliant runs in both parts). *See also* **Performance history from 1695**. *BalMad, HerRec, LeeDon, LS, MacBes, McVCal, PriDon, PriPur, PriThe, RobMan, SpiSon, WinHow.*

'**From silent shades**' Z370 Purcell's first mad song* and his earliest extended multi-sectional song, first published in John Playford's* *Choice Ayres and Songs*, book 4 (1683). The anonymous text, entitled 'Bess of Bedlam', portrays the delusions of madness with bizarre images and disjointed trains of thought. It is related to the poem 'Mad Maulkin' or 'Maudlin', published in 1682, and was apparently written as a counterpart to the ballad 'Forth from the dark and dismal cell', entitled 'Mad Tom of Bedlam', first published with its tune in *Choice Ayres and Songs*, book 1 (1673). Mad Tom is included in *ZimCat* as ZS68 because John Walsh* published it as by Purcell in 1725, though it is actually based on the tune of a Jacobean antimasque dance, originally entitled 'Gray's Inn Masque'. As in other antimasque dances, its unexpected changes of melodic and harmonic direction would have accompanied the capers of comic, exotic or bizarre characters.

Purcell's setting of Bess of Bedlam expands this feature, mixing declamatory passages with snatches of triple time, going through 12 time-changes in 104 bars. It must have been written for a singing actress of great histrionic ability, possibly Charlotte Butler*, and was a favourite recital piece throughout the eighteenth century, normally known as 'Mad Bess'. John Stafford Smith published an imitation of it around 1785, a setting of the broadside ballad 'Grim king of the ghosts', described as 'After Purcell's style'. *See also* **Dance**, **Performance history from 1695**. *BalMad, BurHis, HerRec, HolPur, LanHay, LauSon, MacBes, McVCal, PriThe, RobMad, SimBal, WinHow, WinSoc, WooPoe.*

'**From those serene and rapturous joys**' Z326 Purcell's last welcome song* for Charles II*, a setting of a poem by Thomas Flatman (1635–88), was probably performed in or shortly after 25 September 1684, the date of the king's return from Winchester*. Having weathered the storms of the Popish Plot, Exclusion Crisis and Rye House Plot, Charles was enjoying a political Indian summer, which Flatman reflected in the text, describing the king's return to London 'with an Olive branch adorn'd'. There is an emphasis on four-part string writing, with several extended ritornellos* and a free-standing almand*-like air, which was perhaps danced. The highpoint is 'Welcome, more welcome does he come', a superb tenor solo with a concluding ritornello, inspired by Flatman's striking quasi-religious image of Lazarus rising from the tomb. Purcell fashioned a ground bass* beginning with a rising arpeggio, responding to the line 'The strange surprising word was said: "Come forth"'. *See also* **Odes**. *AdaPur, McGGro, SpiOde, WooEqu, WooOde.*

Frost Scene The masque* near the end of Act III of *King Arthur* Z628/19–27, conjured by the Saxon magician Osmond to advance his evil designs on Arthur's betrothed Emmeline. John Dryden's* fantastic conceit, matched by Purcell's brilliant music, is that Cupid (originally sung by Charlotte Butler*) summons the Cold Genius* (probably sung by John Bowman*) to warm up 'a Prospect of Winter in Frozen Countries'. Osmond's unfulfilled hope is that it will similarly warm Emmeline's heart. Purcell modelled the famous shivering music (repeated notes played by the strings as bow vibrato and imitated by the voices) on Lully's* chorus for the 'Peuples des climats glacez' in *Isis* (1677), Act IV.

Purcell surrounds the extended dialogue between Cupid and the Cold Genius (which comes to a satisfying conclusion with the serene duet 'Sound a parley') with an intricate and tightly organised web of brilliant instrumental and choral passages, so that the masque's Prelude, the opening gesture of a French overture* covered with Italianate semiquavers, has its counterpart in the irresistible ritornello* to the repeated final chorus. The Frost Scene was a highlight of later productions of *King Arthur*. It captivated Roger North* (*NorMus*, 217–18), and the poet Thomas Gray, who saw it in 1735 and thought it 'excessive fine'. He described 'the Genius of Winter asleep & wrapt in furs, who upon the approach of Cupid, after much quivering, & shaking sings the finest song in the Play', with the chorus and dancers 'all rubbing their hands & chattering with cold with fur gowns & worsted gloves in abundance' (*BurRem*, 98–9). *BurArt, HarArt, HolPur, PriPur, SavGen, SawTre.*

Fugeing *See* **Counterpoint**

Full anthem *See* **Anthem**

Funeral sentences *See* **Burial Service**

Funeral Music for Queen Mary *See* **March and Canzona**, **'Thou knowest, Lord'** Z58C

'La Furstemberg' The title of a vigorous *contredanse* popular in eighteenth-century France. It was first published in Paris in 1700 but was already popular as an English country dance, 'St Martin's Lane', published by Henry Playford* in *The Dancing Master*, part 2 (1696). Several manuscripts identify it as the

First Act Tune of Purcell's airs for *The Virtuous Wife** Z611/9, though it was omitted from *A Collection of Ayres**. Purcell's own keyboard setting is in the Purcell-Draghi Manuscript*, and the shapeliness of the melody, with a striking chromatic inflection in the second strain, suggests that it was his original composition (Ex. 3). *SemFur, PriAut, WooKey, ZimCat.*

Ex. 3: Purcell's keyboard setting of 'La Furstemberg'.

Gamut A contraction of *gamma ut*, the lowest note of the scale in medieval music theory, still used in the seventeenth century to mean G; it was defined in the 1671 edition of Edward Phillips's *New World of English Words* as 'the first note in the ordinary scale of Musick' (*StrDic*). This probably explains why contemporary English collections are often ordered by key ascending from G, an organising principle that was probably developed in Baroque lute* and lyra viol* collections to avoid continual retuning. Henry Playford* proclaimed on the title page of *Orpheus Britannicus**, book 1 (1698) that its contents were 'placed in their several Keys according to the Order of the *Gamut*'. Purcell and his contemporaries associated G minor with death and the grave (as did continental composers at least as late as Schubert) which probably explains why collections ordered from Gamut usually begin with G minor rather than G major. *See also* **Key characteristics**, **Pavans**, **Temperament**. *HerThe, HofGam, HolPur, PriPur, SprLut, SteKey.*

The Gentleman's Journal See **Motteux, Peter Anthony (Pierre Antoine Le Motteux)**

George, Prince of Denmark The younger son of Frederick III, King of Denmark and Norway, Prince George (1653–1708) married Princess (later Queen) Anne* in 1683, an occasion marked by Purcell's ode 'From hardy climes'*; their son was Prince William*, Duke of Gloucester. 'The Prince of Denmark's March' by Jeremiah Clarke* (misattributed as 'Purcell's Trumpet Voluntary'*) is named after him. *CudVol, WinAnn.*

Gibbons, Christopher The eldest surviving son of Orlando Gibbons*, Christopher (1615–76), had been organist of Winchester Cathedral before the Civil War. He spent the Commonwealth in London as a teacher, and received court appointments at the Restoration, as a virginal player in the Private Music* and an organist of the Chapel Royal*. He was also organist of Westminster Abbey* from 1660 (and Master of its Choristers from 1664) to 1666. Two contemporary Oxford* writers, Anthony Wood and Thomas Ford, stated that he was Purcell's teacher, and if so this was probably for playing the organ; Purcell's main composition teacher was almost certainly John Blow* – also a former Gibbons pupil. Gibbons was an outstanding keyboard virtuoso, who would have taught the traditional skills of improvising and composing voluntaries*. John Evelyn called him 'that famous *Musitian*' after hearing him play the 'double *Organ*'* at Magdalen College, Oxford in 1654 (*EveDia*, iii. 109), though Wood called him 'a grand debauchee' who 'would sleep at Morning Prayer when he was to play on the organ'. Paul Stubbings (*StuGib*) has recently proposed that Gibbons's music profoundly influenced the young Purcell, a claim that remains to be assessed by scholars, informed by performances of his teacher's music. *BDECM, CBCR, CheChu, CoxOrg, HolPur, RayGib.*

Gibbons, Orlando Purcell engaged with the music of his great predecessor (1583–1625) in several ways. In about 1678 he copied three Gibbons anthems into his scorebook, now GB-Cfm, MS 88, evidently scoring them up with other pre-Civil War anthems from John Barnard's* *First Book of Selected Church Musick* (1641). One of these, 'Hosanna to the son of David', was evidently Purcell's starting point for the 'Amen' of his Jubilate in D major Z232/2; and the madrigal 'What is our life?' apparently inspired the opening of the three-part Fantasia Z734. Gibbons's *Fantazias of III. Parts* (c.1620) were the classics of three-part consort music, and Purcell's Fantasia Z732, with its busy contrapuntal points, several of which use lively syncopated ideas, is particularly close to them. Purcell copied a Prelude from *Parthenia* (1612–13), popular throughout the century as a teaching piece, into the Purcell-Draghi Manuscript*. *BamBar, CheChu, HolPur, HowArt, PriAut, ShaAnc, ShaMan.*

Gildon, Charles Writer and playwright (c.1665–1724), remembered by musicians mainly as the person responsible for the first public performance of *Dido and Aeneas**, inserted into his adaptation of Shakespeare's* *Measure for Measure*, produced at the Lincoln's Inn Fields Theatre early in 1700; it was chopped up, reordered and incorporated into the play as four separate entertainments. In his biography of Thomas Betterton* (1710), Gildon praised Purcell's theatre music (but without mentioning *Dido*) at the expense of the first Italian operas produced in London: 'Let any Master compare *Twice ten hundred Deities*, the Music in the *Frost* Scene, several Parts of the *Indian Queen*, and twenty more Pieces of *Henry Purcel*, with all the *Arrieto's*, *Dacapo's*, *Recitativo's* of *Camilla*, *Pyrrhus*, *Clotilda*, &c. and then judge which excels' (*GilBet*, 167). *HarDid*, *LS*, *PriPur*.

The Glorious Revolution The term, once standard but now largely obsolete, for the events of 1688–9 by which James II* was replaced on the English throne by William III* and his wife Mary II*, James's daughter. For Purcell and many of his colleagues it marked the moment when he ceased to be a full-time court musician. He continued to write birthday odes* for Queen Mary, but he was evidently now free to begin a hectic new career in the theatre, contributing to nearly 50 productions (including four dramatic operas*) in little more than four years.

The Golden Sonata Z810 No. 9 in F major of *Ten Sonata's of Four Parts**, the only Purcell trio sonata* to maintain its popularity after his death. John Walsh* published it separately in 1704 and again in 1707 in an anthology of continental trio sonatas. This must mainly be because it was composed a little later than most of his other trio sonatas, and it uses a more modern idiom, closer to Corelli* and G.B. Bassani than the mid-century composers Purcell had used as models for his earlier trio sonatas. It doubtless helped that it starts with a fast movement using an immediately arresting idea, and it received its nickname early on, possibly in Purcell's lifetime: a manuscript of 'the Golden Sonata drawn out for sev<eral> Inst<uments>' was in Gottfried Finger's* library, left in London when he departed for the continent in 1701. A short score of the Adagio, transposed up a tone with an extra inner part (perhaps derived from the same arrangement), was copied by Edward Finch* into the Armstrong-Finch Manuscript*. Z810 was also influential among Purcell's followers: Christopher Hogwood* described William Croft's* sonata in the same key as 'a gloss, movement by movement'. *HigRec*, *HogTri*, *HolFin*, *HolMan*, *HowArt*, *ShaMan*, *SmiWal*, *ZimCat*.

Goodison, Benjamin A lawyer at Lincoln's Inn, Goodison (b.1736) proposed in 1788 to publish 'The Works of Purcell' by subscription, though he only recruited 105 subscribers rather than the 150 needed and only published nine volumes. However, they included the first publications of the odes 'Celebrate this festival'*, 'Great parent, hail'* and The Yorkshire Feast Song*, as well as the first substantially complete editions of *King Arthur** and *The Indian Queen**. The only instrumental work included was the organ Voluntary in C major ZD241, now thought to be by Purcell's follower John Barrett. *HogCor*, *HumPub*, *JonPub*, *KinGoo*, *ZimCat*.

Goodson, Richard Probably son of an Oxford* innkeeper, Richard Goodson senior (c.1655–1718) was successively choirboy and singing man at Christ Church before succeeding Edward Lowe as Oxford professor of music in 1682; he became organist of New College the following year. His collecting activities suggest direct contact with Purcell: he copied three trio sonatas* and the Fantasia upon one Note* into GB-Och, Mus. 3 and 620 apparently directly from the autograph*, GB-Lbl, Add. MS 30930; while GB-Och, Mus. 1177 is an important early source of Purcell's keyboard music. Goodson copied performing parts for 'Raise, raise the voice'* (GB-Och, Mus. 470), inserting some instrumental movements perhaps for performance by the music club at Oxford's Mermaid Tavern. His son Richard junior (1688–1741) succeeded him as professor of music, and was also an important collector and copyist, adding to the family collection of Purcell.

If Goodson senior was the 'R.G.' who contributed a long poem in memory of Purcell to *Orpheus Britannicus**, book 2, then he was certainly a friend, able to provide a striking pen-portrait of the composer: 'So justly were his Soul and Body join'd, / You'd think his Form the Product of his Mind. / A Conqu'ring sweetness in his Vizage dwelt, / His Eyes wou'd warm, his Wit like Lightning melt, / But those no more must now be seen, and that no more be felt. / Pride was the sole aversion of his Eye, / Himself as Humble as his Art was High'. *CCLMC, CruClu, HerCat, HerCre, HolPur, ShaMan, WolOxf, WooKey.*

***The Gordian Knot Unty'd* Z597** Purcell compiled a set of theatre airs* for this lost play, possibly by William Walsh and probably performed in November or December 1690. It is usually performed today in the version in *A Collection of Ayres**, with the overture heading the sequence. However, the 'Cambury Manuscript'* gives it in the original theatre order (followed in *PS* 20). There the last three movements are placed first: the Chaconne in D minor Z597/6 served as the First Music, and the Second Music consisted of the duple-time Air Z597/7 and the Minuet Z597/8, both in D minor. Purcell must have been pressed for time, for he borrowed heavily from earlier works, including three instrumental passages from court odes of the 1680s. The Fourth Act Tune, the Jig Z597/5, has 'Lilliburlero'* in the bass, suggesting a connection with the Glorious Revolution*, while the Chaconne may have started as a separate consort piece: a variant version of its bass part is in Osborn MS 515* (see Ex. 7, p. 154). The fine overture may therefore be the only movement written specially for the play. *ForOsb, HerCat, HolPur, PriThe, ShaMan, ZimCat.*

Gostling, John The finest bass soloist of the period, Gostling (1649/50–1733), an ordained priest, was a minor canon at Canterbury* Cathedral when Purcell's uncle Thomas wrote to him in 1679 that 'my sonne is Composing: wherein you will be chiefly conserv'd' and that 'F faut: and Double Elamy are preparing for you'. He was sworn in as gentleman of the Chapel Royal* in the same year and soon after also joined the choir of St Paul's Cathedral*, where he became subdean in 1690. He was a member of the Private Music* under James II*, William III* and Mary II*.

From 1682 Purcell began writing solos in odes and anthems fully exploiting Gostling's more than two-octave range, *CC–e'*. John Evelyn described him as 'That stupendious Base' (*EveDia*, iv. 404), and he was a favourite of Charles

II*, who supposedly remarked: 'You may talk as much as you please of your Nightingales, but I have one Gostling that excels them all' (*Gentleman's Magazine* (1777), 148). Famous anecdotes recorded by Sir John Hawkins* include Gostling singing a duet with the king, accompanied on the guitar by James, Duke of York; surviving a storm at sea with them, an event supposedly marked by 'They that go down to the sea in ships'*, with its extraordinary solo bass part written for him (Ex. 4); and his private performance for Queen Mary with Arabella Hunt*, at which the latter sang 'Cold and raw'*. Gostling's exceptional vocal range, dexterity and declamatory skills inspired Purcell's most distinctive solo vocal writing.

Ex. 4: 'They that go down to the sea in ships' Z57, bb. 40–8.

Gostling was a significant copyist and collector of Purcell. His scorebook* US-AUS, HRC 85 (facs., Austin TX, 1977), known as the Gostling Manuscript, includes 16 of Purcell's anthems composed for the Chapel Royal; some are dated and several of them are primary sources, many with solos written specifically for him. He also owned and added to the Bing-Gostling Partbooks, now GB-Y, MSS M1(S), copied mainly by Stephen Bing (an older colleague at St Paul's), containing about 300 anthems and services from Orlando Gibbons* to the 1680s. These include 17 works by Purcell, including the unique copy of the verse anthem* 'Give sentence with me, O God' Z12. Gostling copied services and anthems into two now fragmentary sets of partbooks at St Paul's, part of a project in the late 1690s to create a choral repertory for the new cathedral. Around 1705–15 he copied a score, US-Cn, Case 7A/2, and sets of partbooks now GB-Ob, MSS Tenbury 797–803 and 1176–82, apparently for his own use; they contain 25 Purcell works between them. Gostling seems also to have owned the set of consort partbooks of which Osborn MS 515* is the sole survivor. *BDECM, BoyBin, CBCR, ForCan, GriMan, HawHis, HerCat, ShaBin, ShaMan, SpiPau, WhiPol, ZimCat, ZimGos.*

Grabu, Louis (Luis) This Catalan-born, French-educated violinist and composer arrived in England no later than 1665, and became Master of the King's Music in 1666. As a Catholic, he was a victim of the Test Act, losing his post at the end of 1673. He worked with Robert Cambert to stage Cambert's French opera *Ariane* at Drury Lane* in March 1674, but financial hardship made him leave England with his family for France in 1679. By 1684 he had returned, engaged by Thomas Betterton* to write music for *Albion and Albanius*, a work John Dryden* had originally intended as a prologue to *King Arthur*but subsequently converted into a full-length opera. After the setback of Charles II's* death, whose restoration and reign the opera depicts, the production opened at Dorset Garden* in June 1685.

Purcell clearly knew the opera – he might have played one of the harpsichords, with Grabu leading the orchestra – and aspects of his music for *Dioclesian** and *King Arthur* suggest that he learned from it, and courted comparison with it. Grabu had *Albion and Albanius* printed in lavish full score in 1687, imitating Ballard's editions of Lully's* operas; in turn, Purcell published *Dioclesian* using a similar format. Betterton emulated French operatic staging practice in *Albion and Albanius*: it was his most elaborate and complex production to date, and it was important for developing the methods of staging Purcell's dramatic operas*. Grabu's music was harshly criticised by Edward Dent and his followers, but the quality of its craftsmanship has recently been acknowledged, and movements such as the large-scale Act II chaconne* are recognised as considerable achievements. *HolBat, HolFid, PriPur, ThoOpe, WalDra, WalGra, WalMas, WhiGra, WhiLos, WhiStu.*

Graces *See* **Ornamentation**

'Great parent, hail' Z327 Purcell composed this ode* for the ceremony on 9 January 1694 celebrating the centenary of Trinity College, Dublin; the commission probably came through its poet, the Trinity graduate Nahum Tate*. Its modest musical demands and scoring, with just two recorders, strings and continuo, suggest that Purcell did not know his prospective musicians. It seems that he did not travel to Ireland to direct the performance, for *Dioclesian** was performed in London the following day. The ode's text rehearses the College's founding by Elizabeth I and its flourishing under the Dukes of Ormond and William III* and Mary II*, but also the occupation of the College by James II* in 1689/90 (its 'last distress surviv'd') – words in the first chorus that Purcell set to tensely chromatic ascending lines, the work's most memorable music. The ode has long been dismissed by critics: at the College's tercentenary (held in 1892) it was described as 'curiously poor and perfunctory' and a proposal for a repeat performance was rejected. Nevertheless, there are several attractive passages, such as the string-accompanied bass solo 'Awful matron, take thy seat' and the treble solo with recorders 'The royal patrons sung'. *AdaDub, AdaPur, HolPur, LS, WooOde, WooPur.*

Gresham autograph This large oblong quarto manuscript from Gresham College Library, now deposited in the Guildhall Library in London (GB-Lg, Safe 3), contains 45 pieces in Henry Purcell's hand, with two songs copied by Daniel Purcell* at the end; *PurGre* is a published facsimile. Henry acquired it as a bound music book and used it to copy pieces, mostly from his odes and theatre music, between 1692 (it starts with extracts from *The Fairy Queen**) and shortly before his death in 1695. Most of the music is for treble voice and continuo, arranged, revised and transposed in a few cases from originals written for lower voices or as duets, though he also included a few duets for treble, bass and continuo. These features, together with the oblong format and the fact that Purcell did not copy in the bass part of some of the songs, led scholars to suggest that he wrote it out for his own use to accompany singers, perhaps for an advanced pupil or as part of his employment as a court harpsichordist. However, Robert Thompson has pointed to the significance of the texts of some of its songs, particularly 'I love and I must' Z382 (subtitled 'Bell Barr'*), which he reads as an expression of the close friendship between Lady Annabella Howard* and Sarah Churchill; the song is one of those unique to the manuscript. More broadly, he suggests that the manuscript might have been used in Howard's circle, perhaps in connection with her role as maid of honour to Princess Anne*. HerFow, HerCre, ShaMan, ThoHow.

Ground bass A repeated pattern of notes in the bass, used as the organising principle of a movement, in a concerted work or as a separate vocal or instrumental piece. Ground basses as vehicles for improvised or written-down instrumental variations developed in sixteenth-century Italy, mostly using standard chord sequences (including the *ciacona* or chaconne* and the passacaglia*) rather than an unvaried bass line. This tradition lay behind the English repertories of divisions* on a ground for keyboard, lute* and bass viol*, which Purcell drew on for Three Parts upon a Ground*, and (also informed by a related genre of choral and orchestral ground-bass movements in Lully's* operas) the Chacony*, the Act V chaconne in *Dioclesian** and the Act IV Passacaglia in *King Arthur**.

A second type, ground-bass songs, was introduced to Restoration England from Italy by immigrant singing teachers such as Pietro Reggio*. Reggio's setting of 'She loves and she confesses too'* (using the English variant of the chaconne without the offbeat rhythms) inspired (or rather provoked) Purcell's own setting of 1680. Purcell's early ground-bass songs include 'Let each gallant heart' Z390 (1682–3), based on a seven-bar extended version of the passacaglia in the major, and 'O solitude, my sweetest choice!'* (1684–5). In both the ground is unvaried, leading Purcell to introduce artful modulations in the voice part, a technique much admired today but criticised by Roger North* as 'a wiredrawing of various keys and cadences out of the ground, which the air of it does not in any manner lead to' (*NorMus*, 89). Purcell's later ground-bass airs, such as 'Now that the sun hath veil'd his light'* and 'Wondrous machine' from 'Hail, bright Cecilia'*, followed later Italian practice by introducing graceful modulations, giving these pieces some of the characteristics of da capo* airs.

A third type, apparently invented by John Blow*, is found mostly in Purcell's odes*, though 'Oft she visits this lone mountain' in *Dido and Aeneas** and 'Music for a while'* are famous theatrical examples. It typically consisted of running quavers, sometimes in interlocking *style brisé** patterns devised to suggest two independent contrapuntal lines. Some of them are best termed 'pseudo' grounds because, though they sound like strict ground basses to the casual listener, the ground only fits the first vocal phrase, changing when the voice moves on to the second phrase. Both 'pseudo' and strict grounds of this type often conclude with ravishing string ritornellos*, giving the movements a new lease of life just as the voice finishes.

Purcell is justly celebrated for his ground basses. He claimed (*PlaInt*, 144) that 'Composing upon a *Ground*' was 'a very easie thing to do, and requires but little Judgment', though he acknowledged that 'to maintain *Fuges* upon it would be difficult', and that 'pretty *Dividing Grounds*' (which he thought an Italian genre) 'to do neatly, requires considerable Pains'. Grounds are found in nearly every genre he cultivated (the duet 'The Lord is great' from 'O sing unto the

Lord'* is a fine example in an anthem*), and they have been much imitated in modern times, by Benjamin Britten*, Michael Tippett* and Michael Nyman*, among others. However, ground basses did not appeal to the Enlightenment mind: Charles Burney*, for one, thought them a 'Gothic' practice. *See also* **Italian music**, **Trio sonatas**. *HolPur, HowArt, HowSin, KlaSco, McGGro, RosTet, SchCha, SchGro, SilFre, SilPas, ThoCha, WooEqu.*

Guitar There was a vogue for the five-course Baroque guitar at the Restoration court: it was played by Charles II*, his brother the future James II*, James's children Princess Mary* and Princess Anne*, as well as some courtiers, including Samuel Pepys*. The Italian guitarist Francesco Corbetta came to England with Charles II in 1660; dedicated his collection *La guitarre royale* (Paris, 1671) to the king; and taught Princess Anne – whose later guitar book, now NL–DHnmi, MS Kluis D1, includes arrangements of 22 Purcell pieces. The guitar was also used in the Restoration theatre, particularly accompanying gypsies and other exotic characters or evoking Spanish or north African locations, though Louis Grabu* specified 'gittars' in the Act II chaconne* of his opera *Albion and Albanius* (1685), set in and on the Thames.

The north African location, set in Carthage, is probably why Purcell used a guitar in *Dido and Aeneas**. He provided two solo spots for it: in Act I, after 'Pursue thy conquest, Love' (described in the Chelsea school libretto as '*A Dance Gittars Chacony*' – an unpunctuated phrase probably to be interpreted as possessive, not plural); and in Act II before 'Oft she visits' ('*Gitter Ground a Dance*'). At those places the music is respectively in C major and D minor, keys often associated respectively with the chaconne* (hence its title 'Chacony') and the passacaglia*, so it is likely that the continuo* guitarist played improvised or written-down variations on those two grounds at those points. It is also striking how many sections of *Dido* have continuo lines ideally designed for the guitar's strumming technique, from the fugue of the overture to 'Destruction's our delight'. Purcell probably conceived his opera with a particular guitarist in mind: perhaps the musician who taught the instrument at the school where it was first performed.

Nevertheless, there is little evidence that Purcell generally envisaged guitar continuo in his concerted music; the duet 'In vain the am'rous flute and soft guitar' in 'Hail, bright Cecilia'* might have been an exception. In general, the modern vogue for strumming Baroque guitars in all types of seventeenth-century music seems inspired more by pop music than by the practice of Purcell and other elite musicians at the time. *See also* **Nicola Matteis**. *BalHon, HalPri, HolPur, MaiMor, PagGui, TylGui.*

'Hail, bright Cecilia' Z328 Purcell's setting of Nicholas Brady's* ode for the 1692 Cecilian celebrations* is his longest and most elaborate non-theatrical work. Its rich scoring, with no fewer than 13 soloists and pairs of trumpets*, oboes* and recorders*, 'bass' recorder, kettledrums*, strings and continuo*, allowed him to use a different combination of voices and instruments for each of the 13 movements. The ode is constructed tonally like a great arch, with D major pillars supporting a superstructure of distant keys, reaching to B$^\flat$ major and G minor in the centre. Several movements refer to G.B. Draghi's* setting of Dryden's* *Song for St Cecilia's Day, 1687*, including the great opening choral movement; the superb ground bass 'Hark each tree', with a countertenor* and bass accompanied by pairs of violins and recorders, modelled on Draghi's 'The soft complaining flute'; and ''Tis Nature's voice'*, which develops the highly ornamented solo writing in Draghi's 'What passion cannot music raise'. Purcell took immense care to create musical metaphors for the text's images, perhaps inspired by Dryden's poetic virtuosity, as in the central section of the final chorus, where Brady's commonplace image of Cecilia improving her musical skill in Heaven is transcended by a setting of increasingly complex and skilful counterpoint*.

The ode was immediately and enduringly popular. The autograph score, GB-Ob, Mus. c.26, ff. 21–69, gives the names of the soloists and shows signs of repeated use in performance, and there are a large number of early copies. Peter Motteux* reported that it was encored in full at its first performance in Stationers' Hall*, and Purcell repeated it at York Buildings* in January 1694 for Prince Louis William, Margrave of Baden-Baden. It was performed in Canterbury* in the 1720s, apparently using the set of parts now at GB-Ob, Tenbury MS 1309; and in Oxford* in the 1760s, using parts now in Canada. Michael Tippett's* performances at Morley College during World War II featuring Alfred Deller* were landmarks of the Purcell revival. *AdaPur, ColMor, HolDra, HolPur, HowArt, ManNew, WhiCec, WooOde, WooPur.*

Hall, Henry Composer, organist and poet (*c.*1656–1707), a chorister at the Chapel Royal*, where he was Purcell's friend and contemporary. In his verse tribute to Purcell, published in *Orpheus Britannicus**, book 1, he reflected on their unequal skill: 'We learnt together, but not learnt alike ... For Thou, by Heaven for wondrous things design'd, | Left'st thy Companion lagging far behind'. From 1679 Hall worked at Hereford Cathedral, where he was probably responsible for introducing Purcell's anthems. He wrote the poem and the music of a fine elegy on Purcell's death, the dialogue 'Yes, my Aminta' (ed. in *HowOde*) for treble and bass voices, two recorders and continuo. It includes a descending-scale ground bass* that refers to Purcell's elegy for John Playford*, 'Gentle shepherds, you that know' Z464, as well as 'Rejoice in the Lord alway'*. An earlier version of the poem, 'A Dialogue between Palemon and Alexis Lamenting the Death of the Incomparable Mr. Henry Purcell', is preserved in several manuscripts. Hall also praised Purcell in his commendatory poem to Henry Playford in *Orpheus Britannicus**, book 2, and in his tribute to John Blow* in *Amphion Anglicus* (1700), where he stated that '*Britain's Orpheus* learn'd his Art from You'. *CheChu, PicHal, PicPos, SpiCat.*

Handel, George Frideric Some of Purcell's music must have been known to Handel, since a few of his anthems were still being sung by London's collegiate choirs and plays were still being performed with his music long after the great German composer settled in London in 1712; *King Arthur**, for instance, was revived in 1735. Much of Purcell's domestic music was also readily available in print, notably in *Orpheus Britannicus** and *Harmonia Sacra**, and several of his mad songs* were in the repertory of Handel's solo singers, including Anne Turner Robinson, Giulia Frasi and John Beard. He also contributed to genres of concerted music that Purcell had either created or had dominated: his first large-scale setting of English was the court ode 'Eternal source of light divine', written for Queen Anne's* birthday (6 February 1713), while his Utrecht Te Deum and Jubilate (7 July 1713) was in the tradition initiated by Purcell's Te Deum and Jubilate in D major*. Handel effectively revived the tradition of Cecilian celebrations* with his settings of Dryden's* *Alexander's Feast* (1736), originally set by Jeremiah Clarke*, and 'From harmony, from heav'nly harmony' (1739), originally set by G.B. Draghi*. 'Hail, bright Cecilia'* was still circulating at that time in manuscript.

Nevertheless, Handel does not seem to have borrowed from Purcell directly, as he did from Carissimi, Stradella and other seventeenth-century Italian composers; he also borrowed from John Blow* for his overture to *Susanna* (1749). Some supposed connections between passages in Handel and Purcell were discussed in *ZimPas*, though it is difficult to see any of them as more than commonplaces or coincidences. There are many passages in Handel that sound Purcellian to us, doubtless because he was consciously adopting an English manner, notably in the sublime opening arioso of 'Eternal source of light divine', for countertenor* with obbligato trumpet*, and the fine ground-bass* air 'Let rolling streams'. Several anecdotes record Handel's regard for Purcell, as when, during a performance of *Jephtha*, the singer William Savage (as reported by his pupil R.J.S. Stevens; *BurRem*, 155) remarked to its composer: 'This movement, sir, reminds me of some of Purcell's old music'. 'O got te teffel' (said Handel). 'If Purcell had lived he would have composed better music than this'. *BalMad, BurCha, CHE, LS, HunPat, PurHan, WhiCec, WinAnn.*

Handwriting Purcell's bold and distinctive musical handwriting, with its squat 'H'-shaped treble clefs and its '3' time signatures with an upward loop at the top, has been familiar to musicians interested in his music since the eighteenth century, which has not prevented some non-autograph copies being claimed as autographs* until recently. However, in one of Purcell's earliest autographs, an arrangement of Pelham Humfrey's* symphony anthem* 'By the waters of Babylon' (GB-Lbl, Add. MS 30932, ff. 52–5), Purcell used an 'S'-shaped treble clef and a hook-shaped bass clef – the latter also present in other autographs up to the end of 1677. Attention has recently focussed on the forms of letters in Purcell's text hand as an aid to precise dating. He changed from the secretary form of 'e' to the Italic form by the summer of 1680, and to the Italic 'r' gradually between 1681 and 1685. *ForAut, ShaMan, ThoGlo, ZimHan.*

Harmonia Sacra Henry Playford* published two collections entitled *Harmonia Sacra, or Divine Hymns and Dialogues* by subscription, book 1 on 16 November 1687, book 2 on 13 July 1693; enlarged editions appeared in 1703 (book 1) and 1714 (both books). An anthology dedicated to devotional songs was an innovation, and Playford clearly intended it as a counterpart to his secular song books, appealing to 'the *Musical* and *Devout*' rather than the 'Youthful and Gay', as he put it in the preface to book 1. Purcell 'review'd' (i.e. edited) the contents, 12 of which were his own compositions. He may also have chosen the pieces by other composers, including declamatory songs and duets by Matthew Locke* and Pelham Humfrey* (including Humfrey's remarkable setting of John Donne's Hymn to God the Father), as well as Latin motets attributed to Carissimi and Gratiani. He perhaps collaborated with John Blow*, the second most prolific contributor.

Later editions added pieces by the younger generation, including John Weldon* and Jeremiah Clarke*, as well as several Purcell anthems, including the symphony anthem* version of 'My song shall be alway'*. Purcell published virtually all his later devotional works in *Harmonia Sacra*, some of them probably written especially for the publications. They include such superb songs as the Evening Hymn, 'Now that the sun hath veiled his light'* (book 1) and The Blessed Virgin's Expostulation* (book 2), as well as the dramatic dialogue Saul and the Witch of Endor* (book 2). There were virtually no reprints until Vincent Novello's* edition of *Purcell's Sacred Music*, and this neglect persists to some extent today. CarPub, HarPla, HolPur, LucPla.

Harpsichord Little is known about the plucked keyboard instruments used by Purcell, though in her will his widow Frances left 'the double spinnet' and 'the single spinnet' to their son Edward (*ZimPur*, 282–3), who later became a London organist; they had presumably been her husband's domestic instruments. The latter was doubtless a bentside spinet*, the type made in large quantities in Restoration London by Charles Hayward, Stephen Keene and members of the Hitchcock family, among others. The former may have been an unusual spinet with two registers; one by John Player dated 1680 survives (*BoaMou*, 1423). Few harpsichords seem to have been made in England during Purcell's lifetime; only one survives: a single-manual instrument by Charles Hayward dated 1683 (*BoaMou*, 720). Most must therefore have been imported, probably mainly from the Netherlands; harpsichords by the Ruckers family of Antwerp had been prized in England since at least the 1630s and were beginning to be modernised in London to cope with changing taste and musical requirements.

Purcell's first post as an adult, from 1673, was as assistant to John Hingeston*, tuner and repairer of the court keyboard and wind instruments, which included those variously described as harpsichords, virginals* and 'pedals' – harpsichords with foot-pedals to change registers, invented by John Hayward and described by Thomas Mace*. In 1675 two harpsichords were used for performances in the Great Hall at Whitehall* of John Crowne's masque *Calisto*, with music by Nicholas Staggins*. Purcell may have tuned these instruments, and probably followed suit by using two harpsichords in the continuo* team of his dramatic operas*, directing performances from one of them. Harpsichords were also provided for rehearsals and performances by the Private Music*, presumably of odes* and other court music; 'From hardy climes'* has a short written-out prelude to a solo passage marked 'for the Harpsichord'. Hawkins's* famous anecdote about 'Cold and raw'* (*HawHis*, ii. 564) has Purcell accompanying his songs 'on the harpsichord' at court in the 1690s.

Purcell's early songs and dialogues work well accompanied just by lute-family instruments, though he increasingly wrote active and wide-ranging bass lines implying harpsichord continuo. Much of his time must have been spent teaching his aristocratic female pupils the keyboard, and much of his solo music was doubtless written for them. His more elaborate keyboard pieces, particularly the *style brisé** almands* and corants*, sound best on harpsichords, though the simple arrangements of songs and consort pieces come alive on the small single-strung virginals and spinets of the period. *See also* **Continuo, Figured Bass, Keyboard music, Orchestra**. BoaMou, HolBat, HolPur, KosHar, MolPur, MolSpi, RECM, WooPer.

Harris, Renatus (René) A member of the famous Dallam family of organ* builders (his father Thomas Harrison or Harris was Robert Dallam's apprentice and married his daughter), Renatus Harris (c.1652–1724) was born in Brittany, where members of the family were building organs while in exile during the Commonwealth. They returned to England after the Restoration, and Renatus worked initially with his father, mostly building and repairing organs in the west country. His son Renatus junior (b. ?1678) was apparently a keyboard student of G.B. Draghi*. With his bitter rival Bernard Smith* (the victor of the Battle of the Organs*), he dominated organ building in Restoration England, making about 30 new organs, over half of them in London, of which the three-manual instrument in St Botolph, Aldgate (c.1704) is the only one surviving substantially complete. Harris's organ for St Bride's, Fleet Street* was used when new for the first performance of the Te Deum and Jubilate in D major* on St Cecilia's Day in 1694. The 'chappell-pitch' (about a'=423 Hz) he used, incompatible with woodwind instruments at the lower Consort Pitch, probably explains why Purcell scored the work only with trumpets and strings. Harris and Smith built much larger organs than in earlier English practice, with more varied stops: the one in St Bride's had three manuals and 20 stops. Harris's instruments were renowned for their brilliant tone, with reeds voiced in the French manner. *See also* **Pitch**. *BicOrg, DunSmi, GwyPur, HolBat, KniBat, KniHar.*

Hautboy (Hoboy) *See* **Oboe**

Hawkins, James Hawkins (c.1662–1729) was organist of Ely Cathedral from 1682, having been briefly at St John's College, Cambridge. In addition to his copying work for the Ely choir, he was an industrious collector, sometimes supplying material to Thomas Tudway*; his scores include GB-EL (deposited in GB-Cu), MSS 5–12, 16–20 and GB-Lbl, Add. MSS 31444–5. Among them are copies of Purcell's 1685 coronation anthem 'I was glad'* and the verse anthem* 'O consider my adversity' Z32, as well as the only non-autograph copy of the earliest version of the Funeral Sentences Z17A, 58A from the Burial Service*. As a composer, Hawkins was a competent and sometimes imaginative Purcell follower. 'Behold, I bring you glad tidings'* and 'Rejoice in the Lord alway'*, both of which Hawkins copied, provided him with the starting point for the text and music of his verse anthem 'Rejoice in the Lord alway'. Ian Spink wrote that Hawkins was capable of taking 'an independent line despite reminiscences of Purcell that must have kept crowding in'. *HerCat, ShaSuc, ShaMan, SpiCat, ZimCat.*

Hawkins, Sir John The lawyer and writer John Hawkins (1719–89), knighted in 1772 for his work as a London magistrate, is mainly known today for *HawHis*, his five-volume history of music published in 1776, the first work of its sort in English. The section on Purcell (ii. 743–59) was the first substantial account of the composer, though it was soon eclipsed by Charles Burney's* far more comprehensive and balanced treatment, published in 1789. Nevertheless, Purcell scholars value Hawkins for the anecdotes he published about the composer and his circle. Some of them, such as the story of the origin of the symphony anthem* 'They that go down to the sea in ships'* and the description of the private concert for Mary II* in which Arabella Hunt* sang 'Cold and raw'*, feature the bass John Gostling* and were probably given to him by his friend William Gostling, John's son. Hawkins may have picked up other anecdotes at meetings of the Academy of Ancient Music*, which in its early days included musicians with connections to Purcell's circle. He was also a friend of the composer John Stanley, who, according to Charles Burney (BurHis, iii. 493), was 'justly admired for his ingenious and masterly manner' of accompanying the soprano Giulia Frasi in Purcell's mad songs*. See also **Biography**.

Hayes, Philip Composer and organist (1738–97), professor of music at Oxford* from 1777 (in succession to his father William), and the leading Purcell expert of his time. He copied six scorebooks of Purcell's music, four now at GB-KNt, MR 2–5 and two now in GB-Lcm, MS 518. He used autographs as sources where possible, including GB-Lbl, Add. MS 30930 and GB-Lbl, R.M. 20.h.8 (he owned the latter and presented it to George III in 1781), and those in the Flackton collection*, which he borrowed from their owner. Among his Purcell copies are some unique pieces: the incomplete ode 'The noise of foreign wars'*, copied from an unknown source; the Staircase Overture*, copied from the set of partbooks of which Osborn MS 515* is now the sole survivor; and the devotional part-song 'O that my grief was throughly weigh'd'*, perhaps copied from pages now missing from Add. MS 30930. It is not clear why Hayes made his Purcell collection. He made no effort to publish any of it; it does not seem to have influenced his own music; and he is known to have directed a performance of only one Purcell work, the Te Deum in D major* (in William Boyce's* modernised version), during the annual service for the benefit of the Radcliffe Infirmary in Oxford on 2 July 1778 and 3 July 1783 (Oxford Journal, 4 July 1778, 5 July 1783). He gave a bust of Purcell to the Oxford Music School. See also **Autographs**, **Portraits**. ForSou, HeiHay, HerHay, PooPor, ShaMan, ShaSuc, WolOxf.

'Hear my prayer, O Lord' Z15 This superb eight-part setting of the opening verse of Psalm 102 seems to be the first section of a planned full-with-verse anthem. Purcell copied it into GB-Cfm, Mu. MS 88 around 1685, ending it without a double bar after 34 bars and leaving blank pages for the rest of the anthem. Its date of copying, its incomplete state and the absence of other contemporary copies suggests that Purcell planned it to mark the death of Charles II* in February 1685, but left it unfinished when the king was buried without a state funeral. Alternatively, Purcell might have completed it on loose sheets now lost and for some reason never copied the other sections into his autograph scorebook*. It is perhaps the finest passage of counterpoint* in Purcell's sacred music. Building from the entry of a single voice, it weaves together two points of imitation (both presented in prime and inversion), culminating in dissonances* of agonising intensity at the approach to the final cadence. It is now one of the most performed of Purcell's anthems, though it was virtually unknown until Vincent Novello* published it. See also **Autographs**. ShaAnc, ShaMan, VanChu, WooPur.

Henstridge, Daniel Successively cathedral organist of Gloucester (1666), Rochester (1674) and Canterbury (1698), Daniel Henstridge (c.1650–1736) was an important Purcell collector and copyist. He may have assembled the autographs of Purcell's anthems in the Flackton Collection*, and he made several important copies, including 'The Lord is king and hath put on glorious apparel' ZN69 and 'Turn thou us, O good Lord' Z62. He may also have been responsible for developing Cecilian celebrations* in Canterbury*, featuring 'Welcome to all the pleasures'* and 'Hail, bright Cecilia'*. *CheChu, ForCan, HerCat, HerCre, HerHen, ShaMan, SpiCat, WhiCec, WooKey, ZimCat.*

Heptinstall, John A London printer (c.1657–1732), who developed the 'new tied note' typeface that approximated to features of handwritten music, with round-head notes and a degree of beaming of quavers and semiquavers, making it a little easier to read than John Playford's* Granjon typeface with its separate lozenge-shaped notes. Heptinstall tried it out in John Carr's* aptly named series *Vinculum societatis, or The Tie of Good Company* (1687–91), and subsequently used it for collections of Purcell, including the score of *Dioclesian** (1691) and the 'memorial' volumes issued by Henry Playford (from 1696). Heptinstall's apprentice William Pearson improved the typeface a little with his 'new London character', though both were superseded by engraved editions, developed in London by Thomas Cross* and John Walsh*. *See also* **Editions from 1695, Printing and Publishing**. *CarPub, DaySon, HarPla, HigRec, HumPub, KruPri, MPP, ThoSou.*

Herbert, George Purcell set one poem by the metaphysical poet (1593–1633): the declamatory devotional song 'With sick and famish'd eyes' Z200, from Herbert's collection *The Temple*. He has sometimes been confused with a later Mr Herbert (first name unknown) who wrote the words of 'Incassum, Lesbia, incassum rogas' Z383, one of the elegies on the death of Queen Mary* (1695), as well as its English translation, 'No, Lesbia, no, you ask in vain', set by John Blow*. This Mr Herbert also presumably wrote the Pindaric ode in praise of Blow in *Amphion Anglicus* (1700).

'Hey, boys, up go we' A popular tune associated with Thomas D'Urfey's* ballad satirising the pretensions of the Whigs in the Exclusion Crisis of 1679–81. By using it in two compositions Purcell was probably conveying a hidden message of support for Charles II* and his brother the Duke of York, the future James II*. It comes in the bass as the last movement of his incomplete Suite* in G major Z770/4, perhaps written for court string players around 1682, and then in the solo and chorus 'Be lively, then and gay' Z344/5 in the 1686 ode 'Ye tuneful Muses'*; its concluding ritornello* is a revised version of Z770/4. Purcell applied the same unusual stratagem, apparently also conveying coded messages, to 'Lilliburlero'* and 'Cold and raw'*. *HolPur, ShaMan, SimBal.*

Hingeston, John This Yorkshire organist, viol player and composer (c.1606–83) came to London during the Civil War after service with the Clifford family at Skipton Castle. His role as Cromwell's organist and Master of the Music did not prevent him from receiving court posts at the Restoration, as a viol player and 'keeper, maker, repairer and mender and tuner' of the keyboard and wind instruments. Purcell became his assistant in this role after leaving the Chapel Royal*, his first adult court post, and succeeded him in 1683. To judge from Purcell's appointment document (*RECM*, i. 210) it would have involved overseeing the work of instrument makers, including the virginal* maker Charles Hayward and the organ* builder Bernard Smith* in 1674–5 (*RECM*, i. 156–7), as well as doubtless tuning instruments and carrying out running repairs. Hingeston left £5 in his will to 'my godson Henry Pursall (son of Elizabeth Pursall)' – a crucial piece of evidence helping to establish Purcell's parentage. *BDECM*, *ZimPur*.

Hodgson (Hudson), Mary, née Dyer Probably the daughter of the dancing master Benjamin Dyer, baptised at St Andrew's, Holborn 26 December 1673. Her first-known stage appearance was on 2 May 1692 in *The Fairy Queen**; she married the actor John Hodgson or Hudson a fortnight later. In *The Fairy Queen* she sang 'I am come to lock all fast' as Mystery and 'If love's a sweet passion' as a Nymph, and subsequently took part in the 1693 revival of *Dioclesian** and *Don Quixote**, Part 2 (May 1694), among other productions with Purcell's music. Hodgson became unavailable to Purcell after the break-up of the United Company* in 1695, though she probably sang Dido when *Dido and Aeneas** was performed at the Lincoln's Inn Fields Theatre in 1700. She continued as a stage and concert singer until 1719. The music Purcell wrote for her shows that in modern terms she was a mezzosoprano, with a range c'–f'' sometimes extending to g''. *BalBir*, *BalSin*, *BalSop*, *BalSta*, *BDA*.

Hogwood, Christopher Harpsichordist, conductor and musicologist (1941–2014), with a particular interest in Purcell. He used the name of the Academy of Ancient Music* for his pioneering ensemble using what were then called 'authentic instruments'. Founded in 1973, it was initially a house orchestra for the Éditions de l'Oiseau-Lyre label of the Decca Recording Company, issuing many notable Purcell recordings* from 1974, culminating in *The Indian Queen** (1995). His published editions of Purcell include *Ten Sonata's of Four Parts** (1978) and 'Hail, bright Cecilia'* (2009). His new edition of the keyboard music for the Purcell Society* (*PS* 6) remained incomplete at his death, and is being finished by Andrew Woolley and David J. Smith. *See also* **Recordings**. *HogCor*, *HogMan*.

Hornpipe One of Purcell's favourite types of dance, with more than 20 examples in his theatre airs*. They typically consist of two strains of four and eight bars, notated in 3/2 (3/4 is a less common option); with the phrases ending on the third beat of the bar; and with busy, often syncopated writing in the upper parts, implying a slow tempo and a vigorous style of performance. In the Hornpipe on a Ground from *The Married Beau** Z603/9, Purcell tapped into a tradition going back to the sixteenth century of hornpipes as rustic divisions* on four-bar ground basses*. Purcell's hornpipes are far removed from the Lancashire village dance, and do not seem to have been originally intended to be danced to, though several of them were subsequently used as country dances*. *PlaDan*.

Howard family Purcell had connections with at least three members of the Howard family of Ashtead in Surrey and Duke Street in London. The playwright and politician Sir Robert (1626–98) wrote *The Indian Queen** (1664) with some contribution from his brother-in-law John Dryden*, adapted in 1695 as a dramatic opera* for Purcell. Annabella Dyve (1676–1728) became Sir Robert's fourth wife in 1693 and was apparently the Lady Howard who paid for Purcell's

Illus. 5: Annabella Howard.

memorial tablet in Westminster Abbey. Dedicating *Orpheus Britannicus**, book 1 (1698) to her, Frances Purcell mentioned that she had been her husband's pupil and praised her 'extraordinary skill in Musick, beyond most of either Sex'. Robert Thompson argued that the text of 'I love and I must' Z382 was an expression of her close friendship with Sarah Churchill, and explained its title 'Bell Barr'* as referring to the Howards' country retreat near Hatfield. He also raised the possibility that Purcell copied the Gresham autograph* for her. The Miss Howard who received lessons from Purcell in 1694 and 1695 seems to have been Diana (*c.*1686–1709), Sir Robert's granddaughter. *HowMou, HunPat, ThoHow, ZimPur.*

Humfrey (Humphrey), Pelham A tenor, lutenist and composer (1647/8–74), one of the original group of boys recruited by Henry Cooke* for the Restoration Chapel Royal* in 1660. He had already composed anthems for the Chapel before spending the years 1664–7 abroad, apparently studying in France and Italy at royal expense. Samuel Pepys* dined with him soon after his return, on 15 November 1667, memorably describing him (*PepDia*, viii. 529–30) as 'an absolute Monsieur ... full of form and confidence and vanity', who 'disparages everything and everybody's skill but his own'. Humfrey was certainly precociously talented, and in his symphony anthems* he established an attractive, cosmopolitan mixture of idioms: expressive Italianate vocal writing, French-style dance-like instrumental passages, and angular, dissonant harmony in the English vein. Purcell's score of Humfrey's 'By the waters of Babylon' (GB-Lbl, Add. MS 30932, ff. 52–4), with the string passages arranged rather ineptly for organ, is one of his earliest autographs. They would have been master and pupil

Illus. 6: Arabella Hunt.

between 1672 (when Humfrey succeeded Cooke as Master of the Children) and December 1673 (when Purcell left the Chapel). Humfrey's influence can be heard in Purcell's earliest symphony anthems, particularly in 'My beloved spake'*, though Purcell's interest in counterpoint* soon made Locke* and Blow* more fruitful models. Humfrey married Cooke's daughter Katherine in 1672 but died on 14 July 1674, aged only 26. *See also* **Harmonia Sacra**, **The Tempest**. *BDECM, CBCR, CheChu, DenHum, HolPur, LocDra, ShaMan, SpiSon.*

Hunt, Arabella Though never formally a royal musician, this singer and lutenist (1662–1705), the daughter of a Buckinghamshire landowner, worked entirely at court, apparently starting with Nicholas Staggins's* masque *Calisto* in 1675. She taught Princess Anne* to sing and was a favourite with Mary II*, who granted her a £100 pension. Hawkins* (*HawHis*, ii. 564) described an occasion when Hunt and John Gostling* sang some Purcell songs in private to Mary with the composer at the harpsichord, though the queen, 'beginning to grow tired', asked her to sing instead the Scots ballad 'Cold and Raw'*, accompanying herself on the lute. Hawkins (*HawHis*, ii. 761) also asserted that Blow* and Purcell wrote many of their songs for Hunt, and reported Gostling's opinion that her voice was 'like the pipe of a bullfinch'. William Congreve's* description of cherubs sipping 'Sweet Hallelujahs from her lip' in his ode 'On Mrs Arabella Hunt Singing' may refer to her performance of 'Now that the sun hath veil'd his light'*. *BalSop, BDECM*.

Hymn tunes Of the various hymn or psalm tunes associated with Purcell, the best-known is 'Burford' Z125, first published by John Cheltham in 1718 and said to have been used by the Rev. Samuel Wesley (grandfather of Samuel Wesley*) for his hymn 'Behold the saviour of mankind', though it was not until Edward Miller's *Psalms of David* (1790) that it was 'Said to be Purcell's'. 'Westminster Abbey', used today for J.M. Neale's 'Christ is made the sure foundation', was adapted from the final section of the anthem 'O God, thou art my God'*. *See also* **Chants**.

'If ever I more riches did desire' Z544 The largest, last and greatest of the group of symphony songs* Purcell wrote in the reign of Charles II*, apparently for performance by the Private Music* at Whitehall*. It is scored for four voices, two violins and continuo and may have been written in the spring of 1687, judging from its position in the autograph scorebook GB-Lbl, R.M. 20.h.8. Its immediate model was John Blow's* symphony song 'Awake my lyre', also setting Abraham Cowley* and scored for the same ensemble. Purcell's text combines lines from two of Cowley's 'Several Discourses by Way of Essays in Verse and Prose' (no. 6 'Of Greatness' and no. 3 'Of Obscurity'), which deal in quasi-religious terms with moral questions: the futility of pride and ambition and the virtue of a humble, obscure life. Highlights of Purcell's sober but consistently inspired setting are the beautiful treble duet 'Me, O ye gods', and the profound ground-bass* movement 'Here let my life with as much silence slide' for tenor, violin and continuo, constructed over a sombre peal of bells in the bass. *HolPur, ShaMan*.

'If love's a sweet passion' Z629/17 The memorable minuet song and chorus in *The Fairy Queen**, Act III, originally sung by 'a Troop of Fawns, Dryades and Naiades' in an entertainment put on by Titania for Bottom, with Mary Dyer (soon to be Hodgson*) as soloist. It was enduringly popular: it was expanded as a broadside ballad* as early as 1692; provided the tune for many other ballads; appeared as an engraved single-sheet song; circulated in keyboard arrangements and tune-books; and appeared in *Pills to Purge Melancholy**. It was arranged several times by Charles Babel*, and two French contrafacta were published in Abel Boyer's *Compleat French-Master* (1694). *BalSop, BalSta, DaySon, LebTra, PriPur, SimBal, WooKey, ZimCat*.

'If music be the food of love' Z379A–C A poem by the soldier and East Anglian MP Henry Heveningham (1651–1700), taking its first line from Orsino's speech at the beginning of Shakespeare's* *Twelfth Night*. It was set by Purcell three times. Z379A (G minor) and Z379B (A minor) are closely related strophic songs set in a suave, melodious duple time; they were first published respectively, by Peter Motteux* in *The Gentleman's Journal* (June 1692) and in John Carr's* *Comes Amoris*, book 4 (1693). However, despite these publication dates, Margaret Laurie argued (*PS* 25) that Z379A is a revision of Z379B, with more polished details, extra ornamentation and a running bass added to the repeat of the final section. Z379C (also G minor), first published in Henry Playford's* *Deliciae musicae*, book 2 (1695), is an Italianate through-composed setting: verse 1 is set as a highly ornamented declamatory passage; verse 2 is mostly in a minuet-like $\frac{3}{8}$ rhythm. *LauSon*.

'**I'll sail upon the dog star**' **Z571/6** The most elaborate of seven songs for the character Lyonel in *A Fool's Preferment, or The Three Dukes of Dunstable* (Thomas D'Urfey's* adaptation of Fletcher's *A Noble Gentleman*), probably first performed in April 1688. Lyonel, played by William Mountfort*, has been driven mad by his lover's suspected infidelity, and this song is a manic assertion of his power. Its position in Act IV is not specified, but it may have closed a passage in which he compares himself to Tamerlane. The freely canonic exchanges between voice and continuo skilfully depict the words 'pursue' and 'chase' in the text, and the song's Italianate style doubtless contributed to its enduring popularity. *AdaPur, BalSta, DayDur, PriPur, SpiSon, WinHow*.

Imitation *See* **Counterpoint**

The Indian Queen **Z630** Purcell's last dramatic opera*, an anonymous adaptation of a play by Sir Robert Howard* (with some contribution by John Dryden*), first performed in 1664. It seems to have been revived with Purcell's music in June 1695, though he may have started work on it before the break-up of the United Company* in March 1695. It was probably first performed without the Act V masque*, which Daniel Purcell* apparently set after his brother's death for a revival early in 1696. The convoluted plot, 'in defiance of history and geography' as Curtis Price put it, involves accepting that the Inca and Aztec empires in ancient Peru and Mexico are adjacent and at war, and centres around the Aztec queen Zempoalla and her unrequited love for Montezuma, a warrior of unknown origin.

Purcell's music, concentrated in four scenes, featured the young singers left with Christopher Rich's* company after most of his experienced soloists joined Thomas Betterton's* company. Instead of the normal spoken prologue, an Indian boy and girl (John Freeman* and Jemmy Bowen*) sing a series of graceful airs alluding to the events of the play and foretelling the eventual Spanish conquest. The Masque of Fame and Envy praising Zempoalla in Act II starts with the symphony from 'Come, ye sons of art, away'* transposed to C major, and contrasts swinging C major music for Fame (Freeman) and the chorus with sinister C minor music for Envy (bass; unknown singer) and two accomplices; these three illustrate 'What flatt'ring noise is this, / At which my snakes all hiss?' with unforgettable hissing.

Purcell's greatest music comes in Act III, in which the conjuror Ismeron (sung by Richard Leveridge* in at least one early production) summons the God of Dreams to reveal Zempoalla's fate by singing 'Ye twice ten hundred deities'*. To console the queen after the god's dire prophecy Ismeron conjures 'Aerial-Spirits'. Their scene starts with the superb Trumpet Overture and includes 'We the spirits of the air', a delicious *gavotte en rondeau** for two trebles with chorus, which encloses 'I attempt from love's sickness to fly' (Letitia Cross*), Purcell's most famous and perfect rondeau song. *The Indian Queen* is unlikely to be revived on the stage, and the music is rarely performed in concert, in part because it ends in anti-climax: the Sacrifice Scene in Act V, Henry Purcell's last contribution, is short and largely conventional, and Daniel Purcell's music for the final Masque of Cupid and Hymen is competent rather than inspired. *See also* **Performing material**. *HolPur, LS, PinInd, PriPur, ShaMan, WalDra*.

'In guilty night' *See* **Saul and the Witch of Endor**

Inequality *See* **Rhythmic alteration**

In nomine The English instrumental genre using a plainsong *cantus firmus* derived from a passage at the words 'In nomine Domini' in the Benedictus of John Taverner's mass 'Gloria tibi trinitas', written probably in the 1520s. Detached from the mass, it became the model for more than 150 consort pieces written from the 1550s onwards. Purcell's two examples, in six parts Z746 and seven parts Z747, copied into GB-Lbl, Add. MS 30930 alongside the fantasias*, were apparently composed in or shortly after 1680, about 40 years after the last examples in the continuous tradition, by John Jenkins* and William Lawes*. Z746 and Z747 reach back past Jacobean and Caroline In nomines to Elizabethan composers such as Robert Parsons and Robert White, who both wrote seven-part examples. In Z747 Purcell followed tradition by placing the *cantus firmus* in even breves in the alto part, surrounding it with smooth counterpoint* largely rising and falling in minims and crotchets. Z746 uses an archaic technique in which the *cantus firmus*, speeded up and partly rhythmicised so it can be heard as a melody, provides the material for the accompanying counterpoint. *HowArt, HolPur, PinNom, SchCon, ShaMan, ThoFan*.

Instruments, symbolic associations Purcell and his contemporaries inherited, and in some cases developed, a set of associations in their use of instruments that would have conveyed specific meanings to their audiences, especially in theatre music. In his dramatic works trumpets* were used to evoke war, heroism, courtly power, ceremony and joy, while flat trumpets*, used in the March and Canzona* and *The Libertine**, had funereal associations. Recorders* were often associated with the pastoral, the supernatural, love and death (the last eloquently in odes marking Purcell's death); while oboes* had wide-ranging associations from war and joy (often combining with, or substituting for, trumpets) to mystery and the supernatural, as well as representing the double *aulos*, the single reed instrument associated with Bacchus, as in the Masque of Cupid and Bacchus in *Timon of Athens**. Trumpets and kettledrums* were often imitated in string writing and keyboard music, and the keys associated with particular instruments contributed to a wider range of key characteristics*. *See also* **Odes on the death of Henry Purcell**. *HolPur, PriThe, SimRec*.

An Introduction to the Skill of Musick A series of popular instruction books on music published by John Playford* from 1654, and continued by Henry Playford and others until 1730; until 1670 it was entitled *A Brief Introduction to the Skill of Musick*. It consisted of three sections: the first introduced the reader to the rudiments, including the gamut*, clefs, solmisation, note values and time signatures; the second consisted of tutors for the bass viol* and (from 1655) the violin; and the third was a brief composition treatise, initially by Thomas Campion, which was replaced for the tenth edition of 1683 by 'A Brief Introduction to the Art of Descant' by Playford himself. The 12th edition of 1694 (*PlaInt*) was '*Corrected and Amended by Mr.* Henry Purcell', and he was certainly responsible for a radical revision of 'The Art of Descant' (described, starting with the 13th edition (1697) as being 'made very Plain and Easie by the late Mr. HENRY PURCELL'); he also probably made the less important revisions to the other sections of the book. Purcell's 'Art of Descant' has been used, notably in *HowArt*, in studies of his compositional strategies. *See also* **Counterpoint**. *HarPla, HerThe, MunPla, SquThe*.

Isaack family The brothers William (1652–1703), Peter (c.1655–94) and Bartholomew (1661–1709) were sons of William Isaack, virger and sexton of St George's Chapel, Windsor*. William junior was a chorister and then an adult singer at St George's and Eton College, while Peter and Bartholomew were choirboys in the Chapel Royal*. Peter was a singer and cathedral organist, working in Dublin from 1672, Salisbury (1687–92), and then Dublin again. Bartholomew, also a singer and organist, joined his brother in Dublin in 1684 after a period as organist of St John's College, Oxford*. He was dismissed from St Patrick's, Dublin in 1687 for neglecting his duties, apparently because he had become a Catholic. He was appointed organist of St Saviour, Southwark (now Southwark Cathedral) in 1705.

William Isaack junior was an important copyist working in Purcell's circle, sometimes collaborating with John Walter*, also a Windsor musician. He made scores of a number of Purcell's odes, some copied stratigraphically* (suggesting they were used for direction at the keyboard), and his great scorebook* GB-Cfm, Mu. MS 117 is a central source of church music from Tallis and Byrd to Blow* and Purcell, with anthems at the front and services at the back. Two important scores, US-NYp, Drexel MSS 3976 and 5061, were also probably copied by a member of the family, perhaps Peter Isaack. MS 3976, The Rare Theatrical, is a collection of Matthew Locke's* violin band music, while MS 5061 is the principal secondary source of Purcell's fantasias* but also has a group of vocal and instrumental pieces partly or wholly by 'Mr Bartholomew Isaack'. One of these, a ground-bass* piece for three violins, bass and continuo (ed. in *HolVio*), was clearly inspired by Purcell's Three Parts upon a Ground*. Bartholomew probably wrote it around 1680 while he was working in Oxford; it shows considerable promise for a teenager, a promise seemingly largely unfulfilled in later life. *BDECM, DexQui, HerCat, HerCre, HolFid, HolPur, ShaMan, SpiCat, WolVio*.

Italian music Purcell acknowledged the importance of Italian music in his preface to *Sonnata's of III Parts**, writing (in the third person): 'he has faithfully endeavour'd a just imitation of the most fam'd Italian Masters', adding: 'he is not mistaken in the power of the Italian Notes, or elegancy of their Compositions, which he would recommend to the English Artists'. This has been taken to apply to the trio sonatas* that circulated in Restoration England, by Cazzati*, Legrenzi*, Vitali* and others, that Purcell apparently used as models for his own sonatas. However, the Italian influence in Restoration England went much further than consort music. Some Italian singers and singing teachers settled in England in the 1660s and 70s, bringing with them their native vocal music and, presumably, a system of voice training that enabled English pupils to cope with its novel demands. They included the organist Vincenzo Albrici (an ex-pupil of Carissimi), Pietro Reggio* and Girolamo Pignani, who published a book of Italian songs, *Scelta di canzonette italiane* in London in 1679. It transmitted a largely Roman repertory, by Carissimi, Luigi Rossi, Pasquini, Stradella and others. A good deal of other Italian vocal music arrived in England by other routes.

In the 1670s John Blow* seems to have studied and copied earlier Italian music in Henry Aldrich's* collection at Christ Church, Oxford*, formerly in the possession of the Hatton family. He apparently used the collection to provide models for his own Latin motets (ed. *BloMot*), in turn the starting point for Purcell's Latin motets 'Jehova, quam multi sunt hostes mei'* and 'Beati omnes qui timent Dominum' Z131 – the latter also partly inspired by a motet by Giovanni Felice Sances*. John and Henry Playford* included some Italian vocal music in their publications, among which were motets attributed to Carissimi and Bonifacio Graziani in *Harmonia Sacra**, book 2, perhaps chosen by Purcell himself.

Purcell also assimilated the Italian style through music written by expatriate Italians in London. He may not have been much influenced by the idiosyncratic violin music of Nicola Matteis* (which was popular among English amateurs), and Reggio probably had more impact as a singer-lutenist and the author of a singing treatise than as a composer. However, G.B. Draghi* was a profound and enduring influence. His great *Song for St Cecilia's Day, 1687* was responsible (more than any other single work, so far as is known) for Purcell's turn from a French-influenced dance-based idiom to a more Italianate musical language around 1690.

Purcell's awareness of Italian music was largely retrospective, harking back as far as Monteverdi*; he seems to have had little interest in Italian composers of his own generation, such as Arcangelo Corelli* or his near contemporary Alessandro Scarlatti (1660–1725) – though that was thought to be the case when John Weldon's* music for *The Tempest**, with its modern da capo* airs, was thought to be by him. *DixIta, HerCre, HolDra, HolPur, HowArt, JohSon, LebAlb, LebRom, MabIta, MesAlb, PagGui, SchGro, ThoJen, WaiPat*.

'I was glad' According to Francis Sandford* (*SanCor*, 82), 'I was glad', a full anthem* by Purcell, was sung as the Introit for the coronation of James II* and Mary of Modena in Westminster Abbey* on 23 April 1685. Until 1977 no full anthem by Purcell of that title was known, and it was assumed that his symphony anthem* 'I was glad' Z19 had been performed at that point. However, in that year Bruce Wood drew attention to a five-part full anthem setting the text exactly as printed by Sandford, from Psalm 122, verses 1, 4–7 and the Gloria Patri. It survives in a score copied by the Ely organist James Hawkins* in what is now GB-EL (deposited in GB-Cu), MS 6. Hawkins attributed it to John Blow*, though Wood argued it was Purcell's long-lost coronation anthem and published it as by him (ed. *PurGla*): an attribution that has been generally accepted, with Mathias Range a dissenting voice.

'I was glad' was sung by the choir of Westminster Abbey in procession, preceding the king and queen down the nave. This is presumably why elaborate counterpoint is avoided until the Doxology, by which time the choir would have halted. The main part of the anthem, with its unpredictable and inventive harmonic scheme, full of false relations, could conceivably be by Blow, though the dazzling display of counterpoint at the words 'world without end, Amen', with the imitative point treated in inversion as well as single and double augmentation, is highly characteristic of Purcell, relating to other instances in his works of what he called 'Fugeing ... *Per Augmentation*' (*PlaInt*, 110–12). *See also* **Coronations**, **Counterpoint**, **Dissonance**. *HowArt, RanCor, RanGla, ShaMan, WooCor.*

James II James Stuart (1633–1701), younger brother of Charles II* and father of Mary II* and Anne* by his first wife Anne Hyde, returned to England at the Restoration* after exile in France. Charles created him Duke of York and Lord High Admiral of the fleet, and during the Exclusion Crisis of 1679–81 (caused by James's Catholicism) sent him to Scotland as High Commissioner. The duke was finally welcomed back to Whitehall* in 1682 with Purcell's 'What shall be done in behalf of the man'*. Purcell wrote 'My heart is inditing'* and 'I was glad'* for James's joint coronation* with his second wife, Mary of Modena, in Westminster Abbey* on 23 April 1685. He subsequently wrote the welcome song* 'Why are all the Muses mute?'* (1685), followed by 'Ye tuneful Muses'* (1686) and 'Sound the trumpet, beat the drum'* (1687), all for the king's birthday on 14 October.

Charles Burney (*BurHis*, iii. 484) wrote that James II was 'too gloomy and bigoted a prince to have leisure or inclination for cultivating or encouraging the liberal arts', though in fact he continued his brother's patronage of music and embarked on a thorough reform of the royal household, the first since Henry VIII's reign: a number of traditionally separate groups of court instrumentalists were subsumed into the new Private Music*. As a Catholic, James did not attend the Anglican Chapel Royal*, creating a Catholic chapel in Whitehall, opened on Christmas Day 1686. Nevertheless, the Anglican Chapel celebrated Mary of Modena's pregnancy with a thanksgiving service on 15 January 1688 for which Purcell provided the symphony anthem* 'Blessed are they that fear the Lord' Z5. After his flight to France in December 1688, James continued his patronage of musicians at St Germain-en-Laye near Paris. Innocenzo Fede (who had been Master of the Music of the Whitehall chapel), James Paisible* and François Couperin are among those who worked there in the 1690s. *CorJam, HolFid, HolPur, LeeCat, WhiPol, ZimPur.*

'Jehova, quam multi sunt hostes mei' Z135 Purcell's superb setting of Psalm 3 (in the translation by the Calvinist Immanuel Tremellius) for five voices and continuo was composed in 1678 or 1679. It shares its scoring and idiom with two of the Latin motets John Blow* composed in the 1670s, inspired by Italian models. It is structured in five sections, alternating the full ensemble with tenor and bass solos. Purcell copied it (and the four-part 'Beati omnes qui timent Dominum' Z131) into GB-Lbl, Add. MS 30930 alongside 12 English devotional part-songs*, which suggests he had domestic performance in mind, perhaps by members of the court Private Music*. However, it became a favourite of cathedral choirs in the twentieth century, and in 1929 Edward Elgar orchestrated it for performance at the Three Choirs Festival, a version performed in the 1995 anniversary* concert at Westminster Abbey. *See also* **Italian music**. *AdaPur, BloMot, BurElg, HarChi, HolPur*.

Jenkins, John A viol virtuoso and one of the greatest and most prolific English composers of consort music (1592–1678). He worked for most of his career in the households of members of the East Anglian gentry, including the North family at Kirtling in Cambridgeshire; Roger North* was a pupil. In 1660 he received a post as a lutenist in the court Private Music*, for which he seems to have written his ten fantasia suites for three violins, bass viol and continuo. Their unusual scoring provided Purcell with obvious models for Three Parts upon a Ground* and the Pavan* in G minor Z752. *BDECM, DarCha, HolFid, HolPur, HolVio*.

Jig The word, equivalent to the French *gigue* and the Italian *giga*, was used in English for various types of lively dance music from the sixteenth century. Thomas Mace* (*MacMus*, 129) wrote that jigs are 'of any sort of *Time*', though Purcell's examples are mostly in $\frac{6}{4}$ or $\frac{6}{8}$ with two repeated strains. He included only one in his keyboard suites*, in C major Z665/4; the one in the A minor suite Z663 as transmitted in the Purcell-Draghi Manuscript* may be by John Blow*. However, there are a number of jigs in his sets of theatre airs*, and there are also jig-like stage dances in the dramatic operas*, such as the Chair Dance Z627/17 in *Dioclesian**, Act III and the Dance of the Haymakers* Z629/24a in *The Fairy Queen**, Act III. He often used jig-like compound-time rhythms to signify rustic jollity in vocal music, as in 'Your hay it is mow'd' Z628/37 in *King Arthur**, Act V and the dialogue Coridon and Mopsa* in *The Fairy Queen*. *ChaJig*.

Kettledrums As a Chapel Royal choirboy, Purcell would have been familiar from childhood with pairs of kettledrums or timpani used in the bands of state trumpeters that played fanfares at English court functions. He wrote regularly for trumpets* in his odes and large-scale theatre music from 1690 onwards, though we only have his notated kettledrum parts for two works, both written in 1692: the Act IV Masque of the Seasons from *The Fairy Queen** and the ode 'Hail, bright Cecilia'*; they both have elaborate solo parts for drums in d and A. However, kettledrum parts exist in later sources for other Purcell works with trumpets, including 'Come, ye sons of art, away'* and The Yorkshire Feast Song*, and it is possible that in some circumstances Purcell expected his player to improvise simple parts. *HerPin, SteDru*.

Keyboard music Purcell's keyboard music divides into three main types. (1) Original idiomatic pieces often using the *style brisé** idiom: principally the preludes*, almands* and corants* of his suites* and arrangements of vocal ground basses*, the latter mostly of his own pieces but including his fine keyboard version of Lully's* 'Sccoca pur'*. (2) A much larger corpus of simple keyboard settings of dances and songs, typically with the tune in the right hand and one or two parts in the left hand. Many of these are arrangements of pieces from Purcell's sets of theatre airs*; it cannot be assumed that the keyboard settings of them not in *Musick's Hand-Maid**, part 2 (1689) and the autograph Purcell-Draghi Manuscript* were made by the composer. (3) A few organ* pieces, their number apparently limited because Purcell did not have regular organ pupils and routinely improvised voluntaries*. The standard editions *PurMis*, *PurSui* and *PurOrg* (together with *PurTwe*, an edition of Purcell's section of the Purcell-Draghi Manuscript) will be superseded by the revised collected edition *PS* 6.

Purcell's domestic keyboard music seems mostly to have been written as teaching material after 1689, when he had ceased to be a full-time court musician and had begun to acquire upper-class female pupils, including Rhoda Cavendish* née Cartwright, Diana Howard* and the unknown owner(s) of the Purcell-Draghi Manuscript. It was for pupils, presumably, that he collected and arranged the contents of *Musick's Hand-Maid* and composed the eight suites published posthumously in *A Choice Collection**. Many of his separate keyboard pieces were not published at the time and circulated in manuscript.

The repertory of keyboard music Purcell encountered as a young man (explored in *WooPer*) would have included organ voluntaries in the tradition deriving from Orlando Gibbons*; suites by Matthew Locke*, Albertus Bryan (John Blow's* predecessor as organist of Westminster Abbey*) and others composed in the 1660s; and Blow's own large output of harpsichord and organ music. Purcell was not much influenced by continental keyboard music so far as is known, though he would have been aware of fashionable French dance music from John Playford's* tune-book series *Apollo's Banquet*, and a piece in the Purcell-Draghi Manuscript turns out to be Purcell's metrical version of a French unmeasured prelude*. He was associated, probably as a performer or copyist rather than as its composer, with the fine Toccata in A major*. *See also* **Harpsichord**, **Spinet**. *CooKey*, *FerPur*, *HogCor*, *HogMan*, *HolPur*, *LedSty*, *ShaMan*, *WooKey*.

Key characteristics The idea that composers might choose certain keys for their associations with particular emotions came from Renaissance notions of the character of the modes, and was set out by seventeenth- and early eighteenth-century French and German musicians, including Marc-Antoine Charpentier and Johann Mattheson. No seventeenth-century English writer codified the system, though Roger North* (*NorMus*, 211) recognised that some keys in unequal temperament*, 'by meer out-of-tuned-ness have certein caracters, very serviceable to the various purposes of Musick'. He singled out F minor, a key 'that more resembles a dolorous melancholy than any of the others'. Purcell presumably chose it for that reason for the music he gave to the Sorceress and her witches in *Dido and Aeneas**.

But the system clearly went further than that. Purcell was not alone among English composers in associating G minor (representing *gamma ut*, the lowest note of the scale in medieval music theory) with death and the grave, as in Dido's Lament*. C minor seems to have been Purcell's all-purpose serious key, used for elegies and funerals (the Burial Service* and the elegies for Queen Mary*,

'Incassum, Lesbia, incassum rogas' and 'O dive custos Auriacae Domus'*), but also tragedy (Saul and the Witch of Endor* and 'O lead me to some peaceful gloom' from *Bonduca**), as well as extreme emotion and madness (The Blessed Virgin's Expostulation* and 'From rosy bowers'*). Some key associations were derived from the characteristics of wind instruments: martial and ceremonial music is typically in C major or D major even when trumpets* are absent, while pastoral music is often in F major, associated with the treble recorder*, which goes down to f'. B♭ major, a favourite oboe* key, was often associated with Bacchic jollity, as in the Masque from *Timon of Athens**. *See also* **Gamut, Instruments, symbolic associations**. *HolPur, PriPur, SteKey*.

***King Arthur, or The British Worthy* Z628** The second of Purcell's dramatic operas*, and the only one with a specially written play text, by John Dryden*. It was first performed by the United Company* at Dorset Garden* in May 1691, with Thomas Betterton* in the title role. Dryden originally wrote *King Arthur* in 1684 with an all-sung prologue, but the play was shelved and its prologue converted into the opera *Albion and Albanius*, set by Louis Grabu*. Following the success of his music for Dryden's *Amphitryon** (1690), Purcell was invited to set *King Arthur*, which Dryden claimed to have revised to take account of the new political situation in William III's* reign. The playwright made a determined effort in his play to discover a historical Arthur and his struggles against the Saxons, largely shorn of medieval romance. However, by retaining Merlin, and devising his evil Saxon counterpart Osmond, he created supernatural episodes ideal for elaborate musical setting: notably the Frost Scene* in Act III and the concluding Act V masque, a vision of Britain as a single united, prosperous nation.

Dryden understood, as most of those adapting old plays as dramatic operas did not, that composers needed varied opportunities for music. Thus the musical scenes in *King Arthur* (obeying the principle that supernatural beings sing naturally but humans should only do so in situations that would call for music in real life) include: the solemn yet urgent music of the Saxon sacrifice scene and the rousing 'Song of Triumph' 'Come if you dare', sung by British soldiers (both in Act I); the ethereal spirit music of 'Hither, this way' (Act II), with its remarkable double-choir writing (somewhat garbled in the sources and modern editions); the charming pastoral entertainment of the Pavilion Scene for Emmeline (Act II); and the superb Passacaglia (Act IV), another supernatural episode conjured by Osmond, heavily influenced by the *passacaille* in Act V, Scene 2 of Lully's* *Armide*. The Act V masque starts magnificently with the Locke*-like storm music of 'Ye blust'ring brethren' and includes the evergreen 'Fairest isle'*. However, it lacks dramatic coherence and ends in some sources with the clearly spurious ground-bass* solo 'St George' and the banal (and obviously corrupt) final chorus. Both were probably added after Purcell's death, perhaps in an attempt to replace pieces lost from the autograph score.

Despite its textual problems (there is no single authoritative source of the music), *King Arthur* remained popular, and was repeatedly revived in staged productions until the 1840s, notably in the version devised by David Garrick with Thomas Arne* in 1770. The few sympathetic modern stage revivals of play and music have shown what a wonderful evening in the theatre it can be. *See also* **Political allegory, Stage history from 1695**. *BurArt, BurRem, GilArn, GilGar,*

GreArt, HarArt, HolPur, LamBal, LS, PinArt, PinDou, PriPur, SawTre, SchLul, ShaArt, ShaMan, WalDra, WinArt.

The Knotting Song *See* **Charles Sedley**

Latin motets *See* 'Jehova, quam multi sunt hostes mei'

'Laudate Ceciliam' Z329 In his autograph scorebook* GB-Lbl, R.M. 20.h.8 Purcell headed this work 'A Latine Song made upon St Cecilia, whoes day is commerated yearly by all Musitians made in ye year 1683'. Scored for three voices, two violins and continuo, it is his only concerted setting of a Latin text. It combines a symphony in the Anglo-French mode of Humfrey* and Blow* with Italianate vocal writing influenced by Carissimi and other Roman composers. It falls into two large units of alternating declamatory passages and airs articulated by a repetition of the symphony. Purcell notated the triple-time passages in void crotchets and quavers (modernised in *PS* 10), probably to signal the work's Italianate idiom; he may not have known that French composers also used 'white notation' or *croches blanches*. It is usually described as an ode*, though its unambiguously Catholic text referring to St Cecilia's martyrdom (contrasting sharply with the secular odes for Cecilian celebrations*) suggests it is actually a devotional motet. Its inclusion in R.M. 20.h.8 suggests it was written for court performance, perhaps early on 22 November 1683, preceding the performance of 'Welcome to all the pleasures'* later that day. *See also* **Italian music**. *AdaLau, HolPur, WhiCec.*

Lawes, Henry and William The Lawes brothers Henry (1596–1662) and William (1602–45), both singers, lutenists and composers at Charles I's court, would have been known to Purcell mainly for *Choice Psalmes* (1648) – posthumously in William's case, who was killed at the Siege of Chester. *Choice Psalmes* codified the rich repertory of English three-part devotional part-songs*, to which, among others, John Wilson, George Jeffreys, John Jenkins*, Matthew Locke* and the young Purcell contributed. Purcell would also have known Henry Lawes's secular songs and dialogues, extensively published in John Playford's* song books of the 1650s, taking them as his starting-point for his early essays in these genres. William Lawes's consort music, highly valued today, was outmoded before Purcell was born; there is no sign he knew it. *See also* **Declamatory vocal writing, Dialogues**. *BDECM, CheChu, DaySon, HolPur, HowSin, SpiSon.*

Lee, Nathaniel This poet and playwright, born between 1645 and 1652, studied at Trinity College, Cambridge before moving to London, where his hopes of becoming an actor were undermined by stage fright. He turned to writing plays, enjoying his first significant success with *Sophonisba* in 1675. He achieved another success in 1680 with *Theodosius**, for which Purcell provided music. In 1684 he became mentally ill and was admitted to Bethlehem Hospital, though his plays continued to be performed and reprinted; Purcell may have set 'Beneath the poplar's shadow' Z590 for a revival of *Sophonisba* in 1685. Lee recovered sufficiently to leave hospital in 1688, and the following year he petitioned successfully to allow performances of *The Massacre of Paris* (banned since the early 1680s), in which Purcell's setting of 'Thy genius, lo!' Z604A was performed by John Bowman*. Lee died in 1692, but several of his plays outlived him. Purcell's music for *Oedipus** (written by Lee with John Dryden* in 1678) was composed probably in 1692, while he provided a new setting of 'Thy genius, lo!' Z604B for Jemmy Bowen* in 1695. *PriPur*.

Legrenzi, Giovanni Italian composer (1626–90) from Clusone near Bergamo, who settled in Venice in the 1660s, becoming *maestro di cappella* at San Marco in 1685. His trio sonatas circulated in Restoration England; he was perhaps one of the 'most fam'd Italian Masters' Purcell had in mind as models for *Sonnata's of III Parts**. Purcell's trio sonatas are particularly close to the *sonate à tre* in Legrenzi's Op. 2 (Venice, 1655): he followed Legrenzi by repeating fugal opening themes at the end of sonatas, combining them with new material (see 1683, nos. 5 Z794 and 8 Z797), and by developing a contrapuntal canzona* out of a dance-like passage (Z797 and 1697, no. 10 Z811). *See also* **Italian music**, **Trio sonatas**. *HolPur, KanTri, ThoJen, TilTec*.

Lenton, John Violinist, singer and composer (?1657–1719), a member of the Twenty-Four Violins* from 1681 and a gentleman extraordinary of the Chapel Royal* from 1685. He also wrote at least 12 sets of theatre airs* for the United Company* and then Betterton's* company, and published two collections of consort music (1692, 1697, the former with Thomas Tollett); they only survive incomplete. He was a reasonably competent but unadventurous follower of Purcell, though he is important as the author of *The Gentleman's Diversion* (1693–4), an early violin treatise. Lenton played with Purcell at court for many years, so his advice for holding the violin, fingering, bowing and ornamentation* has a special interest. It includes duets specially written for the book by Lenton himself and a number of colleagues, including 'M[r]. P', who is given pride of place. This can really only be Purcell; his two pieces, an air and minuet in G minor for violin and bass, will be included in the revision of *PS* 31. The 'Rebus on Mr. Hen. *Purcell's* Name' ('The mate to a cock, and corn tall as wheat', also in Latin as 'Galli marita par tritico seges') by the court violinist Richard Tomlinson was set by Lenton as a three-part catch*, first published in 1701. *BDECM, BoyLen, BurRem, DaySon, LowSta, PriThe*.

Leveridge, Richard Bass singer and composer (1670/1–1758), with a remarkably long career on the London stage. He suddenly emerged as one of Purcell's leading theatrical soloists in April 1695, when Thomas Betterton* seceded from the United Company* with most of the experienced actors and singers. Leveridge took the role of Ismeron in *The Indian Queen** in an early production, with its great solo 'Ye twice ten hundred deities'*, and probably played Bacchus in the Masque from *Timon of Athens**. He was also a soloist in Jeremiah Clarke's* *Song on the Death of the Famous Mr Henry Purcell*, performed on the stage at Drury Lane* early in 1696, and he continued to appear in public, often singing Purcell's bass solos, until 1751. Among his compositions are the Purcellian 'Enthusiastic Song', his immensely popular solo in the dramatic opera* *The Island Princess* (1699); and the famous music for *Macbeth* (1702), later misattributed to Matthew Locke* as well as Purcell. *See also* **Performance material**. *BalBir, BalLev, BalSta, BDA, LowSta, LS, HigRec, PriIsl, ShaMan*.

The Libertine **Z600** Purcell's music for Thomas Shadwell's* bloodthirsty tragedy based on the Don Juan legend, first performed in 1675, is conventionally dated to 1692, though it was apparently written for a revival around July 1695, when 'To arms, heroic prince' Z600/3, an elaborate Italianate air with trumpet* obbligato, was published. It was sung, apparently as an entr'acte entertainment, by 'the Boy' – evidently Jemmy Bowen*, who only began his theatre career in April 1695. The rest of Purcell's music is in two scenes. An episode of rustic merriment in Act IV, set in 'a delightful grove', features the famous air 'Nymphs and shepherds, come away'* with its amusing 'Symphony of Rustick Musick' portraying a collective improvisation by a village band. A three-part 'Song of Devils', performed at the end of the play (before Don Juan and his cronies are dragged down to Hell) begins with the March for flat trumpets Z860/1 borrowed from Queen Mary's* funeral music – another reason for favouring 1695 rather than 1692. Four simple settings of lyrics in Acts I, II and III survive in a late manuscript, US-Ws, W.b.533 (ed. in *PS* 20). They are attributed to Purcell but were probably written for a revival after his lifetime. *See also* **March and Canzona**. *HolPur, LS, PriPur, PriThe, SpiLib, WooFun*.

'Light of the world' **Z330** This work is a complicated puzzle. Jacob Tonson published Matthew Prior's ode separately in 1694, heading it 'For The New Year: To The Sun' with the comment: 'Intended to be Sung before their Majesties on *New-Years* Day. 1693/4. Written by Mr. *Prior* at the *Hague*'. There is no evidence that it was set to music at that time, and there is a 1694 New Year ode, 'Sound, sound the trumpet', by Peter Motteux* and John Blow*. When Edward Curll reprinted the ode in 1707 (in an unauthorised collection of Prior's *Poems on Several Occasions*), it was headed '*Intended to be Sung before Their late Majesties, on* New-Year's-Day, 1693/4, *(but here Printed with Alterations; as it was Perform'd lately at a* Consort of Musick, *by the most Eminent Masters.)*', with Queen Anne* and the Duke of Marlborough replacing William III* and Mary II*. William and Mary were restored in Tonson's authorised edition of *Poems on Several Occasions* (1709), now with the heading: 'Set by Dr. *PURCEL, And Sung before their Majesties on New-Year's Day, 1693/4*'. Michael Tilmouth suggested that Purcell's Sonata in D major Z850* was the ode's symphony*, though we doubt that Henry Purcell set the work; Daniel Purcell* might have done so between 1702 and 1707 using Curll's version, though neither of them had a doctorate. *MurOde, TilTec*.

'Lilliburlero' The famous tune associated with the ballad 'Ho, broder Teague, dost hear de decree?', satirising James II's* Irish Catholic supporters during the Glorious Revolution*; it supposedly sang 'a deluded Prince out of Three Kingdoms'. Purcell set it twice, as a simple keyboard piece entitled 'A new Irish Tune' Z646, published in *Musick's Hand-Maid**, part 2 (1689), and in the bass of the Jig from the theatre airs* for *The Gordian Knot Unty'd** Z597/5 (Ex. 5). This set is largely a compilation, so it is possible that its Jig came from a lost work celebrating the accession of William III* and Mary II*. Purcell used the same strategy to convey covert messages with 'Hey, boys, up go we'* and 'Cold and Raw'*. *HolPur, SimBal*.

Ex. 5: Jig from *The Gordian Knot Unty'd* Z597/5.

Lluellen (Llewellyn), George According to Hawkins* (*HawHis*, ii. 749), the clergyman and musician George Lluellen (1668–1739), the son of a Buckinghamshire poet and physician, had been 'a page of the back stairs in the reign of Charles II., and at court became acquainted with Purcell'. He studied at Oxford*, was a member of the city's music club, and while he was there he acquired the early Restoration keyboard manuscript GB-Och, Mus. 1179 from his mother Martha née Long. He dated it 1690, which is probably when the copyist Purcell scholars call FQ4 (perhaps his teacher) added a sequence of pieces mainly by John Blow*, but including the unique copy of Purcell's Voluntary in C Z717. Lluellen was ordained at Oxford in 1695 and later became rector of Pulverbatch in Shropshire. Hawkins wrote that he contributed 'above thirty songs' to the enlarged 1706 edition of *Orpheus Britannicus**, book 1; its index identifies 34 'NEW ADDITIONS'. Charles Burney* (*BurHis*, iii. 495), who knew him as a child in Shropshire, wrote that he was 'often called by the Whigs, "a Jacobitical, musical, mad, Welsh parson"'. *CCED*, *CCLMC*, *HerCat*, *ShaMan*, *WooKey*.

Locke, Matthew Organist and composer (1621/2–77), the leading musician at court and in the theatre in the early Restoration period. He is sometimes said to have been Purcell's teacher, though as a Catholic he was not a member of the Chapel Royal* (despite composing for it); a letter from him to the young Purcell (printed in *CumPur*, 27), long used as evidence of their friendship, seems to be one of Edward Rimbault's* forgeries. Nevertheless, Locke was an important influence on the young Purcell, particularly in anthems, domestic sacred music and consort music. In particular, Locke showed Purcell how to combine the angular lines and unpredictable harmony of declamatory song with traditional imitative counterpoint*.

Purcell probably owned Locke's autograph scorebook of consort music, now GB-Lbl, Add. MS 17801, and its contents also offered important models, though he was much more interested in recondite contrapuntal devices than his mentor. He clearly knew Locke's theatre airs* for *The Tempest* (1674) (ed. in *HolThe*), imitating them in The Staircase Overture* and in the canonic Dance of the Followers of Night from Act II of *The Fairy Queen* Z629/15 – modelled directly on Locke's concluding Canon 4 in 2. Purcell wrote a heartfelt elegy, 'What hope for us remains now he is gone?' Z472, following Locke's death in August 1677. *AdaPur, BDECM, CheChu, HerCre, HolFid, HolPur, LocDra, SpiSon, WalDra, WalMas, WolVio.*

Lonati, Carlo Ambrogio A set circulated in Restoration England of what were thought to be trio sonatas by Lelio Colista*, though about half of them are by the Milanese violinist, singer and composer Carlo Ambrogio Lonati (c.1645–c.1710–15), including the one Purcell used as an example of 'Double Descant' or invertible counterpoint* (*PlaInt*, 124). Lonati came to London with the castrato Marco Godia (known as Marchetti) in 1676, when they performed for Charles II*. According to Hawkins* (*HawHis*, ii. 808) he returned in 1687 in the company of the castrato Siface*. *See also* **Trio sonatas**. *AllSon, HolPur, HowArt, KanTri, MesAlb, TilTec.*

London A The label used by scholars for a prolific music copyist active in Purcell's circle and in the London theatres between about 1685 and 1707. His distinctive, bold hand has been identified in 17 manuscripts to date. He made many additions to Purcell's autograph scorebook* GB-Lbl, R.M. 20.h.8; copied scores of concerted vocal music by Purcell and his followers; and hand-corrected copies of the printed score of *Dioclesian**. He was apparently a house copyist for the Drury Lane Theatre*: his scores include GB-Lcm, MS 1172 (a central source of theatre airs*, all in G minor); primary sources of *The Indian Queen** (the only one with the text and the music); *Timon of Athens** (with the names of the singers included); and the dramatic opera* *The Island Princess* (also with the text and music). His identity was proposed in *ShaMan* as the composer and organist Francis Pigott*, though that has been called into question by the discovery that London A's keyboard manuscript, US-Wc, M21/M185/Case, includes a piece apparently copied from Abiell Whichello's *Lessons for the Harpsichord or Spinett* (1707); Pigott had died in 1704. *HerCat, HerScr, PriIns, PriIsl, ShaMan, WhiCla, WooPer.*

'Lord, how long wilt thou be angry?' Z25 A fine five-part full-with-verse anthem* setting four discontinuous verses from Psalm 79 (5, 8, 9 and 14), suggesting a text devised for a special occasion, perhaps the annual fast on 31 January for the martyrdom of Charles I; Purcell entered it into GB-Cfm, Mu. MS 88 in 1684. He set the penitential text using angular figures and intense chromaticism

Illus. 7: Example of 'Double Descant', chosen by Purcell from Carlo Ambrogio Lonati.

inspired by Matthew Locke* (such as the anthem 'Turn thy face from my sins'), though this anguished part-writing gives way to a final triple-time verse of thanksgiving. A 'remarkable resonance' between a passage in the anthem and a four-part fantasia* by Christopher Gibbons* has recently been identified by Paul Stubbings, leading Robert Thompson to suggest that the work by Purcell's boyhood organ teacher was 'deeply embedded' in his memory. *See also* **Anthem texts, Autographs.** *SpiCat, ShaMan, StuGib, ThoFan.*

'Lovely Albina's come ashore' Z394 This superb song was said in *Orpheus Britannicus**, book 1 to be 'The last Song Mr. *Henry Purcell* Sett before his Sickness'. However, Margaret Laurie pointed out (*PS* 25) that this seems to mean his second-to-last song, because 'From rosy bowers'* was said in the same publication to have been 'the last Song that Mr. *Purcell* Sett, it being in his Sickness'. The allegorical text long puzzled scholars and singers, though James Winn explained that Princess Anne* (Albina) had protested about 'the Belgic lion' (William III*) granting land in Ireland to his mistress Elizabeth Villiers; Anne had expected to inherit it from her father James II*.

The occasion, Winn suggested, might have been Anne's return to London from Windsor* on the Thames, though there are other possibilities, including a visit to the Dorset Garden Theatre* by boat. Whatever the circumstances, Purcell's decision to set such an overtly political text illustrates his closeness to Anne's circle. His setting, in two sections, the first repeated, is remarkable for its brilliant and modern Italianate vocal writing, where the continuo part is virtually an equal partner with the voice, though he reverted to the dissonant English idiom in the wonderful last few bars when setting the words 'and let her grieve'. *AdaPur, WinAnn, WooPoe, ZimPur.*

'Love's goddess sure was blind' Z331 Sir Charles Sedley* marked Mary II's* 1692 birthday with an unusually accomplished and introspective ode, and Purcell matched it with a consistently fine setting, scored just for strings and continuo – forgoing the rich wind writing of most court odes of the period. It begins with a superb overture* (reused in *The Rival Sisters* Z609/1) rather than an Italianate symphony*, and throughout the engagingly melodious writing for solo voices is enhanced by richly detailed string writing in the ritornellos*. An anecdote reported by Hawkins* (*HawHis*, ii. 564) suggests that Purcell's use of the tune 'Cold and raw'* as the bass line to the countertenor solo 'May her blest example chase' was a wry response to Mary preferring that Scots ballad to his songs. The most striking music of the ode is saved for the final chorus in which Sedley's poem anticipates Mary's death. Following a G major section of great contrapuntal ingenuity, a dramatic shift to G minor ushers in four soloists who mourn to intense chromatic harmonies, after which a fugal chorus brings the work to a muted close. *AdaPur, HolPur, MurOde, SmiSed, SpiOde, WooOde, WooPur.*

Lully, Jean-Baptiste Purcell engaged on several levels with the music of the great Florentine violinist, dancer and composer (1632–87). Lully arrived in Paris as a teenager; started to write music for court ballets in 1653; and came to dominate music at the young Louis XIV's court, developing in the early 1670s the French type of court opera, the *tragédie lyrique*. In addition to borrowing ideas from *Le Triomphe de l'Amour* (1681) for *The Fairy Queen**, Purcell wrote direct imitations of two Lully pieces: his Cibell* derives from the 'Descente de Cybelle' from *Atys* (1676), while the famous shivering music in the Frost Scene* Z628/20, 24b, 24c from *King Arthur** was based closely on a chorus in *Isis* (1677). Purcell made a fine *style brisé** harpsichord arrangement of Lully's song 'Scocca pur'*, and used its five-bar ground for his own work, Z807, no. 6 of *Ten Sonata's in Four Parts**. In addition, the Passacaglia* Z628/30 from *King Arthur* was inspired by similar movements in Lully, notably the *passacaille* in *Armide* (1686).

More broadly, Purcell's overtures* mostly take their starting point from the Lully type, popularised in England around 1680, while his fondness for building up large complexes of prelude, vocal solo and chorus from small dance-based units in odes and theatre music was probably also inspired by

Lully, though similar things are found in pre-Civil War masques*. Lully's musical language, particularly embodied in the instrumental music by him that circulated in England (as well as that by his disciple Louis Grabu*), became part of the Restoration idiom when combined with the rugged English harmonic style and then overlaid with Italianate features. With its dance-based patterns and a structure consisting of a (lost) allegorical prologue and three acts, *Dido and Aeneas** is the Purcell work closest to the Lully type of opera, though on a much smaller scale. *HolPur, LS, PriPur, SawTre, SchLul, TupTri, WhiGra, WhiStu, WooSco, ZimCat.*

Lute Purcell would probably have learned hand-plucked instruments as well as the keyboard and bowed instruments while a Chapel Royal* choirboy. The 12-course lute, played from tablature and used mainly for solo music, was in decline while he was growing up: it was largely supplanted by the fashionable five-course guitar*. However, essentially the same instrument, called the theorbo and played from unfigured or figured basses, was the main continuo* instrument for solo vocal music until the 1690s, and was probably included as a matter of course in the continuo section of Purcell's concerted music. A number of his colleagues and prominent contemporaries, such as Henry Cooke*, Pelham Humfrey* and Pietro Reggio*, were singer-lutenists, and would therefore have accompanied themselves – a common practice at the time. The smaller archlute arrived in England from Italy in the 1670s, but does not seem to have been popular until the eighteenth century. Purcell did not write any solo lute music so far as is known, though solo arrangements of ensemble pieces by him are found in several early eighteenth-century manuscripts. *HolPur, MacMus, SayLut, SpeChi, SprLut.*

Lyra viol A mode of playing on the viol* as well as a type of instrument. Lyra viol music, mostly for a solo instrument, was played from tablature using variable tunings. A small bass viol was recommended, with lighter strings and a flatter bridge than on a normal viol. The lyra viol was going out of fashion as Purcell was growing up, and he is not known to have written original music for it, though there are arrangements of two songs from *Theodosius** Z606/5, 9 in the first part of John Playford's* *Musick's Recreation on the Viol, Lyra-way* (1682), and the Leyden Lyra Viol Manuscript (apparently copied by the Glasgow musician Andrew Adam in the 1690s and now in GB-NTu) includes arrangements of six more Purcell songs. *HolLif, MacMus, RobLey, ZimCat.*

Mace, Thomas Writer and musician (1612/13–?1706), singing man at Trinity College, Cambridge from 1635. He is best known for *Musick's Monument* (*MacMus*), published in 1676, an eloquent if eccentric elegy for pre-Civil War musical life, disrupted by the conflict and the closure of cathedral choirs, and then superseded by the fashionable music of the Restoration court – of which Purcell was to be the leading exponent. The book, unsurprisingly published at Mace's own expense, starts with acerbic comments on the deficiencies of 'Parochiall Musick' and 'Cathedrall Music', drawn from his Cambridge experiences. Part 2 is a Baroque lute* tutor claimed in modern times as the only one detailed enough to be of use without a teacher. It includes a continuo* treatise, 'Some *Directions* for *Playing* a *Part* upon a *Theorboe*', important for the practice of Purcell's youth. Part 3, 'The VIOL, AND MUSICK in General', is the best known today, especially for Mace's lament for the viol consort repertory. It may have prompted Purcell to write his pavans* and fantasias* a year or two later. Mace came to London in 1690 to sell his 'whole Stock of *Rich Musical Furniture*', including his instruments, his library and unsold copies of *Musick's Monument*. *BurHis, CarMac, HolBat, HolLif, SprLut*.

Mad songs Portraying madness in English song goes back to Robert Johnson's remarkable 'O let us howl', written for John Webster's *The Duchess of Malfi* (c.1613). However, the tradition Purcell developed so fruitfully started in the 1670s, with the ballad Mad Maulkin and its counterpart Mad Tom, the models for 'From silent shades'* (Bess of Bedlam), first published in 1683. Purcell followed it with 'I'll sail upon the dog star'* (1688) sung by William Mountfort*, and the genre came to maturity in Thomas D'Urfey's* *Don Quixote*✶ plays, which included 'Let the dreadful engines' Z578/3 in Part 1, sung by John Bowman*; and 'From rosy bowers'* in Part 3, sung by Letitia Cross'*. In addition, John Eccles's* 'I burn, I burn' in Part 2 was sensationally sung by Anne Bracegirdle. Eccles wrote other mad songs for Bracegirdle, and there are also fine examples by Blow*, Daniel Purcell*, Finger* and Weldon* (ed. *RobMad*). The vogue for the genre waned soon after 1700, though there is a parallel with the mad scene in Handel's* *Orlando*, Act II (1733). Purcell's mad songs were favourite recital pieces for leading singers throughout the eighteenth century and have resumed that status today. It was essentially a theatrical genre, though The Blessed Virgin's Expostulation* is a remarkable extension of elements of it into devotional song*. *See also* **Performance history from 1695**. *BalMad, CHE, HolPur, MacBes, PriPur, PriThe, SpiSon, WinHow*.

Maidwell, Lewis *See* **'Celestial music did the gods inspire'**

March and Canzona Z860 Purcell wrote these pieces for four flat trumpets* to be played during Mary II's* funeral in Westminster Abbey* on 5 March 1695. According to a manuscript source, GB-Ooc, MS U.a.37, the simple but powerful march was 'sounded before her chariot' (the queen's horse-drawn hearse), while the canzona was 'sounded in the Abby after the Anthem'. The march was possibly accompanied by military drums, though this has been the subject of controversy, as has the exact pattern that might have been used; Thurston Dart's* arrangement of both pieces with four timpani (published in *PurMar*) is memorable but unhistorical. Purcell reused the march in *The Libertine*✶, lowering the range of the fourth trumpet part to make it suitable for a bass violin or bassoon. These two pieces have no connection with Purcell's early setting of the Burial Service*, despite the impression given by some modern performances and recordings. *See also* **Canzona**. *ByrMar, HolPur, PriPur, ShaMan, SteDru, WooFun*.

The Married Beau, or The Curious Impertinent Z603 Purcell wrote a set of theatre airs* and a song for John Crowne's comedy, first produced at Drury Lane* probably in late April 1694. The fine extended minuet song 'See where repenting Celia lies' was sung in Act V by Mrs Ayliff* as Mrs Lovely's maid. It expresses the contrition felt by her mistress ('a witty, beautiful Coquet') for her adultery with Polidor. The original order of movements of the airs is unknown since the primary source is *A Collection of Airs**, which presents the sets reordered for domestic or concert use. However, Ian Spink (*PS* 20) suggested that the Hornpipe on a Ground Z603/9 (a brilliant mixture of hornpipe rhythms, the rondeau* pattern and chaconne* harmonies) was the First Music, and that the Jig Z603/6 was used for the dance at the end of the play. Purcell took the soulful Slow Air Z603/2 from *Circe**, transposing it up a fifth and adding some expressive ornamentation to the top part. *See also* **Hornpipe**. *LS, PriPur, PriThe.*

Mary II, Queen The elder daughter of James, Duke of York (later James II*) and Anne Hyde, Princess Mary (1662–94) married her cousin, Willem Hendrik, Prince of Orange and Stadtholder of the Dutch Republic, in 1677. They became joint English monarchs as William III* and Mary II after the Glorious Revolution* of 1688–9. They were crowned in Westminster Abbey* on 11 April 1689, when Purcell's new anthem 'Praise the Lord, O Jerusalem'* was performed. They cut back the activities of the royal music early in their reign, leaving Purcell's main duty at court to provide odes for Mary's birthday on 30 April: 'Now does the glorious day appear'* (1689), 'Arise, my muse'* (1690), 'Welcome, glorious morn'* (1691), 'Love's goddess sure was blind'* (1692), 'Celebrate this festival'* (1693) and 'Come, ye sons of art, away'* (1694).

Hawkins's* anecdote (*HawHis*, ii. 564) about Mary's preference for Arabella Hunt's* lute-accompanied singing of 'Cold and raw'* to Purcell's songs provides a valuable glimpse of informal court music-making, but insinuates that her musical taste was unrefined. Like the rest of her family, she played the guitar*, and she granted Hunt a pension of £100, probably as her singing teacher. For her funeral in Westminster Abbey on 5 March 1695 Purcell composed the March and Canzona* as well as 'Thou knowest, Lord'* Z58C. The elegies 'Incassum, Lesbia, incassum rogas' Z383 and 'O dive custos Auriacae domus'* were written in her memory. *HolPur, MurOde, PagGui, SpiOde, WinAnn, WooPur, ZimCat, ZimPur.*

Masque The main type of pre-Civil War court entertainment, treating mythological or allegorical subjects through speech, dancing, vocal music and elaborate stagecraft. Masques continued to be performed at court after the Restoration, though the mainstream became the masque-like scenes in plays and dramatic operas*, usually conjured up by magic and performed by supernatural characters; they often take the form of a dialogue between two mythological characters or personifications and their respective supporters. An important prototype was the Masque of Neptune and Amphitrite conjured up by Prospero at the end of Thomas Shadwell's* 1674 version of *The Tempest**. Important examples in Purcell are the Act V Masque of Cupid and Bacchus in *Dioclesian**; the Frost Scene* and the Act V masque in *King Arthur**, summoned up by Osmond and Merlin respectively; the Masque of the Four Seasons in *The Fairy Queen**, Act IV; the Masque of Cupid and Bacchus in *Timon of Athens**; and the Masque of Fame and Envy in *The Indian Queen**, Act II; Daniel Purcell* set its concluding Masque of Cupid and Hymen. In addition, John Blow's* *Venus and Adonis* and *Dido and Aeneas** were both described as masques despite being all-sung operas because they descended from a tradition of private masques put on during the Commonwealth, and because dance is an important element in both of them. *HolPur, LS, PriThe, PriPur, WalDra, WalMas.*

Matteis, Nicola Neapolitan violin virtuoso, guitarist and composer active in London between at least 1674 and 1693. His four books of *Ayrs for the Violin* (1676, 1685) were evidently very popular, to judge by the number of surviving printed and manuscript copies, though his idiosyncratic musical idiom (consisting mostly of dances, character pieces and divisions for violin and continuo with optional second violin parts) apparently had little impact on Purcell. North* wrote that Matteis was 'a consumate master' on the Baroque guitar*, who 'had the force upon it to stand in consort against an harpsicord' (*NorMus*, 357). Matteis explained continuo* playing on the guitar in his treatise *Le false consonanse della musica* (c.1680), translated as *The False Consonances of Music* (1682), and it is possible that Purcell conceived *Dido and Aeneas** with his guitar-playing in mind. *GoeHar, HolPur, JonMat, NorMus, PagGui.*

Minuet The triple-time dance (*menuet* in French; *minuetto* in Italian), popular at the French court from the 1660s and imported into England in the following decade; an early example is Robert Smith's* Second Act Tune in the airs for the 1674 production of *The Tempest** (ed. in *HolThe*). There are 12 named examples in Purcell's theatre airs*, notated in ¾ with commonly two repeated eight-bar strains starting and finishing on the first beat of the bar. There are also many more examples by Purcell of what Roger North* called the 'step-tripla' (*NorMus*, 300), favoured for vocal music at Charles II's* court, including the famous minuets 'Fairest isle'*, 'If love's a sweet passion'* and 'What shall I do to show how much I love her?' Z627/18 from *Dioclesian**. Purcell used the rondeau* pattern for some memorable minuet-like pieces, such as 'Fear no danger to ensue' Z626/7 from *Dido and Aeneas** and 'I attempt from love's sickness to fly' and the Third Act Tune Z630/18 from *The Indian Queen**. His minuets, like many at the time, often have only one or two chords per bar, suggesting they were performed rather faster than the familiar eighteenth-century type. *See also* **Dance**.

Mock-song The practice of adding words to existing music goes back to the sixteenth century (some of John Dowland's songs are adaptations of instrumental dances), and lies behind the broadside ballad and the metrical psalm. Adaptations of songs and dances by Purcell and his contemporaries were often called mock-songs, and writers such as Thomas D'Urfey* and Peter Motteux* were skilled at creating them, presumably with the acquiescence and sometimes the collaboration of the original composers. A famous example is 'O! how happy's he' Z403, adapted and performed by William Mountfort* using the Hornpipe from *Dioclesian** Z627/4. 'When first Amintas sued for a kiss' Z430 is apparently D'Urfey's adaptation of an instrumental Scots jig by Purcell, while Anthony Henley did a similar thing with the Hornpipe Z629/1b from *The Fairy Queen**, making 'There's not a swain on the plain' Z587; it was sung by Mary Hodgson* in a revival of Fletcher's *Rule a Wife and Have a Wife* probably in December 1693. Purcell copied his own version into the Gresham autograph*, in E minor with a new bass and a variant text (Ex. 6). *See also* **Broadside ballads**. *ArkGen, BalSta, DayDur, DaySon, LS, PurGre, SimBal, SpiSon.*

Ex. 6: Purcell's version of 'There's not a swain on the plain'.

Monteverdi, Claudio Purcell's interest in earlier music is exemplified by a fragment in his hand of Monteverdi's madrigal 'Cruda Amarilli' from *Il quinto libro de madrigali* (Venice, 1605), wordless except for the incipit. It survives because he used the back of the sheet as a correction slip for his score, now GB-Ob, MS Mus.a.1, of the Benedicite from his Service in B$^\flat$ Z230M (3) (*c*.1680). He may have come across the madrigal in a much earlier manuscript that evidently passed through his hands. It includes his copy of a canon by John Bull* as well as 'Cruda Amarilli' and two other madrigals from *Il quinto libro*. Italian madrigals by Monteverdi and his contemporaries had long circulated in England in wordless versions as viol consort music, though Purcell was probably more interested in them as compositional models. *DarBul, ShaMan, ZimMon.*

Morgan, Thomas Appointed organist of Christ Church, Dublin from Christmas 1690, Thomas Morgan was paid £5 in March 1691 to travel to England 'to use his best endeavours to attain the perfection of an organist'. He can be identified with the Mr Morgan who wrote music for at least ten productions at Drury Lane* and Dorset Garden* between September 1695 and February 1699 because his song 'Cease thy suit unhappy swain' was said to be 'the last he made in *Ireland*' when it was published (*Mercurius Musicus*, August 1699). His mad song* 'Come, ye inhabitants of heaven' was said to be 'the last he made' when John Walsh* published it on 16 November 1699, and therefore he was apparently the Thomas Morgan buried at St Sepulchre, Holborn on 8 October 1699. He was probably still in his twenties.

Morgan was a close follower of Purcell, and included the eloquent slow triple-time movement 'Mr H. Purcells Farewell' in his theatre airs* for Aphra Behn's *The Younger Brother, or The Amorous Jilt* (Drury Lane, ?February 1696). A lively duple-time air by Morgan (ed. in *MorLov*) from a set only entitled 'Matchless' (evidently a code-word for a lost play) exists in a keyboard transcription in GB-Lbl, K.1.c.5 mislabelled 'Jegg' and misattributed to Purcell (ZS123). Morgan composed a remarkable amount of music during his short career, and it shows some promise. *See also* **Recordings**. *BoyChr, DawMor, LowSta, LS, PriIsl, PriThe, ShaMan, WooKey, ZimCat.*

Morley, Thomas Purcell would have known this Elizabethan composer (*c*.1557–1602) mainly for *A Plaine and Easie Introduction to Practicall Musicke* (1597), the most famous music treatise in English, still studied in the Restoration period; Francis Withy* copied extracts into his commonplace book and it was thought worthy of a reprint in 1771. Purcell apparently composed 'Thou knowest, Lord' Z58C* to fit into Morley's setting of the Burial Service*, which circulated in the Restoration period with that sentence missing. *BDECM, HerCre, HerThe, ShaMan, ThoWit, WooFun.*

Motteux, Peter Anthony (Pierre Antoine Le Motteux) Journalist, playwright and auctioneer (1663–1718), a French Huguenot from Rouen. He came to London after the Revocation of the Edict of Nantes in 1685, and achieved prominence as the editor, publisher and chief author of *The Gentleman's Journal, or The Monthly Miscellany* (January 1692–November 1694), the first English general-interest periodical. The music supplements added at the end of most issues contain 20 Purcell songs, nearly all published for the first time. Among them are a number of mock-songs*, in which new verses (mostly by Motteux) were added to existing music. They include 'No watch, dear Celia, just is found' Z401, based on 'Thou tun'st this world' Z328/6 from 'Hail, bright Cecilia'*; and 'Celia's fond, too long I've lov'd her' Z364, with words fitted to an otherwise lost Purcell song.

Motteux was an informed observer of theatrical and musical affairs. In January 1692 he published a defence of dramatic opera*, praising Purcell for joining 'the Delicacy and Beauty of the *Italian* way' to 'the Graces and Gayety of the *French*'. In the same month he published a famous description of Cecilian celebrations*, adding in November 1692 the information that ''Tis Nature's voice'* had been sung in 'Hail, bright Cecilia'* with 'incredible Graces by Mr. *Purcell* himself' – which started the hare running that Purcell was a countertenor* and had sung the elaborate solo himself. Motteux wrote a Cecilian ode set by John Blow*; texts for a number of masques and musical interludes set to music by John Eccles*, Gottfried Finger*, Jeremiah Clarke*, Daniel Purcell* and others; and libretti for some of the pasticcios in the first phase of Italian and Italianate opera in London. His death in a brothel caused a scandal during which several of those present were tried for murder and acquitted. *ArkGen, BalBir, DaySon, BurRem, PriIsl, RadGen, ZimCat, ZimPur, WhiCec.*

Mountfort, William Actor, playwright and singer, who came to London from his native Staffordshire and was a member of the Duke's Company from 1678, when he was about 14. He was a leading member of the United Company* until his murder during the night of 9–10 December 1692, defending the honour of the actress and singer Anne Bracegirdle. He was an accomplished countertenor*, and in 1688 Purcell wrote a sequence of songs for him in the role of the jealous madman Lyonel in Thomas D'Urfey's* *A Fool's Preferment, or The Three Dukes of Dunstable*, including 'I'll sail upon the dog star'*. Mountfort's popular mock-song* 'O! how happy's he' Z403 is an adaptation of the Hornpipe from *Dioclesian** Z627/4. He was also a composer, writing theatre airs* for his own play *Greenwich Park* (Drury Lane*, April 1691) as well as some songs. He was buried in St Clement Danes, 'Mr. *Purcell* performing the Funeral Anthem', according to a memoir included in his *Six Plays* (1720). *BalCou, BalSta, BDA, LS, PriThe, WalSon, ZimPur, ZimCat.*

Musical Antiquarian Society A society for 'the publication of scarce and valuable works by the early English composers', founded by the writer and publisher William Chappell in 1840, with Edward Francis Rimbault* as secretary. Before its demise in 1848 it had published 19 large folio volumes, including four major Purcell works: *Dido and Aeneas** (1841), ed. George Alexander Macfarren; *Bonduca** (1842), ed. Rimbault; *King Arthur** (1843), ed. Edward Taylor; and 'Hail, bright Cecilia'* (1848), ed. Rimbault. The editions are variable: *Dido and Aeneas* and *King Arthur* derive from their modernised late eighteenth-century concert versions, though Rimbault edited *Bonduca* and 'Hail, bright Cecilia' from early manuscripts. Edward Taylor was also President of the Purcell Club*, which seems to have acted as a performing outlet for the Society's editions. *AndRim, JonPub, PinPhe, RimBon, ShaMan.*

The Musical Society *See* **Cecilian celebrations**

'Music for a while' Z583/2 This famous ground-bass* air comes from the incantation scene in *Oedipus**, sung by a countertenor* priest to persuade the Furies to release the ghost of King Laius. It uses an arpeggiated rising chromatic ground portraying the inexorable and eerie rise of the dead king with the singer's gentle descending phrases soothing him. The ground begins to modulate soon after the singer begins the second phrase of the text, and it returns to the opening words and music as the ground returns to C minor, giving it the character of a da capo aria*. It was popularised in the twentieth century by Alfred Deller*, starting with his first recording of it in 1949. *HolPur, PriPur.*

Musick's Hand-Maid Henry Playford* published *The Second Part of Musick's Hand-Maid* in 1689, the sequel to a collection published by his father John in 1663; it was reissued in 1690 and 1705. The collection (ed. complete in *DarMus*) consists of 35 pieces 'Set for the VIRGINALS, HARPSICHORD, and SPINET' and 'carefully Revised and Corrected' by Purcell; 18 of them are attributed to him or are arrangements of his music. Other composers include John Blow*, William Turner*, Francis Forcer* and the London organist Moses Snow. Playford described the collection in the preface as 'useful not only for Beginners, but the more Skilful in the Art', and it ranges from simple arrangements of songs, consort dances and popular tunes (such as Purcell's setting of 'Lilliburlero'* Z646) to more demanding idiomatic keyboard music*, such as the Suite in C major Z665 and the *style brisé** arrangements of the ground-bass* songs 'Here the deities approve' from 'Welcome to all the pleasures'* and Lully's 'Scocca pur'*. The setting of the last was not attributed to Purcell but is almost certainly by him; he may have composed or arranged all the anonymous pieces in the publication. *CarPub, HarPla, WooKey, WooSco*.

'My beloved spake' Z28 One of Purcell's earliest symphony anthems*, composed by the end of 1677. He submitted it to serial revisions: the earliest version is in the surviving autograph score, GB-Lbl, Add. MS 30932 (*PS* 13, 5b), while a revised symphony with a different and longer first strain prefaces the later version (*PS* 13, 5a), itself in two different states (with minor differences in voice leading) in GB-Ob, Tenbury MS 1031 and GB-Cfm, Mu. MS 117, each of which probably derives from separate lost autographs. The influence of Pelham Humfrey* is strong in the anthem's sectional structure, featuring repetitions of the delightful minuet*-like symphony, part of the first verse and the following ritornello*. The young Purcell skilfully evoked the vernal images of the text (from the Song of Solomon) with expressive harmony, while a triple-time 'Alleluia' offers a foretaste of his lasting preoccupation with counterpoint*. The anthem's modern popularity is well deserved. *AdaPur, HolPur, HowCre, ShaMan*.

'My heart is inditing' Z30 Purcell's longest and grandest symphony anthem* was written for the coronation of James II* and Mary of Modena in Westminster Abbey* on 23 April 1685. According to Francis Sandford* (*SanCor*, 100–2), it was performed after the queen's crowning 'by the whole *Consort of Voices* and *Instruments*': 44 singers from the Chapel Royal* (in a gallery on the south side of the altar); 26 from the Abbey choir (in a gallery further down the north side); with about 30 royal string players (in a gallery opposite the Chapel Royal choir). One of Sandford's illustrations (see the detail in *HolBat*, 70) shows John Blow* beating time among the Chapel Royal singers. Purcell evidently planned the anthem in conjunction with Blow, whose 'God spake sometime in visions' (performed after the king's crowning) uses the same unusual eight-part vocal scoring, with three bass parts. There are no passages for solo voices, and the verse passages may have been sung with more than one voice to a part, possibly by the entire Chapel Royal choir with the Westminster Abbey choir joining in for the full sections.

The text, compiled by Archbishop William Sancroft (1617–93) from Psalms 45 and 147, and Isaiah 49, is a selection of passages suitable for a queen.

Purcell's setting is appropriately delicate, particularly in the ravishing verse passage beginning 'Hearken, O daughter', a foil for Blow's magnificently robust anthem. As with some of his other large-scale anthems, Purcell articulates the structure by repeating the opening symphony complete in the middle, so that the surrounding vocal sections form a great musical diptych. There are a number of thematic connections with Blow's anthem, and both composers set the final 'Alleluia' as seven bars of grand block chords, repeating the word six times in the same rhythm over similar harmonies. *See also* **Coronations**. *BurCha, HolFid, HolPur, RanCor, ShaMan.*

'**My song shall be alway**' Z31 This popular work appears as a continuo anthem in US-AUS, HRC 85, copied by John Gostling*, probably the earliest source. Its position there suggests it was composed no later than the end of June 1688. The text, a discontinuous selection from Psalm 89, was seemingly composed for a special occasion, perhaps the thanksgiving service held on 17 June 1688 for the birth of James Edward Stuart, son of James II* and Mary of Modena and heir to the throne. Purcell subsequently expanded it as a symphony anthem*: a score of this version, copied by the Oxford* musician Francis Withy*, is dated 9 September 1690, and a partly autograph set of string parts, GB-Och, Mus. 1188/9, may have been copied for a performance in the Oxford Music School around then.

The anthem is a display piece for a virtuoso bass; Hawkins* claimed it was 'composed on purpose for Mr. Gostling' (*HawHis*, ii. 753), though it lacks the low notes associated with him. It also circulated in a treble version (first published in the 1703 edition of *Harmonia Sacra**, book 1), sometimes wrongly associated with the castrato Siface*. The anthem consists of a sequence of discrete solo sections, analogous to the recitative-and-aria pairings of Italian cantatas, with only a short choral Alleluia at the end of each half. *See also* **Performing material**. *HolPur, ShaMan, SpiCat, WhiPol, WooAut.*

'**The noise of foreign wars**' This ode by an anonymous poet was written to mark the birth of the Duke of Gloucester* to Princess Anne* on 24 July 1689. Philip Hayes* copied a setting of the poem, unfortunately incomplete, into one of his scorebooks, now GB-KNt, MR 2.3. He did not attribute it to Purcell, though he included it in a set of volumes devoted almost exclusively to his music, suggesting he believed it to be by the composer. Nigel Fortune and Bruce Wood (*PS* 18) argued on stylistic grounds that it is more likely to be by Purcell than John Blow* (the other main composer of court odes* at the time), though a lack of logical harmonic planning in the surviving torso casts doubt on this. The music begins part-way through the opening symphony* and sets the first one-and-a-half of the poem's four stanzas, ending with a C major chorus. The one complete source of the poem states it was 'sung att Hampton Court', which suggests that Hayes copied it from an incomplete source of a complete work, as does the presence of part of the opening symphony – which Restoration composers often added after they had composed the vocal sections. *ForSou, HerHay, MurOde, WhiNoi.*

North, Roger This lawyer, writer and amateur musician (1651–1734) came from East Anglian gentry, spending much of his childhood at his grandfather's

Illus. 8: Roger North.

house at Kirtling near Newmarket. After a year at Cambridge, he entered the Middle Temple in 1669 and was called to the bar in 1674, thereafter acting as a lawyer and courtier mainly in the entourage of his eldest brother Francis (1637–85) – likewise a gifted musician, who rose from Attorney General in 1673 to Lord Keeper in 1682. In 1686 Roger became Attorney General in turn, though he retired from public life after the accession of William III* and Mary II*, refusing as a Nonjuror to accept their legitimacy. He purchased an estate at Rougham near King's Lynn in 1690, where he lived for the rest of his life, though his writings suggest he continued to spend some of his time in London.

North is our most important witness of music and musical life in Purcell's lifetime. He had a much more advanced knowledge of music theory than Samuel Pepys* (whose Diary stops at 1669), having been taught by John Jenkins* and other household musicians at Kirtling. He also had access to the large family music library; was on the spot for many great musical events; and had a much more consuming interest in the subject than Pepys's fellow diarist John Evelyn. He had a lively, enquiring mind, writing on subjects ranging from fishponds to Descartes, and approached musical theory, history, aesthetics, acoustics and performance practice free from the received assumptions of professional musicians. He complained, for instance, of children being made to learn 'the sour'd and misterious gamut'* by heart 'without the least proffer to them of an explanation of it' (NorMus, 59). He also had the priceless ability to turn a memorable phrase, as when he explained why 'Musick held up her head' during the Civil War: 'many chose rather to fidle at home, than to goe out, and be knockt on the head abroad' (*NorMus*, 294).

North knew Purcell personally and his music well, describing occasions (apparently around 1683) when the *Sonnata's of III Parts** were played 'more than once' at his brother's house, with 'myself and another violin', his brother playing the bass viol and 'the devine Purcell' at the harpsichord (*NorMus*, 47). Nevertheless, he could be critical, as when he commented on 'diversifications upon grounds, especially of Mr Purcell's, which shew the many ways a base may be handled (or tormented)': 'there is one excess seldome wanted in them, which is a wiredrawing of various keys and cadences out of the ground, which the air of it doth not in any manner lead to' (*NorMus*, 89).

His comments on Purcell's dramatic operas*, apparently based on first-hand knowledge of early productions, are justly famous, as when he described Charlotte Butler* as Cupid in the Frost Scene* from *King Arthur** facing away from the audience to conceal the distortion of her face from 'her gallants' (*NorMus*, 217–18). Sometimes, however, remembering in old age events long ago, he became confused, as with his reference to *King Arthur* being lost rather than *The Fairy Queen** (*NorMus*, 353); or in his memorable descriptions of Sleep's entrance in Act II of *The Fairy Queen*, singing 'Hush, no more, be silent' in 'a lowd base': 'Your fancy carrys the ratle of the instruments into those vacant spaces … nothing can be greater and nobler than this was' (*NorMus*, 220, 261). He misremembered the work as *Prince Arthur*; the character as Hymen and 'a rurall Deity'; and the words as 'Hush, peace, silence'.

Nevertheless, our understanding of Purcell and his milieu would be immeasurably weaker without Roger North's writings, which he never published, and which remained unknown until Charles Burney* used *The Memoires of Musick* (1728) for *BurHis*; it was first published by Edward Rimbault* in 1846. Their extent and importance were only revealed in 1959, when John Wilson published *NorMus*, a 'comprehensive anthology', as he styled his invaluable edition. *BurFai, HerThe, HolPur, NorCur, SavGen.*

Notes inégales See **Rhythmic alteration**

Novello, Vincent This organist, choirmaster, composer and publisher (1781–1861) developed an interest in editing music from his work as organist of the Portuguese Embassy Chapel, which required him to collect pieces suitable for the Catholic liturgy for its choir. It led to publications of Mozart and Haydn masses (from 1819); to *The Fitzwilliam Music* (1825–7); and then to a near-complete edition of *Purcell's Sacred Music* (1828–32), published by subscription in 72 parts collected in five volumes. An extra part contains an index, 'A Biographical Sketch of Henry Purcell' and much other contextual material. *Purcell's Sacred Music* was reissued in four volumes (1846) by Vincent's son J. Alfred Novello, who developed Novello & Co. – the publisher of the Purcell Society* edition from 1878 to 2007. Vincent Novello was the first Purcell editor to name his sources; to accompany scores with editorial notes; and to try to find the best sources, using a range of private collections and institutional libraries. *See also* **Biography, Editions, from 1695, York Minster**. *GriMan, JonPub, MPP, PalNov, ZimCat.*

'**Now does the glorious day appear**' Z332 According to Thomas Shadwell's* published text (*Poems on Affairs of State*, ii, 1697), Purcell's first ode for Mary II* was performed '*before their Majesties at* Whitehal', presumably on her birthday, 30 April 1689. Purcell used the Italianate five-part string writing of G.B. Draghi's* *Song for St Cecilia's Day, 1687*, and Draghi also inspired the bipartite Italianate symphony and the simple but irresistibly energetic contrapuntal chorus that follows. The chorus is repeated after a duet and a countertenor solo over a 'pseudo' ground bass* to create a structural unit akin to the opening of Draghi's ode, though without an equally compelling textual imperative. The recitative for John Gostling*, 'It was a work of full as great a weight', shows Purcell's matchless facility in capturing what Henry Playford* termed '*the Energy of* English *Words*'. The countertenor ground-bass solo 'By beauteous softness' returns to Purcell's practice in earlier court odes, though the rich five-part ritornello* contributes greatly to a movement of exquisite beauty. The concluding movements are less interesting, but all in all this work was an important prototype for Purcell's later odes in its structure and style. *AdaPur, HolPur, MurOde, SpiOde, WooOde, WooPur*.

'**Now that the sun hath veil'd his light**' Z193 Headed 'An Evening Hymn', this serene ground-bass* air sets words by William Fuller (1608/9–75), Bishop of Lincoln – one of six Purcell settings of verses by this literary and musical High Church clergyman. Henry Playford* chose to open *Harmonia Sacra**, book 1 (1688) with it, a position its modern popularity reflects, though it was not a favourite recital item in the eighteenth and nineteenth centuries. It uses a five-bar elaboration of the passacaglia* ground in G major, modulating to D major by way of E minor and B minor before returning to the tonic and the joyful final Hallelujah. At one point in this last section Purcell uses his favourite device of introducing part of the ground in the voice part in imitation with itself. *See also* **Arabella Hunt**. *AdaPur, HolPur, HowArt*.

Nyman, Michael This English composer (b.1944) has engaged with Purcell throughout his career. He studied musicology with Thurston Dart*, subsequently producing the first edition of the catches* with unbowdlerisd texts (*PurCat*). He came to prominence with his score for Peter Greenaway's film *The Draughtsman's Contract* (1982), set in a Wiltshire country house in 1694. It features pieces by Purcell (but including the Ground in C minor D221, actually by William Croft*), notably the Prelude to the Frost Scene* Z628/19a in *King Arthur**. This was arranged in minimalist fashion for the Michael Nyman Band and was subsequently much quoted and sampled as *Chasing Sheep is Best Left to Shepherds*. Nyman used a similar technique in his funeral march *Memorial* (1985), using the Prelude while the Cold Genius rises Z628/20a, also from the Frost Scene. More recently, he has set Vera Pavlova's Prologue to *Dido and Aeneas** (2011), an operatic 'reconstruction' of the circumstances of the opera's first performance in Chelsea. The recording *If* (Signum Records SIGCD586, 2019) by the countertenor Iestyn Davies and the viol consort Fretwork juxtaposes works by Nyman with arrangements for viols of three ground-bass* songs by Purcell.

'**Nymphs and shepherds, come away**' Z600/1b This song, from Purcell's music for *The Libertine**, became famous through the recording made on 24 June 1929 in the Free Trade Hall, Manchester by the Manchester Children's Choir (60 boys and 190 girls from local schools) with the Hallé Orchestra conducted by Sir Hamilton Harty. Issued on the Columbia label, it sold more than a million copies and was enduringly popular over the following decades.

Oboe Usually called 'hautboy' or 'hoboy' in Purcell's time (from the French *hautbois*), the Baroque oboe was apparently introduced to London in 1673 with the Baroque recorder* by a group of French wind players including the young Jacques or James Paisible*. They were in the vanguard of a movement that took the revolutionary new instrument from France to all parts of Europe within a few decades. The group played at least two sizes of oboe (soprano in c and tenor in f), as well as recorders. They must have initially played French instruments, similar to those ordered by Lully* from the Hotteterre family for the French court, but Peter Bressan* made them in London and soon had English followers, including Thomas Stanesby senior, whose excellent one-keyed oboes have been widely copied in the modern revival.

John Blow* and Purcell introduced oboes and recorders into their court music around 1680; Purcell's first use seems to have been in 1681, in 'Swifter, Isis, swifter flow'*. They were normally deployed so that the two instruments do not play at the same time, implying they were played by the same musicians; recorders mostly accompanied voices in solo sections with oboes reserved for orchestral or tutti sections. However, perhaps following Gottfried Finger's* example, Purcell began to experiment in the 1690s with giving solos to pairs of oboes. He used them in surprisingly varied contexts, ranging from the warlike prelude to 'Let the soldiers rejoice' Z627/9a in *Dioclesian**, Act II to the striking evocation of mystery and the supernatural in the symphony for the entrance of the God of Dreams Z630/14 in *The Indian Queen**, Act III. An obvious role for oboes was to represent the double *aulos*, associated with Bacchus, as in the Masque of Cupid and Bacchus in *Timon of Athens**, and by extension in other scenes of jollity.

Four-part oboe bands with two oboes, tenor oboe and bassoon* were established in the military during the 1680s, in England as elsewhere. Purcell used them in his grandest orchestral passages (producing double-choir effects with the strings), as in the Second Music of *Dioclesian* Z627/2a (see Illus. 3, p. 59); the chaconne* that concludes its Act V masque*; the Passacaglia from *King Arthur**, Act IV, with its quick-fire interchanges with the strings; and the choral and orchestral chaconne that concludes 'Who can from joy refrain?'*. Some indications for oboe solos in eighteenth-century Purcell sources, such as in 'Bid the virtues' in 'Come, ye sons of art, away'* and in 'Hither, this way' from *King Arthur*, Act II, should be treated with caution, and may be later reallocations of violin parts. However, it should not be assumed that oboes were only used where specified. Surviving performing material* of the period from all over Europe shows that they routinely doubled tutti string parts, and it is likely that some of Purcell's concerted works seemingly scored just with recorders were performed with the players changing to oboes for full sections. Alternatively, Purcell used oboes to double trumpets*, apparently intending for them to provide notes not available on the natural instrument. *See also* **Instruments,**

symbolic associations, **Orchestra**, **The Plaint**. *HayHau, HolCla, HolFid, HolPur, LasHau, OweObo, SmiPer*.

Odes In England the musical ode (usually called 'song' at the time) originated as an offering to the monarch on his birthday or the New Year. There were pre-Civil War antecedents, but the genre came to the fore after the Restoration with works by Henry Cooke*, Matthew Locke* and especially Pelham Humfrey*. They set texts modelled on Pindaric odes – derived from those by the Greek poet Pindar as reimagined by Abraham Cowley*. Purcell's first ode, 'Welcome vicegerent of the mighty king'* (1680), described as a welcome song*, marked Charles II's* return to Whitehall* following his summer progress. This was a new genre, perhaps created to exploit Purcell's rapidly developing talents. Purcell's early odes, following models set by Humfrey and John Blow*, are multi-movement works for soloists, chorus, strings and continuo, with a symphony* (often a French-type overture*) followed by a sequence of short vocal and instrumental sections predominantly in dance rhythms. In 'Swifter, Isis, swifter flow'* (1681) and 'What shall be done in behalf of the man'* (1682) Purcell experimented with combining recorders* and oboes* with strings for the first time, and 'Swifter, Isis' also includes a ground-bass* air, a type appearing in almost every subsequent ode.

Purcell composed at least one court ode a year from 1680 until his death, with the possible exception of 1688 ('The noise of foreign wars'* may be by Blow), and he used it as a compositional testing ground, continually vying with and borrowing from Blow. He brought a greater range of musical styles to the genre, introducing anthem-like contrapuntal passages and an air exploiting John Gostling's* talents in 'Fly, bold rebellion'* (1683). He then steadily increased the length and seriousness of his odes, with fewer but longer movements and declamatory solos and ground basses rather than dance-based movements. There were also new opportunities for odes: 'What shall be done in behalf of the man' (1682) celebrated the future James II's* return from exile; 'From hardy climes'* (1683) marked the wedding of George, Prince of Denmark* and Princess Anne*; while 'Welcome to all the pleasures'* (1683) was written for the new Cecilian celebrations*, the first outside the court.

G.B. Draghi's* *Song for St Cecilia's Day, 1687* revolutionised the English ode, with five-part writing for two violins, two violas and bass; an Italianate opening symphony; extended contrapuntal choruses; virtuosic solo writing; and trumpets* added to the strings and recorders. Purcell followed suit in his first of six odes for Mary II's* birthday, 'Now does the glorious day appear'* (1689), with five-part strings, an Italianate symphony and a contrapuntal chorus. In 1690 he wrote for pairs of trumpets, recorders and oboes in The Yorkshire Feast Song* and that year's birthday ode, 'Arise my muse'*. The genre reached its apogee with 'Hail, bright Cecilia'*, the 1692 Cecilian ode. It is his longest, most varied and greatest ode; he added kettledrums* to the trumpets, recorders, oboes and strings and conceived it for as many as 13 soloists. His subsequent odes, notably 'Welcome, glorious morn'* (1691) and 'Come, ye sons of art, away'* (1694), contain some superb music but do not advance the genre much further. *AdaOde, AdaPur, BalWho, HolFid, HolPur, MurOde, SpiOde, WooEqu, WooOde, WhiCec*.

Odes on the death of Henry Purcell Purcell's unexpected death on 21 November 1695 produced many poetic tributes, at least five of which were set to music. Two of them relate to the symphony song* tradition: John Blow's* superb setting of John Dryden's* ode 'Mark how the lark and linnet sing', scored for two countertenors*, two recorders* and continuo*, and Henry Hall's* setting of his own poem, 'Yes my Aminta, 'tis too true', a dialogue for treble and bass voices, two recorders and continuo. Jeremiah Clarke's* 'Come, come along for a dance and a song' is a remarkable large-scale work for soloists, chorus and orchestra, mixing the idiom of court and Cecilian odes* with a theatrical setting: it has stage directions and (according to William Croft*) was performed on the stage of the Drury Lane Theatre*. Daniel Purcell's* setting of Nahum Tate's* 'Lamentation for the Death of Mr. Henry Purcell' is lost, as is Gottfried Finger's* choral and orchestral setting of James Talbot's* ode 'Weep, all ye Muses', though a four-movement 'Farewell' suite by him survives; it was probably performed with the ode at York Buildings on 13 January 1696. *HowOde* is a critical edition of the surviving settings. *See also* **Poems praising Purcell**. *HolCla, WhiCla.*

'**O dive custos Auriacae domus**' Z504 A duet for two treble voices and continuo setting the first four stanzas of a poem on the death of Mary II* by Henry Parker, a student at New College, Oxford*. It was published in 1695 in *Three Elegies upon the Much Lamented Loss of Our Late Most Gracious Queen Mary*, along with two solos, John Blow's* setting of 'No, Lesbia, no, you ask in vain' and Purcell's 'Incassum, Lesbia, incassum rogas' Z383, setting the same text by a Mr Herbert in English and Latin. Drawing on conventional notions of female lamentation, Purcell fashioned a duet of extraordinary expressivity in which, Alan Howard argued, the entwining vocal lines and voluptuous harmony suggest a homoerotic union resonating with the implied sensuality of female grief expressed in other art forms. He also suggested it was written for Arabella Hunt* and Annabella Howard*, both singers closely connected with the queen. *See also* **George Herbert**. *HowMou, ThoHow, WooPur.*

Oedipus, King of Thebes Z583 Purcell wrote music for the incantation scene in Act III, Scene 1 of this tragedy by John Dryden* and Nathaniel Lee*. It was first produced in 1678, but Purcell's contribution was evidently for a revival, possibly in 1692, the date given by Charles Burney* (*BurHis*, iii. 489); the play was reprinted in that year and a performance is recorded for 13 October. The blind seer Tiresias and two priests, accompanied by two violins and continuo, summon up the ghost of King Laius, hoping he will identify his murderer. They begin by addressing the Furies, detailing their unpleasant treatment of the damned in declamatory solos framed by tutti invocations. Then the first priest persuades the Furies to release Laius in the famous ground-bass* air 'Music for a while'*, and the scene ends with a tutti section commanding the ghost to appear. The scene is rarely performed but makes a compelling concert item. *LS, HolPur, PriPur, PriThe.*

'**Of old when heroes thought it base**' *See* **The Yorkshire Feast Song**

'**O God, thou art my God**' Z35 This full-with-verse anthem* setting vv. 1–5 and 8 of Psalm 63 was probably composed not later than 1682 as a companion to the

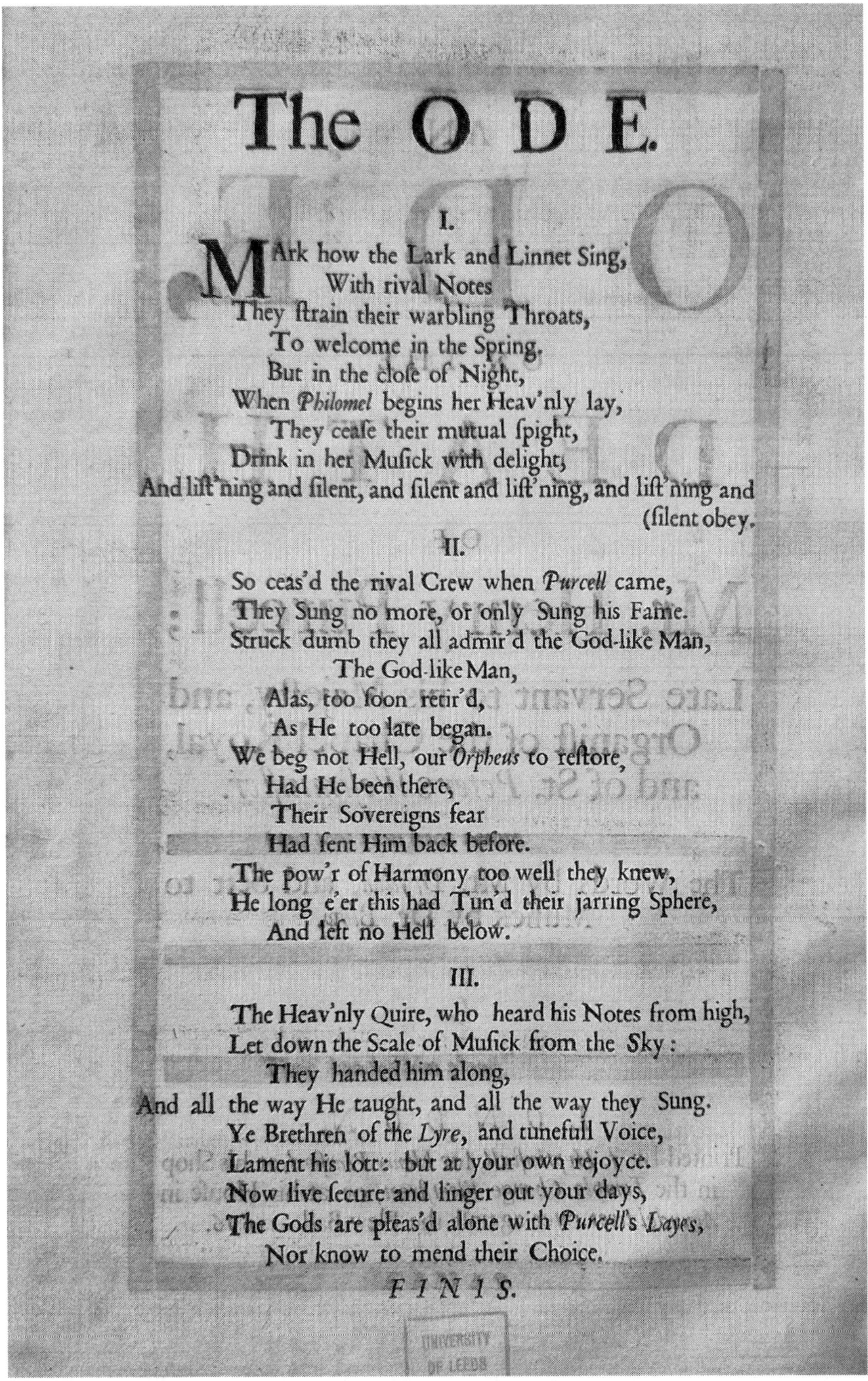

The ODE.

I.

Mark how the Lark and Linnet Sing,
With rival Notes
They strain their warbling Throats,
To welcome in the Spring.
But in the close of Night,
When *Philomel* begins her Heav'nly lay,
They cease their mutual spight,
Drink in her Musick with delight;
And list'ning and silent, and silent and list'ning, and list'ning and
(silent obey.

II.

So ceas'd the rival Crew when *Purcell* came,
They Sung no more, or only Sung his Fame.
Struck dumb they all admir'd the God-like Man,
The God-like Man,
Alas, too soon retir'd,
As He too late began.
We beg not Hell, our *Orpheus* to restore,
Had He been there,
Their Sovereigns fear
Had sent Him back before.
The pow'r of Harmony too well they knew,
He long e'er this had Tun'd their jarring Sphere,
And left no Hell below.

III.

The Heav'nly Quire, who heard his Notes from high,
Let down the Scale of Musick from the Sky:
They handed him along,
And all the way He taught, and all the way they Sung.
Ye Brethren of the *Lyre*, and tunefull Voice,
Lament his lott: but at your own rejoyce.
Now live secure and linger out your days,
The Gods are pleas'd alone with *Purcell's Layes*,
Nor know to mend their Choice.

FINIS.

Illus. 9: John Dryden, *An Ode, on the Death of Mr. Henry Purcell.*

B♭ Service*; it shares musical ideas with several of its movements. It consists of three choral sections enclosing two three-part verse passages, a scheme Purcell exploits with great skill. The verse passages contrast low- and high-voice groups, with the musical affect closely matching the text. The first two choral sections are contrasted in metre; the third introduces antiphonal exchanges between the *cantoris* and *decani* divisions of the choir*. It was first published in William Boyce's* *Cathedral Music*, vol. 2 (1768). Hawkins* thought it one of Purcell's finest anthems; and it has remained in the cathedral repertory. The concluding section is well known as the hymn tune* 'Westminster Abbey'. *ShaAnc, ShaMan, VanChu, ZimSer.*

'Oh that my grief was throughly weigh'd' ZD42 A devotional duet for two tenors and continuo (with a bass voice joining in the repeated refrain), setting words from the Book of Job in the King James Bible. It survives only in a late source, a score made by Philip Hayes* in the mid-1780s, so it was ignored by scholars and performers until Stainer & Bell* published Rebecca Herissone's edition in 2019. She argued convincingly that it is a genuine early work, perhaps copied from pages now missing from Purcell's autograph scorebook*, now GB-Lbl, Add. MS 30930. *See also* **Autographs**. *HerCat, HerHay, ShaMan.*

***The Old Batchelor* Z607** William Congreve's* first play was produced at Drury Lane* on 9 March 1693 to great acclaim. Purcell's music consists of a set of theatre airs* and two songs, 'Thus to a ripe consenting maid', sung by a 'Musick master' in Act II; and the delightful and popular duet 'As Amoret and Thyrsis lay', sung for Heartwell (the title role) in Act III, Scene 2 as an aphrodisiac for his sweetheart Sylvia. The theatre airs were apparently not new: three tunes were published in 1691, and a manuscript (GB-Lcm, MS 1144) has the title 'Mʳ Purcells Tunes in the Husbands Revenge' – that is, Thomas D'Urfey's* play *Bussy d'Ambois, or The Husbands Revenge*, first performed in March 1691. The only complete source of the set is *A Collection of Ayres**, printed in concert order with the overture first; the theatre order is not known. It is a deservedly popular set, with a large-scale overture (the fugue is a fine example of the thematic manipulation of a three-note rhythmic cell) and a number of witty and tuneful airs, including the rustic but highly sophisticated Rondeau Z607/5 and a contrapuntal triple-time March Z607/8. *LS, PriPur.*

'O let me weep' *See* **The Plaint**

'O Lord God of hosts' Z37 Purcell probably composed this magnificent eight-part full-with-verse anthem* in 1681–2. His model was John Blow's* anthem 'God is our hope and strength', also in A major and with the same vocal scoring; Purcell copied an organ part for it around 1675–6 (GB-Och, MS 554). 'O Lord God of Hosts' is a tour de force of dramatic contrasts, harmonic ingenuity and contrapuntal skill, exemplified in the closing section, in which a supplicating figure for 'O let us live' is first juxtaposed and then worked together with a vigorous triadic figure setting 'and we shall call upon thy name', the latter eventually prevailing in the approach to the final cadence. Charles Burney* (*BurHis*, iii. 482) rightly called it 'one of the finest compositions of the kind which our church, or perhaps any church, can boast'. *HolPur, ShaAnc, ShaMan, SpiCat, VanChu.*

Orchestra The development of the full Baroque orchestra, with trumpets*, kettledrums*, oboes* doubling recorders*, bassoon*, strings and continuo*, occurred in England during Purcell's working life. It was partly his creation, working at court with John Blow* and with talented instrumentalists including the oboist and recorder player James Paisible* and the Shore* family of trumpeters. The process began in the 1670s, when the Twenty-Four Violins* adopted the four-part Italianate 'string-quartet' scoring instead of traditional formats with two or three violas. Blow and Purcell started to feature pairs of oboes and recorders in their odes* and other court concerted music around 1680, using oboes largely to reinforce tutti sections, their players changing to recorders for obbligato roles in vocal solos. Trumpets were added a little later, initially in G.B. Draghi's* *Song for St Cecilia's Day*, 1687, and then in court and theatre works, starting in 1690 with the Yorkshire Feast Song* and the dramatic opera* *Dioclesian**. A feature of the latter, repeated in *King Arthur**, was the use of double-choir effects with a four-part oboe consort (including tenor oboe and bassoon) contrasted with the strings, a type of writing probably brought to England from central Europe by Gottfried Finger*. The finishing touch came in 1692 with Purcell's elaborate written-out kettledrum parts for the Act IV Masque of the Seasons in *The Fairy Queen** and the ode 'Hail, bright Cecilia'*.

Little is known about the size of Purcell's various orchestras, though his earlier odes may have been performed with half the Twenty-Four Violins, and the whole group augmented with extras played in the symphony anthems* during the 1685 and 1689 coronations*; it is likely that large string groups also took part in Cecilian celebrations* and later court odes. However, the size of the orchestra in Purcell's dramatic operas was probably limited by the capacity of the pit in the Dorset Garden Theatre*, though some instrumentalists might have been placed in boxes or even aloft in the stage machinery. By contrast, Purcell's symphony anthems were played in the small chapel at Whitehall* with single strings, and the same is probably true of the theatre airs* played in ordinary spoken plays in the Drury Lane Theatre*.

Purcell's orchestral bass lines were played by large bass violins* without reinforcing contrabasses, but with the continuo team in concerted music probably including a bass viol* and lute*-family instruments, with two harpsichords in dramatic operas and an organ in odes. Purcell was a bold and innovative writer for the orchestra, on a par with Lully* in France, and his approach was continued by his followers, including Jeremiah Clarke* and John Weldon*. *BurBan, HolCla, HolFid, HolPur, HolThe, LasHau, OweObo, WhiCec, WolOve, WolVio.*

Organ English church organs in the 1660s were markedly old-fashioned in European terms. They typically had 15–20 stops played from one or two keyboards (the latter often called double organs*), with the 'chair' department hanging over the organ gallery, behind the organist's seat; no pedals; stops largely confined to a chorus of metal pipes and a few ranks of wooden 'recorder' stops; a high sounding pitch*; and even the archaic system by which organs were built a fourth higher than choir pitch, so that accompaniments had to be transposed.

Things began to change when Renatus Harris* (a member of the Dallam family that had dominated English organ building before the Civil War) began to build much larger and more colourful organs, with reeds voiced in the French manner – his family had been in exile in Brittany during the Commonwealth. His bitter rival Bernard ('Father') Smith* introduced elements of Dutch practice, and also began to increase the size and power of his instruments. Between them, they dominated organ building in Purcell's lifetime and long after. Their instruments were highly prized until the early nineteenth century, when most were replaced or rebuilt because of the changing role of the organ in the liturgy, and the need to make them suitable for German solo music, notably the works of J.S. Bach and Mendelssohn.

Purcell's training in the Chapel Royal* was partly as an organist, and his first adult post was as John Hingeston's* assistant as curator of the court keyboard instruments, which involved overseeing Smith's work on the Chapel organ, lowering its pitch and probably modernising its temperament*. He doubtless could carry out running repairs and was paid for tuning the Dallam organ in Westminster Abbey*; he presumably arranged for Smith to rebuild it in 1694. None of the church organs Purcell played survive in more than fragments, though he might have played some of the many surviving chamber organs built by associates of Smith; his own domestic organ was left by his widow to their son Edward (*ZimPur*, 283). He followed English tradition by seemingly preferring chamber organs to harpsichords* for the accompaniment of his consort music*. *See also* **Continuo**. *BicOrg, CoxOrg, DunSmi, FreSmi, GwyPur, GwyWes, HolBat, KniHar, KniWes, ParPer, RosPer, StuGib, WooKey*.

Ornamentation Purcell would have expected two types of ornamentation to be applied to his music, associated respectively with Italian and French music. Italian singers and instrumentalists used a form of florid ornamentation preserving some features of Renaissance *passaggi*, a semi-improvised technique that divided long notes into short ones (hence the English word 'divisions'*), connecting them with florid runs. An idiosyncratic form of *passaggi* had been used in English song since the reign of James I, and a more modern type was apparently taught and demonstrated by the Italian singing teachers active in Restoration London. Traces of it can be found in such things as Daniel Henstridge's* attempt to notate Pietro Reggio's* singing of his own setting of 'Arise ye subterranean winds' from the 1674 production of *The Tempest**; the florid solo writing in G.B. Draghi's* *Song for St Cecilia's Day, 1687*; and, above all, in the extraordinary Draghi-inspired florid ornamentation in "'Tis Nature's voice'* from 'Hail, bright Cecilia'*, written out by Purcell for John Pate*. However, there was English resistance to such extravagance: Matthew Locke* asked performers of his *Little Consort* (1656) 'to play plain, not *Tearing* them in pieces with *division,* (an old custome of our *Countrey Fidlers,* and now under the title of *A la mode* endevoured to be in[t]roduced)'. Roger North* (*NorMus*, 161) condemned the famous florid ornamentation added to Corelli's* Op. 5 sonatas as 'so much vermin'.

The other type, called *agréments* in French or 'graces' in contemporary English, typically decorated single notes rather than groups. Again, this was nothing new: copyists often covered Elizabethan and Jacobean keyboard and lute music in ornament signs; and Charles Coleman codified a table for the benefit of viol players, published by Christopher Simpson* in 1659. They include various types of 'Shaked Graces' or trills, and appoggiaturas from below and above the note, called 'Beat' and 'Backfall'. Coleman's table shows that appoggiaturas were played quite short (unlike the long ones of the mid-eighteenth century); while the example in John Lenton's* *Gentleman's Diversion* (see *HolFid*, 377) gives the impression that court string players covered Purcell's French-style music with them. A number of early ornamented versions of Purcell's songs, some written by the composer in the Gresham autograph* (discussed in *RosPer*, 146–50), suggests that singers were taught to add graces as a matter of course – a feature still not sufficiently adopted in modern performances.

A good deal has been written about ornamentation in Purcell's keyboard music, though, as Roger North warned (*NorMus*, 149): 'It is the hardest task that can be, to pen the manner of artificiall Gracing an upper part. It hath bin attempted, and in print, but with woefull effect'. He was perhaps thinking partly of the 'Rules for Graces', first published in *The Harpsicord Master* (1697); John Walsh* claimed that they had been 'written by ye late famous M^r H Purcell at the request of a perticuler friend, & taken from his owne *Manuscript*'. This is open to question, and the sources give the impression that Purcell and other leading keyboard players in Restoration England ornamented their music with panache but were not much concerned with devising systems for codifying ornament signs – unlike their French counterparts, with their sophisticated and precise tables. Nevertheless, performers of Purcell's keyboard music will need to consult *JohOrn* (the most detailed treatment of a complex and sometimes perplexing subject), together with the practical advice in *PurMis* and *PurSui*; *WooPer* offers useful perspectives from Purcell's contemporaries. See also **Italian music**. *FerPur, HerCre, HogCor, HolNot, JonSon, RosPer, SpiSon, StuGib*.

Orpheus Britannicus The last, most successful and influential of the memorial collections of Purcell, *OB* for short. The original *OB*, printed for Henry Playford* by John Heptinstall*, was published in February 1698; subscriptions had been sought since 1696. It is a well-chosen anthology of 'single' (i.e. separate) songs and duets from across Purcell's composing career mixed with solo sections from the odes and theatre works. Purcell's widow Frances dedicated it to Lady Annabella Howard[A], while Playford stated on the title page that it was ordered by key ascending from Gamut* and that the 'Symphonies for *Violins* or *Flutes*' (i.e. recorders*) from the parent works would be included, a promise kept to a remarkable extent.

OB, book 1 was a resounding success: it was immediately mined by Thomas Cross* for his single-sheet editions; John Blow* imitated it in *Amphion Anglicus* (1700); and Playford produced a sequel, *OB*, book 2 (1702) 'which renders the First Compleat', printed by Heptinstall's apprentice William Pearson using his 'new London character'. Some 'single' songs and duets missed in *OB*, book 1 were included, though book 2 is focussed on sections from post-1690 odes and theatre works (notably 'Music for a while'* Z583/2), but also including the possibly inauthentic trio ''Tis wine was made to rule the day' Z546. Pearson collaborated with John Young* and John Cullen to reissue *OB*, books 1 and 2 in 1706, with additions from *'several Gentlemen who had Original Copies by them'* – among them Purcell's friend George Lluellen*. Included in them are evergreens such as 'Britons, strike home!'* and 'Nymphs and shepherds, come away'*, but at the expense of omitting some pre-1690 songs included in the 1698 edition. Subsequent editions appeared in 1711 and 1712 (book 2) and 1721 (books 1 and

2), these with further additions and one notable omission: Purcell's fine early elegy on Matthew Locke*.

OB transmits texts of variable quality, presumably dependent on the sources available to Playford's editor (often thought to be Daniel Purcell*), and the continuo* figuring cannot be assumed to derive from the composer. Modern editors and performers often rely on *OB* without realising that the autographs are more trustworthy, as are some secondary manuscript sources. The various editions also include many verse tributes to Purcell; those by his friends and colleagues contain some valuable biographical information. *OB* popularised the idea that Purcell could stand comparison with the legendary Thracian musician, as well as with Corelli*. Eighteenth-century musicians mostly encountered Purcell from it, or from editions derived from it. *See also* **Editions, from 1695, Poems praising Purcell, Printing and publishing**. *CarPub, HarPla, HigRec, HolPur, KruPri, LucPla, MPP, ZimCat, ZimPur.*

Osborn MS 515 A folio partbook, now US-NHb, Osborn MS 515. It is a guardbook containing bass parts of consort music compiled and partially copied by an unidentified individual who was probably an associate of John Gostling* in London or the Canterbury* area. Originally one of a set of probably four or five books (there were still three in 1848), it contains music ranging from William Lawes* and John Jenkins* to Henry and Daniel Purcell*, apparently copied over a long period and bound around 1700. It includes nine consort pieces by Henry Purcell otherwise unknown; six of them are in his autograph, copied in the mid-1670s, including two pavans* and an overture*. Luckily, Philip Hayes* scored up The Staircase Overture* from the set before the books containing its violin parts were lost. *See also* **Autographs**. *BroSta, ForOsb, HerHay, HolPur, ShaMan.*

'O sing unto the Lord' Z44 The last of Purcell's Chapel Royal* symphony anthems*, dated 1688 in John Gostling's* scorebook US-AUS, HRC 85. It is one of his most modern church works, with its Italianate symphony*; its division into separate movements; and its clear and directional harmonic language. Its seven movements form a musical arch, with the third and fifth in D minor and F minor surrounding a central ground-bass* duet and ritornello* in the home key, F major. Purcell explores a wide expressive range, encompassing the bold imperative of the opening bass solo; the reverential awe of the F minor verse and chorus; and the joyful choral acclamations of 'the Lord is king'. Equally impressive is the way Purcell uses direct or close motivic relationships to link the two sections of the symphony, the opening bass solo and the D minor verse quartet. The last chorus is full of ingenious counterpoint*: the subject is explored in prime and inversion, with independent upper string parts producing massive seven-part writing towards the end. *AdaPur, HolPur, VanChu, SpiCat, ZimGos.*

'O solitude, my sweetest choice' Z406 This superb ground-bass* air sets excerpts from 'La solitude' by Antoine Girard de Saint-Amant as translated in Katherine Philips's *Poems* (1667). It can be dated by its position in the largely autograph scorebook GB-Lbl, R.M. 20.h.8, ff. 174–173v to the winter of 1684–5, and it uses the same shapely ground in the same key, C minor, as the

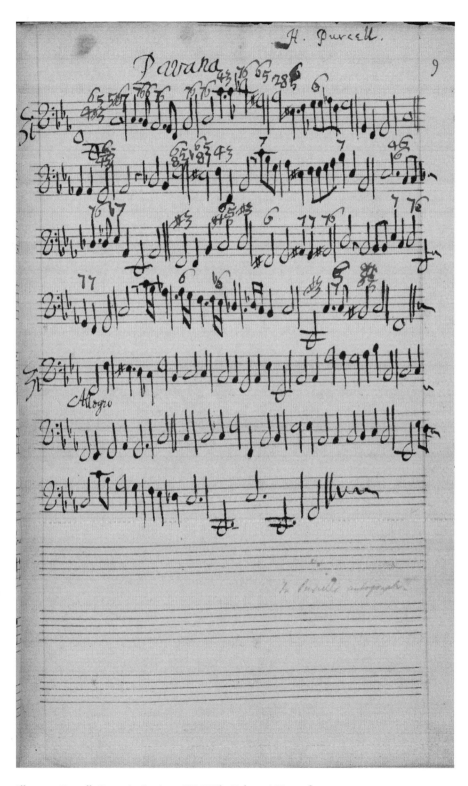

Illus. 10: Purcell, Pavan in F minor, US-NHb, Osborn MS 515, f. 9r.

symphony* to the then recently composed anthem 'In thee, O Lord, do I put my trust' Z16. The song is marked 'Very slow', an instruction reinforced by the fact that the ground is notated in 3/2, rather than 3/4 as in the anthem. It consists of 28 statements of the ground, unvaried but with fleeting modulations to G minor, F minor, A♭ major and E♭ major artfully introduced in the vocal part, a technique admired today but criticised by Roger North*. The voice part is beautifully varied, mixing declamatory gestures (particularly the three statements of 'O solitude' set respectively to a falling seventh, minor sixth and diminished fifth), with gravely tuneful elements. *AdaPur, HolPur, SchGro, ShaMan.*

Overture Purcell wrote more than 50 examples of the French type of overture associated with Lully*, with a duple-time first section typically featuring dotted rhythms, sharp dissonances* and bursts of semiquavers, and a contrasted fugal section usually in triple or compound time. Purcell used the word 'Overture' for those movements in his sets of theatre airs*, though he entitled those prefacing symphony anthems* and odes* 'Symphony'* – a word he also used for the Italianate type without the dotted first-section rhythms and often with a duple-time fugue or canzona*.

Sometimes, as in The Staircase Overture* or 'Laudate Ceciliam'*, the second section consists of a two-strain minuet*-like passage rather than a fugue, recalling a type popular in England and France before the Lully model became established in England. Conversely, the overtures to *King Arthur** and *Abdelazer** have energetic duple-time canzonas akin to those in Purcell's trio sonatas*. Not all of Purcell's first sections conform to the Lullian dotted type. Sometimes, as in the symphony anthem 'Behold, now praise the Lord' Z3 or the overture to *Distressed Innocence**, they are closer to almands* or duple-time airs*, with little or no scope for rhythmic alteration*. Occasionally, as in 'Welcome to all the pleasures'*, overtures start with a contrapuntal passage, and there are several symphony anthems (such as 'Unto thee will I cry, O Lord' Z63) where Purcell plays with the listener's expectations by starting with a contrapuntal first strain, which leads to a two-strain minuet – apparently without the customary repeat of the first section.

The fugal second sections are equally varied, though a near constant (following Lully) is the orderly succession of initial entries from treble to bass. Some are closely argued virtually monothematic fugues, as in the overture to *The Virtuous Wife**, though Purcell also favoured a type in which the first contrapuntal idea gives way halfway through to a second, as in *The Double Dealer** or *The Married Beau**, enabling him to expand the dimensions of his fugues without inserting episodes. In the overture to 'My heart is inditing'* (reused in 'Celestial music did the gods inspire'*) he combined the first idea halfway through with two new ones in a contrapuntal tour de force. Purcell expanded the dimensions of some of his later overtures by adding a concluding passage returning to the duple-time dotted notes of the opening. *AdaPur, HolPur, HolThe, PriPur, WolOve, WolVio.*

Oxford Purcell had a number of connections with the University of Oxford. He seems to have performed in the Music School at least once: Francis Withy's* score of the symphony anthem* version of 'My song shall be alway'* is dated 9 September 1690, perhaps indicating that it was performed around then under the composer's direction. William Heather's endowment of the music professorship, held during Purcell's working life by Edward Lowe (1661–82) and Richard Goodson* senior (1682–1718), provided for weekly practical music sessions. Visiting London musicians, including Matthew Locke* and John Blow*, wrote music to be performed there. The original sets of parts for Oxford academic odes, now in the Music School collection of the Bodleian Library, form the largest corpus of performing material surviving from Restoration England; they have important implications for the performance of Purcell. The Music School once owned a bust of the composer.

Oxford libraries contain many important Purcell sources, including those collected by Henry Aldrich*, whose library is a main component of the Christ Church music collection (catalogued in *CCLMC*); Richard Goodson, apparently a friend of Purcell with access to his autographs; and James Sherard, whose collection was a subsequent addition to the Music School collection. Other Purcell manuscripts at Oxford include three autographs* in GB-Ob, Mus.c.26; GB-Och, Mus. 628, Blow's score with most of Purcell's devotional part-songs; GB-Ob, MS Tenbury 1266, an important score of *Dido and Aeneas**; and four scores of Purcell's odes and theatre music in the library of Oriel College, GB-Ooc, MSS Ua 34–7, copied by the unidentified individual (an associate of Daniel Purcell*) labelled London E by Purcell scholars. *CruClu, HerCat, HolPar, PooPor, ShaMan, ShaSuc, SmiPer, SpiCat, ThoCha, ThoWit, WolOxf, WooAut, ZimPur.*

Paisible, James (Jacques) A French wind player, bass violinist and composer (*c.*1656–1721). He apparently first came to London in 1673 as a member of the group that introduced the Baroque oboe* and recorder* to England. He seems to have been in Scotland with James, Duke of York (the future James II*) between 1678 and 1682, and was one of the instrumentalists in James's Catholic Chapel in 1687 and 1688, following the king into exile and serving him at St Germain-en-Laye. He returned to London in 1693, developing a career in the household of Prince George* and Princess Anne* and in the theatre, writing at least 11 sets of theatre airs* for Drury Lane*. He continued to play in theatre bands long after 1700, and was a prominent recorder soloist in entr'acte entertainments during plays and in public concerts.

Paisible was almost certainly one of the recorder players who took part in Purcell's welcome songs* and other court music written during the reigns of Charles II* and James II, and he probably had an important influence on the development of Purcell's wind writing. He has been underestimated as a composer: he developed an effective synthesis between French and English idioms in his theatre airs, with fluent and thoroughly competent writing, beautifully conceived for the instruments. His airs for *Timon of Athens** were once thought to be by Purcell. *BDECM, BalBir, CorJam, HolFid, HolPur, HolThe, LasHau, LasRec, LeeCat, PriPur, PriThe, ThoIsa.*

Paspe The title given to the danced 'Entry of Hero's' in the Act V Masque from *Dioclesian**. Its binary form and rapid triple-time rhythmic patterns (notated in compound time) suggest that Purcell intended its title as an English variant of *passepied*, the fast dance popular at the French court from the 1680s. *See also* **Dance**.

Passacaglia (*passacalle, passacaille*) The name, apparently of Spanish origin, was originally used in Italian guitar* books for various strumming chord-sequence formulas. However, in the early seventeenth century, partly through Frescobaldi's influence, it became associated with a triple-time, minor-mode ground bass* of four notes descending from tonic to dominant, often elaborated, diversified with complementary ascending progressions and provided with modulations into related keys. In its chromatic form the descending-fourth bass was a potent emblem of love and death in seventeenth-century opera, exemplified by Dido's Lament*. The passacaglia was often paired and contrasted with the major-mode chaconne*, and after 1650 they began to converge, so that composers often forgot (or disregarded) the differences between the two archetypes. Thus Purcell's Chacony* in G minor and the Chaconne in D minor Z597/6 in the airs for *The Gordian Knot Unty'd** are essentially passacaglias rather than chaconnes. Purcell used the title Passacaglia only once, for the magnificent ground bass 'How happy the lover' Z628/30 in *King Arthur**, Act IV. With its mixture of vocal solos, choruses and orchestral passages accompanying dancing, it clearly refers to similar movements by Lully*, particularly the massive *passacaille* in Act V, Scene 2 of *Armide* (1686). HolPur, RosTet, SchCha, SchGro, SchLul, SilFre, SilPas, TylGui.

Pate, John The high tenor or countertenor* John Pate (d.1704) came to public attention in May 1692 in *The Fairy Queen**, taking the roles of Mopsa '*in Woman's habit*' ('Now the maids and the men' Z629/22) and Summer ('Here's the Summer sprightly gay' Z629/33). Purcell evidently valued him highly as a singer, giving him the spectacular solo '"Tis Nature's voice'* in 'Hail, bright Cecilia'* the following November. Pate was one of the most prominent English concert and theatre singers of the 1690s, though he repeatedly got into trouble. He was temporarily dismissed from Drury Lane* in June 1695 for taking part in a Jacobite riot and was briefly imprisoned in the Bastille in 1700 for killing a man in Paris. John Evelyn wrote on 30 May 1698 that, dining with Samuel Pepys*, he had heard 'that rare Voice, Mr. *Pate*, who was lately come from *Italy*, reputed the most excellent singer, ever England had: he sang indeede many rare Italian Recitatives, &c: & severall compositions of the last [late] Mr. Pursal, esteemed the best composer of any Englishman hitherto' (*EveDia*, v. 289). See also **Coridon and Mopsa**. BalCou, BalDel, BalSta, BDA, PriIsl.

Patrick, Dr John A Church of England clergyman (1632–95), from 1671 until his death the preacher at the London Charterhouse (a charitable hospital and school) and the author of *A Century of Select Psalms and Portions of the Psalms of David* (1679). These metrical psalm paraphrases were developed for use at the Charterhouse chapel to be sung to common psalm tunes. Around 1679–80 Purcell set nine of them as devotional part-songs*, copying them into his autograph* scorebook*, GB-Lbl, Add. MS 30930. There is no evidence they were sung at the Charterhouse, nor any evidence of direct contact between Purcell and Patrick. However, gentlemen from the Chapel Royal* sang from time to time at the annual Charterhouse Founder's Day, an event at which Patrick preached and for which Purcell (probably in 1688) composed the anthem 'Blessed is the man' for two voices and organ (*PS* 29, no. 4A), later adapted for cathedral use as a verse anthem Z9 (*PS* 29, 4B). *See also* **'Since God so tender a regard'**. *ForDom, HowSin, PorCha, ShaMan*.

Pavan Originally 'a kind of staide musique, ordained for graue dauncing' according to Thomas Morley*, pavans are typically in duple time with a minim beat and three repeated strains. Around 1600 the pavan became a genre of serious abstract instrumental music, cultivated particularly by English and north German composers. Purcell's Pavan in G minor Z752 for three violins and bass harks back to large-scale Jacobean pavans, using sharply contrasted material in each strain; a contrapuntal idea in the third undergoes subtle melodic and rhythmic changes in the manner of John Jenkins*. Its scoring relates it (and Three Parts upon a Ground*) to an early Restoration court tradition of three-violin music, notably including a suite by the expatriate German violinist Thomas Baltzar (including a splendidly expansive pavan) and ten fantasia suites by Jenkins.

Thurston Dart* suggested that Z752 was written in memory of Matthew Locke*, though if it is a memorial pavan (which is questionable), then Jenkins (d.1678) is the obvious candidate. Locke's influence is much stronger in Purcell's four pavans for two violins and bass, written around the same time. They are more modern and shorter, with a crotchet beat; they still have three strains but are closer to solemn almands*, with a single mood mostly prevailing and the interest maintained by angular melodic lines. They appear as a sequence in the sole source, GB-Lbl, Add. MS 33236: G minor Z751, A minor Z749, A major Z748 and B♭ major Z750, and may therefore be part of a projected collection in common keys ascending from Gamut*. The bass partbook Osborn MS 515* also contains autograph bass parts of two large-scale pavans in the then unusual key of F minor. It is difficult to say much about them just from a figured bass, though the second strain of one is in triple time – a feature of some earlier German and English pavans.

Purcell's enthusiasm for the pavan shows his early interest in old music: there do not seem to be standalone examples by other English composers after about 1640, and he must have been the last to show any interest in the genre before modern times. According to Thomas Mace* (*MacMus*, 129), pavans were 'very *Grave*, and *Sober*, Full of Art, and Profundity, but seldom us'd, in These our Light Days'. *DarCha, ForOsb, HolPur, HolVio, SchCon, ShaMan*.

Pearson, William *See* **John Heptinstall**

Pepys, Samuel The famous diary of this courtier and naval administrator (1633–1703) features in every account of music in Restoration England for his passionate love of the subject: 'music and women I cannot but give way to, whatever my business is'; 'music is the thing of the world that I love most' (*PepDia*, vii. 69–70, 228), as well as his detailed descriptions of music in the home and at court. He also left us precious glimpses of Purcell's older colleagues, used here for G.B. Draghi*, Henry Cooke*, Pelham Humfrey* and Pietro Reggio*. However, Pepys ended the Diary in 1669, when Purcell was still a choirboy, and we glimpse his musical activities thereafter mainly through letters, notably from the Flemish lutenist Cesare Morelli (calendared in *PagGui*, 242–5); Morelli, his household musician, was exiled to Brentwood between

1678 and 1682 because of the Popish Plot furore. There are some music manuscripts and printed collections of music in the Pepys Library at GB-Cmc, notably three anthologies of songs (including pieces by Lully* and a complete transcription of Reggio's *Songs*), copied and adapted by Morelli for Pepys's bass voice with guitar* accompaniment. They remain to be explored in detail, but they do not seem to contain any Purcell. However, Charles II's* presentation copy of *Sonnata's of III Parts** somehow came into his possession and is in the Pepys Library. *HerCat, MaiMor, ThoSou.*

Per arsin et thesin *See* **Counterpoint**

Performance history from 1695 Purcell's music continued in the repertory after his death in several performing situations. A few anthems, notably the organ-accompanied versions of 'Rejoice in the Lord alway'* and 'I was glad' Z19, continued to be performed by collegiate choirs, while the Te Deum and Jubilate in D major* was long a mainstay of national thanksgiving services, the Festival of the Sons of the Clergy, the Three Choirs Festival and provincial Cecilian celebrations*. Purcell's catches* continued to be reprinted, implying a continuing performing tradition; some of them were in the repertory of the Noblemen and Gentlemen's Catch Club, founded in 1761. Songs and excerpts from the stage works continued to be a regular feature of London public concerts and theatrical entr'actes in the early eighteenth century. Two of Purcell's mad songs*, 'From rosy bowers'* and 'From silent shades'* (normally called 'Mad Bess' in later times), had the longest life and were still favourite recital pieces in the early nineteenth century. Haydn took part in the concert in Oxford on 7 July 1791 when Nancy Storace sang 'Mad Bess', and probably accompanied her. He certainly accompanied Gertrude Elisabeth Mara in 'From rosy bowers' during her London benefit concert on 1 June 1792, describing it as 'a very difficult English aria by Purcell'.

The early music revival, led by the Academy of Ancient Music* (1726–1802) and the Concerts of Ancient Music* (1776–1848), overlapped to some extent with the continuous tradition. The former was responsible for some important revivals, including concert versions of *King Arthur** and *Dido and Aeneas**, while the latter had 'Celebrate this festival'* in its repertory, a rare complete revival of a Purcell ode. In the nineteenth century Purcell performances seem only to have been sporadic before the anniversary celebration of 1895 with its associated concerts, though the Purcell Club* had put on regular private performances between 1836 and 1863. Arnold Dolmetsch* began the revival of Purcell's consort music in the 1890s in his early music concerts, and he and his wife Elodie played harpsichords in Hans Richter's landmark concert performance of *King Arthur* in Birmingham in 1897. Gustav Holst directed the first complete revival of *The Fairy Queen** in 1911, made possible by the rediscovery of the complete score and its publication in 1903.

Most of the high-profile Purcell performances before the 1940s were of his theatre works, either in stage productions or in concerts, but Michael Tippett's* activities, initially at Morley College, brought the odes to the fore, notably 'Hail, bright Cecilia'*. Tippett's collaborations with Alfred Deller*, and Benjamin Britten's* performances with Peter Pears, also greatly increased concert performances of the songs, particularly in two concerts at the Wigmore

Hall in 1945, marking the 250th anniversary of Purcell's death. Eight concerts put on during the Festival of Britain in 1951 included rare performances (some probably the first in modern times) of *The Indian Queen**, the Act V masque from *Dioclesian**, the masque from *Timon of Athens** and Purcell's music for the *Don Quixote** plays. The number of Purcell performances increased steadily with the development of period-instrument groups in the 1970s, though there is still a tendency to repeat the same few symphony anthems*, odes and songs. Neglected pieces usually appear only in recordings*, to satisfy the demand for complete box sets of particular areas of the repertory. *See also* **Anniversary celebrations**, **Stage history from 1695**. *BalMad, ColMor, GroPur, HerRec, HigRec, HolLif, JohAca, LanHay, McVCal, PikRej, PurCon, RobCat, TupEig, WebCla, WhiCec.*

Performance practice Purcell, like other seventeenth-century composers, has suffered from the tendency to perform his music in a mid-eighteenth-century style. This was partly inherited from that period, with its modernisations of works such as 'Come, ye sons of art, away'*, the Te Deum and Jubilate in D major* and *Dido and Aeneas**. However, it was aggravated by the twentieth-century concept of 'Baroque music', which assumed a common idiom and performing style from 1600 to 1750, with the detailed treatises by Quantz, Geminiani and C.P.E. Bach routinely applied to seventeenth-century music. Until recently, for instance, it was assumed that Purcell's orchestral bass lines were played by violoncellos and double basses, and one still hears singers applying to his solo vocal music the long appoggiaturas recommended by Quantz.

More recently there has been an equally anachronistic tendency to apply the continuo* scoring of Monteverdi* and his contemporaries to Purcell, with harps, regals and strumming guitars*. Thankfully, the 1960s fashion for applying overdotting to Purcell's overtures has receded, though the rhythms of his carefully conceived declamatory vocal writing are still altered without justification, and it is open to question to what extent the French system of *notes inégales* should be applied to his music. Our performance practice desiderata for the future include performers taking Purcell's time signatures seriously for determining tempo* and tempo relationships; using organs at high pitch* for his church music; encouraging the application of 'graces' (trills and appoggiaturas) to his vocal and instrumental music; and high tenors rather than falsettists singing his 'countertenor'* parts. *See also* **Orchestra**, **Ornamentation**, **Rhythmic alteration**. *HolNot, JonSon, LauCon, MorVoi, ParPer, RosPer.*

Performing material The manuscripts Purcell's performers sang or played from divide into two main types: (1) what has been termed 'single-occasion' sets of parts, prepared for a specific performance and usually copied onto loose sheets; and (2) sets of partbooks intended for repeated use. Sets of printed parts, such as *Sonnata's of III Parts**, are effectively an extension of the second type. Singers normally read from individual voice parts in concerted music. Scores were used in performance for directing from the keyboard, and for solo instrumental or vocal music, as in the Gresham autograph*.

Hardly any material of the first type survives, in part because the performing material for Purcell's concerted music written for the court was apparently consumed in the fire that destroyed Whitehall* in 1698. A lucky survival is the part-autograph set of string parts (GB-Och, Mus. 1188/9) for 'My song shall be alway'*, perhaps prepared for a performance in Oxford* in 1690. Nothing survives of the original material for Purcell's non-court odes, and the only single-occasion part for his theatre music seems to be GB-Ob, MS Tenbury 1278, a voice part copied for Richard Leveridge* to learn his roles in *The Indian Queen**. It is likely that the original sets of parts for Purcell's dramatic operas* were not collected and preserved from production to production; revisions and cast changes would often have prevented their reuse. Tellingly, *The Fairy Queen** could no longer be staged once the original theatre score (now GB-Lam, MS 3) disappeared in or shortly after 1695. Purcell probably used the autograph* scores of his concerted music to direct performances from the keyboard, though he might have preferred a copy in stratigraphic* format, such as GB-Cfm, Mu. MS 684, William Isaack's* early loose-leaf score of 'Who can from joy refrain?'*.

There is a little more early performing material for Purcell's church music. Important items are the first layers of the Chapel Royal* partbooks, GB-Lbl, R.M. 27.a.1–8; sets, now fragmentary, copied for the Chapel and Westminster Abbey* by William Tucker*; an autograph fragment of a bass vocal part from 'I was glad' Z19 (current whereabouts unknown); and GB-Cfm, Mu. MS 152, the remains of one or more Chapel Royal organ books with two pieces in Purcell's hand. GB-Mp, BRm370Bp35, a collection of organ parts copied by John Blow*, probably for St Paul's Cathedral* in the late 1690s, includes eight Purcell works. The bass partbook Osborne MS 515* includes some early autographs, virtually the only performing material of Purcell's consort music demonstrably from his milieu. *See also* **Autographs**. *HerCat, HerCre, HerOrg, HolBat, HolPar, HolPur, ShaMan, SmiPer, ThoSou, WhiPre, WooAut, ZimCat.*

Pigott (Pickett), Francis Organist and composer (1665/6–1704), probably from a musical London family. He was a Chapel Royal* choirboy (1678–83) and did brief stints as organist of St John's College and Magdalen College, Oxford* before becoming in 1688 the first organist of the Temple Church. There he played the new instrument by Bernard Smith* – the victor of the Battle of the Organs*. Pigott also became a Chapel Royal organist in 1695 despite having promised the Temple authorities he would not be 'organist in any other church or chapel whatsoever'. He died on 15 May 1704 and was succeeded at the Temple by his son John (d.1762). His small surviving output (a few songs and a duet from his otherwise lost 1694 Cecilian ode*; a few keyboard pieces; and a full anthem, 'I was glad', for Queen Anne's* coronation in 1702) is of high quality. His early death was clearly a serious loss. Pigott has been proposed as London A*, an important copyist of Purcell's works, though one London A manuscript includes a piece apparently copied from a collection published in 1707, after his death. *BDECM, CBCR, HerCat, HolCla, PriIsl, RanCor, RanPig, SpiCat, SpiSoc, ShaMan, WhiCec, WhiMer.*

Pills to Purge Melancholy *Wit and Mirth, or Pills to Purge Melancholy*, the immensely popular collection of 'the best Merry BALLADS and SONGS, Old and New', was published by Henry Playford* in 1699 in duodecimo format; it was intended to compete with Thomas Cross's* single-sheet songs. Further volumes, with many reprints and enlarged editions, appeared up to 1720, when in its final six-volume form it consisted of more than 1,100 songs and poems, mostly printed with their tunes. Thomas D'Urfey*, often credited with collecting and editing the whole collection, was an important contributor, but apparently only acted as editor in 1719, when the first five volumes were briefly renamed *Songs Compleat, Pleasant and Divertive*. Many of Purcell's more popular songs were included in the various editions, as well as some mock-songs* based on his theatre airs*, such as the ballad 'Enfield Common', set to the Hornpipe Z572/7 from *Amphitryon**. *CarPub, DaySon, HerCro, MPP, SimBal, ZimCat.*

Pindar, Robert Cambridge academic (1739–95), Fellow of King's College, Cambridge from 1765 to 1776. He was the copyist of a manuscript dated 1765, now GB-Lcm, MS 993, containing modernised versions of Purcell's odes 'Welcome to all the pleasures'*, The Yorkshire Feast Song*, 'Hail, bright Cecilia'* and 'Come, ye sons of art, away'*. Authoritative sources survive for the first three, showing that Pindar made drastic and sometimes inept changes to them. These included adding new instrumental movements, amplifying the scoring and modernising the word-setting and underlay. However, Pindar's score is the only surviving complete source of 'Come, ye sons of art, away', and was therefore the basis of all editions, performances and recordings until Rebecca Herissone published her reconstruction of Purcell's original version. It is likely that Pindar made his versions of Purcell for a performing group in Cambridge, though there is no record of performances there of these odes at that time. *BroFac, HerPin, ShaMan, TalPin.*

Pitch There was no fixed pitch standard in seventeenth-century Europe: it varied from place to place and between different performing situations. Purcell would have been familiar with two main pitches, a high one for sacred music and a much lower one for secular music. The evidence from surviving organ* pipes and documentary evidence suggests that what Bruce Haynes labelled Quire Pitch (about $a' = 473$) was a common English church pitch. Bernard Smith* lowered his organ in the chapel at Whitehall* to it in 1676, and it was therefore the one used for Purcell's Chapel Royal* anthems. Much of Purcell's secular music from the early 1680s, including court odes*, symphony songs* and theatre music, requires woodwind instruments, and therefore its pitch can be determined from surviving recorders* by Peter Bressan*. Many of these play at about $a' = 405$, a minor third lower than Quire Pitch; it was called Consort Pitch and was about the same as the French *Ton de la chambre du Roy*.

Today's all-purpose 'Baroque pitch' of $a' = 415$ is therefore a little too high for Purcell's secular works and much too low for his church music. For this reason, Purcell's anthems are sometimes transposed today up a tone or a minor third from the original keys, which helps with the ranges of the voice parts, particularly if the countertenor* parts are sung by falsettists. However, transposition changes the sonority of the string parts of symphony anthems*, and works put as a result into a remote key can cause problems when accompanied by an organ in unequal temperament*. *GwyPur, HayPit, MorVoi, ParPer, RosPer.*

The Plaint Z629/40 Few pieces in the Purcell canon have aroused as much controversy as 'O let me weep', entitled The Plaint. It was added in 1693 to Act

V, Scene 1 of *The Fairy Queen**; is not in the part-autograph score; and was not published until *Orpheus Britannicus**, book 1 (1698). For one thing its scoring is uncertain: the obbligato part, assigned to a violin in *Orpheus Britannicus*, has a simple 'vocal' quality that suggests a wind instrument, and one now-lost manuscript (see *PS* 12, 268) apparently specified an oboe*. However, some of the oboe indications in late Purcell sources cannot be taken at face value, and the restricted range of the part ($f'–b^{b\,\prime\prime}$) suggests the treble recorder*, often associated at the time with despairing love.

More important, critics are divided about the quality of the Plaint, an extended ground bass* on a freely varied and modulating version of the passacaglia*, organised like a da capo aria*. Some see it as one of Henry Purcell's finest achievements: Ian Spink compared it to Dido's Lament*, while Bruce Wood and Andrew Pinnock characterised it as 'in Purcell's best melancholy manner'. However, Curtis Price thought it 'an over-indulgence; interminable, especially at the slow tempo at which it is usually performed'. We agree with Price, and wonder whether it was actually written by one of Henry Purcell's followers. *HolPur, PriPur, SpiSon, WooFai*.

Playford, John and Henry 'Honest' John Playford (?1621–87) was effectively the father of the London music-publishing trade. He came from his native Norwich in 1640 to be apprenticed to a London bookseller, and set up his own shop at the porch of the Temple Church in 1647, starting to publish music in 1651. He took advantage of the fact that the twin monopolies on metrical psalm books and polyphonic part-music, established under Elizabeth I, had been abolished by Parliament during the Civil War. He cannily began to cater systematically for amateur musicians, issuing cheap instruction books-cum-anthologies for cittern and gittern, lyra viol*, treble viol or violin, keyboard and flageolet. There are also collections of simple consort music; several types of theory books (notably the long-lived series *An Introduction to the Skill of Musick**); and *The Dancing Master*, the latter with choreographies as well as tunes. In addition, he published several types of metrical psalm books; collections of devotional part-songs*; and simple glees and catches*. Most important for the young Purcell, he started a rolling series of handsome folios anthologising the rich repertory of English 'ayres and dialogues' from Jacobean composers to his own time.

Playford began to include substantial numbers of Purcell's songs in *Choice Ayres and Songs*, books 2 (1679), 3 (1681) and 4 (1683), developing a close relationship with the young composer. He prompted Purcell's setting of Cowley's* 'She loves and she confesses too'* as a corrective to faulty accentuation in Pietro Reggio's* setting; and doubtless encouraged the composer to employ Thomas Cross* to engrave *Sonnata's of III Parts** (1683), which he sold in conjunction with John Carr*. He has been criticised for undermining the market for serious and ambitious collections: he only published two- and three-part consort music and mostly only the solo sections of odes* and symphony songs*. However, that overlooks his role as a music copyist and the organiser of an active scriptorium. A more pertinent criticism is that he relied too long on traditional typesetting, using his old-fashioned Granjon font with individual lozenge-shaped notes; he reserved engraving mostly for *Musick's Hand-Maid** and *The Division-Violin* (1684 onwards). Only the simplest keyboard music could be typeset, and divisions* are more legible with proper

Illus. 11: John Playford.

beaming, easily achieved by an engraver imitating hand-written music. Cross apparently imitated Playford's own hand when engraving *Sonnata's of III Parts*.

John Playford announced in 1684 that he was handing the business over to 'two young men': his only surviving son Henry (1657–1709) and the court violinist Robert Carr*; the music printer John Playford junior (1650–85) was his nephew. John senior died in January 1687, leaving Purcell a mourning ring in his will, and the composer reciprocated with a superb elegy to words by Nahum Tate*, 'Gentle shepherds, you that know' Z464, published separately by Henry Playford in 1687. Henry and Robert Carr evidently resolved to continue the various lines developed by John Playford, starting ambitiously with *The Theater of Music* (1685–7). They made a point of including '*Symphonies* and *Retornels* in 3 Parts ... for the *Violins* and *Flutes*' (i.e. recorders*), which enabled theatre songs and symphony songs to be printed complete, a policy maintained with *The Banquet of Music* (1688–92) and *Deliciae musicae* (1695–6). However, Carr soon dropped out and it became apparent that Henry lacked his father's business acumen. He remained wedded to typesetting in the face of the cheap engraved editions produced in the 1690s by Cross and John Walsh*, relying instead on the 'new tied note' developed by his printer John Heptinstall*, an imperfect solution at best. He seems to have diversified into promoting concerts and dealing in fine art, but to little effect, and he apparently ceased commercial activity in 1707.

Henry Playford's memorial is his loyalty to, and support for, the Purcell family. The composer featured prominently in his song books; in *Musick's Hand-Maid*, part 2 (1689), which he 'carefully Revised and Corrected'; and in *Harmonia Sacra** (1688, 1693 and later editions), superb collections of devotional songs and dialogues. Playford also collaborated with the family in the memorial volumes of his music: *A Choice Collection** (1696) of keyboard music; *A Collection of Ayres**, the collected theatre airs*; *Ten Sonata's in Four Parts**; the Te Deum and Jubilate in D major* (all 1697); and the various editions of *Orpheus Britannicus** (from 1698). He also published John Blow's* *Ode on the Death of Henry Purcell** (1696) and the song book *Amphion Anglicus* (1700), the latter a worthy imitation of *Orpheus Britannicus*. Had Henry Playford embraced Thomas Cross and his engraving when he inherited the business in 1684, then the subsequent history of music publishing in London (and the reception of Purcell's music) would have been rather different. *See also* **Editions from 1695, Printing and Publishing**. *CarPla, CarPub, ChaMee, DaySon, HarPla, HerCro, HerPla, HerThe, HolPur, HumPub, KruPri, LucPla, MPP, MunPla, SchAyr, SpiSoc, SpiSon, TemPla, ThoMan, ThoPla, ThoSou, TilCha.*

Poems praising Purcell Henry Purcell's unexpected death on 21 November 1695 inspired an unprecedented number of poetic elegies for a musician, by, among others, John Dryden*, Nahum Tate*, James Talbot*, Henry Hall* and the poet and politician John Sheffield, Duke of Buckingham, as well as anonymous authors or those hiding behind initials. Many were printed in the two volumes of *Orpheus Britannicus**, including those by 'H.P.' (doubtless Henry Playford*) and 'R.G' (probably Richard Goodson* senior), though the satirist Thomas Brown* had already published a poem, *'To his unknown Friend, Mr.* Henry Purcell', in *Harmonia Sacra**, book 2 (1693). Later poetic tributes include a section of Christopher Smart's *Ode for Musick on St Cecilia's Day* (1746), set to music by William Russell (?1803), and Gerard Manley Hopkins's sonnet *Henry Purcell* (April 1879). *See also* **Odes on the death of Henry Purcell**. *BurRem, PicHal, HigRec, HowOde, LucSha, PinPhe, WhiCec, ZimPoe, ZimPur.*

Political allegory The practice of identifying living people with characters from myth, history or the Bible was common in Restoration literature. Such parallels were drawn in two ways. In an allegorical work specific one-to-one correspondences were made between fictional characters, groups or ideas and living people, as in Louis Grabu's* opera *Albion and Albanius*, in which John Dryden* intended the title characters to represent Charles II* and his brother the future James II*. In court odes* references to 'Caesar' routinely signified the current monarch. Anthem texts* were sometimes chosen to create an analogy between King David (traditionally believed to be the Psalmist) and the monarch, or were assembled to reflect great events such as coronations*. More commonly, parallels were drawn in general terms, by which a pattern or situation in a text was 'applied' to a contemporary situation. Such readings might be intended by the author, might arise serendipitously (or otherwise) through changed circumstances, or might be created independently by audiences. In the case of Saul and the Witch of Endor*, some people in the 1690s might have associated Saul with the deposed James II, whether or not Purcell intended this application when choosing the text and setting it to music.

The existence of allegorical schemes in Purcell's theatre works, especially covert or subversive ones, has been hotly debated. Changing and competing allegorical readings of *Dido and Aeneas**, several of which have been invalidated by new information about its date, demonstrate the danger of such interpretations. Several allegorical readings of *Dioclesian** have been proposed even though it was a minimally altered adaptation of a Jacobean play. Allegorical and applied readings have been suggested more plausibly for *King Arthur**, but no scholarly consensus has been reached. *HumPol*, *PinDou*, *PriPur*, *WalAll*, *WalPol*, *WhiPol*, *WooDid*.

Portraits Of the large number of portraits said to represent Purcell, only three seem to be true-to-life images, the apparent sources for most of those reproduced and discussed in *ZimPur*, 349–88:

(1): National Portrait Gallery, NPG 2150, an anonymous and rather poor oval head-and-shoulders painting of Purcell as a young man, said to have been given by him to the singer, composer and copyist John Church (1674–1741). It was evidently the model for many later images, including a late eighteenth-century watercolour now at the Royal Academy of Music; see *SnoPor*.

Illus. 12:
Henry Purcell (1683).

(2): The oval head-and-shoulders engraving of Purcell in his 24th year, used for the frontispiece of *Sonnata's of III Parts** (1683) and probably engraved by Robert White. Among the later images connected with it is the engraving by Charles Grignion printed in *HawHis*, ii. facing 742.

(3): NPG 4994, John Closterman's* fine head-and-shoulders chalk drawing, done in 1695. Images derived directly or indirectly from it include: NPG 1352, a painting perhaps executed after Purcell's death by Closterman's brother John Baptist; British Museum, 1885.0509.1897, an anonymous drawing; and Robert White's reversed engraving, published in *Orpheus Britannicus**, book 1 (1698).

Paintings too often presented as portraits of Henry Purcell include NPG 1463 and Royal Society of Musicians, AS33/ART7. Neither is at all convincing in this role, and they seem to depict different people, though they have both been said to be of Daniel Purcell*. AS33/ART7, a man with a long, thin face holding a roll of paper, is the more convincing in this latter role. In 1920 W.A. Shaw (*ShaPor*) included photographs of three paintings he claimed were of Henry Purcell, though without revealing their provenance or ownership; they do not seem to have surfaced since. From Shaw's commentary (and what can be deduced from the poor images) it seems that nos. 1 and 2 show young musicians in what may be court uniform, one at a table with papers and a stringed instrument, the other seated at a music desk holding a large viola with an organ behind; no. 3 clearly derives from Closterman's drawing, though also with an organ behind. Nos. 1 and 2 show individuals clearly too young to be Purcell for 1685 and 1689 (the dates given by Shaw) and are not convincing likenesses. A bust of Purcell by John Bacon senior (1740–99), now lost, was given by Philip Hayes* to the Oxford* Music School (*PooPor*, 165). *DunSon, HolPor, LucSha, RogClo.*

'Praise the Lord, O Jerusalem' Z46 It was only recognised in the 1970s that Purcell wrote this expansive symphony anthem* for the coronation* of William III* and Mary II* in Westminster Abbey* on 11 April 1689. It was performed after their joint crowning, so Henry Compton, Bishop of London, compiled a text including a slightly altered version of Isaiah 49:23: 'For kings shall be thy nursing fathers, and queens thy nursing mothers'. It would have been sung by the joint Chapel Royal* and Westminster Abbey choirs, probably with about 30 royal string players, and it is likely that the verse passages (there are none for single voices) were sung more than one to a part. The primary source, a contribution apparently made by London A* to GB-Lbl, R.M. 20.h.8, does not always distinguish between verse and full passages, an issue not resolved satisfactorily in modern editions. Purcell used a suitably grand but rather impersonal idiom, though there are some memorable moments, including the mysterious opening to the Symphony*, indebted to the opening of G.B. Draghi's* *Song for St Cecilia's Day, 1687*; the powerful setting of the words 'Be thou exalted, Lord'; and the conclusion to the Alleluia, with its wild C♮s and F♮s in D-major tonic pedal harmonies. *See also* **Coronations**. *BurCha, HolBat, RanCor, ShaMan.*

Prelude Purcell started a number of his keyboard suites* with preludes, ranging in nature from a short and simple series of arpeggiated chords, as in the Prelude in G major Z660/1, to the brilliant toccata-like movement Z662/1, also in G major. Of the four preludes in Purcell's section of the Purcell-Draghi Manuscript*, three are clearly didactic: no. 1 is a simple exploration of scale-passages in C major, probably for a pupil's first lesson; no. 8 is a version of a famous G major teaching piece by Orlando Gibbons*, exploring runs in semiquavers; while no. 18 turns out to be a metrical version of an anonymous French unmeasured prelude, with Purcell's detailed fingering. Purcell also used the word 'prelude' for single-section instrumental ensemble pieces introducing vocal works, such as the famous passage imitating bells in 'Rejoice in the Lord alway'*, or the movement introducing the incantation scene in *Oedipus**. *CooKey, HogCor, HogMan, HolPur, LedSty, ShaMan, WooKey, ZimCat.*

Priest, Josias Dancer and dancing master (buried 3 January 1735). He is first heard of in August 1667, when he danced in John Dryden's* play *Sir Martin Mar-All*. John Downes* (*DowRos*, 63, 89) wrote that he devised dances for the spectacular production of *Macbeth* at Dorset Garden* in February 1673, as well as for Purcell's dramatic operas* *Dioclesian**, *King Arthur** and *The Fairy Queen**, while Thomas Bray* also credited him with devising a dance for *The Indian Queen**. He is last known to have danced on stage in the dramatic opera *The Island Princess* (February 1699). In 1712 John Weaver, writing about 'GROTESQUE *Dancing*' (*WeaDan*, 164–7), described him as 'the greatest Master of this kind of *Dancing*, that has appear'd on our Stage'.

Documents refer to Josiah, Josias, Joseph and Jonas Priest, though they probably all denote the same man. He is best known as the proprietor of the 'Boarding-School of Gentlewomen' at Gorges House in Chelsea, where John Blow's* *Venus and Adonis* and Purcell's *Dido and Aeneas** were performed respectively in 1684 and 1687–8. He had moved his school from Leicester Fields in 1680; it was at Lawrence Street in Chelsea from January 1712 to 1714. *See also* **Dance**. *BalHon, BDECM, LS, SemDan, ThoOpe, ThoPri, WhiAle.*

Printing and publishing English music publishing, stymied by court monopolies and then the Civil War, lagged far behind developments abroad. In the 1650s John Playford* began to cater systematically for amateur musicians, issuing series of cheap instruction books-cum-anthologies for various instruments, collections of songs and dialogues and some simple consort music. In addition, *An Introduction to the Skill of Musick** and *The Dancing Master* (with its choreographies for country dances*) became institutions and were continued by other publishers into the eighteenth century. Playford largely issued typeset editions, though single-composer publications, such as Purcell's *Sonnata's of III Parts**, were usually produced at the authors' expense, supported through subscription and/or patronage and often engraved to allow short print runs.

John Playford's business was continued by his son Henry, who lacked his father's business acumen. Henry remained largely wedded to typesetting in the face of the cheap engraved single-sheet editions, produced in the 1690s by Thomas Cross* and then John Walsh*; Walsh was the first London publisher to engrave music on a large scale. By contrast, Henry Playford employed the printer John Heptinstall* to use his 'new tied note' typeface to produce the full score of *Dioclesian** (1691) and then the 'memorial' Purcell collections (1696–8). Nevertheless, most of Purcell's concerted works remained unpublished until much later, and eighteenth-century musicians mostly encountered Purcell's music through the various editions of *Orpheus Britannicus** or reprints derived from them. *See also* **Editions from 1695**. *CarPla, CarPub, DaySon,*

HerCro, HerPla, HigRec, HumPub, HunPri, KruPri, LucPla, MPP, SchDio, SmiWal, ThoSou, ZimCat.

The Private Music The select group that had access to the Privy Chamber, the collective name for the private apartments at Whitehall* and other palaces. There they taught the royal family music and entertained them with solo performances and varied vocal and instrumental ensembles. At the Restoration it initially consisted of solo singers, lutenists, viol players, two or three violinists, several keyboard players and a harpist, though Charles II's* fondness for French-style orchestral music soon ensured that this heterogeneous group was quickly supplanted by a section of the Twenty-Four Violins*. In 1685 James II* embarked on a reform of the royal household, the first since the reign of Henry VIII, abolishing the Tudor distinction between Privy and Presence Chamber. Most of the court instrumentalists were combined into a new Private Music, effectively turning it into an up-to-date Baroque orchestra* of wind, strings and continuo. This institution, later called the Royal Band, lingered on into the nineteenth century, at least on paper. *HolFid, HolPur, RECM.*

The Prophetess See **Dioclesian** Z627

Prompter This crucial figure in the Restoration theatre helped the actors with their lines, but also fulfilled (in modern terms) the roles of librarian, publicist, producer and stage manager. He stood in the wings stage left (later known as the Prompt side) with a marked-up copy of the wordbook in his hand; a whistle on a chain around his neck to signal scene changes to the stagehands; and a little bell hanging from his arm to cue the music. It is possible that John Downes*, prompter for the United Company*, had a role in directing Purcell's dramatic operas* by beating time for the chorus and dancers, though this was probably done, in the Dorset Garden Theatre* at least, from the orchestra pit. *HolBat.*

Purcell Club Formed in 1836 with James Turle (organist of Westminster Abbey*) as conductor, this group met twice a year for a dinner in a London tavern followed by a concert of Purcell's works; its summer meetings followed a morning service in the Abbey. In 1842 the singer and editor Edward Taylor (1784–1863) was elected president; he apparently organised the Purcell anniversary celebration* in 1858. The club was wound up after Taylor's death and its library deposited at Westminster Abbey. Its name is currently used by a male-voice choir, formed in 1927 by former Westminster Abbey choristers. *See also* **Musical Antiquarian Society**. *GroPur, PinPhe.*

Purcell, Daniel The organist and composer Daniel Purcell (c.1664–1717) was consistently said in early sources to have been Henry's younger brother, though it has been argued (wrongly in our opinion) that he was actually the youngest son of Thomas Purcell (d.1682) and was therefore Henry's cousin. Daniel was a Chapel Royal* choirboy, known to have attended at Windsor* in the summers of 1678, 1679 and 1682. His whereabouts are unknown from then until late 1688, when he was appointed organist of Magdalen College, Oxford*, though he was already writing music, contributing a song to *Vinculum societatis*, book

1 (June 1687). He developed rapidly as a composer at Oxford, writing anthems and the Cecilian ode 'Begin and strike th'harmonious lyre' (1693), possibly for the music club at the Mermaid Tavern.

Daniel evidently returned to London after Henry's death in November 1695 to provide music for the Drury Lane Theatre*, completing *The Indian Queen** by writing the Act V masque and probably contributing a duet to *Pausanias*, Richard Norton's tragedy, for which Henry had written 'Sweeter than roses'*. He set Nahum Tate's* 'Lamentation on the Death of Mr. Henry Purcell' (the music is lost), and was probably the compiler and editor of the memorial volumes of Henry's music, published by Henry Playford* between 1696 and 1698. He collaborated with Jeremiah Clarke* in writing theatre music for Christopher Rich's* company, notably for the dramatic opera* *The Island Princess* (1699). He continued to write theatre music, coming third in the competition to set William Congreve's* masque *The Judgment of Paris* (1701), though he was also organist of St Dunstan-in-the-East (from at least 1698) and later also of St Andrew, Holborn. He published sonatas and cantatas suitable for amateurs, suggesting a sideline as a music teacher.

Daniel Purcell is suspected as the author of some works listed in *ZimCat*, including 'When Night her purple veil'* and the Magnificat and Nunc Dimittis in G minor Z231. Hawkins* (*HawHis*, ii. 759) wrote that he 'derived most of that little reputation which as a musician he possessed' from his brother. Henry certainly provided fatally attractive models, such as the canzona* from the symphony to 'Come, ye sons of art, away'*, slavishly but flat-footedly imitated in the equivalent movement of Daniel's 1698 Cecilian ode 'Begin the noble song' (ed. *WhiCec*, 149–51). Daniel's music is often unambitious and derivative (Clarke was another influence), though it is rarely technically incompetent, and in his best works, such as *The Judgment of Paris* (1701), there are glimpses of a potential never fully realised. *See also* **Portraits**, **Purcell family**, **Services**. *BalBro, BDECM, HerCre, HowOde, PriIsl, PriPur, PriThe, WhiCec, ZimPur.*

Purcell-Draghi Manuscript This oblong quarto, the first substantial Purcell autograph* to be discovered for more than a century and the only one for solo keyboard, was sold at Sotheby's on 26 May 1994 and was subsequently acquired by the British Library; it is now MS Mus. 1. It consists of two sequences: 21 pieces in Purcell's hand (ed. *PurTwe*) and (at the other end with the volume reversed) 17 pieces composed and copied by G.B. Draghi* (ed. *WooPer*), Purcell's court colleague. It is likely that they were both working for an unidentified pupil, or perhaps several pupils in a single family, Purcell probably in 1693–4, Draghi a little later. Purcell's section was clearly intended to instruct a beginner, with simple preludes* (one a long-lived teaching piece by Orlando Gibbons*); arrangements of pieces from theatre airs* (including a hornpipe* by John Eccles*); and, at the end, variant versions of two suites published in *A Choice Collection**. Nine pieces were previously unknown. Draghi's section of the manuscript, less obviously didactic, includes four pieces previously unknown. *PriAut, HogCor, HogMan.*

Purcell family Henry Purcell was the son and nephew of two singers in the Chapel Royal* and the Private Music*: he was the son of Henry (?1624–64) and Elizabeth (d.1699). However, Thomas (1627–82) referred to him as 'my sonne

Henry' in a letter of 8 February 1679 (transcription in *WesPur*, 305), probably because he acted as parent to Henry junior and his brothers Edward and Daniel, securing court positions for them after Henry senior's death. Henry senior and Thomas were only minor composers (the part-song 'Sweet tyranness, I now resign my heart' ZS69, published in 1667 with an attribution to 'Mr. Hen. Pursell' is probably by him rather than his precocious son), while only an Anglican chant and a catch* survives attributed to Thomas, despite him being a composer to the Twenty-Four Violins* – one of no fewer than seven court posts held by this extraordinary pluralist. Only Daniel Purcell* became a musician among Henry junior's siblings and cousins.

In 1679 or 1680 Henry Purcell married Frances (d.1706), the daughter of John Baptista Peters or Pieters, a leather merchant of Flemish extraction working in London. Only one of their children was a musician: Edward (1689–1740) became organist of St Clement Eastcheap in 1711, adding St Margaret's, Westminster in 1726; he was the author of two published songs. Edward's son Edward Henry (d.1765) succeeded his father at St Clement Eastcheap. Frances stated in her will (*ZimPur*, 282–3) that, 'according to her husband's desire' she had given Edward a 'good education' and left him 'all the books of music in general, the organ, the double spinnet, the single spinnet'. Frances played an important role preserving and disseminating Purcell's music by initiating the series of 'memorial' publications with Henry Playford*. *See also* **Editions, from 1695**. *BalBro, BDECM, DufPur, DunNew, ThoGlo, WesPur, WooPur, ZimPur.*

Purcell, pronunciation of his name Today, the surname Purcell is often stressed on the second syllable, but we know from the scansion of a line from John Dryden's* poem on Henry's death ('So ceas'd the rival Crew when *Pur*cell came', see Illus. 9, p. 125), and from parallel cases such as 'violin' and 'pavan', that such two-syllable words were generally stressed on the first syllable in the seventeenth century. So: *Pur*cell, not Pur*cell*. *HowOde*.

Purcell Society Founded in 1876, it was originally a membership organisation devoted to doing justice 'to the memory of Henry Purcell, firstly by the publication of his works ... and, secondly, by meeting for the study and performance of his various compositions', according to the original prospectus. Performance was quickly forgotten, but publication began in 1878 with the Yorkshire Feast Song*, ed. W.H. Cummings; 25 more volumes followed until 1928, when publication was suspended. Editors included the composers Arthur Somervell, Charles Villiers Stanford and Ralph Vaughan Williams, as well as early-music specialists such as G.E.P. Arkwright, J.A. Fuller Maitland and Edward Dent. The Society was revived in 1950, and between 1957 and 1965 six more volumes were published, edited by Thurston Dart*, Anthony Lewis, Arnold Goldsborough and others, making 32 in all. The Society continues to issue revised volumes more in line with current scholarly standards, and it initiated the Purcell Tercentenary Committee, which coordinated the 1995 anniversary celebrations*. Novello & Co published the Edition until 2007, when Stainer & Bell* took over the role. Between 2008 and 2018 the Society published six volumes of its Companion Series, largely of music by composers who influenced Purcell, including Louis Grabu*, John Blow* and G.B. Draghi*. *See also* **Vincent Novello**. *GroPur*.

'Raise, raise the voice' Z334 This fine but neglected work is usually thought of as a Cecilian ode*, though its anonymous text contains no reference to the saint; it is instead concerned with Apollo and 'Sacred Music's holy day'. Its scoring for three voices, two violins and continuo implies it is really a symphony song*, as does its inclusion in a group of those pieces in a court-related score, now GB-Lbl, Add. MS 33287. Purcell published a keyboard setting of one of its ritornellos* (ZT688) in *Musick's Hand-maid*, part 2 (1689), which reinforces the impression that it dates from early in James II's* reign. A score and set of parts, GB-Och, Mus. 1145, 470, was seemingly copied for a performance in Oxford*. The work is notable for its independent writing for the violins: they fill out the textures in tutti sections rather than doubling, and in the fine ground-bass* treble air 'Mark how readily each pliant string' they alternate with the voice and contribute a fine ritornello. See also **Richard Goodson**. HerCat, HolPur, ShaMan, SpiOde, WhiCec.

Reading, John, organist of Winchester The various Readings active as musicians in Restoration England are hard to disentangle, though this one (c.1645–92) became organist and master of the choristers at Winchester Cathedral in 1675, transferring to Winchester College as organist in 1681. He is probably the person who was a choirboy at St Paul's Cathedral* (1661); a clerk at Lincoln (1667) and Master of the Choristers there (1670); and briefly organist and master of the choristers at Chichester (1675). As a composer, he is mainly remembered for setting 'Dulce domum' (the Winchester College song), though he is more important as a Purcell copyist. He may have had direct contact with the composer between 1682 and 1684, when the court made annual visits to Winchester*. His scorebook* GB-Lbl, R.M. 20.h.9 includes the only copy of Purcell's Overture in D minor Z771; the only complete copies of Three Parts upon a Ground* and the five-part Overture in G minor Z772; and other court instrumental music, including a section from a sonata by G.B. Vitali* which (according to Reading) Nicholas Staggins* 'produced as his own May 29th 1679'. Another scorebook, GB-Lbl, Add. MS 47845, an important source of Purcell's symphony anthems*, includes the only copy of the first version of 'I will give thanks unto thee, O Lord' Z20. See also **Overtures**. HolCom, HolFid, HolRos, ShaMan, ShaSuc, SpiCat, ZimCat.

Reading, John, singer The baritone John Reading (fl.1684–1724) was a theatre singer at least from 1684. Purcell used him in comic dialogues: as Coridon in the Coridon and Mopsa* duet with John Pate* in *The Fairy Queen* (1692); with Mrs Ayliff* as a mad couple in 'Behold the man' Z608/1 from *The Richmond Heiress* (1693); and as a clown (again with Mrs Ayliff as his wife) in 'Since times are so bad' Z578/6 from *Don Quixote*, Part 2 (1694). He was not available to Purcell after the United Company* broke up in the spring of 1695; he continued to sing, mainly at the Lincoln's Inn Fields Theatre, until the 1724–5 season. BalSta, BDA.

Reception The word commonly applied in Purcell studies to 'the broader context in which Restoration music was heard, disseminated and appropriated by later generations and came to shape our own perceptions of it today' (*HerRec*, 303). In practice, it has four main aspects: (1) Purcell's music in performance in the eighteenth century and its subsequent revival; (2) the transmission, arrangement and publication of Purcell's music from the late 1690s to the present; (3) the critical reception of Purcell from the early eighteenth century and the history of writing his biography; and (4) the influence on Purcell on subsequent English composers.

(1) has been surveyed here in **Performance history from 1695**, **Stage history from 1695** and **Recordings**. (2) is surveyed in **Editions, from 1695** and is discussed in the entries for collectors such as Edward Finch*, John Gostling*, Philip Hayes*, Daniel Henstridge* and Thomas Tudway*, as well as those involved with the Academy of Ancient Music* and the Concerts of Ancient Music*. (3) effectively started with poets marking Purcell's death (see **Poems praising Purcell**); was followed by writers such as Tom Brown* and Charles Gildon* (as well as others surveyed in *HigRec* and *LucSha*); and developed with the various attempts to write Purcell's biography*, initiated by Sir John Hawkins* and Charles Burney*.

(4) deserves a full-length study. It would begin with his immediate associates and followers (particularly Jeremiah Clarke*, Daniel Purcell*, John Eccles*, John Weldon* and William Croft*), and would discuss composers (such as Thomas Arne*, Maurice Greene and William Boyce*) who were still working in genres – cathedral music, court odes* and theatre music – that Purcell had cultivated. The subsequent influence of Italian solo vocal and instrumental music meant that English composers tended to be most Purcellian in their choral music, though those connected with the Academy of Ancient Music (notably Greene, J.C. Pepusch and Benjamin Cooke) experimented with a more comprehensive archaic style, which included elements of the Restoration idiom. Samuel Wesley* referred to the Service in B$^\flat$ Z230 and Purcell's odes in several of his major works; however, the Purcell idiom was just one ingredient in his rich stylistic brew.

A much later generation of English composers (including Arthur Somervell, Charles Villiers Stanford and Ralph Vaughan Williams) became involved as editors for the Purcell Society*. Gustav Holst put on pioneering performances (notably *The Fairy Queen** in 1911), and published editions and arrangements of several sets of theatre airs*; while Peter Warlock published the first edition of the fantasias* in 1927 (*PurWar*). However, it was left to Michael Tippett* and Benjamin Britten* to engage seriously with the Purcellian idiom in their own music, a by-product of their work as performers and arrangers/editors of the composer. This tradition has continued to the present, with composers such as Peter Maxwell Davies*, Michael Nyman*, Oliver Knussen and George Benjamin using Purcell works as starting points for free recompositions. *See also* **Fantasia upon One Note Z745**, **Performance history from 1695**. *BurRem, HerRec, HigRec.*

Recitative The word, derived from the Italian *recitativo*, applied to Purcell's declamatory vocal passages. Roger North* (*NorMus*, 217) referred to 'What ho! thou genius of this isle' Z628/19b, sung by Cupid in the Frost Scene* of *King Arthur**, as 'a *recitativo* of calling towards the place where Genius was to rise'. However, English poets at the time did not follow Italian practice by supplying specially written verse with fixed conventional line lengths, limiting and standardising phrase lengths and leading to the formulas of *recitativo semplice*

– which singers could treat freely. However, Purcell's type, derived in part from mid-seventeenth-century Italian recitative and often overlaid with bursts of brilliant runs, was clearly intended to be sung as written, with only the pace varied according to the dramatic situation. *See also* **Song**.

Recorder The Baroque recorder was apparently introduced to England in 1673 by a group of French wind players including the young Jacques or James Paisible*. They brought with them its French name, *flûte douce* or just 'flute' – the word hitherto used in English for the transverse instrument. They presumably brought recorders with them, though Peter Bressan* made recorders in London, as did followers such as Thomas Stanesby senior. Purcell used recorders frequently in his theatre music, odes* and symphony songs*, beginning with *Theodosius** (1680) and 'Swifter, Isis, swifter flow'* (1681). He normally deployed pairs of recorders and oboes* so that the two types do not play simultaneously, implying that the same players doubled on both, with recorders typically used to accompany solo vocal sections and oboes reserved for tutti sections.

Restoration composers nearly always wrote for the treble or alto recorder in *f*', though Purcell also specified a 'bass flute' (apparently a contrabass recorder in *C*) alternating with a bass violin on the bass line of 'Hark each tree' in 'Hail, bright Cecilia'*. He used recorders as an option in only one independent consort piece, the magnificent Three Parts upon a Ground*, though the Chaconne for Flutes Z627/16, played at an unspecified point in *Dioclesian**, Act III, is equally memorable, popular as a concert item today; it is an exact canon for two recorders and continuo over an elaborated passacaglia* bass. Both pieces have alternative versions a third lower for violins, anticipating a common practice with divisions* and sonatas around 1700. Purcell followed convention by associating recorders with the pastoral, the supernatural, love and death. He clearly had a fondness for them; it is significant that John Blow* and Henry Hall* chose them as the obbligato instruments for their pieces in memory of Purcell, and they feature prominently in Jeremiah Clarke's* choral and orchestral ode on the same subject. *See also* **Odes on the Death of Henry Purcell**. *BaiTal, HolFid, HolPur, LasRec, SimRec, ThoCha*.

Recordings The early history of Purcell recordings has yet to be investigated in detail, though landmarks first issued on 78s are 'Nymphs and shepherds, come away'* by the Manchester Children's Choir (Columbia, 1929) and Rudolf Dolmetsch's fine harpsichord recordings (Columbia, 1933) of the Suite in G major Z660 and the 'Overture Air and Jig in Gamut' ZT693, S123 (anonymous transcriptions of *The Virtuous Wife** overture Z611/1 and an air from *Abdelazer** Z570/6 with an air by Thomas Morgan*). They were followed by the first two complete recordings of *Dido and Aeneas**, conducted by Clarence Raybould with Nancy Evans and Roy Henderson (Decca, 1935), and conducted by Constant Lambert with Joan Hammond and Dennis Noble (EMI, 1945); and Alfred Deller's* first recordings, notably of 'Music for a while'* (HMV, 1949).

The development of vinyl LPs from 1948, making recordings of large-scale works and complete collections easier to realise, enabled Purcell's music to be covered more systematically. Landmark early LPs include a complete recording of *Sonnata's of III Parts** (Éditions de L'Oiseau Lyre, 1950) with the Swiss harpsichordist Isabelle Nef; Nef's recording of the eight suites from *A Choice Collection** (L'Oiseau Lyre, 1953); *Dido* again, conducted by Geraint Jones with Kirsten Flagstad and Elisabeth Schwarzkopf (HMV, 1953); and the first complete recordings of the fantasias* and In Nomines* with a Basel viol consort led by August Wenzinger (Archiv, 1954). These were followed by a succession of notable first complete recordings of major works, including 'Hail, bright Cecilia'* conducted by Michael Tippett* with Alfred Deller (Bach Guild, 1956); *The Indian Queen** conducted by Anthony Bernard (Club Françoise du Disque, 1957); and *The Fairy Queen**, 'Come, ye sons of art, away'* (with Alfred Deller) and *King Arthur**, all conducted by Anthony Lewis (L'Oiseau Lyre, 1957, 1958, 1959). These were followed by two ground-breaking recordings by Nikolaus Harnoncourt and his pioneering period-instrument group Concentus Musicus (both Bach Guild, 1965): music from *Dioclesian** including the Act V Masque complete, conducted by Deller; and the complete fantasias and In Nomines.

The change to CDs in the 1980s (with their compact format and much longer playing-time) enabled British period-instrument groups to develop large-scale projects covering complete genres of Purcell's music, so that by the 1995 anniversary celebrations* nearly everything had been recorded. *Purcell: Theatre Music* by Christopher Hogwood* and the Academy of Ancient Music (L'Oiseau Lyre, 1974–83) was originally in LP boxes and was subsequently transferred to CD; Hogwood subsequently added the complete trio sonatas* (1982, 1995), *Dido* (1994) and *The Indian Queen* (1995). Robert King and The King's Consort complemented Hogwood's recordings with three series for Hyperion: *The Complete Odes and Welcome Songs* (1988–92); *The Complete Anthems and Services* (1992–4), including the devotional songs and part-songs*; and *The Secular Solo Songs* (1994). Another notable venture was *Complete Chamber Music* (including most of the keyboard music), recorded by Pieter-Jan Belder and his Dutch group Musica Amphion (Brilliant Classics, 2006). *See also* **Robert (Bob) Thurston Dart**. *CamDol, ClaDel, HarDel, HarDid, MorDar, PerDar.*

Recte et retro *See* **Counterpoint**

Reggio, Pietro Genoese singer, theorbo player and guitarist (1632–85). He seems to have arrived in London in 1660 after working in Spain, Germany, Sweden and France, and established himself as a singer, singing teacher and composer in Oxford* and London. He published *The Art of Singing* (Oxford, 1677) and *Songs Set by Signior Pietro Reggio* (1680). The latter, including many Abraham Cowley* settings, includes 'Arise ye subterranean winds', used in the Masque of Devils in Act I of Thomas Shadwell's 1674 version of *The Tempest**. Reggio probably sang it onstage to his own accompaniment, and several fascinating manuscript copies (discussed in *HerCre* and *HerHen*) illuminate ways in which composer-performers at the time modified their own music in performance.

In the preface to *Choice Ayres and Songs*, book 3 (1681), John Playford* criticised Reggio's English word-setting: he was 'not perfect in the true *Idiom* of our Language' and 'the Air of his Musick' would 'sute far better with *Italian* than *English* Words'. It did not help that Reggio was arrogant, 'disparaging and undervaluing most of the best *English* Masters and Professors of Musick'. Playford emphasised the point by getting Purcell to make a rival and more correct setting of Cowley's 'She loves and she confesses too'*, using the same chaconne*

ground bass*. Nevertheless, Reggio was clearly an important apostle for the Italian style of singing and vocal music, which Purcell developed in his own solo vocal music in the 1680s. *See also* **Italian music**. *BDECM, DixIta, HolPur, JohSon, LebRom, LocDra, MabIta, MaiMor, PagGui, RosPer, SpiSon*.

'Rejoice in the Lord alway' Z49 This symphony anthem* came to be known as the 'Bell Anthem' because of the descending-octave ground bass* in imitation of a peal of bells in the famous opening prelude*. The anthem is notable for its structure, in which a catchy minuet*-like theme setting the opening words recurs in the manner of a rondeau*. Purcell copied the anthem into GB-Lbl, R.M. 20.h.8 in 1683 or 1684, leaving some inner parts incomplete, probably with the unfulfilled intention of revising them; two non-autograph copies preserve a complete but earlier version. The anthem quickly gained popularity, circulating widely as a verse anthem with the prelude and other string passages cut or arranged for organ. *See also* **Edward Finch**, **Henry Hall**, **James Hawkins**. *HolPur, PikRej, ShaMan, VanChu*.

'Remember not, Lord, our offences' Z50 A five-part full anthem*, copied by Purcell into GB-Cfm, Mu. MS 88 not later than 1682, setting a text from the Litany in the Book of Common Prayer. Purcell achieves an extraordinary expressive range in about three minutes, with a central section of anguished counterpoint* using two simultaneous points of imitation framed by consoling homophony. The most affecting moment is the transition from the angular setting of 'but spare us, good Lord', with its tortuous descending tritones, to the solace of the cadence at 'whom thou hast redeem'd with thy most precious blood'. First published by Vincent Novello*, it is one of Purcell's most popular anthems. *ShaAnc, VanChu*.

Restoration Strictly speaking, this word should apply just to the immediate process of restoring the English monarchy after the Civil War and Commonwealth, starting with the Declaration of Breda on 4 April 1660. Charles II* was proclaimed king on 8 May; arrived in London on 29 May (his 30th birthday); and was crowned in Westminster Abbey* on 23 April 1661. However, 'Restoration' is commonly extended to 1688 (taking in the reigns of Charles II and James II*), and is loosely used (particularly in writing about the arts) as a shorthand for the whole period up to the death of Queen Anne* in 1714, which marked the end of the Stuart dynasty.

Restoration Michael Hoffman's 1995 film, based on Rose Tremain's novel, deals with the relationship between Charles II* and Merivel, a fictional medical doctor, set against the events of 1665–6. Its music was assembled and arranged, somewhat anachronistically, by James Newton Howard partly from Purcell's theatre works of the 1690s, including *King Arthur**, *The Fairy Queen** and *The Indian Queen**.

Revisions Scholars have searched for insights into Purcell's development as a composer and a performing musician by studying those works that exist in different versions. Much attention has been given to the Burial Service*, perhaps his earliest large-scale composition, which he revised several times, refining its counterpoint* and improving the word-setting. 'My beloved spake'*, one of his earliest symphony anthems*, was also serially revised and improved. The sources of Purcell's consort music show that he worked hard to improve structural coherence and balance, with the three-part fantasia Z733 given a remarkable chromatic coda, extending and crowning the work. Conversely, in the Golden Sonata*, he replaced a chromatic Adagio at the end of the Canzona* with a more conventional conclusion, apparently to avoid spoiling the effect of the succeeding Grave. Purcell was a habitual reviser: he regularly made small-scale changes when copying his own music, notably in GB-Cfm, Mu. MS 88, which includes revisions to several anthems that never entered wider circulation. It is not always possible to determine the order of revisions of a work, or that Purcell considered one version to supersede another. In the case of nos. 7 and 8 of *Ten Sonata's in Four Parts**, the two extant states of each probably represent 'alternative *finished* versions' (*HowArt*, 28). *See also* **Fantasias**.

Some revisions, such as those carried out on the verse anthem 'Let mine eyes run down with tears' Z24 (*c*.1682), were also apparently for aesthetic reasons, to improve the logic and coherence of the counterpoint and the harmonic scheme. Others had a practical purpose: 'Hear me, O Lord, and that soon' (*c*.1678–81) apparently started out as a domestic part-song for three voices and continuo Z13A, but was revised and completed as the verse anthem Z13B. 'My song shall

Ex. 7 (a) Chaconne from *The Gordion Knot Unty'd* Z597/6, bb. 31–40, compared with (b) the bass part of the version in Osborn MS 515.

be alway'* seems to have originated as a continuo anthem to which Purcell subsequently added string symphonies, probably for an Oxford* performance in 1690. The theatre airs* for *The Gordian Knot Unty'd**, apparently compiled under pressure in the autumn of 1690 largely from existing works, include the Chaconne in D minor Z597/6, revised from an earlier standalone consort piece, now known only from the bass partbook Osborn MS 515* (Ex. 7). The Gresham autograph* includes a number of his songs and duets arranged, revised and transposed in the 1690s, possibly for singers in Princess Anne's* circle. *See also* **Autographs**. *ForFun, HerCre, HerFow, HerRev, HowArt, HowCre, ManRev, PurSon, ShaFun.*

Rhythmic alteration It has been recognised since at least the 1960s that Purcell and his English contemporaries did not always intend their music to be performed exactly as notated. They were heirs to a tradition, associated particularly with dance music, in which passages of the fastest prevailing note-values (usually quavers but sometimes semiquavers) were played slightly unevenly to make them more elegant, with the second of a pair of notes a little late, rather as jazz is 'swung' today. We associate this effect with Lully* and the French convention of *notes inégales*, though there is evidence for it in much earlier English dance music. Conversely, according to the anonymous author of Mary Burwell's lute tutor (*c*.1670), 'the Soule of the lute' consisted of 'stealing halfe a note from one note and bestoweing of it upon the next note' (i.e. a short-long effect) to 'make the playing of the Lute more aerye and skipping'; the author added 'The heareing of Violins and singing is a great helpe to learne this livelines and Sweetnes'.

There is also suggestive evidence of rhythmic alteration in Purcell's music, such as the quavers in the third bar of 'Fairest isle'*, originally written in even notes but printed dotted in *Apollo's Banquet*, book 2 (1691). Similar discrepancies can be found in the keyboard almands* Z662/2 and Z663/2 between *A Choice Collection** and manuscript versions (set out side-by-side in *PurSui*), perhaps attempts to notate an elusive effect poised somewhere between even and dotted notes. Purcell sometimes notated parts for his boys more precisely than for the violinists doubling them, as shown in a revealing triple-time passage in 'My heart is inditing'* (discussed in *RosPer*, 154), suggesting that pairs of slurred quavers falling by thirds were often performed short-long as 'Scotch snaps'. Another type of rhythmic alteration, best called 'incorporation', was made for notational convenience before the double dot became established. It involved playing notes, usually crotchets or quavers, later than notated, to fit into prevailing dotted crotchet-quaver or dotted quaver-semiquaver patterns (see Ex. 8).

Ex. 8: the bass and continuo parts of the Largo from Trio Sonata in E minor Z796/4, bb. 11–14.

In recent years a consensus has emerged that Purcell's music, with its rich mixture of English, French and Italian elements, should not automatically be performed à-la-Lully. Some of his overtures* (such as the ones for *Amphitryon** and *Distressed Innocence**) begin with almand-like passages, best performed more or less as written, without the overdotting promoted by Arnold Dolmetsch*, Thurston Dart* and their followers, but using *notes inégales* and incorporation where necessary. There is certainly no case for altering wholesale the rhythms of Purcell's carefully conceived declamatory vocal writing, as in the 1961 Novello* vocal score of *Dido and Aeneas**. Suggested alterations of vocal rhythms, some misconceived in our opinion, are still found here and there in PS, though distinguished from the original with rhythm flags above the stave. *DarInt, DolInt, FerPur, HefAlt HogCor, HolNot, RosPer.*

Rich, Christopher Lawyer and theatre manager (1647–1714), the business partner of Thomas Skipwith, who had been a shareholder in the United Company*. In 1693 they acquired a controlling interest in the Drury Lane Theatre* when the incompetent manager Alexander Davenant, who was heavily indebted to them, fled to the Canary Islands. Rich's management style, which involved cutting production costs and reducing salaries, provoked a crisis in the winter of 1694–5. It led Thomas Betterton* to establish a rival company at the Lincoln's Inn Fields Theatre in the spring of 1695, taking with him most of the leading actors, singers and musicians, including John Eccles*, Gottfried Finger* and John Lenton*. Purcell stayed loyal to Rich, and had to provide the music for *The Indian Queen**, *Bonduca** and other plays with mostly young inexperienced singers, including Letitia Cross*, Jemmy Bowen* and Richard Leveridge*. Rich's leading composers after Purcell's death were Daniel Purcell*, Jeremiah Clarke*, Thomas Morgan* and James Paisible*. Rich was succeeded as a theatre manager by his better-known son John. *LowSta, LS, PriPur, PriThe, SawRic.*

Rimbault, Edward Francis Organist, collector and editor (1816–76), the leading authority on Purcell in mid-Victorian England. He edited two Purcell volumes for the Musical Antiquarian Society*: *Bonduca** (1842), with a remarkable 'Historical Sketch of the History of Dramatic Music in England', the first treatment of the subject; and 'Hail, bright Cecilia'* (1848). Both were first complete editions, based on early manuscripts. Rimbault's library, sold after his death, included most of the early prints of Purcell's music, together with a large amount of other seventeenth-century English music. Many of his manuscripts, including US-NYp, Drexel MS 5061 (the most important non-autograph source of Purcell's fantasias* (apparently copied by a member of the Isaack family*), were acquired by the banker and collector Joseph William Drexel and are now in the New York Public Library.

Rimbault was less than scrupulous as a scholar: he seems to have stolen books from Oxford and Cambridge libraries; and to have invented imaginary documents, including a letter from Matthew Locke* to the young Purcell (printed in *CumPur*, 27), and the 'Address of the Children of the Chapel Royal to the King, and their master, Capt. Cooke, on his Majesty's birthday, A.D. 1670, composed by master Purcell, one of the children of the said chapel'.

Zimmerman* catalogued this 'work' as ZD120, but pointed out that 'apparently no one besides Rimbault ever saw the work'. *AndRim, HolPur, JonPub, ZimCat.*

Ritornello Purcell used this word (usually abbreviating it as 'Ritor') to mean an instrumental interlude in a concerted vocal work; he used 'symphony'*, 'sonata'*, 'overture'* or 'prelude'* for introductory music. Ritornellos frequently take up and develop the thematic material of the preceding vocal section – there are some ravishing examples in the ground-bass* movements of the odes* – but some are thematically independent of the surrounding vocal material, and occasionally a passage marked 'Ritor' introduces a vocal section, such as the one preceding 'Be thou exalted, Lord' Z46/4a in the symphony anthem 'Praise the Lord, O Jerusalem'*.

Roger, Estienne A French Huguenot, Roger (1665/6–1722) established a printing business in Amsterdam, publishing music from 1697 using engraved copper plates rather than moveable type. His catalogues are full of Italian and French music, though he also published composers working in London, including Gottfried Finger*, Nicola Matteis*, James Paisible*, J.C. Pepusch and William Williams. *Recueil d'airs à 4 parties tirez des opéra, tragédies et comedies* (Amsterdam, 1699) is Roger's two-volume reprint of *A Collection of Ayres*. He did not attempt to improve on the flawed original, confining himself to translating the titles of plays (rendering *The Old Batchelor** as 'Musique du Vieux garson', for instance), though by engraving the music he improved its legibility. It is the only significant continental publication of Purcell's music. However, in Roger's *50 Airs Anglois*, vol. 1 (1701), George Bingham (an English expatriate recorder teacher in Amsterdam) included some movements arranged for recorder and bass from *Abdelazer**, *Amphitryon**, *Bonduca** and *The Old Batchelor*, as well as the Cibell*. *MPP, RasRog, HigRec, ZimCat.*

Rondeau (Round O) The rondeau pattern – normally ABACA (AABACA or AABACAA with the implied repeats) – was applied to dances in mid-seventeenth-century France and came into England in the 1680s; there are several early examples by Thomas Farmer*, including two in his theatre airs* for Nathaniel Lee's* play *The Princess of Cleve* (1680–2). Purcell had a special fondness for the form, often using minuet* patterns to express love and passion, as in 'Fear no danger to ensue' (*Dido and Aeneas** Z626/7) and 'I attempt from love's sickness to fly' (*The Indian Queen** Z630/17h). Gavotte rhythms were also fruitful, as in the delicious duet 'Oh, the sweet delights of love' Z627/30 from *Dioclesian**, Act V, with its delightful hocket-like cooings on the words 'oh' and 'who' and its wide-ranging and varied episodes powerfully suggesting the all-embracing nature of love. There are some beautiful instrumental examples, such as the Rondeau Minuet from *The Gordian Knot Unty'd** Z597/3, originally an instrumental movement in 'Why are all the Muses mute?'*, and the serene Third Act Tune from *The Indian Queen** Z630/18. Purcell's most famous rondeau today is the vigorous one in hornpipe* rhythm in *Abdelazer** Z570/2, made famous by Benjamin Britten*. He always seems to have used the French word *rondeau*, though the English corruption 'Round O' is sometimes found in secondary sources of his music and became common among his followers. *HolPur, PriThe.*

Roseingrave, Daniel According to Hawkins* (*HawHis*, ii. 771), Daniel (d.1727), the father of the composer Thomas Roseingrave, was a choirboy in the Chapel Royal* alongside Purcell. He was subsequently organist of Gloucester, Winchester* and Salisbury cathedrals, ending up at St Patrick's and Christ Church in Dublin. In the early 1680s Purcell copied a wordless stratigraphic score* of Roseingrave's anthem 'Lord, thou art become gracious', now in GB-Och, Mus. 1215, section 1. The composer then added enough words to enable it to be copied into parts for performance. Perhaps Roseingrave found himself without a copy of his own anthem, asking Purcell to copy it from a now-lost source in London to be sent or taken to Winchester. *BoyChr, HerCat, HerFow, HolRos, ShaMan, ShaSuc, SpiCat.*

St Bride's, Fleet Street Christopher Wren's church replaced a fifteenth-century building on the site, destroyed in the Great Fire of London. Renatus Harris* built a new organ for the recently erected west gallery in time for the 1694 Cecilian celebrations*, when the church hosted a morning service preceding the dinner at Stationers' Hall*, including the first performance of Purcell's Te Deum and Jubilate in D major*. Harris's organ was destroyed when the church was bombed in November 1940, but engravings and photos preserve a record of the gallery and the fine organ case. *HolBat, KniHar, WhiCec.*

Illus. 13: St Bride's, Fleet Street (1896).

Saint Cecilia's Day celebrations *See* **Cecilian celebrations**

'St Martin's Lane' *See* **'La Furstemberg'**

St Paul's Cathedral Old St Paul's was badly damaged in 1666 during the Great Fire of London, and Christopher Wren's new building was under construction during Purcell's entire working life. It was formally opened in 1697, though a wooden tabernacle was used for services from 1674 and the choir was brought up to strength in 1687. The cathedral employed some of Purcell's court colleagues, including John Gostling*, William Turner* and John Blow*. Thomas Tudway* wrote that the Te Deum and Jubilate in D major* was 'compos'd principally against ye Opening of St Paul's, but [Purcell] did not live till that time; However, it was sung there, severall times since, before her Majesty Queen Anne upon ye great Events of her Reigne' (*HogTud*, 45). The Te Deum was also often performed at St Paul's in the annual Festival of the Sons of the Clergy (the charity supporting the families of clergymen), particularly after 1755, when it was given a new lease of life in William Boyce's* enlarged and modernised version. As Sub-Dean from 1690, Gostling played an important role in collecting and copying service music for the new cathedral, including many works by Purcell. *HolBat, ShaMan, SpiPau, SpiRes, WhiCec.*

Sances, Giovanni Felice A Roman tenor and composer (c.1600–79), who worked in Vienna for most of his career. Pieces from his *Motetti* (Venice, 1638) circulated in Restoration Oxford*, and Stephan Schönlau has suggested that the Alleluia from 'Laudemus viros gloriosos', for two tenors and continuo, was the starting point for the equivalent section of Purcell's four-part motet 'Beati omnes' Z131. They are both ground-bass* pieces (a favourite genre for Sances) and start with similar rhythms and declamation. The connection illustrates Purcell's interest in earlier Italian sacred music, an interest he shared with John Blow*, among others. *See also* **'Jehova, quam multi sunt hostes mei'**. *SchGro, WaiPat.*

Sandford, Francis Irish herald and genealogist (1630–94), best remembered for his detailed and lavishly illustrated account of James II's* coronation* on 23 April 1685, published in 1687 (*SanCor*). It became the authoritative source of information for organising later coronations, and it tells us a good deal about how Purcell's 1685 coronation anthems, 'My heart is inditing'* and 'I was glad'*, were performed. It is also useful for the lists of the singers and instrumentalists, including the earliest surviving ones (*SanCor*, 69) of the choirboys in the Restoration Chapel Royal* and Westminster Abbey*. *HolBat, HolFid, RanCor.*

Saraband This dance was in transition in Restoration England. Thomas Mace* (*MacMus*, 129) described it 'of the *Shortest Triple-Time*', and Matthew Locke* mostly wrote his examples in compound time (⅜ in modern notation) with two chord changes per bar, implying the fast tempo of the Italian *sarabanda*. However, Purcell's sarabands are in three-crotchet bars (¾ in modern notation), mostly with two or three chord changes per bar, suggesting the influence of the slower and more expressive French *sarabande*. Sarabands do not have initial upbeats and their phrases end on the third beat of the bar, distinguishing them from corants* and minuets*. They usually have two eight-bar strains. All except one of Purcell's sarabands (in the airs for *Amphitryon** Z572/2) are keyboard pieces, four of them ending suites in *A Choice Collection**.

Saul and the Witch of Endor Z134 Purcell apparently found the text of his superb dialogue 'In guilty night' in the setting by Robert Ramsey (*c.*1595–1644), organist of Trinity College, Cambridge. Paraphrasing Samuel 28: 8–20, it dramatises the encounter between Saul (countertenor) and the Witch of Endor (treble), who summons the ghost of Samuel (baritone) to tell the doomed king's fortune before the Battle of Gilboa. The story was used in seventeenth-century England as anti-Catholic polemic, and it has been argued that Purcell's setting, published in *Harmonia Sacra**, book 2 (1693), might have been understood by some as an allegory of James II's* position in 1690 after the Battle of the Boyne. It is not known why Purcell wrote it, though the range of Samuel's part suggests Purcell's favourite baritone John Bowman*, while the Witch's part might have been written for Mrs Ayliff*, and Saul's for a prominent countertenor* such as John Pate* or John Freeman*.

Illus. 14: Saul, the ghost of Samuel and the Witch of Endor.

Purcell's setting, though indebted to Ramsey's in some details of the word-setting, uses Italianate vocal writing to reinvigorate the devotional song tradition: brilliant bursts of semiquavers illustrate phrases (such as 'pow'rful arts', 'raise the ghost' and 'ascending from below'), and repetitions of affecting words (such as 'forbear', 'no, no', 'alas!', 'oh!' and 'tell me') continually raise the emotional temperature. Purcell's masterstroke was to pick out the word 'farewell' for the last chorus, with the singers in character to the end, the witch and the ghost dismissing the shattered king, who can only sob in semitone slides over descending passacaglia*-like harmonies. ChaEnd, HolPur, SmaEnd, SpiSon, ZimPur.

'Scocca pur tutti tuoi strali' Lully's* famous Italian song (LWV 76/3), for three voices with an introductory *ritournelle* for two violins and bass on a ground bass*, was disseminated in Restoration England mostly in vocal and instrumental reductions consisting just of the first treble and bass. There is only one English copy of the complete piece (in GB-Ob, Tenbury MS 1232, copied by London A*; ed. in WooSco). Lully's song clearly appealed to English musicians for its delightful evocation of spurned love and for its ingenious five-bar G minor ground, an elaboration of the descending passacaglia* ground. Purcell almost certainly made the beautiful harpsichord arrangement (published in *Musick's Handmaid**, part 2), which uses his idiosyncratic *style brisé** realisation of the continuo* interludes (see Ex. 9, p. 175). It also influenced a wider group of G minor grounds, including John Blow's* for two violins and bass (ed. in HolTri); the air 'Crown the year'* Z335/3 from 'Sound the trumpet, beat the drum'*; and above all Purcell's great G minor ground Z807, no. 6 of *Ten Sonata's in Four Parts**, based directly on Lully's ground. HolPur, KlaSco, ShaMan.

Scorebook The idea of copying collections of particular genres or the works of a single composer into large, bound music manuscripts goes back in England to the late sixteenth century, though the format was mostly the preserve of lutenists and keyboard players until about 1650, when composers began to use it to assemble their own ensemble works in score. Early examples are those copied by William and Henry Lawes*, and in particular Matthew Locke's* collection of his main sets of consort music, GB-Lbl, Add. MS 17801. Purcell extended the idea, systematically copying particular genres into large folio scorebooks, one genre at the front and the other copied from the back with the book turned upside down: GB-Cfm, MU MS 88 (symphony anthems* | full and verse anthems*); GB-Lbl, R.M. 20.h.8 (symphony anthems | odes* and court vocal music); GB-Lbl Add. MS 30930 (devotional part–songs* | consort music*). Notable examples copied by Purcell's followers include GB-Lbl, R.M. 20.h.9, copied by the organist John Reading* (canonic exercises and church music | court consort music); and US-AUS, HRC 85, John Gostling's* largely chronological anthologies of Chapel Royal* music (symphony anthems | anthems with organ). *See also* **Autographs**. HerCat, HerCre, HolPur, ShaMan, ZimGos.

Scots (Scotch) songs and dances There was a fashion in Restoration London for dances and songs supposedly from Scotland, many of which were given words by the Englishman Thomas D'Urfey*. Tell-tale features are slurred pairs of quavers, often rising or falling by thirds (to be performed short-long as 'Scotch snaps') and unconventional (by the standards of art music) modal progressions and pentatonic melodic shapes. Examples are Purcell's 'When first Amintas' Z430 (a mock-song* on an instrumental jig*) and 'Sawney is a bonny lad' Z412, published in 1687 and 1694 respectively. 'A New Scotch Tune' Z655 in *Musick's Hand-Maid**, part 2, was later associated with Allan Ramsay's words 'Peggy, I must love thee'. Purcell wrote several other pieces using elements of the style, including the Scotch Tune Z572/4 from *Amphitryon** and the dialogue 'Jenny, 'gin you can love' Z571/7 between Jenny and Jockey in D'Urfey's play *A Fool's Preferment, or The Three Dukes of Dunstable* (1688). One of the best-known Scots songs, ''Twas with a furlong of Edinboro' town'* Z605/2 from *The Mock Marriage* (1695), also with D'Urfey's words, may be by Jeremiah Clarke*. *See also* **Songs**. *DayDur, FisSco, HigRec, PriPur.*

Sedley, Charles Politician, wit, poet and playwright (1639–1701), a favourite drinking partner of Charles II*. He supported the Glorious Revolution*, and wrote the 1692 birthday ode* for Mary II*, 'Love's goddess sure was blind'*. With its intimate tone and striking depiction of angels welcoming Mary to heaven, it is one of the finest court ode texts, and it drew from Purcell a setting of the highest quality. Two years later Purcell set Sedley's poem 'Hears not my Phillis' Z371. Its title, 'The Knotting Song', refers to the female pastime of knotting threads, popularised in England by Queen Mary. Purcell's triple-time setting of the refrain ('Phillis without a frown or smile, | Sat and knotted all the while.'), doubtless repeated a number of times for comic effect, perfectly captures the monotonous three-movement action. *BalKno, SmiSed, WooPur.*

Semi-opera The term coined by Roger North* (*NorMus*, 306–7, 353–4) for the elaborate Restoration musical plays he characterised as 'half Musick, and half Drama', such as *Dioclesian**, *King Arthur** and *The Fairy Queen**. However, modern scholars mostly prefer 'dramatic opera'*, the term used by John Dryden* to describe *King Arthur*.

Services Settings of Anglican liturgical texts prescribed by the *Book of Common Prayer* for Matins, Evensong and Holy Communion are known as services. Purcell's Service in B$^\flat$ Z230 sets texts required for the Anglican liturgy over a whole day: Te Deum and Benedictus for Matins, Magnificat and Nunc dimittis for Evensong; and the responses to the Commandments (also known as the Kyrie) and the Creed for Holy Communion; it also provides alternative canticles for Matins (Benedicite and Jubilate) and Evensong (Cantate Domino and Deus misereatur). In several sources the alternative canticles are labelled 'Second Service' and the other settings 'First Service', a division observed in *PS* 23. The First Service was probably composed in the late 1670s, the Second Service a year or two later. The anthem 'O God, thou art my God'*, annotated 'to Mr Purcell's Bmi Service' in GB-Cfm, Mu. MS 117, shares musical ideas with several movements from the Service and was evidently composed to be performed with it.

Z230 is modelled on John Blow's* Service in G major. They are both in the verse style, in which groups of solo voices alternate with the full choir, itself sometimes deployed antiphonally. Blow linked many movements with a head-motive, while Purcell used one head-motive to link the Te Deum,

Benedicite and Cantate Domino and another for the Benedictus and Nunc dimittis. More significant was Blow's use of six canons* (Purcell reproduced one of these in *PlaInt*), while Z230 has no fewer than ten – an exploration of canonic technique that parallels his devotion to counterpoint* in the fantasias* and trio sonatas*. Purcell's service is also notable for its well-proportioned divisions between full and verse sections and between polyphonic and homophonic textures, and for its colourful harmonic and contrapuntal detail. It marks the high point of the Restoration service and was widely disseminated in the eighteenth century; William Boyce* included it in *Cathedral Music*, vol. 3.

Purcell wrote little liturgical music by comparison with Blow, his only other contributions being settings for the Burial Service* and the ceremonial Te Deum and Jubilate in D major*. The Sanctus in G major ZD90 survives in an organ part attributed to Purcell and is related to (and probably derived from) the Third Act Tune from *The Indian Queen** Z630/18. The Magnificat and Nunc dimittis in G minor Z231, attributed to 'Mr Purcell' in most sources, is probably by Daniel Purcell*. *See also* **Samuel Wesley**. *HolPur, SpiCat, VanChu, ZimSer.*

Seymour, Charles *See* **Somerset, Duke of**

Shadwell, Thomas Poet and playwright (c.1640–92), the son of a Norfolk landowner. He came to public attention as the adapter of the 1674 version of *The Tempest** and as the author of *Psyche*, produced the following year. They were among the first dramatic operas*, and Shadwell's musical knowledge (John Jenkins* taught him as a child) is shown by the detailed descriptions of their music in his published texts. Purcell wrote music for two of Shadwell's original plays, a duet 'Leave these useless arts in loving' Z579 for Act II of the comedy *Epsom-Wells* (1672) as revived in 1693, and settings of two scenes for *The Libertine** (1675) as revived in 1695. In addition, he wrote music for Shadwell's 1678 adaptation of Shakespeare's *Timon of Athens**, apparently in the spring or early summer of 1695. A more direct collaboration had come in the spring of 1689, when Shadwell wrote 'Now does the glorious day appear'*, the first of Purcell's odes for Mary II's* birthday. Shadwell, a staunch Protestant and Whig, had replaced the Catholic John Dryden* as Poet Laureate after the Glorious Revolution*. 'Welcome, glorious morn'*, the anonymous ode for Mary's 1691 birthday, was included by Montague Summers in his Shadwell edition. *BDA, LS, PriPur, PriThe, WalDra.*

Shake *See* **Ornamentation**

Shakespeare, William Purcell seems to have set only seven words written by the Bard: Henry Heveningham's verse 'If music be the food of love'* borrows just its first line from Orsino's speech at the beginning of *Twelfth Night*. Purcell wrote music for four Restoration versions of Shakespeare plays, but always setting the words of their adapters: a song for *The Sicilian Usurper* (1680) Z581, Nahum Tate's* version of *Richard II*; *The Fairy Queen**, a dramatic opera* adapted from *A Midsummer Night's Dream*; music for Thomas Shadwell's* version of *Timon of Athens**; and a song, 'Dear pretty youth' Z631/10, for *The Tempest** in Shadwell's adaptation as a dramatic opera. *Dido and Aeneas** was first performed in public in 1700 as part of Charles Gildon's* version of *Measure* *for Measure*. The best-known Shakespeare music attributed to Purcell in the eighteenth century, for *Macbeth* and *The Tempest*, was actually written respectively by Richard Leveridge* and John Weldon*. *ChoSha, LS, PriPur*.

Shaw, George Bernard The Irish playwright (1856–1960) became a Purcell enthusiast while working as a music critic in London in the 1880s and 90s. Reviewing a concert performance of *Dido and Aeneas** in the East End in 1889, he was entertainingly rude about the performance, but wrote that 'Henry Purcell was a great composer: a very great composer indeed; and even this little boarding-school opera is full of his spirit, his freshness, his dramatic expression, and his unapproached art of setting English speech to music'. He also used Purcell as a stick with which to beat Victorian musical life. After attending a concert in March 1894 given by Arnold Dolmetsch*, featuring music by Matthew Locke* and Purcell (including the Golden Sonata*, some songs and keyboard pieces played on the harpsichord), Shaw wrote: 'Mr Dolmetsch has taken up an altogether un-English position in this matter. He says "Purcell was a great composer: let us perform some of his works." The English musicians say "Purcell was a great composer: let us go and do Mendelssohn's Elijah over again and make the lord-lieutenant of the county chairman of the committee"'. *BurRem, CamDol, ShaMus*.

'She loves and she confesses too' Z413 Purcell's song, a setting of lines from Abraham Cowley's* *The Mistresse* using the chaconne* ground, had an unusual origin. It was effectively commissioned by John Playford*, who criticised Pietro Reggio* for his arrogance and his faulty English word-setting in the preface to *Choice Ayres and Songs*, book 3 (1681). Purcell's setting, composed in 1680 and published in *Choice Ayres and Songs*, book 4 (1683), makes the point eloquently: it uses the same ground in the same key as Reggio's setting, alludes to it in places but contradicts its word-setting at every turn. *HerCre, HolPur, LebRom, SchGro, ShaMan, SilPas*.

Sherman, Rowland Born in Leicester in or before 1665, by 1683 Sherman was living in London in the house of the Levant merchant and amateur musician Sir Gabriel Roberts (1629–1715), to whom he was apprenticed. Sherman played the recorder* and the harpsichord*, instruments which he took with him in July 1688 when he travelled to Aleppo as a Levant Company factor. Copies of Sherman's letters sent from Aleppo reveal that he knew Purcell, as did his London correspondents, the cloth trader James Pigott (probably a cousin of Francis Pigott*) and the Levant merchant Philip Wheak. They all seem to have been members with Purcell of a London music club Sherman referred to as 'Brothers of the string'. Sherman's letters show that he tried and failed to obtain from Purcell a copy of his rules for playing thoroughbass, and that he visited the composer's house shortly before leaving for Aleppo. Sherman was aware of *Dido and Aeneas** (he called it 'the mask ... made for Preists Ball'), and hoped he might obtain copies of instrumental movements from it in Purcell's harpsichord arrangements. An inventory of his music library, made after his death in Aleppo in 1748, includes a number of volumes of Purcell's music. *See also* **Continuo**. *WhiAle, WhiMer, WhiShe*.

Shore family Three members of this family, Matthias (d.1700) and his sons William (d.1707) and John (d.1752), were the leading trumpeters in London in the 1690s. Matthias, appointed a trumpeter in ordinary at court in 1682, became Sarjeant Trumpeter in 1687, and as such probably oversaw the introduction of his instrument (traditionally used for fanfares and in trumpet* bands) into concerted music. The process began, several months after his appointment, with G.B Draghi's* *Song for St Cecilia's Day, 1687*, performed on 22 November. William was appointed a trumpeter in ordinary in 1679; served in the First Troop of Horse Guards; was one of 'four of the best of the King's sixteen trumpeters' chosen to attend William III* for the signing of the Peace of Ryswick in 1697; and succeeded his father as Sarjeant Trumpeter in 1700.

John, probably born around 1670, became a trumpeter in ordinary in 1688; he was also a member of Princess Anne's* chamber band. According to Hawkins* (*HawHis*, ii. 752), he 'split his lip in sounding the trumpet, and was ever after unable to perform on the instrument'. This was probably shortly before 1706, when he was appointed the lutenist of the Chapel Royal*. In January 1708 he succeeded William as Sarjeant Trumpeter, presumably as an administrator. According to Hawkins, Matthias's daughter Katherine (1669–1734) was 'a very beautiful and aimable young woman, whom Purcell taught to sing and play on the harpsichord'. She married the actor Colley Cibber in 1693; worked with him at Drury Lane*; and took part in *Don Quixote*, Part 2 (June 1694), singing 'Genius of England' with John Freeman*, her brother John playing 'the symphony on the trumpet'.

The Shores seem to have inspired, enabled and to some extent led the development of the trumpet writing in odes and theatre music by Purcell and his contemporaries, though it is not always clear which members of the family were responsible for the various innovations credited to them. The 'Mr *Showers*' who (according to Peter Motteux*) taught the court trumpeters 'of late years to sound with all the softness imaginable', playing 'some flat Tunes' by Gottfried Finger* at the 1691 Cecilian celebrations*, was presumably Matthias rather than John – as is normally assumed. However, Hawkins wrote that John, 'by his great ingenuity and application had extended the power of that noble instrument', producing from it 'a tone as sweet as that of a hautboy'; and John was probably the 'Mr. Shoar, a most exquisite trumpetter' that Roger North* (*NorCur*, 119) credited with the invention of 'a screw or worme ... by which his exotick notes fall all into use'. Evidently something of an inventor, John produced the first tuning fork, according to Hawkins; and he may also have developed the flat trumpet*, written for by Purcell in the March and Canzona*. The Shores were celebrated by puns on their name, notably in the ode 'Come, ye sons of art, away'*, which includes the couplet 'Sound the trumpet, till around | You make the list'ning shores resound'. BDECM, BaiTal, BalSop, DowExo, HolCla, PinTru, RycTru, SmiTru, SteTru, WebTru, WhiCec.

Siface The castrato Giovanni Francesco Grossi (1653–97) achieved early fame singing the role of Syphax or Siface in Cavalli's opera *Scipio affricano*, hence his nickname. In 1679 he entered the service of Francesco II d'Este, Duke of Modena, who sent him in 1686 to England to entertain his sister, Mary of Modena, James II's* wife. He arrived in London on 16 January 1687 and sang in James's Catholic chapel and other places. Purcell marked his departure from London on 19 June 1687 with an expressive minuet*-like piece, 'Sefauchi's Farewell' Z656. It was published in 1689 in *Musick's Hand-Maid**, part 2 in a keyboard setting, though its textures suggest it was originally a four-part consort piece, as with other examples of the farewell* genre. Its tune was used for a ballad, 'Sefautian's Farewell', and for other ballad verses. It was once thought that Purcell wrote the symphony anthem* 'My song shall be alway'* for Siface, but that probably dates from 1688, after the castrato had left England, and was written for a bass soloist. BDA, DixIta, LeeCat, ShaMan, SimBal, ZimPur.

Simpson, Christopher Composer, viol player and writer (c.1602–69), remembered mainly by Purcell and his contemporaries for his treatises: on playing and composing divisions*, *The Division-Violist* (1659), revised as *Chelys/The Division-Viol* (1665); and on rudiments and composition, *A Compendium of Practical Musick* (1667), an expansion of *The Principles of Practical Musick* (1665). Simpson died when Purcell was still a boy, and as a Catholic (and possibly a Jesuit priest) never held a court post that would have brought them together. However, Purcell recommended the *Compendium* as 'the most Ingenious Book I e're met with upon this Subject' (*PlaInt*, 115). He also took the ground for Three Parts upon a Ground* from the *Compendium*, and doubtless found the instruction and examples in *The Division-Viol* useful when learning how to write ground-bass* compositions. HerCre, HerThe, HolCom, HowArt, SchGro.

'Since God so tender a regard' Z143 Purcell's devotional part-song* for two tenors, bass and continuo, composed around 1678–9, sets John Patrick's* metrical paraphrase of Psalm 116 verses 1–4, 7 and 8. The setting is rooted in the tradition of three-voice devotional works deriving from Henry and William Lawes*, employing an intimate compositional style designed to appeal to sophisticated, mostly amateur, performers in a domestic environment. Using an unvaried eight-note ground bass* throughout, Purcell alternates solo and ensemble textures in each verse. Those for solo voice employ hymn-like melody, triple-time airs and declamatory passages in turn, while the ensembles explore a variety of fugal techniques – processes which Purcell noted in *PlaInt* were 'difficult' to maintain over a ground. Alan Howard's analysis demonstrates his use of self-conscious compositional virtuosity as a means of interpreting the text – an approach in part inspired by the evocation of 'skill' in the third verse: 'But when my skill was at a loss|His kindness rais'd my low estate'. ForDom, HowSin.

Singers Purcell worked closely with the finest singers of his day, primarily in two contexts: at court (where they served in the Chapel Royal* and the Private Music*) and in the theatre. He wrote sophisticated solos in his Chapel Royal anthems, though no sources record names of singers for specific works. However, some have solos with the extreme low bass range associated with John Gostling*; and soloists are known for two sacred works written for other milieux: the Te Deum and Jubilate in D major*, for which ten singers are recorded, and the Charterhouse anthem, 'Blessed is the man' (*PS* 29, no. 4A), for the countertenor Bernard Martin Barenclow or Berenclow and the baritone John Bowman*.

From 1686 onwards singers are sometimes recorded for court odes*, and in 'Hail, bright Cecilia'* they divide into those known to have sung only at court and those who also appeared in the theatre. Of the first sort are four 'countertenors'* (equivalent to French *hautes-contre* or high tenors), Josiah Boucher (d.1695), Alexander Damascene*, John Howell (c.1670–1708) and Anthony Robert (fl.1689–1703). Boucher, a Gentleman of the Chapel Royal from 1682 and a member of the Private Music from 1689, sang in 'Hail, bright Cecilia' ('The fife and all the harmony of war') and 'Arise, my Muse'*. Howell, a Chapel Royal member from 1691, had an unusually high voice; Purcell wrote for him in the C2 clef, as in the duet 'Hark each tree' from 'Hail, bright Cecilia'. Robert, a member of the Private Music from 1689, sang solos in 'Arise, my muse', 'Celebrate this festival'* and 'Who can from joy refrain?'*.

The countertenors John Freeman*, John Pate* and William Turner* performed at court and in the theatre, though Turner is not known to have sung in Purcell's theatre works. John Abell (1653–after 1716), one of the most prominent singers of his day, is known to have sung in two of Purcell's odes: 'Ye tuneful muses'* and 'Sound the trumpet, beat the drum'*. He joined the Chapel Royal and the Private Music in 1679, and in James II's* reign sang in the king's Catholic chapel at Whitehall*. He followed the king into exile in France, returning only after Purcell's death. The singing actor William Mountfort* does not seem to have performed at court.

Purcell also used conventional tenors, more often in ensembles than as prominent soloists. John Church (1674–1741) began in the theatre, singing in the duet 'Ah! how happy are we' from *The Indian Queen**; he joined the Chapel Royal only after Purcell's death. Alphonso Marsh (d.1692) joined the Chapel Royal in 1676 and the Private Music in 1689; he sang solos in 'Sound the trumpet, beat the drum'. Moses Snow (1661–1702) also joined the Private Music in 1689 and the Chapel Royal in 1692; he was a soloist in 'Hail, bright Cecilia' and 'Celebrate this festival'.

Six of the basses named in Purcell's works were court musicians. James Hart (1647–1718) became a priest in the Chapel Royal after joining as a Gentleman in 1670. He sang in *The Tempest** and the court masque *Calisto* in the 1670s, and also ran a girls' school in Chelsea with Jeffery Banister*. Leonard Woodson (1659–1717), Daniel Williams (c.1668–1720) and Thomas Edwards (1658/9–1730) were respectively members of the Chapel Royal from 1681, 1692 and 1700; they, along with Hart, were all soloists in 'Hail, bright Cecilia'. Edwards, Williams and Woodson sang in the Te Deum and Jubilate, and Edwards and Woodson are also named in the scores of court odes. John Bowman*, a member of the Private Music, also worked in the theatre. John Reading* and Richard Leveridge* did not hold court posts but were important theatre singers.

Women did not hold formal posts in the royal music, though Arabella Hunt* received a court pension; and Mrs Ayliff* is named in sources of 'Celebrate this festival' and 'Hail, bright Cecilia'. Mrs Ayliff, Charlotte Butler*, Letitia Cross*, Mrs Dyer/Hodgson* and Katherine Shore (of the Shore family*) are known to have sung in Purcell's theatre music. The only boy treble named in the primary sources of Purcell's music is the theatre singer Jemmy Bowen*. *BalCou, BalSop, BalSta, BDECM, CBCR, RobBow, WhiCec*.

Smith, Bernard ('Father') Organ builder and organist (c.1628/9–1708), possibly an Englishman (rather than a German from Bremen, as is usually stated) who spent the Commonwealth in exile in the northern Netherlands before coming to London after the Restoration*. He was described as 'the Kings organ maker' in 1671, working under John Hingeston*, the keeper of the court keyboard and wind instruments, a post given to Purcell in 1683; Smith (with John Blow*) succeeded Purcell in turn in 1695. In 1676 Smith provided an organ for St Margaret's, Westminster, and served as its organist until his death. Alongside his bitter rival Renatus Harris*, Smith dominated organ building in Restoration England: he produced at least 34 new church instruments. Many more have been attributed to him, including a number of surviving chamber organs, now thought to be by unidentified contemporaries.

Smith seems to have had a close relationship with Purcell. Purcell and Blow played his instrument in the public recitals during the Battle of the Organs* at the Temple Church, and Purcell assessed and reported on his organs at St Katherine Cree (1686) and St James, Piccadilly (1691). Smith and Harris built much larger organs than in earlier English practice, with more varied stops: Smith's Temple Church organ had three manuals and 23 stops with divided accidentals for $E^b/D^\sharp$ and $G^\sharp/A^b$. He was renowned for the power and sweetness of his pipework. *See also* **Organ, Pitch, Temperament.** *BDECM, BicOrg, DunSmi, FreSmi, GwyPur, KniBat, StuGib, ZimPur.*

Smith, Robert A singer, lutenist and composer (d.1675), described as 'one of the Children of his Majesties Chappel' in 1664, when James Clifford printed the words of six of his anthems. It is not known whether he was related to any of the other Smiths employed at the Restoration court as musicians. He succeeded Pelham Humfrey* as a court singer-lutenist on 3 August 1674 but died little more than a year later. He was also active in the theatre, contributing songs to at least ten plays put on by the King's Company and the Duke's Company between January 1672 and the spring or early summer of 1673, as well as act tunes* for the 1674 production of *The Tempest** (ed. in *HolThe*). Smith was an innovative and reasonably accomplished composer of songs and consort music; his anthems are all lost. Purcell seems to have had the prelude to his 'New Year's Day' suite (probably 1 January 1675) in mind when writing the Staircase Overture*. Smith was also apparently the first English composer to write a ground-bass* consort piece; it perhaps gave Purcell the idea of contributing to the genre himself. *BDECM, HolFid, HolPur, HolThe, LS, PriThe, SchGro, SpiSon, WolVio.*

Somerset, Charles Seymour, Duke of The so-called 'proud duke' (1662–1748), sixth Duke of Somerset and great-great-grandson of Edward VI's Lord Protector, inherited the title unexpectedly in 1678, when his elder brother Francis was murdered in Italy. As second duke of the realm, who had married the heiress Elizabeth Thynne née Percy in 1682, he was able to dispense patronage on a grand scale, remodelling Petworth House in Sussex and Syon House in Middlesex, among other properties. He would have encountered Purcell as second mourner for Charles II* and then as a Gentleman of the Bedchamber to James II*. He astutely switched allegiance at the Glorious Revolution*, and in 1692 he sided with Princess Anne* in her conflict with William III* and Mary

II*. Purcell, with John Dryden's* help, dedicated the score of *Dioclesian** to him, doubtless for a suitable reward; and his widow Frances followed that up in 1697 with the dedication of *A Collection of Ayres** – which begins with a set from the same work. *BurRem, HunPat, WinAnn.*

Sonata in D major Z850 Purcell's only independent sonata with an orchestral scoring, for trumpet*, four-part strings and continuo, survives only in a manuscript score in an unidentified hand at York Minster*. Its simple style (though with a characteristically expressive, chromatic slow movement just for the strings) and its fast-slow-fast pattern connects it with Italian operatic overtures and some Bolognese trumpet sonatas, while its brevity suggests it is the symphony* for a concerted vocal work. Michael Tilmouth suggested it came from the ode 'Light of the world'*, supposedly set by Purcell in 1694, though that work may never have been composed. *GriMan, HowArt, ShaMan, SmiTru, TilTec, WooEqu.*

Sonata in G minor Z780 Alfred Moffat first published this fine piece in 1899 as the 'Violin Sonata in G minor'. This was because Edward Finch* had copied it into the sole surviving source, the Armstrong-Finch manuscript*, on two staves, seemingly for violin and continuo. However, Thurston Dart* realised that a number of imitative bass entries in the fast movements were missing or incomplete, and that they could be reinstated by adding a bass viol* part similar to those in continental sonatas for violin, obbligato bass viol and continuo. Perhaps Finch encountered the sonata in a set of loose-leaf parts from which the viol part had become separated. Dart's reconstruction is convincing in the fast movements, though Purcell's probable immediate models, Gottfried Finger's* Op. 1, nos. 1–3, suggest that the part in the slow movements should be more independent, elaborate and chordal than in Dart's version; it will be modified for the forthcoming revision of *PS* 31. Z780's simple slow-fast-slow-fast pattern of sections and its modern style suggests it was written around 1688, the year Finger's Op. 1 was published. *DarCha, HolLif, HolMan, HolPur.*

Songs Henry Playford* wrote in *Orpheus Britannicus**, book 1 (1698) that Purcell *'was especially admir'd for the* Vocal, *having a peculiar Genius to express the Energy* of English *Words, whereby he mov'd the Passions of all his Auditors'*, and Henry Hall* added in a poem a few pages later that his friend had made 'Each Syllable first weigh'd, or short, or long, | That it might too be Sense, as well as Song'. Purcell inherited two main traditions of secular song. One, common since the sixteenth century, borrowed the rhythmic patterns, character and sometimes the structure of dances, often with a high degree of correlation between poetic and musical accent, line endings and phrase endings, rhyme schemes and matching cadences. Minuet* songs were the most popular type, and he wrote them throughout his career: 'I resolve against cringing' Z386 (published 1678) is one of his first, and he left the Congreve* setting 'Ah! what pains, what racking thoughts' Z354 incomplete in the Gresham autograph* at his death. He used the rondeau* pattern particularly for minuet theatre songs, as in 'I attempt from love's sickness to fly' from *The Indian Queen** Z630/17h.

Songs in other dance patterns are less common in Purcell (though 'Phillis, I can ne'er forgive it' Z408 is a delightful example of a gavotte song), and he tended to reserve duple time for settings of serious poetry using the tradition of declamatory song, derived from Henry Lawes* and Jacobean composers. This type mirrors the inflections of speech, illustrating the words with appropriate images, angular melodic lines and often dissonant harmony, though with more melodic coherence than in true recitative*. A fine early example is 'What hope for us remains now he is gone?' Z472 (1677), the elegy for Matthew Locke*. The declamatory principle was later diluted by a fashion for suave melodic writing in patterns of flowing quavers, as in the first two settings of 'If music be the food of love'* (?1691–2).

In the 1680s Purcell mostly preferred to include declamatory passages in extended multi-section songs, as in his Abraham Cowley* settings (some of them symphony songs*); a fine example is 'The rich rival', 'They say you're angry' Z422 (late 1684), which mixes declamatory passages with almand*- and minuet-like sections. The multi-sectional principle was taken to its logical conclusion in mad songs*, notably in the famous Bess of Bedlam, 'From silent shades'*. Purcell added a third ingredient to this mix of idioms with ground basses*. 'Cease, anxious world, your fruitless pain' Z362 (late 1684) is a remarkable early example, though most occur in multi-sectional works, as in the elegy for Thomas Farmer*, 'Young Thyrsis' fate ye hills and groves deplore' Z473 (winter 1688–9). A classic type of late Purcell song is a musical diptych, with a declamatory passage (by then enlivened with bursts of Italianate ornamentation) followed by a matching minuet-like section, as in the third setting of 'If music be the food of love' (?May 1695) or 'The fatal hour comes on apace' Z421 (?1694–5).

Nearly all of Purcell songs deal with some aspect of love, usually written from the male poet's perspective, though there are a few non-theatrical 'female' ones, such as 'How I sigh when I think of the charms of my swain' Z374 (summer 1680). John Playford* printed vocal music in the treble clef to be sung equally at the higher or lower octave, and this usage was followed by Purcell and his colleagues, becoming standard practice in England earlier than other countries. A number of his songs have a 'chorus'* in which the soloist is joined by a bass voice largely doubling the continuo. His duets for treble or tenor, bass and continuo are, along with his dialogues*, among his least-known works, though they include a number of miniature masterpieces such as 'Dulcibella, whene'er I sue for a kiss' Z485 (1694) or 'When Myra sings' Z521 (1695). See also **Devotional songs and part-songs**, **Harmonia Sacra**. *AdaPoe, ArkGen, BalMad, DaySon, HolPur, JonSon, LauSon, RohPoe, SavScu, SpiSon, ZimCat.*

Song tune The Restoration name for instrumental versions of songs and other vocal music. Most of Purcell's examples are four-part consort settings, published in *A Collection of Ayres**, of favourite pieces from the dramatic operas*, such as 'Let the soldiers rejoice' from *Dioclesian**, 'Fairest isle'* from *King Arthur** and 'If love's a sweet passion'* from *The Fairy Queen**. It has been assumed that they served as preludes* or ritornellos* to their parent vocal pieces, though they may have been arranged just as 'hit songs' from the shows, not necessarily by the composer. The two song tunes in *Musick's Hand-Maid**, part 2 are simple keyboard settings of the songs 'Ah! how pleasant 'tis to love' Z353 and 'Sylvia, now your scorn give over' Z420. *HolPur, SchAyr, WooKey.*

Sonnata's of III Parts The first set of trio sonatas* published in England; the first engraved edition of consort music since Orlando Gibbons's* *Fantazias of III. Parts* (c.1620); and the first publication devoted entirely to Purcell's music. The composer published it by subscription, and had it handsomely engraved by Thomas Cross*; it was sold by John Playford* and John Carr*. Cross used an engraving style similar to Playford's own hand and therefore probably worked from a set of parts written out by the publisher rather than the composer. Purcell dedicated it to Charles II* (a presentation copy on special paper belonged to Samuel Pepys*), stating in his famous preface that he had 'faithfully endeavour'd a just imitation of the most fam'd Italian Masters'; he recommended 'the power of the Italian Notes' to English musicians. He also explained Italian tempo* marks and mentioned that he had not originally intended to include a separate continuo* part. Perhaps he had intended keyboard players to play from a manuscript score or may have planned to combine the continuo and bass viol* parts, though that would have been impracticable, so often do they diverge. A second edition was produced in 1684, and copies (probably run off from the original plates) were advertised by Purcell's widow Frances in 1699 and by John Walsh* in 1707. *See also* **Roger North**, **Portraits**, **Trio sonatas**. *DunSon, HarPla, HogTri, HolPur, HowArt, SchSon, ShaMan, SmiWal, ThoSou.*

'Sound the trumpet, beat the drum' Z335 Purcell's use of instruments in this ode, James II's* 'Birthday Song' for 14 October 1687, was ground-breaking in several respects: the bravura bass solo (by then a staple of court odes*) is accompanied by four-part strings, while previous examples only used two solo violins with continuo. The strings do not simply double the voices in the choruses but sometimes expand the texture to as many as seven real parts. Purcell clearly relished the irony that trumpets* and kettledrums* were not yet available for his concerted music; instead, he imitated them in the opening vocal entries and in subsequent string passages. Midway through the ode he inserted a majestic 128-bar chaconne* (later used in *King Arthur**), which, like other ground-bass* orchestral movements in his odes, may have been danced. Three vocal movements stand out. The memorable tenor solo 'Crown the year'* is set to a modulating and flexibly extendable ground bass. Better still is 'Let Caesar and Urania live', the famous countertenor duet over a ground bass that, according to Burney* (*BurHis*, iii. 494), Maurice Greene and William Boyce* inserted into several of their court odes. The string-accompanied 'While Caesar, like the morning star', one of the finest solos Purcell wrote for John Gostling*, exploits the extremes of the singer's range to superb dramatic effect. *AdaPur, HolPur, HolRos, SpiOde, WooOde.*

Southerne, Thomas This Irish playwright (1660–1746), initially a close associate of John Dryden*, had five plays produced at Drury Lane* to which Purcell contributed songs: the comedies *Sir Anthony Love* Z588 (November 1690), *The Wives Excuse* Z612 (December 1691) and *The Maid's Last Prayer* Z601 (February 1693), and the enduringly successful tragedies *The Fatal Marriage* Z595 (February 1694) and *Oroonoko* Z584 (November 1695), both adapted from novels by Aphra Behn. Southerne was clearly knowledgeable about music, though he does not seem to have been particularly interested in exploiting its dramatic potential in his plays. However, *The Wives Excuse* is of particular interest because it opens with a 'Musick-Meeting', probably satirising the concerts at York Buildings*; it features the performance of an unspecified 'Italian song' followed by 'An *English Song*', which turns out to be Purcell's 'Ingrateful Love! thus ev'ry hour' Z612/1, a bipartite minuet-like song with some brilliant Italianate runs.

Curtis Price remarked that Purcell and Southerne 'must have been kindred spirits. Each possessed a faultless technique that was at its best when depicting passion'. He pointed to the superb song (with a prelude for two solo violins and bass) 'Pursuing beauty' in *Sir Anthony Love* Z588/2 and the duet 'No, resistance is but vain' Z601/2 in *The Maid's Last Prayer* as contributions to Southerne's plays that were 'among the composer's finest pieces'. 'No, resistance is but vain' is of particular interest because it is an incongruously beautiful item in another chaotic music meeting: a scene in Act IV set in the house of Sir Symphony, an amateur bass viol player and musical know-all. According to the play text the duet was sung by two of Purcell's leading theatre singers, Mrs Ayliff* and Mary Hodgson*. *LS, PriPur, PriThe, ZimCat*.

Spinet *Spinetta* was the original Italian term for the rectangular type of plucked keyboard instrument, usually called virginal* in English, though in Restoration England 'spinet' was normally used for the compact triangular type; it replaced the virginal during Purcell's lifetime. A single set of strings runs at an angle of about 30 degrees from the keyboard with an abbreviated version of the wing-shaped bentside of a harpsichord – hence the term 'bentside spinet'. The type may have been invented by the Roman harpsichord maker Girolamo Zenti (*c*.1610–67), Charles II's* virginal maker in 1663–4. See also **Harpsichord**. *BDECM, BoaMou, KosHar, MolPur, MolSpi*.

Stage history from 1695 After Purcell's death most of his major stage works continued to be used in stage productions of the parent plays, though the loss of the full score of *The Fairy Queen** around 1695 prevented complete performances of that dramatic opera* until the twentieth century. *Dioclesian** was revived at Drury Lane* in 1700, 1702 and 1705, and at the Lincoln's Inn Fields Theatre in 1715 with 'all the Original Musick'. Purcell's 'original Musick' was also a selling-point for revivals of *The Indian Queen** at Drury Lane in 1706 and 1715. *Dido and Aeneas**, apparently never performed in public in Purcell's lifetime, was inserted into plays at Lincoln's Inn Fields in 1700 and 1704, but was not given another stage production until 1895, when it was revived at the Lyceum Theatre in London by students from the Royal College of Music conducted by Charles Villiers Stanford.

King Arthur* had the longest stage history. After the initial production in 1691 it was revived in 1698, 1701 and 1706, and then at the theatre in Goodman Fields in December 1735; there is a vivid description of the Frost Scene* by the poet Thomas Gray (*BurRem*, 98–9). Later revivals at Drury Lane include David Garrick's adaptation, with a score revised and enlarged by Thomas Arne* (December 1770); and a revival by Richard Brinsley Sheridan and Thomas Linley senior (October 1781); a greatly shortened afterpiece, *Arthur and Emmeline*, adapted by John Phillip Kemble and Thomas Linley (November 1784), was popular until 1791 and was revived in 1803, 1819 and 1827. The last notable production in the continuous tradition was the spectacular version of

King Arthur put on by William Charles Macready at Drury Lane on 16 November 1842, with music arranged by Thomas Simpson Cooke.

Notable productions of Purcell's operas in the twentieth century include *Dido and Aeneas* and the Act V masque from *Dioclesian*, put on by Gordon Craig and the Purcell Operatic Society (1900–2); *The Fairy Queen* and *King Arthur*, given by Edward Dent and Clive Carey at the New Theatre, Cambridge (1920, 1928); *The Fairy Queen* at Covent Garden (1946) conducted by Constant Lambert; *Dido and Aeneas* with Kirsten Flagstad at Bernard Miles's Mermaid Theatre (1951); and Roger Savage's landmark *Fairy Queen* at Edinburgh University (1972), the first revival using the 1692 text of the play. Michael Burden has shown that earlier revivals of the dramatic operas were all travesties to a lesser or greater extent, with the spoken text often omitted or replaced and the music rescored, reordered or even replaced by pieces from other Purcell works. In 1971 M.J. Greenhalgh (*GreArt*) satirised the version of the Britten-influenced *King Arthur*, assembled by Colin Graham and Philip Ledger for the English Opera Group, by imagining a version of *Peter Grimes* treated in a similar fashion. There has been little improvement since, though the *Fairy Queen* first done at Glyndebourne in 2009 mostly used the 1692 text, avoiding the fatal pitfall of trying to marry Purcell's music with Shakespeare's original play. *See also* **Anniversary celebrations**, **Benjamin Britten**, **Recordings**. *BurArt, BurCra, BurDeb, BurGal, GilArn, GilGar, HarArt, HarDid, HerRec, LS, LSNV, PinPhe, SavFai, SquFai.*

Staggins, Nicholas The son of Isaack (a 'common musician of London' according to Anthony Wood), Nicholas Staggins (d.1700) joined his father in the Twenty-Four Violins in 1670; he unexpectedly became Master of the Music in 1674, succeeding Pelham Humfrey*, who had died on 14 July that year. Staggins was not much of a composer: most of his major works, including three court odes*, are lost, and his surviving songs and instrumental pieces are unambitious. He received a doctorate at Cambridge in 1682, but the Vice-Chancellor allowed him to submit an exercise for instruments only rather than the specified eight-part vocal and instrumental composition, a decision that caused 'great murmurings' according to Hawkins* (*HawHis*, ii. 739), though that did not prevent him being appointed the first Cambridge professor of music in 1684. Tom Brown* described him as 'bandy-legged and even contemptuously regarded'. Nevertheless, Staggins served three monarchs as Master of the Music, apparently without complaint, so he must have been a good administrator. He travelled to France and Italy in 1676 probably to study operatic practice, and in 1683 he applied with John Blow* for a licence to develop 'an Academy or Opera of Musick', which may have led that year to the construction of a theatre in Windsor Castle and to the production there of Blow's *Venus and Adonis* – providing Purcell with the model for *Dido and Aeneas**. *BDECM, BloVen, HolFid, MurOde, SpiSon, ThoOpe, WalMas, WooDid.*

Stainer & Bell An independent music publisher, founded in 1907 and based in north London. It took over the publication of the Purcell Society* edition from Novello & Co. in 2007, adding it to a catalogue that also includes the scholarly series Musica Britannica and Early English Church Music. Other notable Purcell publications issued by the firm include Michael Nyman's* edition of the catches* (*PurCat*), the first with unbowdlerised words; and Rebecca Herissone's reconstruction of the lost original version of 'Come, ye sons of art, away'*.

The Staircase Overture Almost certainly Purcell's earliest surviving consort piece, probably written in 1675. Its title refers to the rushing scales of the almand*-like first section, indebted to Matthew Locke's* theatre airs* for *The Tempest** (1674). After a minuet*-like second section, the duple-time conclusion plunges unexpectedly and eloquently from the home key, B^b major, into B^b minor, apparently inspired by a similar move in the Prelude to Robert Smith's* 'New Year's Day' suite, probably written for 1 January 1675. An autograph set of parts was subsequently incorporated into a set of consort partbooks, of which the bass part Osborn MS 515* is the sole survivor. Luckily, Philip Hayes* scored it up before the other books were lost, providing parts for two violins, bass and continuo; there is probably a viola part missing and Hayes may have added the continuo part to compensate for its absence. *BroSta, ForOsb, HerHay, HolPur, PurThe, ShaMan, WolOve.*

Stationers' Hall The livery hall of the Stationers' Company near St Paul's Cathedral*, completed in 1673. It remains little changed from Purcell's day, when it was hired by the Musical Society for the annual Cecilian celebrations*. It measures about 25 by 10 metres with a gallery over the south door. For performances, such as that of 'Hail, bright Cecilia'* in 1692, scaffolding was built in the hall to accommodate the large numbers of performers. The hall was hired regularly by organisations for feasts and concerts and was used in 1702 for Cavendish Weedon's series of Divine Entertainments. *WhiCec.*

Stratigraphic scores The term used for scores printed or copied right across an opening. They were produced in Italy around 1600 and in Germany throughout the seventeenth century so that keyboard players score-reading while accompanying singers would have to move their eyes from system-to-system half the number of times needed for a conventional score; there are some early seventeenth-century English examples, presumably copied for the same reason. Restoration composers used the format for their autograph scores of choral music, usually by extending the staves freehand across the centre of the opening of conventional pre-ruled music paper. Purcell laid out the autographs* of his Benedicite from the Service in B^b Z230M3 (GB-Ob, Mus.a.1) and 'Let mine eyes run down with tears' Z24 (GB-Ob, Mus c.26, ff. 4–9) in this way. He also used it for his score of Daniel Roseingrave's* anthem 'Lord, thou art become gracious' (GB-Och, Mus. 1215, section 1), and for a two-stave organ part for Blow's* anthem 'God is our hope and strength' (GB-Och, Mus. 554, f. 3). GB-Cfm, MU MS 684, William Isaack's* stratigraphic score of 'Who can from joy refrain?'*, originally consisted of unbound leaves and was perhaps used by Purcell in that state to direct the performance from the keyboard. *HerCat, HerCre, HerFow, HolBat, HolRos, ShaMan, ThoSou.*

Style brisé The accepted modern term for a broken texture in lute and keyboard music, in which counterpoint* is suggested by interlocking arpeggios rather than in fully worked-out, continuous part-writing. It was fashionable in French and French-style dances from the 1630s until at least the 1660s. David Ledbetter argued that Purcell 'playfully mocked' poor realisations of the idiom in his Suite in G major Z660, evidently written for beginners, though the composer also had recourse to it in more serious and ambitious solo keyboard pieces, such as the 'Bell Barr'* Almand in D minor Z668/1.

Purcell also seems to have used it when accompanying solo vocal music, to judge from the solo keyboard settings of his ground-bass* songs with *style brisé* realisations of the continuo* interludes. These include 'With him he brings the partner' ZT681 ('Ye tuneful Muses'* Z344/11) and 'Here the deities approve' ZT682 ('Welcome to all the pleasures'* Z339/3). This idiom seems to have been an idiosyncrasy of Purcell (which is apparently why William Croft's* Ground in C minor ZD221 was wrongly attributed to him), so the anonymous settings using the same idiom, of Lully's* 'Scocca pur'* (Ex. 9), and of 'Crown the year'* Z335/3 from 'Sound the trumpet, beat the drum'*, are also probably by him. Roger North* (*NorMus*, 247) was perhaps thinking of Purcell when he wrote that 'the sprinkling or *arpeggio*' was 'the proper genius' of the harpsichord, especially when 'humouring a solo or single voice, where there is much of interlude, which lets that instrument in to shew itself'. HerCre, HogCor, LedSty.

Ex. 9: Purcell's keyboard setting of J.B. Lully, 'Scocca pur tutti tuoi strali', bb. 1–5.

Suite This French word tended to be reserved in Restoration England for a sequence of dances in a single key, with or without a prelude* or overture*. It is therefore best avoided for Purcell's sets of theatre airs*, with their movements in several keys, not originally performed in a continuous sequence. Purcell's harpsichord suites as collected in the posthumous *Choice Collection** have almand*-corant* pairs as core ingredients, prefaced frequently by a prelude and followed by a saraband*; only one, Z665, has a jig* as well, achieving the classic four-movement sequence common in continental Europe. However, Purcell evidently altered the make-up of his suites according to circumstances: manuscripts (including the autograph Purcell-Draghi Manuscript*) preserve versions with a number of alternative movements.

Only two consort suites by Purcell are known, both probably composed in the early 1680s: the four-part Suite in G major Z770 and a recently discovered sequence of dances following the five-part Overture in G minor Z772 in US-NH, Filmer MS 8. Purcell left Z770 incomplete: in the autograph score, GB-Lbl, Add. MS 30930, he reserved a space for a movement between the minuet Z770/3 and the jig Z770/4 (filled in with Z577/7 from *Distressed Innocence** in PS 31), and entered the inner parts only for the Overture Z770/1a, b and the Air Z770/1c. The five-movement suite following Z772 in Filmer MS 8 (consisting of a triple-time rondeau*, a borry, two more triple-time dances and a jig) was presumably written by Purcell in five parts, though only its bass part survives. ChaJig, HogCor, HolPur, MacMus, FerPur, ShaBas, ShaMan, WooKey, ZimCat.

'The summer's absence unconcerned we bear' Z337 Purcell dated the autograph copy of his third welcome song* for Charles II* 'October ye 21 – 1682', the day of the king's return from Newmarket. As with 'What shall be done in behalf of the man'*, the anonymous poet extolled the crown's succession from Charles II to his brother the future James II*, made possible by the king's victory over those determined to exclude James. The opening declamatory bass air is striking for its dramatic plunges to D and E, exploiting John Gostling's* extended low range for the first time. Two sections of Z337 are notable for their similarity to movements in *Dido and Aeneas**. The treble duet 'All hearts should smile', with its minuet* pattern and parallel thirds, is related to the Act I duet 'Fear no danger', while the modulating ground bass* of the fine countertenor solo 'These had by their ill usage drove' corresponds closely to 'Oft she visits', the Second Woman's solo in the Grove Scene. *HolPur, SpiOde, WooDid, WooEqu, WooOde.*

'Sweeter than roses' Z585/1 Purcell wrote this famous song for the tragedy *Pausanias*, probably by Richard Norton; the play may not have been produced at Drury Lane* until the spring of 1696, after the composer's death. The piece was sung at the beginning of Act III to Pandora, the mistress of Pausanias, the regent of Sparta; she is about to try to seduce the youth Argilius. It is in two sections: the first, an Italianate recitative in C minor, has beautiful written-out ornamentation* (Curtis Price describes it as 'an unforgettable evocation of suspended ecstasy'); the second, in minuet rhythm and C major, is mostly taken up with virtuosic passages using the trumpet idiom to illustrate the words 'What magic has victorious love!'. *AdaPur, LS, PriPur.*

'Swifter, Isis, swifter flow' Z336 Purcell's second welcome song* for Charles II* was composed in 1681. The anonymous poet clearly anticipated the king's arrival by barge on the Thames (the river is called the Isis above its meeting with the Thame at Dorchester), and it perhaps marked his return from Oxford* in March after the dissolution of parliament; or (less appropriately) it may have celebrated the king's return from Windsor* in late August of the same year. The work is a marked advance on Purcell's first welcome song, 'Welcome, vicegerent of the mighty king'*: it consists of fewer, longer sections organised in a wider, better-planned tonal scheme. He also expanded the instrumental palette: the bass solo 'Land him safely on her shore' is accompanied by two recorders*; one player also doubled on oboe* in the ritornello* to the tenor solo 'Hark! just now my list'ning ears'. The latter, first of a long series of ground-bass* songs in Purcell's odes, was perhaps inspired by John Blow's* example in 'Great Sir, the joy of all our hearts', composed for the New Year 1681. *AdaOde, AdaPur, HolPur, McGGro, SpiOde, WooEqu, WooOde, WooPur.*

Symphony The word Purcell commonly used for multi-sectional pieces at the beginning of symphony anthems*, odes* and masques* in the dramatic operas*. He also used it for unitary introductory movements (interchangeably to some extent with 'Prelude'*), as in his early symphony anthem 'My beloved spake'*. However, 'Overture'* was the label used for the French type in *A Collection of Ayres** and other sources of Purcell's theatre music, so it makes sense to restrict 'Symphony' to the multi-sectional Italianate type, increasingly common in his later concerted music. It differs from the French type by not starting with a passage of dotted notes (a fanfare passage was a common alternative); by using the canzona* idiom in the second section; and in a few cases by greatly extending the pattern – as in the much-imitated symphony to 'Hail, bright Cecilia'* – in eight sections with all repeats observed. However, the terminology was not always consistent: the superb six-movement piece that begins the Masque of the Four Seasons in *The Fairy Queen**, Act IV is labelled 'Symphony' in the part-autograph score but is described as 'Sonata' in the play's printed text. *HolPur, HowArt, PriPur.*

Symphony anthem The type of verse anthem enhanced with passages for strings (and occasionally other instruments), developed in the Chapel Royal* during the early years of Charles II's* reign. It was strongly encouraged by the king, 'a brisk & Airy Prince' according to Thomas Tudway*, who 'Order'd ye Composers of his Chappell, to add Symphonys &c w<i>th Instruments to their Anthems' (*HogTud*, 25). Tudway added that they were only performed when Charles 'came himself to ye Chapell, w<hi>ch was only upon Sundays in ye morning, on ye great festivals, & days of Offerings'. The genre had antecedents in several anthem-like works by Henry Lawes* composed before the Restoration, and in the Italian and French concerted sacred music Charles would have heard during his years in exile on the continent. Henry Cooke* wrote the earliest (rather poor) examples, but it was Matthew Locke*, Pelham Humfrey* and later John Blow* who made the most important contributions to the genre before Purcell; Locke had also been in exile on the continent, while Humfrey was sent abroad to study in the 1660s. Amongst Purcell's first symphony anthems are 'My beloved spake'*, composed by the end of 1677 and 'Behold, now praise the Lord' Z3.

Purcell's symphony anthems are typically scored for soloists, choir, four-part strings and continuo. At the Chapel Royal the string parts were played one-to-a-part by groups from the Twenty-Four Violins*, with organ and theorbo continuo. These anthems had a spatial dimension in performance not immediately obvious from the scores: the soloists were apparently in the organ loft; the strings in a neighbouring first-floor gallery; and the choir in the stalls on the floor of the Chapel, where the bass voices may have been doubled by bass viols. It was normally only in coronations*, held in Westminster Abbey*, that the full (and even enlarged) Twenty-Four Violins participated in symphony anthems.

As a Catholic, James II* did not attend the Anglican Chapel Royal, so new symphony anthems were only written for occasions when Princess Anne* attended; of the 27 by Purcell (two survive incomplete), all but eight date from Charles II's reign. William III* and Mary II*, strongly Calvinist, banned all instruments but the organ from the Chapel, effectively putting an end to the genre. However, the church services held on St Cecilia's Day from 1693 created a new context for their performance, and for the related genre of concerted settings of the Te Deum and Jubilate*, which Purcell initiated in 1694.

The symphony anthem depended on the availability of court string players, so most of the repertory was not taken up in provincial cathedrals, though 'Rejoice in the Lord alway'* and one or two others did circulate with the string passages omitted or replaced with organ ritornellos*. Conversely, Purcell transformed the verse anthem 'My song shall be alway'* into a symphony anthem, perhaps for a performance in Oxford*, where the university's Music School had a sporadic tradition of performing such works. *HolFid, HolPur, PikRej, ShaMan, SpiRes, VanChu, WhiCec.*

Symphony song A Restoration genre of multi-sectional secular works for two to four voices with obbligato violins or recorders and continuo. Today they are often called 'cantatas' – an inappropriate word for works closer to odes and anthems than to the later Italian cantata, with its formal alternation of recitative and aria. The eight by Purcell had antecedents in concerted madrigals by earlier composers such as Walter Porter and George Jeffreys, though the immediate model was John Blow's* 'Awake, awake my lyre', a setting of verses by Abraham Cowley* for four voices, two violins and continuo; it was probably written in memory of Christopher Gibbons*, who died on 20 October 1676.

Purcell copied his symphony songs into his autograph scorebook, GB-Lbl, R.M. 20.h.8, in a sequence that also includes court odes* with known dates. This apparently means that he copied five of them ('How pleasant is this flow'ry plain' Z543; the unfinished 'We reap all the pleasures' Z547; 'Hark how the wild musicians sing' Z542; 'Hark, Damon, hark' Z541; and 'See where she sits' Z508) between 21 October 1682 and 28 July 1683. He added 'Oh! what a scene does entertain my sight' Z506 and the Serenading Song 'Soft notes and gently rais'd accent' Z510 between 22 November 1683 and the autumn of 1684. 'If ever I more riches did desire'* Z544 came later, copied between odes performed in October 1686 and 1687. A ninth work, 'Raise, raise the voice'* Z334, is usually classified as a Cecilian ode but has more in common with symphony songs.

Purcell's symphony songs were probably performed at Whitehall* by the court Private Music*. Some of them have pastoral texts that refer to the spring and may have been first performed at informal court celebrations akin to the annual Maying ceremonies of Henry VIII's court. On the other hand, Z508 and Z544, both settings of Abraham Cowley, are more serious works: in Z508 Purcell responded to Cowley's dense and extravagant images with dense textures (the outer sections have six-part anthem-like writing with three of the contrapuntal lines taken by instruments and daring harmonies with constant false relations). The finest of the lighter symphony songs is Z543, and it is of particular interest because a contemporary hand squeezed in an elaborate written-out continuo realisation, probably for archlute, between the staves of a copy of Henry Playford's* *The Banquet of Music*, book 1 (1688), now GB-Ob, Harding Mus. E 65. *HolPar, HolPur, ShaMan, SpiSon.*

Talbot, James Clergyman and writer (1664–1708), best known as the compiler of a series of manuscript notes on musical instruments, now GB-Och, MS 1187; they were apparently made in the 1690s for a never-completed treatise. It is our most important contemporary source of information about the instruments written for by Purcell. Talbot probably encountered him as chaplain and secretary to Charles Seymour, sixth Duke of Somerset*: Purcell dedicated the score of *Dioclesian** to Seymour, and an inscription in the copy now at US-NHub records that it had been his gift to 'his friend and admirer James Talbot' ('Amico suo atque Admiratori Jacopo Talbot'). Inserted into this volume is the autograph of Talbot's ode on Purcell's death, set by Gottfried Finger* and subsequently published in *Orpheus Britannicus**, book 1. *See also* **Poems praising Purcell**. *BaiTal, HerScr, HigRec, HowOde, RawFin, UnwTal.*

Tate, Nahum (Nathaniel) Poet, playwright and translator (c.1652–1715). He graduated from Trinity College, Dublin, in 1672 and was established as a writer in London by 1676. In 1680 Purcell set the song 'Retir'd from any mortal's sight' Z581 for *The Sicilian Usurper*, an adaptation of Shakespeare's* *Richard II*, probably performed in December; Tate renamed it to avoid censorship after it was perceived to be a commentary on the Exclusion Crisis. He subsequently adapted his first play, *Brutus of Alba* (1678), based on Virgil's *Aeneid*, book 4, as the opera *Dido and Aeneas**, which Purcell set no later than 1688.

Tate was apparently well respected in musical circles. He provided the 1685 St Cecilia's Day ode for William Turner* and wrote an elegy on the death of John Playford*, 'Gentle shepherds, you that know' Z464, set by Purcell in 1687. In 1689 he may have recommended Purcell to set 'Celestial music did the gods inspire'* for his friend Lewis Maidwell's school; and in 1690 Purcell set his elegy 'Young Thyrsis' fate ye hills and groves deplore' Z473 in memory of Thomas Farmer* – who had provided music for *Brutus of Alba*. He succeeded Thomas Shadwell* as Poet Laureate in December 1692, choosing to write the great majority of court odes* himself, thereby establishing a lasting precedent. In 1693 Purcell set his ode for Mary II's* birthday, 'Celebrate this festival'*; 'Come, ye sons of art, away'* (1694) may also be by him.

Purcell set two of Tate's poems, almost certainly written expressly for him, for *Harmonia Sacra**, book 2 (1693): 'Awake, ye dead' Z182 and 'Tell me, some pitying angel', The Blessed Virgin's Expostulation*. Henry Playford* published Tate's anthology of sacred poetry, *Miscellanea Sacra* (1696), containing most of the verse used in the two books of *Harmonia Sacra*. Tate also probably recruited Purcell to set his ode for the centenary of Trinity College, Dublin, 'Great parent, hail'* (1694); their last collaboration was the 1695 birthday ode for the Duke of Gloucester, 'Who can from joy refrain?'* After Purcell's death, he commemorated their long-standing and fruitful relationship with a lament, 'A gloomy mist o'erspreads the plains', published in *Orpheus Britannicus**, book 1; Daniel Purcell's* setting is unfortunately lost.

Tate's verse has routinely been derided by modern critics, but he was a skilled writer of poetry for music, and he was regularly set by the most significant composers of the day, including John Blow*, Jeremiah Clarke* and John Eccles*; he consistently inspired fine settings from Purcell. The tightly focussed plot and vivid rhyming verse of *Dido and Aeneas* contributes greatly to its dramatic power, while his depiction of the Virgin Mary's mental turmoil in The Blessed Virgin's Expostulation was crucial to the potent psychological depth of Purcell's setting. Tate was the poet with whom Purcell enjoyed the most long-standing relationship – one clearly founded on great mutual respect. Despite all this, he is mainly remembered (with Nicholas Brady*) for *A New Version of the Psalms of David* (1696), which ran to more than 300 editions over 150 years, and for the associated hymn 'While shepherds watched their flocks by night'. BalBir, HarDid, HelPre, HolPur, MurOde, WooDid.

Te Deum and Jubilate in D major Z232 Purcell composed these groundbreaking settings for the service at St Bride's, Fleet Street*, on St Cecilia's Day 1694. In 1693 the Musical Society instituted a service there before their annual Cecilian celebrations*, with a sermon supporting instrumentally accompanied sacred music. Purcell's Te Deum and Jubilate demonstrated its potential: close imitations by John Blow* and William Turner* followed in consecutive years. By using trumpets* (for the first time in English sacred music) with strings and continuo, he was responding to William III* and Mary II's* 1689 ban on orchestral instruments in the Chapel Royal*, probably hoping his settings would be used in the annual thanksgiving services for the king's continental campaigns. However, their use in this role in the Chapel Royal on 11 December 1694 did not lead to a general restoration of concerted music there.

Purcell followed tradition by using a sectional structure for the lengthy Te Deum hymn, and by employing canonic writing at 'O go your way' in the Jubilate, as he had in his B♭ Service*. However, he greatly expanded the scope of the settings with several free-standing movements, notably the extended treatment of 'Vouchsafe, O Lord' in the Te Deum, scored for countertenor*, two solo violins and continuo. He also included several artifice-filled contrapuntal choruses, linking an entry in double augmentation in the bass at 'Ever world without end' in the Te Deum with a bass entry in triple augmentation at 'World without end' in the Jubilate.

Purcell's contemporaries were stunned by the sonic power of these works. Thomas Tudway* described the setting of 'Holy, holy, holy' in the Te Deum in ecstatic terms, marvelling at the 'whole Copia Sonorum, of voices, & instruments', and challenging 'all ye Orators, Poets, Painters &c of any Age whatsoever, to form so lively an Idea, of Choirs of Angels singing, & paying their Adorations' (*HogTud*, 45). Purcell's widow Frances published the settings in 1697 to coincide with a repeat performance on St Cecilia's Day that year, dedicating them to Nathaniel Crew, Bishop of Durham. They were performed regularly at national thanksgiving services; in the Festival of the Sons of the Clergy; at the Three Choirs Festival; and in provincial Cecilian celebrations*. Walsh* reissued the original print with a new title page in 1707 and later issued a newly engraved edition; other editions appeared periodically throughout the century.

Purcell's canticles provided the model for more extended settings by William Croft* (1709, rev. 1715) and Handel* (1713, for the Peace of Utrecht). William Boyce* modernised them in 1755, while Philip Hayes* and John Stafford Smith produced abridged versions. Benjamin Cooke composed a new setting of 'Vouchsafe, O Lord' when the Te Deum was performed for the Installation of the Knights of Bath at Westminster Abbey on 15 June 1772. *See also* **Renatus (René) Harris**. *AdaPur, BurCha, HerRec, HolBat, HolPur, HowArt, LucSha, McVCat, SmiWal, SpiPau, VanChu, WhiCec.*

'Tell me, some pitying angel' *See* **The Blessed Virgin's Expostulation**

Temperament In the seventeenth century keyboard instruments were normally tuned in unequal temperament, specifically quarter-comma meantone, which gives pure thirds in home keys (from E♭ major and C minor to E major and E minor if split keys are provided for the E♭/D♯ and G♯/A♭ keys or those notes are retuned according to the music being played), but gives thirds too sharp in remote keys to be tolerable. Purcell wrote his solo keyboard music within this 'envelope' of keys available in quarter-comma meantone, implying that this is how he expected the spinets* and harpsichords* of his pupils and amateur clientele to be tuned.

However, Purcell clearly expected the keyboard instruments he used in his ensemble music to be tuned in one of the modified meantone systems that were beginning to replace quarter-comma meantone. They enabled all keys to be used, but with progressively sharper thirds in remoter keys. Thus there are trio sonatas* in F minor and B minor (Z800, Z802); an anthem in B minor ('The Lord is my light' Z55); sections of theatre works in F minor (part of the Witches' Scene in *Dido and Aeneas** Z626/14, 16) and B minor ('Thus the ever grateful spring' from *The Fairy Queen** Z629/33). There are also many excursions outside the quarter-comma meantone envelope in other works. For instance, 'Jehova, quam multi sunt hostes mei'* in A minor uses B♭s and A♯s, E♭s and D♯s, A♭s and G♯s, D♭s and C♯s as well as E♯s.

Purcell was John Hingeston's* assistant as court 'keeper, maker, repairer and mender and tuner' from 1673, and therefore may have specified the temperament of the Chapel Royal* organ* when Bernard Smith* lowered its pitch* in 1676. The tuning recipes written down by his contemporaries J.G. Keller (published in 1705) and Roger North* (*NorMus*, 203–12) clearly go beyond quarter-comma meantone, though they do not seem to be precise enough to convey the exact temperaments they favoured; it is not clear whether they correspond to Purcell's practice. However, North was aware that 'meer out-of-tuned-ness have certain caracters, very serviceable to the various purposes of Musick', and it is clear that temperament was an important ingredient of key characteristics*. In particular, the sour D♭s (closer to C♯s) of F minor would have contributed to the horror Purcell powerfully evoked in his music for the Witches in *Dido*. *DufTem*, *MefTem*, *ParPer*.

The Tempest, or The Enchanted Island Shakespeare's* play was adapted by John Dryden* and William Davenant (1667) and then by Thomas Shadwell* as a dramatic opera* (1674), with music by John Banister*, Pelham Humfrey*, Matthew Locke*, Robert Smith*, Pietro Reggio* and others. A later setting of the music required for the Restoration version of the play, principally the devils' music in Act II, Ariel's songs and the Act V Masque of Neptune and Amphitrite, was attributed to Purcell in the late eighteenth century and was generally accepted as genuine (Z631) until the 1960s; it was edited by Edward Dent for the Purcell Society* in 1912. Sir Jack Westrup (*WesPur*, 145–9) thought it 'Purcell's most mature work for the theatre', responding to the striking chorus of 'Full fathom five' with 'first admiration and joy and then a stab of regret that this abounding maturity and mastery was so soon after brought to nothing'.

However, in 1964 Margaret Laurie drew attention to an advertisement for a performance of *The Tempest* at Drury Lane* on 31 July 1716 stating that 'All the musick' for the play had been composed by John Weldon*; she argued convincingly that this charming score, with its da capo arias, Italianate vocal writing and a rather modern harmonic idiom, was too late in style to be by Purcell. Weldon's score, which may have been composed as early as 1706, includes one genuine Purcell song: 'Dear pretty youth' Z631/10, composed for Letitia Cross* as Dorinda in Act IV for an unrecorded 1695 revival. The G minor overture included by Dent in his edition (Z631/1) is also genuine Purcell, but Curtis Price suggested it came from the otherwise lost prologue to *Dido and Aeneas**; it is included in *PS* 3. *ChoSha*, *HigRec*, *LauTem*, *LocDra*, *LS*, *PriIns*, *PriPur*, *RylTem*, *ShaMan*, *WalDra*, *ZimCat*.

Tempo Purcell and his contemporaries inherited the remnants of the Renaissance mensural system in which tempo was essentially indicated by the note values and time signatures chosen. In theory ¢ was twice as fast as C, and 𝄵 twice as fast again, though he just described them respectively (*PlaInt*, 25–7) as 'slowest of all', 'a little faster' and 'quickest of all'; 2 was 'The *French* mark for this retorted *Time*'. This is largely borne out by his use of them in his concerted music. He habitually notated declamatory passages in C, to be sung in a moderate four, changing to ¢ or 𝄵 for faster sections, though he sometimes followed French practice by using 2 for the first section of overtures*, meaning a moderate two-in-a-bar, as with the symphony to 'My heart is inditing'*. Purcell's use of the system is mostly admirably clear (though it is often disregarded in modern performances), with problems largely created by later printers and copyists, who tended to replace C with ¢, obscuring the distinction Purcell made between them. Conversely, the Cold Genius's* shivering music in The Frost Scene* from *King Arthur** is often performed at half speed today because two early but non-autograph scores notate it in C rather than ¢ – the time signature used when the chorus sings its own version of the shivering music.

The mensural system also provided for the relationship between duple and triple time, though by the early seventeenth century these proportional relationships – three triple-time notes in the time of two (*sesquialtera*) or one (*tripla*) – broke down as the semibreve beat or *tactus* gave way to a minim beat and then to the modern crotchet beat – changes largely caused by composers including faster and faster note-values in florid passages. In *A Choice Collection** Purcell (or his posthumous editor) merely wrote that 3/2 is 'commonly play'd very slow'; 3i has 'three Crotchets in a barr, and they are to be play'd slow; 3 also has three-crotchet bars but 'is play'd faster' (though he apparently made little or no distinction between 3i and 3 in practice), and both are normally rendered today as 3/4; while 6/8 'is Commonly to brisk tunes such as Jiggs and Paspys' – a hint here that dance rhythms and patterns were also used to define tempo.

Purcell wrote much of his early concerted music in short, contrasted but linked sections, often alternating duple and triple time and best performed using proportional relationships. This is suggested by his revealing habit of notating the transitions between sections so that performers are led through them without stopping, as at the beginning of 'Fear no danger to ensue' in *Dido and Aeneas** Z626/7, where the last bar of the preceding duple-time declamatory passage is notated in triple time. Most if not all of *Dido*, Act II, Scene I Z626/14–21 seems intended to be performed at a single tempo, with the Sorceress's declamatory passages (notated with a 2 time signature to indicate a moderate two-in-a-bar) contrasted with 'Harm's our delight' (3 with three-crotchet bars) and the 'Ho, ho, ho' choruses (also 3, but with three-quaver bars) in *sesquialtera* and *tripla* proportions respectively. In his later concerted music Purcell tended to write longer, separate movements, though a work such as the Te Deum and Jubilate in D major* can seem incoherent unless its 'patchwork' of short, contrasted sections is mostly performed with proportional relationships.

The introduction of Italian and English tempo marks during Purcell's lifetime was a symptom of the breakdown of the mensural system. He was the first Englishman to explain the Italian terms, in the preface to *Sonnata's of III Parts**: 'Adagio *and* Grave, *which import nothing but a very slow movement*: Presto

Largo, Poco Largo, or Largo *by it self, a middle movement*: Allegro, *and* Vivace, *a very brisk, swift, or fast movement'*. The idea of *largo* as 'a middle movement' (not slower than *adagio*, as in later practice) is important for the triple-time passages marked thus in Purcell's trio sonatas*, particularly the many notated in ³⁄₂, which are often taken too slowly today. Performers should be alert to the possibility that, when a tempo mark coincides with a change from fast to slow notes or vice-versa, it often seems to be describing what is happening rather than prescribing a change of pace – as may be the case with some of the 'Quick', 'Brisk' and 'Slow' indications in the fantasias*.

Another way of defining tempo (used by Purcell in *PlaInt*, following a precedent set by Christopher Simpson*) was to relate them to the motions of clocks and watches, though modern attempts to do so, particularly with the fantasias, are not entirely convincing. The choice of tempo in Purcell will depend, as it must have done at the time, on the type of music, the type of ensemble, the acoustic, the way words are set, and the harmonic movement. Even experienced performers sometimes forget that a movement with one chord per bar, as in many of Purcell's minuet*-like triple-time passages, must have been taken much faster than a movement with three or even six chord-changes per bar, as in many of his hornpipes*. *See also* **Jig**, **Paspe**. *BoaClo, CyrTem, HerThe, HolNot, LauCon, ParPur, RosPer.*

Tenor oboe *See* **Oboe**

Tenor, term for the viola *See* **Violin family**

Ten Sonata's in Four Parts The third of the memorial publications of Purcell's music, published in July 1697 by Henry Playford* for his widow Frances; it was printed by John Heptinstall*. Subscribers had been sought more than a year earlier, in April 1696; they were doubtless headed by the dedicatee, Purcell's ex-pupil Lady Rhoda Cavendish*. Purchasers of *Sonnata's of III Parts** must have been disappointed that Thomas Cross* was not again asked to engrave the collection: Heptinstall's typesetting is much less elegant and more difficult to read than the earlier collection, his continuo part 'garbling any but the most elementary figuring into a heap of unaligned numerals', as Christopher Hogwood* put it (*PurSon*). Frances Purcell and the volume's editor – probably Daniel Purcell* – doubtless felt the absence of the composer to guide them over such things as the choice of versions and the order of the sonatas, as well as detailed proofreading questions: it is much less accurate than *Sonnata's of III Parts*, particularly for nos. 9 and 10. *See also* **Trio sonatas**, **Editions, from 1695**. *HarPla, HogTri, SchSon, ShaMan.*

Theatre airs Restoration plays were routinely provided with instrumental music of three types. Two groups of preliminary pieces, called First and Second Music*, were played before the play began, followed by the curtain tune* or overture*, and then by four act tunes* played between the acts. This typically made a sequence of eight or nine movements, though the extended sets for Purcell's dramatic operas* included in *A Collection of Ayres** also include some song tunes* and theatrical dances. When sets of theatre airs were performed in plays the overture came in the middle of the sequence, an ordering preserved in some manuscripts, though they were reordered in *A Collection of Ayres* with the overtures placed first, presumably for domestic or concert performances. Purcell's sets are often called 'incidental music' or 'theatre suites' today, though the word 'suite'* is anachronistic in this context and is best avoided. *HolPur, HolThe, PriPur, PriThe.*

Theodosius Z606 According to John Downes*, Purcell's music for *Theodosius, or The Force of Love* was 'the first he e'er Compos'd for the Stage'; Nathaniel Lee's* tragedy was first performed by the Duke's Company at Dorset Garden* in the spring or early summer of 1680. Purcell's main contribution was music for a religious ceremony in Act I, welcoming the early Christian emperor Theodosius and his sisters, who are retiring to a monastery. The music, a sequence of short sections scored for solo and tutti voices with two recorders and continuo, avoids complex counterpoint and virtuosic solo writing, presumably to evoke the simplicity of early Christian ceremonies, though a stream of melodic and harmonic twists and turns in the vein of Matthew Locke* keeps up the interest. Lee and Purcell also provided five simple songs to be sung between the acts, apparently replacing the instrumental act tunes*; no set of theatre airs* is known for the play. The songs were printed in the play text (which names John Bowman* as Atticus, the chief priest), and the tunes of three of them, 'Now the fight's done', 'Hail to the myrtle shade' and 'Ah! cruel bloody fate', passed into the popular repertory and were used for broadside ballads*. *BalSta, HolPur, LamBal, LS, PriPur, PriThe, SimBal.*

Theorbo *See* **Lute**

'They that go down to the sea in ships' Z57 Hawkins* (*HawHis*, ii. 693) printed an anecdote in which John Gostling* chose the text of this symphony anthem* to mark his deliverance from a storm at sea with Charles II* and his brother James* on the royal yacht *Fubbs*. No other source corroborates the story, but it could refer to an outing in the summer of 1682. Purcell vividly depicts the dramatic text, the imagery of which provided abundant opportunity to exploit Gostling's extensive vocal range, so that, in Hawkins's words, 'hardly any person but himself was then, or has since been able to sing it' (see Ex.4, p. 81). *ShaMan, VanChu.*

Thoroughbass *See* **Continuo**

'Thou knowest, Lord' Z58C Purcell's simple but memorable setting of one of the grave-side sentences from the Burial Service* (not to be confused with his early settings, Z58A and B) was composed for Mary II's* funeral in Westminster Abbey* on 5 March 1695. It seems to have been written to fit into Thomas Morley's* setting of the Burial Service, which had been used for state funerals before the Civil War but was transmitted in the Restoration period with that sentence missing. Thomas Tudway* wrote that it was accompanied with 'flat Mournfull Trumpets' and that it 'drew tears from all' who heard it, showing 'ye pow'r of Music, when tis rightly fitted, & Adapted to devotional purposes'. It was performed again at Purcell's own funeral on 26 November 1695, and William Croft* subsequently inserted it into his own Burial Service, for reasons 'obvious

to every Artist', as he put it when he published it in *Musica sacra* (1724). *See also*
Flat trumpet. *HogTud, HolPur, ShaMan, WooFun.*

Three Parts upon a Ground Z731 This remarkable piece has been labelled a fantasia and a chaconne in modern editions, though to judge from the only complete source, GB-Lbl, R.M. 20.h.9 (a score in the hand of the organist John Reading*), Purcell just called it '3 parts upon a Ground', defining it by texture rather than idiom. Reading copied it in D major, for three violins and continuo, but added the note 'playd 2 notes higher for F[lutes]', and an autograph fragment of the second treble part headed 'flut' (GB-Lbl, Add. MS 30932, f. 121*v) confirms the authority of the alternative F major version for three recorders*; they will both be included in the revision of *PS* 31. Purcell seems to have taken care to cater for both alternatives, not going below the range of the treble recorder or out of first position on the violin.

The work draws on three distinct idioms. He took the ground bass* from an example in Christopher Simpson's* *Compendium of Practical Music* (1667) showing how to make a three-part canon* on a ground; its similarity to Pachelbel's famous Canon, also in D major and for three violins and bass, seems to be just a coincidence. Purcell punctuated the work with four passages of strict canon, in one of which the second violin plays the first part upside down (inversion) while the third part plays it backwards (retrograde). There are also passages influenced by French orchestral chaconnes* and passacaglias*, with sighing suspensions and restrained writing in dotted rhythms; as well as sections of canonic or semi-canonic divisions* in the style of John Jenkins*. Purcell probably wrote the work around 1678, perhaps in an attempt to revive the court tradition of contrapuntal consort music, which had included ten fantasia suites by Jenkins for the same scoring. *See also* **Counterpoint**, **Dissonance**. *DarCha, HolCom, HolPur, PurGro, SchCon, ShaMan, ZimCat.*

Tierce de Picardie The practice of ending a composition or a movement in the minor with a major third. It was the dominant practice in European music from about 1500 to 1700 and continued even later in conservative genres of church music. Friederich Erhardt Niedt (Hamburg, 1700) stated: 'Even if the entire preceding piece [*Gesang*] has been in minor the composition will ultimately conclude in major', though he added: 'French composers do the opposite, but not everything is good simply because it originates in France or has a French name' (*NieGui*, 40). Purcell's practice, shown most clearly in his full-voiced anthems and consort music, was either to end pieces with major thirds or with just an octave or an octave and a fifth, with the third omitted. Minor chords are sometimes found in Purcell at section endings, and very occasionally at the end of complete pieces, as in the five-part Overture in G minor Z772 – which might have been Purcell's nod to French practice in a French-derived genre. Continuo* players should certainly think twice about adding minor chords at final cadences where they are not present in the music they are accompanying. *ArnAcc.*

Time signatures *See* **Tempo**

***Timon of Athens, the Man-Hater* Z632** Purcell wrote music for a revival of Thomas Shadwell's* 1678 adaptation of Shakespeare's play, apparently for Drury Lane* in the spring or early summer of 1695. His main contribution was a new setting (replacing one by Louis Grabu*) of the Masque in Act II, Scene 2, performed during a banquet thrown by Timon for his opportunistic cronies. This delightful miniature drama embodies the popular theme of a debate over the merits of love and wine, conducted by Cupid (a boy named George in London A's* score) and Bacchus (Richard Leveridge*), supported respectively by Nymphs and Shepherds and a trio of Bacchanals. Purcell appropriately associates recorders* and strings with Cupid's party (the masque starts with the charming duet with recorders 'Hark! how the songsters of the grove'), while Bacchus and his crew are consistently accompanied by oboes*, evoking the god's double *aulos*. Other highlights are the fine chorus 'Who can resist such mighty charms?', Bacchus's amusing 'Return, revolting rebels' and Cupid's dazzling recitative 'The cares of lovers'.

The instrumental music associated with the play (all ed. in *PS* 2) includes the overture to 'Who can from joy refrain?'*, transposed from C major to D major (and probably added after Purcell's lifetime); a set of theatre airs* apparently by James Paisible* Z632/2–9; and the superb Ground in G minor Z632/20. This last was labelled 'Courtin Tune' (i.e. curtain tune* or overture*) and assigned to *Timon of Athens* in the only complete source, London A's* score GB-Lcm, MS 1172. However, Curtis Price argued that it was actually played in Act IV, Scene 3 while Timon throws stones at his tormentors. *HolPur, LS, PriIns, PriPur, PriThe, ZimCat*.

Timpani *See* **Kettledrums**

Tippett, Michael Introduced to Purcell's music in the 1930s by his friend Francesca Allinson, the composer Michael Tippett (1905–98) became intensely engaged with it after rescuing several volumes of the Purcell Society* edition from the rubble at Morley College in south London following its bombing in October 1940; he conducted the College's choir. He subsequently directed ground-breaking Purcell performances there, including 'My beloved spake'*, 'Welcome to all the pleasures'* and 'Hail, bright Cecilia'*. Walter Bergmann* became his continuo* player, and they went on to produce practical editions of Purcell for Schott & Co., including 'Come, ye sons of art, away'*, 'Hail, bright Cecilia' and many songs.

In 1944 Tippett visited Canterbury* Cathedral for the première of his motet 'Plebs Angelica', where he first heard the falsetto countertenor* Alfred Deller*. He 'recognised absolutely' Deller's voice as the one for which Purcell had written, and immediately engaged him for his performances. They included 'Come, ye sons of art, away' in a Purcell concert for the Festival of Britain in 1951, and the first recording of 'Hail, bright Cecilia' in 1956. Tippett's enthusiasm for Purcell also drew Benjamin Britten* and Peter Pears to Morley College, and in 1945 he collaborated with them in two concerts at the Wigmore Hall marking the 250th anniversary of the composer's death. In 1947 he gave two series of talks on Purcell for the BBC's Third Programme, and wrote repeatedly about his music (*TipMus*); he was a member of the Purcell Society from 1951.

Tippett acknowledged Purcell as an influence on a number of his own compositions, including *A Child of Our Time* (1939–41); *Boyhood's End* (1943), modelled on The Blessed Virgin's Expostulation*; and String Quartet no. 2 (1942). Purcellian features of Tippett's vocal writing include a sensitivity to word-setting, with exuberant melismas on affective words. His fascination with Purcell's ground basses* was expressed in the first of the Ritual Dances from *The Midsummer Marriage* (1946–52) and the slow movement of Symphony no. 1 (1955–7). Furthermore, he based the second movement of *Divertimento on 'Sellinger's Round'* (1953–4) on the ground-bass air 'Ah, Belinda' from *Dido and Aeneas**, composing it as he was preparing to direct the opera for Swiss Radio. He used the catch* 'Fie, nay, prithee John' ZD100 (now thought to be by Christopher Fishburn) in the third movement of *The Shires Suite* (1965/69/70); and the ritornello* from the opening chorus of 'Welcome to all the pleasures' in the second movement of String Quartet no. 5 (1990–1). BurRem, ColMor, ColTip, MarBer, PurCon, TipBlu, TipCon.

''Tis Nature's voice' Z328/4 The spectacular declamatory solo for countertenor* and continuo in the 1692 St Cecilia ode 'Hail, bright Cecilia'* was sung by John Pate* in the original performance on 22 November 1692, according to Purcell's autograph. However, Peter Motteux* wrote in *The Gentleman's Journal* for November 1692 that it 'was sung with incredible Graces by Mr. *Purcell* himself', which presumably led Thomas Cross* to publish it as having been '*Sung by himself at St Caecelia's Feast*'. This led in turn to the notion gaining ground in the twentieth century that Purcell had been a countertenor, though he was listed amongst the basses in the Chapel Royal choir at James II's* coronation (*SanCor*, 71). Motteux's ambiguous sentence probably means that the graces were composed rather than sung by Purcell, for the piece has most unusual and elaborate written-out ornamentation*. Equally remarkable is the passage of vocal 'sighing & languishing by degrees' at the word 'charms', underpinned by clashing descending harmonies. *See also* **Dissonance**. BalSta, GoeHar, HolPur.

Toccata in A major ZD229 This extended and brilliant keyboard piece, ascribed variously to Michelangelo Rossi, J.S. Bach (BWV Anh. 178) and Purcell, has long baffled scholars. However, Barry Cooper pointed out that it is too late in style to be by Rossi (d.1656); and its presence in manuscripts dated 1698 and 1702 means that it is too early to be by Bach. It survives in five English sources, two attributed to Purcell, suggesting he played it and/or copied it. Its style rules him out as the composer. It is probably by a north German organist, possibly one resident in London, though Jonathan Baxendale made a good case for Dieterich Buxtehude – or perhaps someone imitating him. It is a pity that its dubious status has prevented it becoming popular with harpsichordists or organists (it is equally suitable for both), because opportunities to hear it well played on historical instruments would help decide the issue. Meanwhile, George Malcolm's dashing 1963 recording makes a good case for it, despite being played on a heavily built mid-twentieth-century harpsichord. BaxToc, CooKey, CoxOrg, HogCor, HolPur, ShaMan, WooKey.

Treble Purcell and his contemporaries used this word to mean the G clef; as well as the voices and instruments reading from it; and, by extension, the parts written for them. However, they did not use 'treble' and 'soprano' to distinguish between a boy and an adult as we do – which is why we have largely avoided using 'soprano' in this book. John Evelyn, writing on 27 January 1682 (*EveDia*, iv. 270), described the countertenor* John Abell as 'the famous Trebble', adding: 'I never heard a more excellent voice, one would have sworne it had ben a Womans it was so high, & so skillfully manag'd'.

Trio sonatas The combination of two violins*, bass viol* and organ* (or harpsichord*), used in Purcell's two sets of trio sonatas, *Sonnata's of III Parts** (1683) and *Ten Sonata's in Four Parts** (1697), was established in English consort music in James I's reign, a tradition reflected in his three-part pavans*. However, according to the famous preface of the 1683 set, Purcell 'faithfully endeavour'd a just imitation of the most fam'd Italian Masters'; these seem to have been mostly composers born early in the century, such as Cazzati*, Legrenzi*, Colista* and G.B. Vitali*, rather than his near-contemporaries Corelli* and G.B. Bassani. In his trio sonatas, mostly composed between about 1678 and 1683, Purcell imitated the Italian *à tre* sonata, the contrapuntal genre descended from the canzona*, in which the bowed bass contributes to the musical argument on near-equal terms with the violins, rather than the more modern 'à due' type, with the violins accompanied just by continuo* instruments. Of the trio sonatas composed in England during Charles II's* reign (collected in *HolTri*), the closest to Purcell and the finest is John Blow's* in A major. The Sonata in G minor Z780*, Purcell's only trio sonata outside the published sets, belongs to the northern European variant of the genre for violin, obbligato bass viol and continuo, though the bass viol part is lost and has had to be reconstructed.

Purcell's trio sonatas mostly consist of five or more short, linked sections, as in mid-century Italian works, rather than the more modern sequence of four discrete movements that predominates in Corelli's Op. 1 (1681). There is no sign of Corelli's distinction between the *da chiesa* and *da camera* types: dance-like passages are freely mixed with 'abstract' movements. Purcell seems to have been attracted to the trio sonata mainly because of the possibilities it offered for formal counterpoint*; he wrote in *PlaInt* about Italian sonatas: 'you will find *Double* and *Treble Fuges* also reverted and augmented in their *Canzona*'s, with a good deal of Art mixed with good Air, which is the Perfection of a Master'. Purcell's canzona sections are closely modelled on those by Colista and Carlo Ambrogio Lonati*; he quoted from one by Lonati in *PlaInt* (wrongly attributing it to Colista) as an example of 'Double Descant' or invertible counterpoint. They often present two themes combined in various ways, including inversion, augmentation and stretto. Alternatively, the themes are presented successively, the second arriving just as the ear tires of the first. Purcell sometimes followed Legrenzi in placing a triple-time canzona so that it emerges out of, and is effectively the second section of, a dance-like passage.

Roger North* wrote that Purcell's 'noble set of sonnatas' were 'very artificiall and good musick', but admitted they were 'clog'd with somewhat of an English vein, for which they are unworthily despised' (*NorMus*, 310–11). In the 1690s Corelli's trio sonatas 'cleared the ground of all other sorts of musick whatsoever', and the next generation of English trio sonata composers, including William Williams, William Corbett, Matthew Novell and James Sherard, mostly imitated Corelli rather than Purcell. However, the Golden Sonata* (1697, no. 9 in F major), one of four apparently composed rather later than the others and rather more modern than them, remained popular. It was reprinted twice by John Walsh* and was imitated by William Croft*, among others. *AllCor, AllSon, CunSon, CyrTem, HogTri, HolPur, HolTri, HowArt, HowPoe, KanCor, KanTri, SchCon, SchSon, ShaMan, TilTec, TalFug, ThoJen.*

Trumpet Natural trumpets, normally pitched in C or D, were used in bands with kettledrums* to play improvised or semi-improvised flourishes and fanfares at the English court until after the Restoration. The first English concerted work with surviving trumpet parts is G.B. Draghi's* *Song for St Cecilia's Day, 1687*, first performed on 22 November 1687. Draghi's trumpet writing reflects established continental practice, though it was evidently also inspired and enabled by members of the Shore family*, the leading royal trumpeters; Matthias Shore had become Sarjeant Trumpeter that summer. Draghi inspired Purcell, John Blow* and their followers to incorporate trumpets into their odes and theatre music. Gottfried Finger's* trumpet writing seems to have been another influence in the 1690s. Purcell wrote for trumpets in 18 concerted works, beginning in the spring of 1690 with The Yorkshire Feast Song*, the birthday ode for Queen Mary 'Arise, my muse'* and the dramatic opera* *Dioclesian*.

Purcell followed convention in using trumpets, usually in pairs, to evoke war, heroism, courtly power, ceremony and joy, though his writing for the instrument was ground-breaking and highly inventive. In *Dioclesian* and *The Fairy Queen** he required his players to change between C and D trumpets, evidently for tonal variety in large-scale works. There is evidence from Purcell's scores and an early set of parts for 'Hail, bright Cecilia'* that trumpets could be doubled by oboes*, enabling notes outside the harmonic series to be included in their parts. However, several other techniques were associated with the Shore family that enabled non-harmonic tones to be played; see **Flat trumpet**. Overtures* and symphonies* with trumpets in Purcell's concerted vocal works, notably the Trumpet Overture from *The Indian Queen** Z630/16 and the Sonata in D major* Z850, have become mainstays of concerts and recordings of Baroque trumpet music. *DowExo, HolCla, HolFid, HolPur, PinTru, RawFin, RycTru, SmiTru, SteTru, WebTru, WhiCec.*

Trumpet Voluntary This piece, popularised as 'Purcell's Trumpet Voluntary' in Sir Henry Wood's overblown orchestral arrangement, is in fact 'The Prince of Denmark's March' ZS125 by Jeremiah Clarke*. A lively and unassuming piece in rondeau* form, it seems to have been originally a consort piece, though it circulated in a keyboard arrangement, first published in 1700 and transmitted in several contemporary manuscripts. It seems to have been first misattributed to Purcell and given the inappropriate title 'voluntary' by William Spark, City Organist of Leeds, in one of his collections of *Short Pieces for the Organ*, published in the 1870s. *CudVol, TayCla, WhiCla, ZimCat.*

Tucker, William Clerical singer, copyist and composer, a minor canon of Westminster Abbey* and a gentleman of the Chapel Royal* from shortly after the Restoration. He was an important copyist for both institutions, and his work in GB-Lwa, Triforium Set I, in which he styled John Blow* 'Mr' rather than 'Dr', apparently means that some Purcell anthems, including 'Blow up the trumpet in Zion'*, 'I will sing unto the Lord' Z22 and 'O Lord our governor' Z39, were composed before December 1677, when Blow received his Lambeth doctorate. One of them, 'Let God arise' Z23, has autograph revisions. Tucker also used the 'Mr Blow' label in his copies for the Chapel Royal, including a set of partbooks of symphony anthems* (of which the bass books GB-Lbl, Add. MS 50860 and J-Tn, MS N5/10 are the sole survivors), which means that the same dating mechanism applies to a revised version of 'My beloved spake'* and the fragmentary anthems 'If the Lord himself' ZN66 and 'Praise the Lord, ye servants' ZN68. Tucker died on 28 February 1679. *BCECM, CheChu, HowCre, ShaMan, SpiRes, ZimCat.*

Tudway, Thomas Organist and composer (c.1650–1726), the son of a lay clerk at St George's Chapel, Windsor*. He was a choirboy in the Chapel Royal* until 1668 and became organist of King's College, Cambridge in 1670, subsequently adding other Cambridge posts. In 1705 he was awarded a Cambridge Mus.D. with the honorary title 'Professor of Music', in abeyance since Nicholas Staggins's* death in 1700. Tudway composed a fair amount of church music, though he is mainly remembered as the copyist of a six-volume historical anthology of English church music from the Reformation to the death of Queen Anne*, now GB-Lbl, Harley MSS 7337–42; it was copied for Edward, Lord Harley (later Earl of Oxford) between 1714 and 1720. It includes the Service* in B$^\flat$, 'Thou knowest, Lord' Z58C* and the Te Deum and Jubilate in D major*, which Tudway accompanied with rapturous descriptions of their performances. He drew on his experiences as a Chapel Royal choirboy for his well-known description of music there in Charles II's* reign. *BalBir, BDECM, DexQui, HogTud, ShaMan, SpiCat, WebCla.*

Turner, William Composer and countertenor* singer (1651/2–1740), a Chapel Royal* chorister from soon after the Restoration. In 1667 he was appointed Master of the Choristers at Lincoln Cathedral but became a Gentleman of the Chapel in 1669 and a member of the Private Music* in 1672; he was active as a singer and composer in both. He also worked in the theatre, composing for plays and singing in *The Tempest** at Dorset Garden* in 1674 and in the court masque *Calisto* in 1675. Turner was the most prominent court composer in the 1680s after Purcell and John Blow*. He composed two anthems for James II's* coronation* in 1685, and in the same year composed the ode for the annual Cecilian celebrations*; all three are lost. In 1696 he was awarded a Cambridge Mus.D. and composed orchestrally accompanied settings of the Te Deum and Jubilate for the Cecilian service at St Bride's, Fleet Street*, modelled on those by Purcell.

Turner was not an important influence on Purcell as a composer, though a section of his theatre airs* for *Pastor Fido* (1676) (ed. in *HolThe*) seems to have been the starting point for the Chaconne in *The Fairy Queen** Z629/51. However, Turner was a constant as a singer throughout Purcell's court career, named as a soloist in 'Why are all the Muses mute?'*, 'Ye tuneful Muses'*, 'Sound the trumpet, beat the drum'*, 'Arise, my muse'*, 'Hail, bright Cecilia'*, 'Celebrate this festival'* and the Te Deum and Jubilate*. Burney* described him as 'a countertenor singer, his voice settling to that pitch; a circumstance which so seldom happens, *naturally*, that if it be cultivated, the possessor is sure of employment'

(*BurHis*, iii. 460). In modern terms he was a high tenor with a range occasionally extending to *c"*. *BalCou, BDECM, CBCR, SpiCat, SpiSon, WhiCec*.

"Twas with a furlong of Edinboro' town' Z605/2 The best-known piece in the Restoration Scots song* idiom. Setting words by Thomas D'Urfey*, it was originally sung by 'the Girl', Letitia Cross*, in Thomas Scott's comedy *The Mock-Marriage*, probably first performed at Drury Lane* in the summer of 1695. The music, its swinging tune signalling its Caledonian credentials with falling thirds and Scots snaps, is attributed to Purcell in a single-sheet edition, but to Jeremiah Clarke* in a keyboard version in GB-Lbl, Add. MS 22099. It was enduringly popular: the words were expanded as a broadside ballad* while the tune was used in eight eighteenth-century ballad operas. It is sometimes confused with James Hook's song 'Within a mile of Edinburgh town' (1794), which sets a text partly derived from D'Urfey. *DayDur, FisSco, LS, PriPur, SimBal, TayCla, ZimCat*.

The Twenty-Four Violins The pre-Civil War court violin band, with its roots in Henry VIII's reign, was revived at the Restoration, enlarged from about 14 to 24 in imitation of the French court's *Vingt-quatre Violons*. It continued to provide daily dance music at Whitehall*, but was soon given several new roles, reflecting Charles II's* musical taste. Groups from it accompanied anthems in the Chapel Royal*; partially supplanted the Private Music* in the Privy Chamber; and accompanied court odes* and welcome songs*. Divided into two, it was also placed at the service of London's two theatre companies, the King's Company and the Duke's Company, from 1664–5 until, probably, 1677. The Twenty-Four Violins was directed informally by its leading members, including John Banister*, Louis Grabu* and Nicholas Staggins*, but also doubtless by court and theatre composers when it played in their concerted music, notably Pelham Humfrey*, Matthew Locke*, John Blow*, G.B. Draghi* and Purcell.

Until 1642 the violin band still used the Renaissance-style five-part scoring, with a single violin part, three violas and bass violins*, but the Twenty-Four Violins used the more modern four-part scoring (though sometimes reverting to five parts under Grabu), initially with violin and two violas but changing to the modern 'string quartet' scoring in the 1670s. Purcell wrote for its members in Chapel Royal symphony anthems*, in welcome songs and other court odes, and apparently in a few independent consort pieces such as the Chacony*. In 1685, as part of James II's* reforms of the royal household, the group was combined with wind and continuo players to form a new Private Music, effectively an up-to-date Baroque orchestra*. *HolFid, HolPur, HolThe, RECM, WolOve, WolVio*.

United Company Formed by a merger in 1682 of the King's Company and the Duke's Company, the United Company had a monopoly over theatrical productions in London until the spring of 1695, when the senior actors and singers led by Thomas Betterton* seceded from it in protest at Christopher Rich's* management style. It mostly used the Drury Lane Theatre* for ordinary spoken plays and the better equipped Dorset Garden Theatre* for spectacular productions requiring stage machinery, including Purcell's dramatic operas*. *LS, PriPur, PriThe, SawRic*.

Verse Purcell and his contemporaries used this word (usually spelt 'vers') to mean a passage for a solo voice or group of solo voices, contrasted with 'full' or 'chorus' passages. It derives from the word for a section of a chapter in the Bible, which is why it was mostly used in church music, though it is also found by extension in Purcell's odes*, welcome songs* and similar works.

Verse anthem This type of anthem*, accompanied by organ* or continuo*, consisting largely of passages for single soloists or small vocal ensemble (the verse*); the choir* ('full') typically makes short contributions in the middle and at the end of the work. Despite being the most numerous type of Purcell anthem (29 surviving complete or incomplete), the genre has been overshadowed by the more glamorous symphony anthem* with strings, and by the full or verse-with-full type, more useful to modern choirs. However, the best of them, such as 'Let mine eyes run down with tears' Z24 and 'O consider my adversity' Z32, are among his finest church works. Perhaps recordings will eventually redress the balance. *SpiCat, VanChu.*

Viol (viola da gamba) The complete consort made up of three sizes of six-string, flat-backed, fretted viols (treble: d–g–c'–e'–a'–d''; tenor: G–c–f–a–d'–g'; bass: D–G–c–e–a–d') was passing out of use in England before Purcell was born, rather later than in most parts of Europe. Roger North* wrote that Matthew Locke's* *Consort of Four Parts*, probably written in the 1650s, was 'the last of the kind that hath bin made' (*NorMus*, 349). Nevertheless, the lyra viol* and the bass viol continued in use; the latter was used as a continuo* instrument until about 1710 and in solo and obbligato roles much later, with prominent players such as Gottfried Finger* and Francis Withy* continuing to add to the repertory. Viol makers working in Restoration London, such as Barak Norman, Richard Meares senior and junior and Edward Lewis, concentrated on basses. Lewis also made contrabass-size instruments, probably originally set up as 'great bass viols' tuned AA–D–G–B–e–a, and presumably used for the AAs in orchestral music by Jeremiah Clarke* and William Croft*.

Purcell wrote bass viol parts in his trio sonatas*, often more elaborate than the continuo part, and the instrument's use can be assumed in the pavans*, Three Parts on a Ground* and his other early consort music, and as an option in the songs, with or without a continuo instrument; his Sonata in G minor Z780* had an obbligato bass viol part, now lost. It is also likely that a bass viol was part of the continuo group in Purcell's odes and theatre music, as viols were in the *petit choeur* of French opera orchestras. However, the bass part of pieces in orchestral idioms such as the Chacony in G minor*, The Staircase Overture* and Purcell's theatre airs* were probably played on bass violins*, at least at court and in the theatres, as were the string passages of symphony anthems*. There is some evidence for the use of bass viols in the Chapel Royal*, perhaps doubling the bass of the *decani* and *sub-decani* sections of the choir.

The instrumentation of Purcell's fantasias* is a problem. They are a central part of the modern viol consort repertory, and recordings have demonstrated how well they work on these instruments, despite their angular and high-lying writing for the trebles. There were still viol players at court in 1680 (when most of the fantasias were written), though there is no evidence that a complete consort functioned there or anywhere else in London at the time, and it is significant that all the viols purchased for court use in the Restoration period were basses or lyra viols rather than trebles and tenors. If Purcell's fantasias were performed then, it is likely they were played with a mixed consort of violins and viols – an option demonstrated successfully by several recordings*. Hawkins* (*HawHis*, ii. 747) wrote that John Gostling* 'played on the viol de gamba, and loved not the instrument more than Purcell hated it', using the catch* 'in Commendation of the Viol' 'Of all the instruments that are' Z263 to illustrate his point. However, this 'mock eulogium', as Hawkins called it, is extremely gentle satire, and the idea that Purcell hated the viol is belied by its prominent role in his music. See also **Violin family**. *DilVio, HofGam, HolCla, HolCon, HolFid, HolLif, MacMus, RECM, RobLey*.

Violin family A complete violin consort or band, consisting of violins, violas and bass violins*, was an important part of the royal music from the reign of Henry VIII to the Civil War. When the group was revived at the Restoration it was enlarged and named the Twenty-Four Violins* in imitation of the French court *Vingt-quatre violons*. Purcell wrote for members of the group playing in four parts (two violins, viola and bass violin) in symphony anthems* and in court odes*, and later for string groups working in the theatre and for Cecilian celebrations*. He also wrote for mixed groups of violins and bass viol in his trio sonatas* and in much of his early consort music, including the pavans* and Three Parts upon a Ground*; it is likely that bass viols were used as a continuo* instrument in his symphony songs* and other small-scale concerted music.

Purcell probably learned the violin as a child in the Chapel Royal* (he holds a viola in a portrait* supposedly depicting him), and he wrote for the instrument with assurance, though he avoided the virtuosic techniques such as multiple stopping and high positions that had been introduced to England by the German violinist Thomas Baltzar and the Neapolitan Nicola Matteis*. Italian violins had long been imported into England, and were highly prized, though there was also a flourishing native violinmaking tradition, represented by Ralph Agutter, Thomas Urquhart, William Baker and members of the Pamphilon family, among others. See also **Viol (viola da gamba)**. *DilVio, HolFid, HolVio, JonMat, TilCha, WolVio*.

Virginal A word of obscure origin used in sixteenth- and seventeenth-century England as a generic term for all types of domestic keyboard instrument, but also specifically for the plucked type in a rectangular box with a single set of strings running parallel to the keyboard. 22 English virginals survive, ranging in date from *c*.1580 to 1684; the type was gradually replaced during Purcell's lifetime by the more fashionable and compact bentside spinet*. See also **Harpsichord**. *BoaMou, KosHar, MarVir*.

***The Virtuous Wife, or Good Luck at Last* Z611** Purcell contributed a set of theatre airs* to Thomas D'Urfey's* play, probably for a revival in 1695. It was published in a reordered form for concert use in *A Collection of Ayres**, though the original theatrical order (with the Overture preceded by pairs of movements in C major and C minor serving as First and Second Music*) is found in the near-contemporary violin book GB-Lbl, Add. MS 35043; it is followed in *PS* 21. The G minor overture* is one of Purcell's finest, with a fiercely energetic and dissonant first section and a closely argued fugue, both founded on a fifth rising from the tonic. Of the act tunes, the first (Z611/9) is the fine bourrée-like movement published as the country dance 'St Martin's Lane' and known in France as 'La Furstemberg'*. The third (Z611/2) is a beautiful arrangement of the song 'Ah! How sweet it is to love' Z613/2 from John Dryden's* play *Tyrannic Love*, probably written for a revival in the autumn of 1694; it may originally have been the Dance of Spirits that followed the song in Dryden's play. The minuet*-like Fourth Act Tune (Z611/7) was used by D'Urfey for the mock-song* 'New reformation sweeps through the nation' in his play *The Campaigners* (June 1698). LS, ZimCat.

Vitali, Giovanni Battista Bolognese cellist, singer and composer (1632–92), pupil of Maurizio Cazzati*. He was probably one of 'the most fam'd Italian masters' Purcell mentioned as his models for *Sonnata's of III Parts**: sonatas from his Op. 2 (Bologna, 1667), Op. 5 (Bologna, 1669) and Op. 9 (Venice, 1684) are found in Restoration manuscripts. In particular, Vitali's Op. 5, no. 8 'La Guidoni' (evidently a model for Purcell's Golden Sonata*) was copied by the Winchester organist John Reading* into GB-Lbl, R.M. 20.h.9 alongside some unique Purcell pieces and other court instrumental music. Vitali's Op. 5, no. 12, the five-part sonata 'La Scalabrina', may have been the model for the writing for two violins, two violas and bass in Purcell's Overture in G minor Z772, composed in the early 1680s. HolFid, KanTri, ShaMan, ThoJen, TilTec.

Voices *See* **Singers**

Voluntary An improvised or composed keyboard piece typically performed on the organ* in a church service. Roger North* (*NorMus*, 135–45) treated 'The Excellent Art of Voluntary' as a genre for improvisation, writing that 'the great performers upon organs will doe voluntary, to a prodigy of wonder, and beyond their owne skill to recover and set downe'. This presumably explains why we have only a few voluntaries by Purcell. Of the prominent organists in Restoration England, only John Blow* left a sizeable body of organ music, and that can be explained by his need for teaching material while training generations of Chapel Royal* boys. Several voluntaries once attributed to Purcell are now thought or known to be spurious: the Voluntary in C major ZD241 is probably by John Barrett; the Verse in the Phrygian Mode ZS126 is by Nicolas Lebègue; while the Voluntary on the 100th Psalm Z721 exists in two versions – one attributed to Blow, the other to Purcell – and could be by either composer.

Of the remaining five works in *PurOrg*, two, Z717 in C major and Z720 in G major use the common Restoration pattern, in which a full-voiced passage gives way to a point of imitation. In Z720 the first section is in the *durezze e ligature* (dissonances and ties) idiom that English organists derived from Frescobaldi. By far the most important is the Voluntary in D minor Z718 and its cousin the Voluntary for Double Organ Z719; the two pieces gradually diverge, going their separate ways about half-way through. It is not clear which came first or whether Purcell was responsible for both of them, though they are striking pieces, with lavishly ornamented imitative passages giving way to bursts of florid passagework. They provide tantalising glimpses of the organ music

Purcell might have left had it been the practice for Restoration organists to write down their improvisations. *CoxOrg, HolPur, WooKey, ZimCat*.

Walsh, John Music publisher, music seller and musical instrument maker (or dealer) of supposed Irish origin (1665/6–1736). He established himself in London around 1690, became the court 'musical instrument maker' (or probably supplier of instruments) in 1692 and began publishing in 1695. The Walsh firm under him and his son John dominated the London music trade until the 1760s. From the start Walsh senior used engraving rather than the typesetting still favoured by Henry Playford*, John Carr* and others, soon changing to the use of punches and pewter plates rather than the hand-engraving and copper plates used by his rival Thomas Cross*. Walsh mostly avoided direct competition with Playford and the Purcell family, preferring to compete with Cross in the publication of single-sheet engraved editions of Purcell's songs. He also reprinted The Golden Sonata* and eventually produced his own engraved edition of the Te Deum and Jubilate* Z232; in 1707 he had reissued unsold copies of the original 1697 edition, just adding his own title page. In 1724 he published a selection from *Orpheus Britannicus**. *See also* **Editions, from 1695**, **Printing and publishing**. *BDECM, DaySon, HerPla, HigRec, HolPur, HumPub, HunPri, KruPri, MPP, SmiWal, ThoSou, TilCha, WooKey*.

Walter (Waters), John Singer and music copyist (c.1660–1708), a choirboy in the Chapel Royal* until 1677. As an adult he worked at Windsor and Eton*: clerk at George's Chapel; organist and 'informator choristarum' at the College from 1681. Walter's copying activities, often in collaboration with his Windsor colleague William Isaack*, suggest he was a member of Purcell's circle. Scores in his hand include GB-Ob, MS Mus. c.28, ff. 100–24, an important secondary source of Purcell's devotional part-songs; and GB-Lbl, Add. MS 22100, a score of vocal music with mostly court associations: it begins with Purcell's 'Welcome, vicegerent of the mighty king'* (1680) and ends with John Blow's* *Venus and Adonis* (1683), perhaps performed at Windsor. *See also* **John Weldon**. *BDECM, BloVen, DexQui, HerCat, HerCre, HolPur, ShaMan*.

'Welcome, glorious morn' Z338 This fine but rarely performed ode for Mary II's* 1691 birthday, setting an anonymous text possibly by Thomas Shadwell*, is closely related in its musical material to *King Arthur**, produced the following month. It is richly scored, with the orchestra deployed during the Italianate symphony in antiphonal fanfares between trumpets*, oboes* and strings. It is noteworthy for its large-scale organisation, achieved through careful tonal planning, cunningly varied scorings and subtle musical repetition. Purcell's increasingly expert handling of the last is exemplified by the ingenious treatment of the countertenor solo and first chorus, set to a modulating ground bass*. When the chorus is repeated, shorn of the prefatory solo, it is subtly expanded with a brief verse passage. No soloists are named in the sources, though the declamatory solo 'My pray'rs are heard' and the following ground-bass solo 'I see the round years' require musical and technical skills that suggest an adult female singer. Queen Mary's favourite Arabella Hunt* is a likely candidate. *AdaPur, HolPur, MurOde, SpiOde, WooOde*.

Welcome song The term used by Purcell and his colleagues for the odes* performed when Charles II* and then James II* returned to Whitehall* usually after absence in the summer; they were officially on progress around their realm, but they often arrived just from Windsor* or from the races at Newmarket. The genre may have been invented to give Purcell a new role at court; John Blow* had the task of setting odes for the New Year and the king's birthday. Purcell's welcome songs are: 'Welcome, vicegerent of the mighty king'* (1680); 'Swifter, Isis, swifter flow'* (1681); 'What shall be done in behalf of the man'* (1682); 'The summer's absence unconcerned we bear'* (1682); 'Fly, bold rebellion'* (1683); 'From those serene and rapturous joys'* (1684); and 'Why are all the Muses mute?'* (1685). After that the genre was merged with odes for James's birthday, which conveniently fell on 14 October; it was discontinued after the Glorious Revolution*.

'Welcome to all the pleasures' Z339 Purcell's 1683 setting of verses by Christopher Fishburn inaugurated the series of annual Cecilian celebrations* in London. It draws heavily on court odes*, particularly 'Welcome vicegerent of the mighty king'*, the 1680 welcome song*. The closest point of contact is the pair of tenor solos, 'Music, the food of love' from the 1680 ode and 'Beauty thou scene of love' in the Cecilian ode. Fishburn praised St Cecilia rather than Charles II* using the same rhyme scheme and some of the same rhymes, while Purcell set the two texts to similar minuet* songs. 'Welcome to all the pleasures' is indistinguishable from contemporary court odes in idiom and scoring, though it lacks the logical structure of 'Fly, bold rebellion'*, composed two months earlier. However, there are several excellent movements: the opening symphony* begins with a double canon*; and the composer gave the famous ground bass* 'Here the deities approve' the accolade of a *style brisé** keyboard setting (ZT682). It was the only Purcell ode published complete in his lifetime: in full score in 1684 with a dedication to the Musical Society. Its availability in print, and its modest scoring and technical demands, enabled it to be taken up for the Cecilian celebrations that developed throughout Britain in the 1690s; it has become popular in modern times for the same reasons. *AdaPur, HolPur, SpiOde, WhiCec, WooOde.*

'Welcome, vicegerent of the mighty king' Z340 Purcell's first ode* was a welcome song* for Charles II*, probably marking his return from Windsor* in September 1680. Its anonymous text deploys seasonal imagery to equate the king's absence with winter and his presence with spring. John Blow's* court odes inspired Purcell to create a work with a wider range of movement types than hitherto, and he began with a remarkable innovation: the first choral entry is superimposed on the repeated second section of the French-style symphony*, creating a sophisticated and rich seven-part texture. The rest of the ode is a patchwork of short vocal movements in dance rhythms, often rounded off with string ritornellos*. The most successful are the gavotte-like treble duet 'When the summer, in his glory'; the minuet* for tenor and chorus 'Music, the food of love'; and the brief but densely contrapuntal final chorus. Nevertheless, Purcell's inexperience in the genre is betrayed by the work's structure, with many short sections; and by a lack of clear direction: an unbalanced tonal scheme is awkwardly articulated in several places with continuo* links. *AdaPur*, *AdaOde*, *HolPur*, *SpiOde*, *WooEqu*, *WooOde*.

Weldon, John Composer and organist (1676/7–1736), a choirboy at Eton College from at least Lady Day 1693; its organist John Walter* had the College pay Purcell £5 for teaching him between Michaelmas 1693 and Lady Day 1694. At Michaelmas 1694 Weldon became organist of New College, Oxford*, where he produced some early works, including a Purcellian song on the Peace of Ryswick (1697). He came to prominence in 1701 by unexpectedly winning the competition to set William Congreve's* masque *The Judgment of Paris*, which established his career in London, enabling him to relinquish his Oxford post that Christmas. He became a gentleman of the Chapel Royal* that year, and on 18 June 1702 he was appointed organist of St Bride's, Fleet Street*, with its three-manual Renatus Harris* organ. By then he also had a flourishing career in public concerts and at Drury Lane*, where he wrote among other things a new setting of the music for *The Tempest** – evidently the one long thought to be by Purcell (Z631). Weldon was appointed an organist and composer in the Chapel Royal in 1708 and seems to have spent most of his later career writing church music.

Early in his career Weldon was a composer of considerable promise – a promise seemingly never wholly fulfilled. His Suite in D minor for two violins and bass (ed. *WelSui*), surviving in Oxford and doubtless written while he was at New College, combines a mastery of Purcellian idioms (it ends with a fine 'Two in One on a Ground' inspired by *Dioclesian** Z627/16) with slightly more modern writing apparently inspired by French and Italian models. A similar synthesis can be heard in his highly effective and tuneful setting of *The Judgment of Paris*, as well as in his *Tempest* music, which was accepted as by Purcell for more than 200 years. *BDECM*, *BulWel*, *CBCR*, *ChoSha*, *DexQui*, *LauTem*, *LSNV*, *SpiCat*, *ZimPur*.

Wesley, Samuel (1766–1837), the leading English organist and composer around 1800, was a Purcell enthusiast. He included 'From rosy bowers'*, 'From silent shades'* and other Purcell songs in the concerts he gave with his brother Charles at the family home in London between 1779 and 1787. In a lecture, given probably in 1828, Samuel suggested that the ideal public concert should mix old instrumental and vocal music (including 'a Cantata of Purcell') with modern operatic music and symphonies. Purcell was an important model for his own vocal music, particularly in his *Ode to St Cecilia* KO 207 (1794), which sets a text by his grandfather and namesake and uses a Purcellian idiom in several movements; they were probably inspired by the three odes published by Benjamin Goodison* around 1790.

Wesley was also strongly influenced by Purcell in his Morning and Evening Service in F KO71 (1824), which takes the B$^\flat$ Service* Z230 as its starting point; he would have known it from Boyce's* *Cathedral Music*. He responded in print to a critical review of his own service by quoting twice from Z230, and complained in a letter to Vincent Novello* in 1830 that 'Henry Purcell's immortal Church Service in B flat is very rarely (if ever) sung at St. Paul's Cathedral, at Westminster Abbey or at the Chapel Royal; whereas all the harmless and hackneyed Chords of [Charles] King and [James] Kent are in Constant Request at the Cathedrals all over England'. *HolWes, OllWes.*

Westminster Abbey St Peter at Westminster was the main collegiate church in London during Purcell's working life; St Paul's*, destroyed in 1666, was not formally reopened until 1697. He grew up near the Abbey (see the map in *WooPur*, 3), where his father Henry was Master of the Choristers as well as a gentleman of the Chapel Royal*, and he was paid for tuning the Abbey organ* and copying music between 1674 and 1678. He succeeded John Blow* as its organist in 1679, with Blow taking over again after his death. It is not known who built the Abbey organ Purcell played, though George Dallam tuned it until 1665 and Bernard Smith* thereafter. In 1694 Purcell was a signatory to Smith's contract to 'make new the present Organ', but did not live to see its completion. A painting of the Abbey made no earlier than 1695 shows the instrument Purcell played (a detail is in *GwyWes*) in a gallery projecting into the north side of the Choir; he is buried in the north aisle near where it stood. Two vocal partbooks from a large set, GB-Lwa, Triforium Set 1, discovered in the Triforium of the Abbey in 1972, were largely copied by William Tucker* (d.1679) and include nine works by Purcell. Nothing survives of Purcell's own copying for the Abbey, which included a large project in 1688 for 'makeing ye Service Bookes' and having them bound (*ShaMan*, 198). *HolPur, KniWes, ShaMan, ShaSuc, SpiRes, ZimPur.*

'What shall be done in behalf of the man' Z341 Purcell composed this ode to celebrate the future James II's* return to London from Scotland; it was probably performed at Whitehall* on 29 May 1682. The anonymous poem staunchly defends the Duke of York's position as heir to the throne, ridiculing his foes (who had tried to exclude him from the succession) and praising his loyalty to his brother Charles II*: 'York the obedient, grateful, just | Courageous, punctual, mindful of his trust'. The work is notable for the quality of the opening symphony*, especially the virtuosic handling of cross accents in its compound-metre second section, and for the composer's first brief and tentative experiment in concerto-like alternations between recorders and strings in one of its ritornellos*. Purcell later reused the bourrée-like tune for the solo and chorus 'All the grandeur he possesses' as the First Act Tune of *The Gordian Knot Unty'd**. *AdaPur, HolPur, SpiOde, WooEqu, WooOde.*

'When I am laid in earth' *See* **Dido's Lament**

'When Night her purple veil' ZD201 This cantata-like work for baritone, two violins and continuo survives in an early eighteenth-century score, GB-Ob, MS Tenbury 1175, entitled 'The Musick In the Play' and attributed to 'H.P.' It was included among Purcell's theatre music in the original edition of *PS* 21, though it was probably an independent concert piece, possibly used as a theatrical entr'acte. It has some expressive word-setting, though it is generally too drawn-out and late in style to be by Henry Purcell; it was omitted from the revised *PS* 21. Daniel Purcell* has been suggested as its composer, and significantly its unidentified copyist (labelled London E in *ShaMan*) was Daniel's close collaborator; MS Tenbury 1175 is an important source of his music. Benjamin

Britten* had an affection for the work, evidently accepting the attribution to Henry. His performing edition (Faber Music, 1977) was used for a BBC recording made in Aldeburgh on 24 June 1965 by Dietrich Fischer-Dieskau with Britten at the piano; it was also included on *Dietrich Fischer-Dieskau singt Barock-Kantaten*, a 1969 EMI Electrola LP. John Shirley-Quirk included it on a 1966 Saga LP.

Whitehall The collective name for the buildings once ranged along the Thames north of Westminster; it served as the main palace for English monarchs from 1530, when Henry VIII appropriated Cardinal Wolsey's York Place. Purcell would have known it from boyhood as a Chapel Royal* choirboy, singing in Wolsey's small chapel in the middle of the site. Later he played its Robert Dallam organ* as a Chapel organist and wrote anthems for its choir. In verse anthems* the soloists were apparently placed in the organ gallery, with the instrumentalists for symphony anthems* in an adjacent gallery and the choir in stalls on the floor of the chapel.

The large-scale concerted odes* and welcome songs* Purcell wrote for Charles II* and James II* were most likely performed in Wolsey's Great Hall, next to the chapel. For small-scale music he would have had access to the Privy Chamber, the collective name for the royal family's private apartments, housed in a rabbit-warren of buildings of different periods to the south of the chapel and the great hall. However, William III* and Mary II* preferred to live at Kensington Palace and Hampton Court, and Whitehall was destroyed by fire on 4–5 January 1698. The sole surviving part (apart from fragments incorporated into later buildings) is Inigo Jones's Banqueting House, subsequently converted to serve as the Chapel Royal. It is thought that the accumulated royal music

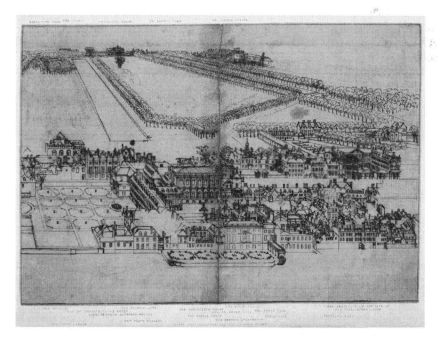

Illus. 15: Whitehall Palace (c.1695).

library, including the original performing material for the concerted music Purcell wrote as part of his court duties, was destroyed in the fire. The present Royal Music Library, now at *GB-Lbl*, is an eighteenth-century creation. *HolFid, HolPur, SpiRes, ThuWhi.*

'Who can from joy refrain?' Z342 Purcell's last court ode* sets a text possibly by Nahum Tate* celebrating William, Duke of Gloucester's* sixth birthday on 24 July 1695, a task that seems to have been a replacement for his duties as the composer for Mary II's* birthday odes; she had died the previous December. It was probably performed at Camden House, Kensington, where the duke's household had been established. The household musicians of his mother Princess Anne* included the trumpeter John Shore* and an oboe* band largely of French musicians, which explains why Purcell scored the work with a single trumpet*, a four-part oboe consort and strings. Purcell's autograph names four vocal soloists, all countertenors*. The martial cast of the text, and Purcell's prominent use of wind instruments, reflects the young duke's interest in soldiering: he drilled his own regiment of boys armed with wooden swords.

If none of the ode's movements are on the level of the best of those in Mary's birthday odes, the music is consistently appealing, beginning with a fine trumpet sonata (later used in *Timon of Athens**) and ending with an extended chaconne* that mixes rondeau* and ground-bass* patterns with a kaleidoscopic variety of vocal and instrumental combinations. Two of the airs stand out: the ground bass 'A prince of glorious race descended' for a countertenor (Anthony Robert) with its beautiful string ritornello*; and 'Sound the trumpet and beat the warlike drums', for countertenor (John Freeman*) and trumpet (doubtless Shore). The latter is a fine example of its type, mixing declamatory and tuneful elements and adroitly progressing from antiphonal exchanges to a full-blown duet. *See also* **Performing material.** *AdaPur, BalWho, HolPur, MurOde, ShaMan, WooPur.*

'Why are all the Muses mute?' Z343 Purcell's first welcome song* for James II* may have been the 'mighty Musique-Entertainment at Court for the welcomeing home the King and Queene' that Samuel Pepys* witnessed on 10 October 1685. Establishing the model for future odes, the anonymous poet represented the king as Caesar, while making extended reference to the crushing of Monmouth's Rebellion that summer. Purcell responded to the opening rhetorical question by keeping back the symphony* until after a countertenor* and the choir had commanded the sleeping viol, lute and lyre to awaken, a gesture also used in his earlier symphony anthem* 'My heart is fixed, O God' Z29.

Purcell's dramatic engagement with the text extended to the wide-ranging tonal planning. After the D minor opening a countertenor ground-bass* solo in D major proclaims Britain's greatness, followed by a descent to G minor for 'Accurs'd Rebellion' (a daring solo for John Gostling*), a treble duet, and a beautiful free-standing minuet* in rondeau* form (reused in *The Gordian Knot Unty'd**), which may have been danced. E^b major restores the blessings of peace in a countertenor and bass duet with obbligato violin, followed by a triumphant song and chorus (C major), a bass duet (A minor), and the final solo and chorus (returning to D minor). Purcell saved his most powerful musical gesture for this chorus: James's fame endures in long held notes, while all else decays in wilting chromatic lines. *AdaPur, HolPur, SpiOde, WooOde, WooPur.*

William III Willem Hendrik, Prince of Orange and Stadtholder of the Dutch Republic (1650–1702), was the son of Mary, Princess of Orange, daughter of Charles I, and was therefore the nephew of Charles II* and James II*; he married his first cousin Mary, James's daughter, in 1677. They became joint monarchs of England as William III and Mary II* following the Glorious Revolution* of 1688–9. They were crowned in Westminster Abbey* on 11 April 1689, when Purcell's anthem 'Praise the Lord, O Jerusalem'* was performed. Mary was musical, like the other Stuarts, though William's musical interests were apparently limited to martial music – reflected in the prominent use of oboes* and trumpets* in court odes* of the 1690s. After 1689 music at court was sharply reduced: Purcell lost his post as harpsichordist in the Private Music*, and symphony anthems* were no longer required for the Chapel Royal*, enabling him to devote most of his time to the theatre. However, he continued as a Chapel organist, composing several verse anthems* celebrating William's military campaigns. He also retained his post as curator of the court keyboard instruments and began a series of odes for Queen Mary's birthday. *HolFid, HolPur, MurOde, SpiOde, WhiPol, ZimPur.*

William, Prince, Duke of Gloucester Born on 24 July 1689 to George* and Anne*, Prince and Princess of Denmark, William stood in direct line of succession to the English throne: his aunt and uncle, the joint monarchs William III* (his godfather) and Mary II* were childless. The ode 'The noise of foreign wars'*, by Purcell or John Blow*, marked his birth, while Purcell's last court ode*, 'Who can from joy refrain?'*, celebrated his sixth birthday. The boy was obsessed with the military, an interest reflected in works for him by Blow*, John Church, Jeremiah Clarke* and Daniel Purcell*. Thomas Bray* may have been his dancing master. He died in 1700, a few days after his eleventh birthday, probably of smallpox. *BalWho, MurOde, WhiNoi, WinAnn.*

Winchester Three successive organists of Winchester Cathedral had connections with Purcell. John Reading* (organist 1675–81 and then of Winchester College 1681–92) was an important Purcell copyist, of consort music as well as church music, some of it probably obtained directly from the composer. Daniel Roseingrave* (organist 1681–92) was reportedly a choirboy in the Chapel Royal* alongside Purcell, who later copied out a verse anthem* by him. Roseingrave may have been a source of information about Purcell, transmitted to Hawkins* through his son Thomas. Vaughan Richardson (c.1670–1729, organist from 1692) had also been a Chapel Royal choirboy (he sang in the 1685 coronation*), and became a Purcell follower as a collector and a composer; he may have owned GB-Ob, Mus.c.26, an important source of odes by John Blow* and Purcell. Towards the end of his life Charles II* was much concerned with his project to build a palace in Winchester, staying there in the summers of 1682–4. Nicholas Staggins* and a group of unnamed musicians, perhaps including Purcell, attended him there between 29 August and 25 September 1683. *HerCat, HolPur, HolRos, RECM, ShaMan, ShaSuc, SpiRes.*

Windsor and Eton The two neighbouring collegiate foundations, at St George's Chapel, Windsor and Eton College, were theoretically independent but many of their adult members held places in both choirs, with the former the dominant institution during Purcell's lifetime. St George's had strong court links: several of its leading singers were also members of the Chapel Royal*, while two of them, William Isaack* and John Walter*, sometimes working together, were also important Purcell copyists, making scores of his odes* and other court secular music as well as devotional part-songs* and church music. Access to the court repertory was facilitated by the presence of the Chapel Royal (with a group of court string players provided for symphony anthems*) in Windsor during most summers of Charles II's* reign starting from 1671. It mostly performed in a chapel inside Windsor Castle, not in St George's Chapel. As organist and 'informator choristarum' at Eton, Walter arranged in 1693–4 for Purcell to teach John Weldon*. There are a number of Purcell works in manuscripts used in St George's Chapel (catalogued in *DexQui*), including the B$^\flat$ Service* Z230, 'Behold, I bring you glad tidings'*, 'My song shall be alway'* and 'Rejoice in the Lord alway'*. *DexQui*, *HerCat*, *RECM*, *ShaMan*, *ShaSuc*, *SpiRes*.

Wit and Mirth See *Pills to Purge Melancholy*

Withy, Francis A singing man at Christ Church, Oxford* from 1670 until his death in 1727, as well as a bass viol player and prolific collector and copyist of consort music. His commonplace book, GB-Och, Mus. 337, bound in with a copy of Christopher Simpson's* *Compendium of Practical Music* (1667) and compiled *c*.1670–95, contains hundreds of brief extracts taken from contemporary English, French and Italian music, including Purcell's *Sonnata's of III Parts** (1683), which he analysed and compared for their contrapuntal technique and handling of chromatic harmony. GB-Ob, MS Mus. Sch. C.61, mainly an anthology of bass viol and violin solos, includes among several Purcell items a score of the symphony anthem* version of 'My song shall be alway'* dated 9 September 1690. Withy probably copied it from Purcell's lost autograph in connection with an Oxford performance around then. *CCLMC*, *HolLif*, *ShaMan*, *ThoWit*.

Word-setting Purcell's word-setting can be understood on several levels. Large-scale rhythmic frameworks were governed largely by formulaic responses to the poetic metre of the verses. Iambic (weak–strong) and mixed iambic and trochaic (strong–weak) metres elicited both declamatory and lyrical treatment. For the latter, common mismatches of stress patterns prompted characteristic duple- or triple-time settings; for instance, lines beginning with three unstressed syllables almost invariably attracted triple-time settings. Trochaic, dactylic (strong–weak–weak) and anapaestic (weak–weak–strong) metres were almost always set as airs*, often in appropriate dance rhythms.

Purcell had an acute sense of the stress profiles of words and phrases, which he captured frequently in minute detail. His approach was not always to replicate natural accentuation, but often to heighten (or even intentionally distort) it, almost always prioritising expressive variety; he rarely fell into repetitive rhythmic patterns, except in some settings using dance rhythms. He revelled in word-painting, emphasising individual words through melisma and affective intervals, details which interacted subtly with word repetition and harmonic devices, always governed by a fine sense of melodic line.

'From rosy bowers'*, singled out by Burney* for its 'exquisite expression of the words' (*BurHis*, iii. 493), encapsulates Purcell's methods at their most sophisticated. The declamatory sections employ kaleidoscopic word-painting devices, combined with highly detailed declamation (Ex. 10), while of the two lyrical sections, one is in a bourrée rhythm, and the other in a contrasting triple time. In *Orpheus Britannicus**, book 1 Henry Playford* acknowledged Purcell's *'peculiar Genius to express the Energy of English Words, whereby he mov'd the Passions of all his Auditors'*. Purcell's text setting was a significant influence on British twentieth-century composers of solo vocal music, especially Britten* and Tippett*. BurRem, PinMan, RohPoe, SavScu, SpiSon, TipMus, WooPoe.

Ex. 10: 'From rosy bowers' Z578/9, bb. 1–14.

'Ye tuneful Muses' Z344 James II's* 1686 'Birthday Song' was performed on 14 October; the anonymous poem refers to the king's review of his troops that morning. It opens with a fine two-section symphony*, the second of which begins with some ingenious double counterpoint*. The countertenor* solo, chorus and ritornello* sequence 'Be lively then and gay' uses the tune 'Hey, boys, up go we'*, first as a bass line to the solo, then as a violin obbligato in the chorus, returning to the bass in the concluding ritornello. The tune was associated with Thomas D'Urfey's* ballad attacking the Whigs during the Exclusion Crisis, so Purcell probably intended it to recall James's ultimate triumph over his opponents. 'From the rattling of drums and the trumpet's loud sounds', a C major ritornello and chorus in rondeau* form, seems to depict James reviewing the troops, with trumpets* and kettledrums* imitated by the strings. It is juxtaposed with 'To music's softer but yet kind', a superb C minor paean to music replete with exquisite suspensions and chromatic colouring, in which two countertenors and a bass gently alternate with two recorders*. Purcell made a fine keyboard arrangement (ZT681) of 'With him he brings the partner', the ensuing ground-bass* countertenor solo. *AdaPur, HolPur, SpiOde, WooOde.*

'Ye twice ten hundred deities' Z630/13 This great solo for bass with two violins and continuo is Purcell's most awe-inspiring conjuring trick; Charles Burney* (*BurHis*, iii. 492) called the opening 'the best piece of recitative in our language'. It comes from Act II, Scene 2 of *The Indian Queen*, sung by the conjurer Ismeron, played in an early production by the young Richard Leveridge*. He summons up the God of Dreams for the Aztec queen Zempoalla, who seeks solace for her unrequited love for the warrior Montezuma. In the following air 'By the croaking of the toad' he recites a litany of charms, each one despatched with a sinister, jerky figure in the violins. Then the god begins to rise through the theatre trapdoor, illustrated by a slow, ascending, chromatic and increasingly dissonant passage as Ismeron commands him to 'open thy unwilling eyes'. He concludes by illustrating the 'bubbling springs ... That use to lull thee in thy sleep' with a passage of graceful triple time, harmonised in sweet sixths and thirds. *BalLev, BalSta, HolPur, PriPur.*

York Buildings The name given to the streets between the Strand and the Thames built in the 1670s on the site of York House, which included the eponymous concert room in Villiers Street. Roger North* (*NorMus*, 305, 352–3) wrote that it was 'built express and equipt for musick'. It is first heard of as a venue in 1685, and a weekly concert was first advertised there in 1689. Gottfried Finger*, John Banister* junior and Robert King were among those promoting weekly concerts in the 1690s, and it was also used for repeat performances of odes* originally performed at court or for Cecilian celebrations*. For instance, on 25 January 1694 'Hail, bright Cecilia'* was performed, presumably directed by Purcell himself, with 'some other Compositions of his, both Vocal and Instrumental, for the Entertainment of his Highness Prince Lewis of Baden'. A benefit concert for Richard Leveridge* on 28 May 1698 consisted of 'an Entertainment of Vocal and Instrumental Musick' by Purcell, with John Pate* and Jemmy Bowen* as soloists. Later repeat performances of Purcell's odes included two of the Yorkshire Feast Song*, on 10 March and 18 June 1701. York Buildings was small: in 1724 an advertisement stated it was '32 Foot 4 Inches long, 31 Foot 6 broad, 21 Foot high', with a performing area in an alcove large enough for about 11 musicians and a harpsichord. However, there is evidence that groups of about 60 performed odes and other large-scale music there around 1700, so it must have been rebuilt at some point. It seems to have been last used for public performances in April 1738. *HolBat, HolFin, LS, LSNV, ScoCon, TilCha, WhiCec.*

York Minster was a centre for performing and collecting Purcell's music in the early eighteenth century. Purcell enthusiasts there included Edward Finch*, a prebendary from 1704; the Subchanter Valentine Nalson (1683–1723); William Knight (1684–1739), Nalson's successor as Subchanter; and John Cooper, a singing man from 1721 to 1730. Many of the manuscripts and prints containing Purcell, copied or owned by Knight and Cooper, are still in the Minster library, though Finch's manuscripts are mostly at Durham and Glasgow. Other notable Purcell manuscripts at York include the Bing-Gostling* Partbooks; and the sole source of the Sonata in D major Z850*. Vincent Novello* transcribed three Purcell anthems and the Magnificat and Nunc Dimittis in G minor Z231 (now thought to be by Daniel Purcell*) in the Minster library just before the fire of 1829, claiming that otherwise they would have been 'entirely & irretreivably [sic] lost to the world', though all but one of the manuscripts he used are still in the library. *BoyBin, GriMan, GriMin, HerCat, HolMan, SpiRes, ShaBin, ShaMan, ZimCat.*

The Yorkshire Feast Song Z333 When Thomas D'Urfey* published 'Of old when heroes thought it base' (*Pills to Purge Melancholy*, i. 114–16), he described it as '*An ODE on the Assembly of the Nobility and Gentry of the City and County of York, at the Anniversary Feast,* March *the* 27th. 1690. Set *to Musick by Mr.* Henry Purcell. *One of the finest Compositions he ever made, and cost* 100l. *the performing*'. County feasts were a regular part of London's cultural calendar, but performing elaborate music during them was an innovation, probably imitating the Cecilian celebrations*. D'Urfey's poem combines (rather unconvincingly) an evocation of Yorkshire's stirring early history with effusive praise of William III*. Purcell wrote for his largest forces yet outside the court: pairs of trumpets*, oboes* and recorders* supplement the four-part strings and continuo.

The work opens with an Italianate trumpet sonata, probably the first by an Englishman, showing that Purcell had fully assimilated the Italianate writing of G.B. Draghi's* *Song for St Cecilia's Day, 1687*. Individual movements are mostly in extended, standalone forms, several of which begin with lengthy instrumental preludes. The finest is 'So when the glitt'ring queen of night', a mysterious tenor ground-bass* solo accompanied by hushed four-part strings. Some sections use the warlike idiom of Purcell's later court odes*, concerned with cheering-on the king's military exploits. However, the Yorkshiremen gathered that day in Merchant-Taylors' Hall would doubtless have responded more to the grandeur and novelty of the orchestral writing, combined with the extravagant praise of their native county. *AdaPur, HolPur, HowArt, SpiOde, WooPur, WooOde.*

Zimmerman, Franklin Bershir American musicologist (b.1923), latterly at the University of Pennsylvania. He revolutionised Purcell studies with *ZimCat* (1963), the first and only thematic catalogue of Purcell's music; and *ZimPur* (1967; revised 1983), still the most comprehensive biography* of the composer. Zimmerman announced his intention in the 1967 edition of *ZimPur* to write a third book, 'Henry Purcell, 1659–1695: Analytical Essays on his Musical Forms', but it never appeared. *ZimCat* is still in everyday use, with the 'Z' catalogue numbers used particularly to identify works with multiple generic titles, such as the sonatas and the fantasias*. However, it is now seriously out of date: subsequent research has modified the dates or the status of the authenticity of many works, and a number of new works have come to light since the 1960s.

Works

Introductory notes

1. The following list includes only works by Henry Purcell we consider genuine, or at least plausibly attributed to him. However, some misattributions are discussed in individual entries in the *Dictionary*.
2. Z numbers are taken from F.B. Zimmerman: *Henry Purcell, 1659–1695: an Analytical Catalogue of his Music* (London, 1963).
3. PS numbers refer to the volumes of the scholarly collected edition, *The Works of Henry Purcell* in the rev. 2nd edn. (London, 1961–).
4. The categories under which works appear largely follow those of Zimmerman's catalogue, though we have introduced a few modifications to reflect more closely the musical genres as understood by Purcell and his contemporaries.
5. Works should be understood as complete and preserved in their entirety (or virtually so) unless otherwise stated.
6. Titles given to works observe the modernised spelling and punctuation commonly used in the Purcell literature.
7. Sources are only given for works omitted, or for primary sources not listed, in Z or PS.
8. Major keys are indicated by capitals, minor keys by lower case. Keys are only given for opening and concluding sections, ignoring internal key changes.
9. Precise dates are for first known performances, except for those for the fantasias in section 8, Consort music, which appear in Purcell's autograph score and are assumed to be dates of composition or copying.

Abbreviations

→	after / or later
←	by / before
arr.	arranged / arranger
attrib.	attributed to
aut	autumn
b	bass voice (solo)
B	bass voice (choral)
bc	basso continuo
bn	bassoon
bs	instrumental bass
bv	bass viol
c.	circa
can	cantoris
ct	countertenor (solo); see the entry in the *Dictionary* for a discussion of the contemporary and modern meanings of the term.
Ct	countertenor (choral)
dec	decani

	ed./eds.	editor/editors
	edn.	edition
	frag	fragmentary (with one or more parts missing)
	full a4	four-part choir (Tr Ct T B)
	full a5	five-part choir (Tr Tr Ct T B)
	full a8	eight-part choir (Tr Tr Ct Ct T T B B)
	fwv	full with verse
	inc	incomplete (with bars missing)
	kdr	kettledrums
	keybd	keyboard
	MS	manuscript
	org	organ (an extant contemporary written-out organ part, or vestige of one)
	ov	overture
	pub	published / publication
	rec	recorder
	recon	reconstructed
	rev	revised / revision(s)
	spr	spring
	str a3	three-part strings (2 vn, bs)
	str a4	four-part strings (2 vn, vla, bs)
	str a5	five-part strings (2 vn, 2 vla, bs)
	sum	summer
	sym	symphony (anthem, service, song)
	t	tenor (solo)
	T	tenor (choral)
	tpt	trumpet
	tr	treble (solo), including parts for adult female sopranos as well as boys
	Tr	treble (choral)
	trv	treble viol
	tv	tenor viol
	vla	viola
	vn	violin
	vv	voices (unspecified)
	win	winter

Contents

The list of works is divided into the following sections:
1   Anthems
2   Liturgical music
3   Domestic sacred music
4   Catches
5   Domestic secular vocal music
6   Welcome songs and extended occasional works
7   Stage works
8   Consort music
9   Keyboard music
10 Theoretical works

1 Anthems

Z	Title	Genre	Key	Date	Scoring	Edition	Comment
1	Awake, put on thy strength	sym	D	1681–2	ct ct b, [full a4], str a4, bc	PS 14	inc: final chorus missing
2	Behold, I bring you glad tidings	sym	C	25/12/1687	ct t b, full a4, str a4, bc	PS 13	
3	Behold, now praise the Lord	sym	D	c.1678	ct t b, full a4, str a4, bc	PS 13	
4	Be merciful unto me	verse	c–C	c.1693	ct t b, full a4, bc	PS 29	
5	Blessed are they that fear the Lord	sym	g	15/1/1688	tr tr ct b, full a4, str a4, bc	PS 13	thanksgiving for the queen's pregnancy
6	Blessed be the Lord my strength	verse	g	←12/1677	ct t b, full a4, org	PS 28	
7	Blessed is he that considereth the poor	verse	a	?1690–4	ct t b, bc	PS 29	
8	Blessed is he whose unrighteousness is forgiv'n	verse	a–A	c.1679–81	tr tr ct t b, full a4, bc	PS 32	
9	Blessed is the man that feareth the Lord	verse	c–C	c.1688	t b, full a4, org	PS 29	Anthem for the Charterhouse, chorus probably inauthentic
9	Blessed is the man that feareth the Lord	verse	c–C		ct t b, full a4, org	PS 29	cathedral rev of Anthem for the Charterhouse with different chorus, chorus probably inauthentic
10	Blow up the trumpet in Sion	fwv	C–c	←aut 1677	tr tr tr ct t t b, Tr Tr Ct Ct T T B B, bc	PS 32	
11	Bow down thine ear, O Lord	verse	a	c.1679–81	tr ct t b, full a4, bc	PS 32	
12	Give sentence with me, O God	verse	A	c.1679	ct t b, full a4, bc	PS 28	
13B	Hear me, O Lord, and that soon	verse	d–D	c.1678–81	tr ct t b, full a5, bc	PS 32	?rev and completion of the domestic part-song Z13A

Z	Title	Genre	Key	Date	Scoring	Edition	Comment
14	Hear my prayer, O God	verse	c	?early 1685	ct t b, full a4, bc	PS 28	Tr inc
15	Hear my prayer, O Lord	?fwv	c	?1685	full a8, bc	PS 32	inc: probably opening of a fwv anthem; ?planned for Charles II's funeral
N66	If the Lord himself had not been on our side	sym	c	←12/1677		PS 32	frag: only B part survives
16	In thee, O Lord, do I put my trust	sym	c	1682–3	ct t b, full a4, str a4, bc	PS 14	
18	It is a good thing to give thanks	sym	g	1680–1	ct t b, full a4, str a4, bc	PS 14	
19	I was glad when they said unto me	sym	G	1682–3	ct t b, full a4, str a4, bc	PS 14	
	I was glad when they said unto me	full	G	23/4/1685	full a5, bc	PS 32	coronation of James II; attrib. John Blow in the principal source
20	I will give thanks unto thee, O Lord	sym	G	c.1683	tr tr ct t b, full a4, str a4, bc	PS 17	
21	I will give thanks unto the Lord	sym	g	c.1684	t b b, full a4, str a3, bc	PS 13	
N67	I will love thee, O Lord	verse	g	c.1679	b, full a4, bc	PS 28	
22	I will sing unto the Lord	fwv	a	←12/1677	tr tr ct t b, full a5, bc	PS 32	
23	Let God arise	verse	C	←12/1677	t t, full a4, bc	PS 28	
24	Let mine eyes run down with tears	verse	g	c.1682	tr tr ct t b, full a5, bc	PS 28	
25	Lord, how long wilt thou be angry?	fwv	g	c.1683	ct t b, full a5, bc	PS 32	
N69	The Lord is king, and hath put on glorious apparel	verse	G	c.1682	tr, full a4, bc	PS 28	
53	The Lord is king, be the people never so impatient	verse	d	?1690→	tr tr, full a4, bc	PS 29	

Works

211

Z	Title	Genre	Key	Date	Scoring	Edition	Comment
54	The Lord is king, the earth may be glad	verse	G	1688	b, full a4, org	PS 29	
55	The Lord is my light	sym	b	1682–3	ct t b, full a4, str a4, bc	PS 14	
26	Lord, who can tell how oft he offendeth?	verse	a?	c.1676	t t b, full a4, org	PS 28	
28	My beloved spake	sym	F	←12/1677	ct t b b, full a4, str a4, bc	PS 13	
29	My heart is fixed, O God	sym	A	1682–3	ct t b, full a4, str a4, bc	PS 14	
30	My heart is inditing	sym	C	23/4/1685	tr tr ct ct t b b b, Tr Tr Ct Ct T B B, str a4, bc	PS 17	coronation of James II and Mary of Modena
31	My song shall be alway	verse/sym	G	←6/1688	B, full a4, str a4, bc	PS 13	?str added for Oxford (?9/9/1690)
32	O consider my adversity	verse	c?	?1694–5	ct t b, full a4, org	PS 29	
33	O give thanks unto the Lord	verse	C	?12/11/1693	tr ct t b, full a4, org	PS 29	?for William III's return from Flanders
34	O God, the king of glory	?verse	b	←12/1677	?solo vv, full a4, bc	PS 32	inc: only two full sections; probably from a lost verse anthem
D4	O God, they that love thy name	?verse	g		?full a4, org	PS 32	frag: only b and org survive
35	O God, thou art my God	fwv	B♭	c.1681–2	tr tr ct t b, full a4 *can*, *dec*, bc	PS 32	related to the Service in B♭ Z230; apparently performed with sections of it
36	O God, thou hast cast us out	fwv	c?	c.1679–81	tr tr ct ct t b, Tr Tr Ct Ct T B, bc	PS 32	
37	O Lord God of hosts	fwv	A	←9/1682	tr tr ct ct t b, full a8 ?*can*, *dec*, bc	PS 32	
38	O Lord, grant the king a long life	sym	F	c.1684	ct t b, full a4, str a3, bc	PS 13	

Z	Title	Genre	Key	Date	Scoring	Edition	Comment
39	O Lord our governor	verse	c	←12/1677	tr tr tr b b, full a4, org	PS 28	
40	O Lord, rebuke me not	verse	g	1690–3	tr tr, full a4, org	PS 29	
41	O Lord, thou art my God	verse	a–A	c.1684	ct t b, full a4, bc	PS 28	
42	O praise God in his holiness	sym	B$^\flat$	1680–1	ct t b b, full a4, str a4, bc	PS 14	
43	O praise the Lord, all ye heathen	verse	a	c.1679	t t, full a4, bc	PS 28	
44	O sing unto the Lord	sym	F	1688	tr ct t b b, full a4, str a4, bc	PS 17	
45	Out of the deep have I called	verse	c–C	c.1685	tr ct b, full a4, bc	PS 28	
46	Praise the Lord, O Jerusalem	sym	d–D	11/4/1689	tr tr ct t b, full a5, str a4, bc	PS 17	coronation of William III and Mary I
47	Praise the Lord, O my soul, and all that is within me	sym	F	1682–3	tr tr t t b b, full a4, str a4, bc	PS 14	
48	Praise the Lord, O my soul, O Lord my God	sym	G	1687	ct b, full a4, str a3, bc	PS 17	
N68	Praise the Lord, ye servants	sym	d	←12/1677		PS 32	frag: b, B parts only
49	Rejoice in the Lord alway	sym	C	1683–4	ct t b, full a4, str a4, bc	PS 14	the Bell Anthem
50	Remember not, Lord, our offences	full	a	c.1679–81	full a5, bc	PS 32	
51	Save me, O God, for thy name's sake	fwv	g–G	1677	tr tr ct t b, Tr Tr Ct T T B, org	PS 32	
52	Sing unto God, O ye kingdoms of the earth	verse	D	1687	b, full a4, bc	PS 29	
57	They that go down to the sea in ships	sym	D	c.1682–3	ct b, full a4, str a3, bc	PS 13	

Works

Z	Title	Genre	Key	Date	Scoring	Edition	Comment
59	Thy righteousness, O God, is very high	?full	a		?full a4, org	PS 32	frag: only org survives
60	Thy way, O God, is holy	sym	d	1688	ct b, full a4, str a3, bc	PS 13	
61	Thy word is a lantern	verse	C	c.1690–4	ct t b, full a4, bc	PS 29	
62	Turn thou us, O good Lord	verse	c	?c.1674	ct t b, full a4, org	PS 28	
63	Unto thee will I cry, O Lord	sym	d–D	1684–5	ct t b, full a4, str a4, bc	PS 17	
56	The way of God is an undefiled way	verse	D	11/11/1694	ct ct b, Tr Ct Ct Ct T B, org	PS 29	William III's return from Flanders
64	Who hath believed our report	verse	c	c.1674–5	ct t t b, full a4, bc	PS 28	
65	Why do the heathen so furiously rage together	sym	c	1683–4	ct t b, full a4, str a4, bc	PS 17	

2 Liturgical music

Z	Title	Genre	Key	Date	Scoring	Edition	Comment
17A, 58A	Funeral sentences	fwv, full	c	?1672–6	tr ct t b, full a4, bc	PS 32	1st version; ?for Henry Cooke, Pelham Humfrey or Christopher Gibbons
	In the midst of life we are in death Thou knowest, Lord, the secrets of our hearts						
27, 17B, 58B	Funeral sentences	fwv	c	?1676–9	tr ct t b, full a4, bc	PS 32	2nd version; last rev c.1679–81
	Man that is born of a woman In the midst of life we are in death Thou knowest, Lord, the secrets of our hearts						
58C	Funeral sentences	full	E^b	5/3/1695	full a4, 4 flat tpt, bc	PS 32	funeral of Mary II
	Thou knowest, Lord, the secrets of our hearts						
230	Morning and Evening Service	fwv	B^b	c.1680	tr ct t b can, dec, full a4 can, dec, bc	PS 23	

	1st Service
	  Te Deum (We praise thee, O God)
	  Benedictus (Blessed be the Lord God of Israel)
	  Responses to the Commandments (Lord have mercy upon us)
	  Nicene Creed (I believe in one God)
	  Magnificat (My soul doth magnify the Lord)
	  Nunc Dimittis (Lord, now lettest thou thy servant depart in peace)
	2nd Service (alternative Morning and Evening Canticles)
	  Benedicite (O all ye works of the Lord)
	  Jubilate Deo (O be joyful in the Lord)
	  Cantate Domino (O sing unto the Lord)
	  Deus misereatur (God be merciful unto us)						

232	Morning Service	sym verse	D	22/11/1694	tr tr ct ct t b, full a5, 2 tpt, str a4, bc	PS 23	St Cecilia service, St Bride's Church
	Te Deum (We praise thee, O God) Jubilate Deo (O be joyful in the Lord)						
D90	Sanctus (Holy, holy, holy)	full	G		full a4, org	PS 23	inc: recon from org; related to (?and arr. from) The Indian Queen, Z630/18

3 Domestic Sacred Music

Z	Title	Key	Date	Scoring	Edition	Text author; (title); comment
						bracketed dates are of 1st pub within Purcell's lifetime
						tr/t + b, bc: a solo song with a bass (or other voices) entering for the 'chorus'
130	Ah! few and full of sorrow	e	1678–9	tr ct t b, bc	PS 30	George Sandys inc: final section missing
101	Alleluia	c		tr ct t b	PS 32	canon 4 in 2 'recte et retro'; late sources only
181	Awake, and with attention hear	F	1685	b, bc	PS 30	Abraham Cowley
182	Awake, ye dead, the trumpet calls	C	(1693)	b b, bc,	PS 30	Nahum Tate (A Hymn upon the Last Day)
131	Beati omnes qui timent Dominum	g	1678–9	tr tr ct b, bc	PS 30	
183	Begin the song, and strike the living lyre!	C	c.1688	b, bc	PS 30	Cowley (The Resurrection)
184	Close thine eyes and sleep secure	c	(1688)	tr/t b, bc	PS 30	Francis Quarles (Upon a Quiet Conscience)
102	Domine non est exaltatum cor meum	D	1678–9	ct t, bc	PS 30	inc: opening only
132	Early, O Lord, my fainting soul	e	1678–9	tr tr ct b, bc	PS 30	John Patrick
103	Gloria Patri et Filio	c	1678–9	tr ct t b, bc	PS 30	
104	Gloria Patri et Filio	g	c.1677–80	3vv	PS 32	canon 3 in 1
105	Gloria Patri et Filio	g	c.1677–80	4vv	PS 32	canon 4 in 1 'per arsin et thesin'
106	Glory be to the Father	G	c.1677–80	4vv	PS 32	canon 4 in 1
107	God is gone up with a merry noise	C	c.1677–80	7vv, bc	PS 32	canon 7 in 1
186	Great God and just	f	?1680–3	tr + tr tr b, bc	PS 30	Jeremy Taylor (A Penitential Hymn)
13A	Hear me, O Lord, and that soon	d	c.1678–81	tr ct t b, bc	PS 32	inc: opening section only; rev and completed as the anthem Z13B

Works	Z	Title	Key	Date	Scoring	Edition	Text author; (title); comment
216	133	Hear me, O Lord, the great support	c	1678–9	ct t b, bc	PS 30	Patrick
	187	Hosanna to the Highest	c		b + ct, bc	PS 30	William Fuller; on a ground; c.1750 MS only
	188	How have I stray'd, my God	c	(1688)	tr/t + b, bc	PS 30	William Fuller
	189	How long, great God	a	c.1683	tr/t, bc	PS 30	John Norris (The Aspiration)
	134	In guilty night	c	(1693)	tr ct b, bc	PS 30	Saul and the Witch of Endor; biblical scene using text set by Robert Ramsey and others
	190	In the black, dismal dungeon of despair	e	(1688)	tr/t, bc	PS 30	Fuller
	D71	It must be done, my soul	f	?1680–3	b, bc	PS 30	Norris (The Meditation); also attrib. Francis Bragge
	135	Jehova, quam multi sunt hostes mei	a	1678–9	tr tr ct t b, bc	PS 30	
	108	Laudate Dominum	G	c.1677–80	3vv	PS 32	canon 3 in 1
	191	Let the night perish	c	1682–3	tr/t + b, bc	PS 30	Taylor (Job's Curse)
	136	Lord, I can suffer thy rebukes	g–G	1678–9	tr tr ct b, bc	PS 30	Patrick
	137	Lord, not to us, but to thy name	d	c.1680	ct t b, bc	PS 30	Patrick; inc: opening only
	192	Lord, what is man	g	(1693)	tr/t, bc	PS 30	Fuller (A Divine Hymn) ?early version with different bass in GB-Ob, Mus. C.26.
	109	Miserere mei	d	c.1677–80	tr ct t b	PS 32	canon 4 in 2
	193	Now that the sun hath veil'd his light	G	(1688)	tr/t, bc	PS 30	Fuller (An Evening Hymn on a Ground)
	138	O all ye people, clap your hands	C	1678–9	tr tr t b, bc	PS 30	Patrick
	139	O happy man that fears the Lord	a	c.1680	tr tr ct b, bc	PS 30	Patrick; inc: opening only

Z	Title	Key	Date	Scoring	Edition	Text author; (title); comment	Works
140	O, I'm sick of life	c	1678–9	ct t b, bc	PS 30	Sandys	217
141	O Lord our governor	B♭	1678–9	tr tr ct b, bc	PS 30	Patrick	
194	O Lord, since I experienc'd have	c	?1680–3	tr/t, bc	PS 30		
D42	Oh that my grief was throughly weigh'd	g	?1678–9	t t b, bc	PS 30	survives only in Philip Hayes's 1780s copy, ?made from a now-lost autograph	
142	Plung'd in the confines of despair	d	1678–9	t t b, bc	PS 30	Patrick	
143	Since God so tender a regard	F	1678–9	t t b, bc	PS 30	Patrick; on a ground	
195	Sleep, Adam, sleep and take thy rest	c	1677	tr/t, bc	PS 30	(Adam's Sleep)	
196	Tell me, some pitying angel	c	(1693)	tr, bc	PS 30	Tate (The Blessed Virgin's Expostulation)	
197	The earth trembled	A–a	?1680–3	tr/t, bc	PS 30	Quarles (On our Saviour's Passion)	
198	Thou wakeful shepherd	g	(1688)	tr/t, bc	PS 30	Fuller (A Morning Hymn)	
199	We sing to him whose wisdom form'd the ear	c	←1685	tr/t + b, bc	PS 30	Nathaniel Ingelo	
144	When on my sick bed I languish	a	1678–9	t t b, bc	PS 30	Thomas Flatman (A Thought on Death)	
200	With sick and famish'd eyes	g	?1682–3	tr/t, bc	PS 30	George Herbert (A Religious Elegy)	

4 Catches

Z	Title	Key	Date	Scoring	Text author; (title); comment
\multicolumn{6}{l}{bracketed dates are of 1st pub within Purcell's lifetime; all edited in PS 22A}
241	An ape, a lion, a fox and an ass	d	(1686)	3vv	
242	As Roger last night to Jenny lay close	c		3vv	
244	Call for the reck'ning	G	(1695)	3vv	(The Careless Drawer)
245	Come, come, let us drink	C	(1695)	3vv, bc	Alexander Brome
246	Come, come my hearts	F	(1685)	3vv	(A Loyal Catch); refers to the Exclusion Crisis (1679–81)
247	Down, down with Bacchus	F	(1693)	3vv	refers to the raising of the Siege of Charleroi (10/1692)
248	Drink on till night be spent	C	(1686)	3vv	Philip Ayres
249	Full bags, a brisk bottle	e/G	(1686)	3vv	Jacob Allestree
250	God save our sov'reign Charles	C	(1685)	3vv	(A Loyal Catch); refers to the Duke of York's absence in Scotland (1679–82)
251	Great Apollo and Bacchus	C	←1688	3vv	
240	A health to the nut-brown lass	F	(1685)	4vv	Sir John Suckling
252	Here's a health, a health	d		3vv	
253	Here's that will challenge all the fair	C	1681–2 (1685)	3vv	(Bartholomew Fair)
254	He that drinks is immortal	G	(1686)	3vv	
255	If all be true that I do think	g	(1688–9)	3vv	?Henry Aldrich
256	I gave her cakes	C	(1689–90)	3vv	
257	Is Charleroy's siege come too?	g	?1692	3vv	for the raising of the Siege of Charleroi (10/1692)
258	Let the grave folks go preach	G	1681–2 (1685)	3vv	(The Jovial Drinker)
259	Let us drink to the blades	C	?1690–1	3vv	refers to the Sieges of Limerick (1690–1)
276	The Macedon youth	C	(1686)	4vv	after Suckling

Works

218

277	The miller's daughter riding to the fair	a	(1686)	3vv	also set by Blow
260	My lady's coachman, John	C	(1687)	3vv	
261	Now England's great council's	G	c.1679 (1685)	3vv	(A Catch Made in the Time of Parliament, 1676 [*sic*]) refers to the 1679 Parliament and the Popish Plot
262	Now, now we are met	C	(1687–8)	3vv	
263	Of all the instruments that are	C	(1693–4)	3vv	(In Commendation of the Viol)
264	Once in our lives	c	(1686)	3vv	(A Farewell to Wives)
265	Once, twice, thrice, I Julia tried	g		3vv	
266	One industrious insect	a		3vv	R. Tomlinson (A Rebus on Mr. Anthony Hall [d. 10/1691] who keeps the Mermaid Tavern in Oxford, and plays his part very well on the Violin)
267	Pale faces, stand by	d	(5/1688)	3vv	Mr. Taverner
268	Pox on you for a fop	C		3vv	
269	Prithee ben't so sad and serious	a		3vv, bc	Alexander Brome
270	Room for th'express	C	?1691	3vv	(On the Fall of Limerick); for the end of the Siege (7/1691)
271	Since the duke is return'd	B$^\flat$	?1682 (1685)	3vv	?Thomas Jordan (On the Duke's Return) for the Duke of York's return from Scotland (10/3/1682); ?for the Lord Mayor's show (30/10/1682)
272	Since time so kind to us does prove	a	←1688	3vv	
D104	Since women so false	c	1681–2	3vv	
273	Sir Walter enjoying his damsel one night	D	←1688	3vv	after John Aubrey
274	Soldier, soldier, take off thy wine	C	(1695)	4vv	
275	Sum up all the delights	F	(1687–8)	3vv	
278	The surrender of Lim'rick	g	?1691	3vv	for the end of the Siege (7/1691)

Works	279	'Tis easy to force	C	1681–2 (1685)	4vv	(A Catch on a Horse)
220	280	'Tis too late for a coach	C	(1686)	3vv	
	281	'Tis women makes us love	C	c.1682 (1685)	4vv	
	282	To all lovers of music	c	(1686–7)	3vv	John Carr (A Catch by Way of Epistle)
	283	To thee, to thee, and to a maid	g	c.1682 (1685)	3vv	
	284	True Englishmen drink	g	?1688	3vv	refers to the acquittal of the seven bishops (30/6/1688)
	285	Under a green elm	G	(1686)	4vv	
	286	Under this stone lies Gabriel John	a	(1686)	3vv	(An Old Epitaph)
	287	When V and I together meet	d	(1686)	3vv	
	288	Who comes there? Stand!	C	(1685)	3vv	(The London Constable)
	289	Wine in a morning	C	(1686)	3vv	Thomas Brown
	290	Would you know how we meet	D	(1684–5)	3vv	Thomas Otway
	291	Young Colin cleaving	C	(1690–1)	3vv	after Thomas D'Urfey
	292	Young John the gard'ner	B$^\flat$	1681–2 (1683)	4vv	

5 Domestic Secular Vocal Music

Z	Title	Key	Date	Scoring	Edition	Text author; (title); comment
			bracketed dates are of 1st pub within Purcell's lifetime tr/t + b, bc: a solo song with a bass voice entering for the 'chorus'			
351	Aaron thus propos'd to Moses	B♭	1687 (1688)	tr/t, [bc]	PS 25	inc: bc and ?tr/t b lost; only attrib. Purcell in late sources
480	Above the tumults of a busy state	d	1682–3	tr/t b, bc	PS 22B	
352	Ah! cruel nymph!	g	4 or 5/1693	tr/t, bc	PS 25	
353	Ah! how pleasant 'tis to love	C	win 1687–8 (1688)	tr/t, bc	PS 25	keyd arr. (T694) pub 1689
354	Ah! what pains, what racking thoughts	g	aut 1695	tr, [bc]	PS 25	William Congreve; inc: bc lost or never composed; last section missing
482	Alas, how barbarous are we	a	c.1679	tr/t b, bc	PS 22B	(Katherine Philips)
355	Amidst the shades	a	spr/sum 1683 (1687)	tr/t, bc	PS 25	
356	Amintas, to my grief I see	d	?1678 (1679)	tr/t, bc	PS 25	
357	Amintor, heedless of his flocks	c	sum 1680 (1681)	tr/t, bc	PS 25	
358	Ask me to love no more	B♭	early 1694 (1694)	tr/t, bc	PS 25	Anthony Hammond
359	A thousand sev'ral ways I tried	B♭	win 1683–4 (1684)	tr/t, bc	PS 25	
360	Bacchus is a pow'r divine	D	?1687–9	b, bc	PS 25	
461	Beneath a dark and melancholy grove	d	?1680–3	tr/t + b, bc	PS 25	(Sappho's Complaint)
361	Beware, poor shepherds!	d	win 1683–4 (1684)	tr/t, bc	PS 25	(The Caution)
362	Cease, anxious world, your fruitless pain	g	late 1684 (1687)	tr/t, bc	PS 25	Sir George Etherege (Song on a Ground)
363	Cease, O my sad soul	c	(1678)	tr/t, bc	PS 25	Charles Webbe; ?by Henry Purcell snr

Works	Z	Title	Key	Date	Scoring	Edition	Text author; (title); comment
222	364	Celia's fond, too long I've lov'd her	d	mid 1694 (1694)	tr/t, bc	PS 25	Peter Anthony Motteux; mock-song on lost Purcell piece
	483	Come, dear companions of th'Arcadian fields	C	early 1686 (1686)	tr/t b, bc	PS 22B	
	484	Come lay by all care	F	sum 1685 (1685)	tr/t b, bc	PS 22B	(Adieu to a Mistress)
	365	Corinna is divinely fair	g	(1692)	tr/t, bc	PS 25	
	367	Cupid, the slyest rogue alive	g	early 1685 (1685)	tr/t, bc	PS 25	John Dryden after Anacreon
	462	Draw near, you lovers that complain	d	spr/sum 1683	tr/t + b, bc	PS 25	Thomas Stanley
	485	Dulcibella, whene'er I sue for a kiss	d	(10–11/1694)	tr/t b, bc	PS 22B	Anthony Henley
	486	Fair Cloe my breast so alarms	C	early 1692 (1692)	tr/t b, bc	PS 22B	John Glanvill
	368	Farewell, all joys!	g	spr 1684 (1685)	tr/t, bc	PS 25	
	463	Farewell, ye rocks	d	late 1684 (1685)	tr/t + b, bc	PS 25	Thomas D'Urfey (The Storm)
	421	The fatal hour comes on apace	e	?1694–5	tr/t, bc	PS 25	
	487	Fill the bowl with rosy wine	C	aut 1687 (1687)	tr/t b, bc	PS 22B	Abraham Cowley
	369	Fly swift, ye hours	d	win 1691 (1692)	tr/t, bc	PS 25	
	370	From silent shades	C	win 1682 (1683)	tr/t, bc	PS 25	(Bess of Bedlam)
	464	Gentle shepherds, you that know	a	early 1687 (1687)	tr/t + b, bc	PS 25	Nahum Tate (A Pastoral Elegy on the Death of Mr. John Playford)
	489	Go tell Aminta, gentle swain	e	1683–4	tr/t b, bc	PS 22B	Dryden

Z	Title	Key	Date	Scoring	Edition	Text author; (title); comment	Works
481	A grasshopper and a fly	g	(1686)	tr/t b, bc	PS 22B	(An Allegory); on the Monmouth Rebellion (6–7/1685)	223
541	Hark, Damon, hark	G	?spr 1683	tr tr b, 2 rec, str a3, bc	PS 27		
542	Hark how the wild musicians sing	B♭	?spr 1683	t t b, str a3, bc	PS 27		
490	Haste, gentle Charon	F	1682–3	b b, bc	PS 22B	(A Dialogue between Charon and Orpheus)	
491	Has yet your breast no pity learn'd	g	?1680–3 (1688)	tr b, bc	PS 22B	(A Dialogue between Strephon and Dorinda)	
371	Hears not my Phillis	F	aut 1694 (1695)	tr/t, bc	PS 25	Sir Charles Sedley (The Knotting Song)	
372	He himself courts his own ruin	F	win 1683–4 (1684)	tr/t, bc	PS 25		
492	Hence, fond deceiver!	d	aut 1687 (1687)	tr/t b, bc	PS 22B	(A Dialogue. Love and Despair)	
493	Here's to thee, Dick	G	1685–6 (1688)	tr/t b, bc	PS 22B	Cowley	
465	High on a throne of glitt'ring ore	G	1689	tr/t + b, bc	PS 25	D'Urfey; on Mary II	
373	How delightful's the life of an innocent swain	G	?c.1685	tr/t + b, bc	PS 25	Cowley	
S57	How happy are they	C		tr/t, bc		Attrib. 'HP' in GB-Lbl, Mus. Dep. 2016/52; pub version (1688) with different bc attrib. Mr Marsh	
374	How I sigh when I think of the charms	c	sum 1680 (1681)	tr/t, bc	PS 25		
D133	How peaceful the days are	c	1678–9 (1679)	tr/t, bc	PS 25		

Works	Z	Title	Key	Date	Scoring	Edition	Text author; (title); comment
224	543	How pleasant is this flow'ry plain	g	win 1682–3	tr t, 2 rec, bc	PS 27	Cowley
	495	How sweet is the air and refreshing	G	aut 1687 (1687)	tr/t b, bc	PS 22B	
	375	I came, I saw, and was undone	a	mid 1685	tr/t, bc	PS 25	Cowley (The Thraldom)
	377	I fain would be free	C	?5/1694	tr, [bc]	PS 25	inc: bc lost or never composed
	544	If ever I more riches did desire	G	?spr 1687 (1688)	tr tr t b, str a3, bc	PS 27	Cowley
	378	If grief has any pow'r to kill	d	early 1685 (1685)	tr/t, bc	PS 25	
	379B	If music be the food of love	a	?1691–2 (1693)	tr/t, bc	PS 25	Henry Heveningham; 1st setting, 1st version
	379A	If music be the food of love	g	?1691–2 (1692)	tr/t, bc	PS 25	Heveningham; 1st setting, 2nd version
	379C	If music be the food of love	g	?5/1695 (1695)	tr/t, bc	PS 25	Heveningham; 2nd setting
	380	If pray'rs and tears	c	?2/1685	tr/t, bc	PS 25	(Sighs for our late Sovereign King Charles the Second)
	381	I lov'd fair Celia	d	?1692–3 (1694)	tr/t, bc	PS 25	Bernard Howard
	382	I love and I must	c	win 1693	tr, bc	PS 25	(Bell Barr); ?for Lady Annabella Howard
	545	In a deep vision's intellectual scene	a	?1683	tr/t tr/t b, bc	PS 27	Cowley (The Complaint)
	383	Incassum, Lesbia, incassum rogas	c	early 1695 (1695)	tr/t, bc	PS 25	Mr Herbert (The Queen's Epicedium); for Mary II (d. 28/12/1694)
	384	In Cloris all soft charms agree	G	win 1683–4 (1684)	tr/t, bc	PS 25	John Howe
	497	In some kind dream	d	1685 (1687)	tr/t b, bc	PS 22B	Etherege
	385	In vain we dissemble	d	early 1684	tr/t, bc	PS 25	

Z	Title	Key	Date	Scoring	Edition	Text author; (title); comment	Works
386	I resolve against cringing	a	(1678)	tr/t, bc	PS 25		225
498	I saw fair Chloris all alone	a	early 1686 (1686)	tr/t b, bc	PS 22B	William Strode; variant of text in Walter Porter, *Madrigales and Ayres* (1632)	
387	I saw that you were grown so high	d	(1678)	tr/t, bc	PS 25	?by Henry Purcell snr	
499	I spy Celia, Celia eyes me	d	?1690s	tr/t b, bc	PS 22B		
388	I take no pleasure in the sun's bright beams	a	sum 1680 (1681)	tr/t, bc	PS 25		
500	Julia, your unjust disdain	a	?1690s	tr/t b, bc	PS 22B		
389	Leave these useless arts	g	early 1694	tr/t, bc	PS 25	solo arr. of duet Z579	
390	Let each gallant heart	C	win 1682–3 (1683)	tr/t, bc	PS 25	John Turner; on a ground	
391	Let formal lovers still pursue	a	early 1687 (1687)	tr/t, bc	PS 25		
501	Let Hector, Achilles, and each brave commander	C	(1689)	tr/t b, bc	PS 22B	(On Celia's Charms)	
466	Let us, kind Lesbia		win 1683–4 (1684)	tr/t + b, bc	PS 25		
502	Lost is my quiet forever	c	aut 1691 (1691)	tr/t b, bc	PS 22B		
392	Love arms himself in Celia's eyes	C	?1695	tr/t, bc	PS 25	?Matthew Prior	
393	Love is now become a trade	g	early 1684 (1685)	tr/t, bc	PS 25		
394	Lovely Albina's come ashore	C	?10–11/1695	tr/t, bc	PS 25	'the last song the author set before his sickness'; ?allegory of Princess Anne's (Albina) and William III's (the Belgic Lion) relationship	

	Z	Title	Key	Date	Scoring	Edition	Text author; (title); comment
Works 226	395	Love's pow'r in my heart	C	win 1687–8 (1688)	tr/t, bc	PS 25	
	396	Love, thou can'st hear	c	early 1695 (1695)	tr/t, bc	PS 25	Sir Robert Howard
	397	More love or more disdain I crave	G	(1678)	tr/t, bc	PS 25	Charles Webbe; ?by Henry Purcell snr
	467	Musing on cares of human fate	a	early 1685 (1685)	tr/t + b, bc	PS 25	D'Urfey
	399	My heart, whenever you appear	d	early 1684 (1685)	tr/t, bc	PS 25	
	503	Nestor, who did to thrice man's age attain	d	(1689)	tr/t b, bc	PS 22B	Daniel Kenrick
	468	No, to what purpose should I speak?	d	?spr/sum 1683	tr/t + b, bc	PS 25	Cowley (The Concealment)
	400	Not all my torments can your pity move	c	late 1693	tr/t, bc	PS 25	
	504	O dive custos Auriacae domus	c	(1695)	tr/t tr/t, bc	PS 22B	Henry Parker; for Mary II (d. 28/12/1694)
	505	Oft am I by the women told	d	aut 1687 (1687)	tr/t b, bc	PS 22B	Cowley
	402	Oh! fair Cedaria, hide those eyes		?c.1689–92	tr/t, bc	PS 25	
	506	Oh! what a scene does entertain my sight	D	win 1683–4	tr b, vn, bc	PS 27	
	404	Olinda in the shades unseen	G	?5/1694	tr/t, bc	PS 25	
	405	On the brow of Richmond Hill	B$^\flat$	win 1691	tr/t, bc	PS 25	D'Urfey (An Ode to Cynthia, walking on Richmond Hill)
	406	O solitude, my sweetest choice!	c	win 1684–5 (1687)	tr/t, bc	PS 25	Philips (Solitude); on a ground
	407	Pastora's beauties when unblown	c	sum 1680 (1681)	tr/t, bc	PS 25	
	408	Phillis, I can ne'er forgive it	g	win 1687–8	tr/t, bc	PS 25	

Z	Title	Key	Date	Scoring	Edition	Text author; (title); comment	Works
409	Phillis, talk no more of passion	c	early 1685 (1685)	tr/t, bc	PS 25		227
410	Pious Celinda goes to prayers	d	early 1695 (1695)	tr/t, bc	PS 25	Congreve	
334	Raise, raise the voice	d–D	?c.1685	tr t b, str a3, bc	PS 10	?symphony song celebrating music, not a St Cecilia ode	
411	Rashly I swore I would disown	B♭	win 1682 (1683)	tr/t, bc	PS 25		
507	Saccharissa's grown old	d	(1686)	tr/t b, [bc]	PS 22B		
412	Sawney is a bonny lad	G	1/1694 (1694)	tr/t, bc	PS 25	Motteux (Scotch Song); ?mock-song on lost Purcell piece	
469	Scarce had the rising sun appear'd	g	1678 (1679)	tr/t + b, bc	PS 25		
470	See how the fading glories of the year	e	early 1689 (1689)	tr/t + b, bc	PS 25		
508	See where she sits	g	sum 1683	tr b, str a3, bc	PS 27	Cowley	
413	She loves and she confesses too	C	aut 1680 (1683)	tr/t, bc	PS 25	Cowley (A Song upon a Ground); response to Pietro Reggio's setting	
414	She that would gain a faithful lover	B♭	early 1695 (1695)	tr/t, bc	PS 25	'Lady E–M–'	
415	She, who my poor heart possesses	g	sum 1682 (1683)	tr/t, bc	PS 25		
416	Since one poor view has drawn my heart	C	sum 1680 (1681)	tr/t, bc	PS 25		
471	Since the pox or the plague	F	1678 (1679)	tr/t b, bc	PS 25		
509	Sit down, my dear Sylvia	F	early 1685 (1685)	tr b, bc	PS 22B	D'Urfey (A Dialogue betwixt Alexis and Sylvia)	

	Z	Title	Key	Date	Scoring	Edition	Text author; (title); comment
Works 228	510	Soft notes, and gently rais'd accent	g	win 1683–4 (1685)	tr b, 2 rec, bc	PS 27	Howe (A Serenading Song)
	417	Spite of the godhead, powerful Love	e	early 1687 (1687)	tr/t, bc	PS 25	Anne Wharton
	444	Stripp'd of their green	C	late 1691 (1692)	tr/t, bc		Motteux; also attrib. Raphael Courteville
	418	Sweet, be no longer sad!	a	(1678)	tr/t, bc	PS 25	Webbe; ?by Henry Purcell snr
	420	Sylvia, now your scorn give over	C	win 1687–8 (1688)	tr/t, bc	PS 25	keybd arr. (T695) pub 1689
	511	Sylvia, thou brighter eye of night	c	win 1683–4	tr/t b, bc	PS 22B	(A Serenading Song)
	512	Sylvia, 'tis true you're fair	C	late 1685 (1686)	tr/t + b, bc	PS 25	
	422	They say you're angry	B$^\flat$	late 1684 (1685)	tr/t, bc	PS 25	Cowley (The Rich Rival)
	423	This poet sings the Trojan wars	C	1687 (1688)	b, bc	PS 25	(Anacreon's Defeat)
	514	Though my mistress be fair	g	win 1683–4 (1685)	tr/t b, bc	PS 22B	
	424	Through mournful shades and solitary groves	c	win 1683–4 (1684)	tr/t, bc	PS 25	Richard Duke
	546	'Tis wine was made to rule the day	C		tr/t tr/t b, bc	PS 22B	(A Drinking Song); only late sources; ?inauthentic
	516	Underneath this myrtle shade	d	1682–3 (1692)	tr/t b, bc	PS 22B	Cowley (The Epicure)
	426	Urge me no more, this airy mirth	c	1680	tr/t, bc	PS 25	
	547	We reap all the pleasures	d	win 1682–3	tr t b, 2 rec, bc	PS 27	inc: sym and opening tutti only
	517	Were I to choose the greatest bliss	d	aut 1689 (1689)	tr/t b, bc	PS 22B	
	428B	What a sad fate is mine	c	?1692	tr/t, bc	PS 25	(A Song on a Ground); 1st version

Z	Title	Key	Date	Scoring	Edition	Text author; (title); comment	Works
428A	What a sad fate is mine	a	?1693–4	tr/t, bc	PS 25	2nd version; bc missing	229
518	What can we poor females do	a		tr/t b, bc	PS 22B	?original version of Z429	
429	What can we poor females do	a	c.12/1693 (1694)	tr/t, bc	PS 25	?solo arr. of Z518	
472	What hope for us remains now he is gone?	d	?8/1677 (1679)	tr/t + b, bc	PS 25	('On the Death of his worthy friend Matthew Lock ... who dyed in August 1677')	
430	When first Amintas	A	?5/1686 (1687)	tr/t, bc	PS 25	D'Urfey; mock-song of ZN774	
431	When first my shepherdess and I	a	sum 1686 (1687)	tr/t, bc	PS 25		
519	When gay Philander left the plain	a	(1684)	tr/t b, [bc]	PS 22B		
432	When her languishing eyes said 'Love!'	e	sum 1680 (1681)	tr/t, bc	PS 25		
433	When I a lover pale do see	C	(1678)	tr/t, bc	PS 25	?by Henry Purcell snr	
520	When, lovely Phillis, thou art kind	d	sum 1685 (1685)	tr/t b, bc	PS 22B		
434	When my Acmelia [Aemelia] smiles	b	?1690–5	tr/t, bc	PS 25		
521	When Myra sings	c	sum 1695 (1695)	tr/t b, bc	PS 22B	George Granville	
435	When Strephon found his passion vain	G	win 1682 (1683)	tr/t, bc	PS 25	?tr/t b, bc	
522	When Teucer from his father fled	g–G	win 1684–5 (1686)	tr/t b, bc	PS 22B	Daniel Kenrick after Horace (Teucer's Voyage)	
D172	When the cock begins to crow	F		ct t b, bc	PS 22B	?inauthentic, after *The Fairy Queen* Z629/5	

Works	Z	Title	Key	Date	Scoring	Edition	Text author; (title); comment
230	436	When Thirsis did the splendid eye	d	(1675)	tr/t, bc	PS 25	?by Henry Purcell snr
	523	While bolts and bars my days control	g	?1690s	tr/t b, bc	PS 22B	late source only
	437	While Thyrsis, wrapp'd in downy sleep	F	early 1685 (1685)	tr/t, bc	PS 25	(A Pastoral Coronation Song); celebrates the accession of James II
	524	While you for me alone had charms	C	?spr 1683	tr b, bc	PS 22B	John Oldham (The 9th Ode of Horace Imitated, a Dialogue betwixt the Poet and Lydia)
	438	Whilst Cynthia sang	d	late 1685 (1686)	tr/t, bc	PS 25	
	440	Who but a slave can well express	g	?1682	tr/t, bc	PS 25	
	441	Who can behold Florella's charms	F	early 1695 (1695)	tr/t, bc	PS 25	
	525	Why, my Daphne, why complaining?	d	?11/1690 (1691)	tr b, bc	PS 22B	(A dialogue between Thirsis and Daphne); sung in a play, possibly *The Gordion Knot Unty'd* Z597
	442	Why so serious, why so grave	a	?c.1680	tr/t, [bc]	PS 25	Thomas Flatman (The Whim); inc: bc lost
	443	Ye happy swains, whose nymphs are kind	d	early 1684 (1685)	tr/t, bc	PS 25	
	473	Young Thyrsis' fate ye hills and groves deplore	c	win 1688–9 (?1689)	tr/t + b, bc	PS 25	(An Elegy on the Death of Mr. Thomas Farmer); composer and court violinist, buried 5/12/1688

6 Welcome songs and extended occasional works

Z	Title	Key	Date	Scoring	Edition	Text author; comment
			ordered by probable date of first performance			
340	Welcome, vicegerent of the mighty king	C	?9/1680	tr tr ct t b, full a4, str a4, bc	PS 15	to welcome Charles II from Windsor
336	Swifter, Isis, swifter flow	G	?29/3 or 27/8/1681	tr tr ct t b, full a4, 2 rec, ob, str a4, bc	PS 15	to welcome Charles II from the Oxford Parliament or from Windsor
341	What shall be done in behalf of the man	B♭	?27/5/1682	tr tr ct t b, full a4, 2 rec, str a4, bc	PS 15	to welcome James, Duke of York from Scotland
337	The summer's absence unconcern'd we bear	C	21/10/1682	tr tr ct ct t b b, full a4, str a4, bc	PS 15	to welcome Charles II from Newmarket
325	From hardy climes	D	28/7/1683	tr tr ct t b, full a4, str a4, bc	PS 15	marriage of Prince George of Denmark and Princess Anne
324	Fly, bold rebellion	F	?25/9/1683	tr tr ct ct t b b, Tr Tr Ct Ct T B, str a4, bc	PS 15	?to welcome Charles II from Winchester
329	Laudate Ceciliam	C	22/11/1683	ct t b, str a3, bc	PS 10	unidentified St Cecilia celebration
339	Welcome to all the pleasures	e–E	22/11/1683	tr tr ct t b, full a4, str a4, bc	PS 10	Christopher Fishburn; Musical Society's St Cecilia celebration
326	From those serene and rapturous joys	d–D	25→/9/1684	tr tr ct t b, full a4, str a4, bc	PS 18	Thomas Flatman; to welcome Charles II from Winchester
343	Why are all the Muses mute?	d	?10/10/1685	tr tr ct t b b, full a5, str a4, bc	PS 18	to welcome James II from Windsor
344	Ye tuneful Muses	g	14/10/1686	tr tr ct ct t b b, full a4, 2 rec, str a4, bc	PS 18	James II's birthday
335	Sound the trumpet, beat the drum	a	14/10/1687	ct ct t t b b, full a4, str a4, bc	PS 18	James II's birthday

Works	Z	Title	Key	Date	Scoring	Edition	Text author; comment
232	332	Now does the glorious day appear	D	30/4/1689	tr ct t b b, full a4, str a5, bc	PS 11	Thomas Shadwell; Mary II's birthday
		The noise of foreign wars	?G	24→/7/1689	tr tr ct ct t b, full a4, 2 rec, str a4, bc	PS 18	for birth of Duke of Gloucester; inc: only end of sym and opening vocal sections; possibly by Blow
	322	Celestial music did the gods inspire	C	5/8/1689	tr ct t b, full a4, 2 rec, str a4, bc	PS 1	for Lewis Maidwell's school; text by 'one of his scholars'
	333	Of old when heroes thought it base	D	27/3/1690	tr ct ct t b b, full a5, 2 rec, 2 ob, 2 tpt, str a4, bc	PS 1	Thomas D'Urfey; the Yorkshire Feast Song
	320	Arise, my muse	D	30/4/1690	ct ct t b, full a4, 2 rec, 2 ob, 2 tpt, str a5, bc	PS 11	D'Urfey; Mary II's birthday; ?inc: poem not set complete
	338	Welcome, glorious morn	C	30/4/1691	tr ct t b b, full a4, 2 ob, 2 tpt, str a4, bc	PS 11	?Shadwell; Mary II's birthday
	331	Love's goddess sure was blind	g	30/4/1692	tr ct ct t b, full a4, str a4, bc	PS 24	Charles Sedley; Mary II's birthday
	328	Hail, bright Cecilia	D	22/11/1692	tr ct ct t b b, Tr Tr Ct Ct T B, 2 rec, bs rec, 2 ob, 2 tpt, kdr, str a4, bc	PS 8	Nicholas Brady; Musical Society's St Cecilia celebration
	321	Celebrate this festival	C	30/4/1693	tr tr ct t b, full a5, 2 rec, 2 ob, tpt, ?bn, str a4, bc	PS 24	Nahum Tate; Mary II's birthday
	327	Great parent, hail	C	9/1/1694	tr ct t b, full a4, 2 rec, str a4, bc	PS 1	Tate; centenary of Trinity College, Dublin

Z	Title	Key	Date	Scoring	Edition	Text author; comment	Works
323	Come, ye sons of art, away	D	30/4/1694	tr ct ct b, full a4, 2 tpt, kdr, 2 rec, 2 ob, str a4, bc	PS 24	?Tate; Mary II's birthday; survives complete only in modernised form in 1765 source; possible original scoring (tpt, 2 rec, 2 ob, str a4, bc) reconstructed and ed. R. Herissone (London, 2010)	233
342	Who can from joy refrain?	C	24/7/1695	tr tr ct ct b, full a4, tpt, 2 ob, tenor ob, bn, str a4, bc	PS 4	?Tate; Duke of Gloucester's birthday	

7 Stage works

DG: Dorset Garden Theatre   DL: Drury Lane Theatre
com: comedy   do: dramatic opera   trag: tragedy   tragcom: tragicomedy
ta: set of theatre airs

Z	Title	Genre	Author	First production	Purcell's contribution	Scoring	Editions	Comment
570	Abdelazer, or The Moor's Revenge	trag	Aphra Behn	DL, ?25/3/1695	ta; song	str a4; tr, bc	PS 16	
572	Amphitryon, or The Two Sosias	com	John Dryden	DL, 10/1690	ta; 4 nos.	str a4; tr t b, str a3, bc	PS 16	
573	Aureng-Zebe, or The Great Mogul	trag	Dryden	?DL, 1693	song	tr, bc	PS 16	2 versions
574	Bonduca, or The British Heroine	trag	George Powell after John Fletcher	DL, 10/1695	ta; 8 nos.	tpt, str a4; 3vv, tr tr ct t b, full a4, tpt, 2 rec, 2 ob, str a4, bc	PS 16	
591	The Canterbury Guests, or A Bargain Broken	com	Edward Ravenscroft	DL, 10–11/1694	dialogue	tr tr ct b, bc	PS 16	
575	Circe	trag	Charles Davenant	?1689–90	temple scene	tr ct t b, full a4, str a4, bc	PS 16	
576	Cleomenes, the Spartan Hero	trag	Dryden	DL, 4/1692	song	tr/t, bc	PS 16	
494	Cuckolds–Haven, or An Alderman no Conjurer	com	Nahum Tate	?7/1685	song	tr/ct, bc	PS 16	2 versions
626	Dido and Aeneas	all-sung masque	Tate	Chelsea, Josiah Priest's school, ←7/1688, ?or earlier court production		tr tr tr tr tr tr tr/t tr/b t/b, full a4, str a4, bc	PS 3	

Z	Title	Genre	Author	First production	Purcell's contribution	Scoring	Editions	Comment
627	Dioclesian (The Prophetess)	do	Thomas Betterton after Philip Massinger and Fletcher	DG, 5/1690		tr tr ct b b, full a4, 2 tpt, 2 rec, 2 ob, tenor ob, bn, str a4, bc	PS 9	
577	Distress'd Innocence, or The Princess of Persia	trag	Elkanah Settle	DL, 10-11/1690	ta	str a4	PS 16	
578/1-4	Don Quixote I	com	Thomas D'Urfey	DG, 5-6/1694	4 nos.	tr tr ct b, str a3, bc	PS 16	
578/5-8	Don Quixote II	com	D'Urfey	DG, 6/1694	3 nos.	tr ct b, tpt, bc	PS 16	
578/9	Don Quixote III	com	D'Urfey	DG, 12/1695	song	tr, bc	PS 16	
592	The Double Dealer	com	William Congreve	DL, 11/1693	ta; song	str a4; tr, bc	PS 16	2 versions of song
594	The English Lawyer	com	Ravenscroft	?1684	catch	3vv	PS 16	
579	Epsom Wells	com	Thomas Shadwell	?1693	duet	tr b, bc	PS 16	arranged for tr solo in Gresham manuscript
629	The Fairy Queen	do	after Shakespeare, A Midsummer Night's Dream	DG, 2/5/1692; enlarged version DG, 2/1693		tr tr ct b, full a4, 2 tpt, kdr, 2 rec, 2 ob, str a4, bc	PS 12	
595	The Fatal Marriage, or The Innocent Adultery	trag	Thomas Southerne	DL, ?2/1694	2 songs	tr, bc	PS 20	
596	The Female Virtuosos	com	Thomas Wright	DG, ?5/1693	duet	tr tr, bc	PS 20	
571	A Fool's Preferment, or The Three Dukes of Dunstable	com	D'Urfey	DG, spr 1688	8 songs	tr t, bc	PS 20	

Works

235

Z	Title	Genre	Author	First production	Purcell's contribution	Scoring	Editions	Comment
597	The Gordian Knot Unty'd	com	?William Walsh	?11–12/1690	ta	str a4	PS 20	
580	Henry the Second, King of England	trag	?William Mountfort and John Bancroft	DL, ?8/11/1692	song	tr, bc	PS 20	
598	The Indian Emperor, or The Conquest of Mexico by the Spaniards	trag	Dryden and Robert Howard	?12/1691	song	t, bc	PS 20	
630	The Indian Queen	do	Dryden and Howard	DG, ?6/1695 and/or early 1696		tr tr ct t b, full a4, tpt, 2 rec, 2 ob, str a4, bc	PS 19	Act V masque by Daniel Purcell
628	King Arthur, or The British Worthy	do	Dryden	DG, 5/1691		tr tr ct t b, full a8, 2 tpt, 2 rec, 2 ob, ten ob, bs, str a4, bc	PS 26	tpts probably added later
581	King Richard the Second (The Sicilian Usurper)	trag	Tate after Shakespeare	DL, 12/1680	song	tr/t, bc	PS 20	
599	The Knight of Malta	tragcom	Fletcher	?1690–1	catch	3vv	PS 20	
600	The Libertine	trag	Shadwell	c.7/1695	2 scenes; song	tr ct b, full a4, 4 flat tpt, str a4, bc; tr, tpt, bc	PS 20	
582	Love Triumphant, or Nature Will Prevail	tragcom	Dryden	DL, 1/1694	song	tr, bc	PS 20	
601	The Maid's Last Prayer, or Any rather than Fail	com	Southerne	DL, ?2–3/1693	3 nos.	tr tr, bc	PS 20	
602	The Marriage-Hater Match'd	com	D'Urfey	DL, ?1/1692	song; duet	tr, bc; tr/ct b, bc	PS 20	
603	The Married Beau, or The Curious Impertinent	com	John Crowne	DL, 4/1694	ta; song	str a4; tr, bc	PS 20	

Z	Title	Genre	Author	First production	Purcell's contribution	Scoring	Editions	Comment
604	The Massacre of Paris	trag	Nathaniel Lee	DL, ?11/1689; revival 1695	song (2 settings)	b, bc; tr, bc	PS 20	
605	The Mock Marriage	com	Thomas Scott	DL, ?sum 1695	3 songs	tr, bc	PS 20	1 song also attrib. Jeremiah Clarke
583	Oedipus	trag	Dryden and Lee	?1692	incantation scene	ct t b, str a3, bc	PS 21	
607	The Old Batchelor	com	Congreve	DL, 9/3/1693	ta; song; duet	str a4; tr/t, bc; tr/ct b, bc	PS 21	?ta originally for D'Urfey's com *Bussy d'Ambois* (DL, 3/1691)
584	Oroonoko	trag	Southerne	DL, ?11/1695	duet	tr tr/t, bc	PS 21	
585	Pausanias, the Betrayer of his Country	trag	?Richard Norton	DL, ?4/1696	song; duet	tr/t, bc; tr t, bc	PS 21	duet also attrib. Daniel Purcell
586	Regulus, or The Faction of Carthage	trag	Crowne	DL, 6/1692	song	tr, bc	PS 21	
608	The Richmond Heiress, or A Woman once in the Right	com	D'Urfey	DL, 5/1693	dialogue	tr b, bc	PS 21	two versions
609	The Rival Sisters, or The Violence of Love	trag	Robert Gould	DL, ?10/1695	ov; 3 songs	str a4; tr t, bc	PS 21	ov from 'Love's goddess sure was blind', Z331/1
587	Rule a Wife and Have a Wife	com	Fletcher	win 1693–4	mock-song; duet	tr/t, bc; tr/ct b, bc	PS 21	mock-song, *The Fairy Queen*, Z629/1b
588	Sir Anthony Love, or The Rambling Lady	com	Southerne	DL, 11/1690	ov; 2 songs; dialogue	str a4; tr, str a3, bc; tr b, bc	PS 21	

Works

Z	Title	Genre	Author	First production	Purcell's contribution	Scoring	Editions	Comment
589	Sir Barnaby Whigg, or No Wit like a Woman's	com	D'Urfey	DL, ?6/1681	song	tr/t b, bc	PS 21	
590	Sophonisba, or Hannibal's Overthrow	trag	Lee	?c.1685	song	tr, bc	PS 21	
610	The Spanish Friar, or The Double Discovery	tragcom	Dryden	DL, ?3–4/1695	song	tr/t, bc	PS 21	
631/10	The Tempest, or The Enchanted Island	do	William Davenant, Dryden and Shadwell after Shakespeare	?spr–sum 1695	song	tr, bc	PS 21	other music attrib. Purcell by John Weldon
606	Theodosius, or The Force of Love	trag	Lee	DG, ?spr–sum 1680	ceremonial scene; 5 songs	tr tr ct t b, full a4, 2 rec, bc; tr tr/t ct b, bc	PS 21	
632	Timon of Athens, the Man-Hater	trag	Shadwell, after Shakespeare	DL, spr 1695	Masque of Cupid and Bacchus; Curtain Tune	tr tr t b, tpt, full a4, 2 rec, 2 ob, str a4, bc	PS 2	ov ('Who can from joy refrain?, Z342/1); ta ?by James Paisible) ?all added later
613	Tyrannic Love, or The Royal Martyr	trag	Dryden	DL, ?aut 1694	duet; song	tr b, bc	PS 21	
611	The Virtuous Wife, or Good Luck at Last	com	D'Urfey	?1695	ta	str a4	PS 21	
612	The Wives Excuse, or Cuckolds Make Themselves	com	Southerne	DL, ?12/1691	4 songs	tr/t ct, bc	PS 21	

8 Consort music

A. Fantasias (all in PS 31)

Z	Title	Key	Scoring	Date	Comment
732	Fantasia a3	d	trv/vn, tv/vla, bv	c.1679–80	
733	Fantasia a3	F	trv/vn, tv/vla, bv	←c.1679–80	early version lacks last section
734	Fantasia a3	g	trv/vn, tv/vla, bv	c.1679–80	
735	Fantasia a4	g	trv/vn, tv/vla, tv/vla, bv	10/6/1680	
736	Fantasia a4	B$\flat$	trv/vn, tv/vla, tv/vla, bv	11/6/1680	
737	Fantasia a4	F	trv/vn, tv/vla, tv/vla, bv	14/6/1680	
738	Fantasia a4	c	trv/vn, tv/vla, tv/vla, bv	19/6/1680	
739	Fantasia a4	d	trv/vn, tv/vla, tv/vla, bv	19, 22/6/1680	
740	Fantasia a4	a	trv/vn, tv/vla, tv/vla, bv	23/6/1680	
741	Fantasia a4	e	trv/vn, tv/vla, tv/vla, bv	30/6/1680	
742	Fantasia a4	G	trv/vn, tv/vla, tv/vla, bv	16, 18–19/8/1680	
743	Fantasia a4	d	trv/vn, tv/vla, tv/vla, bv	31/8/1680	
744	Fantasia a4	a	2 trv/vn, tv/vla, bv	24/2/1683	inc: first section only
745	Fantasia upon One Note	F	2 trv/vn, 2 tv/vla, bv	c.1680	
746	In Nomine a6	g	2 trv/vn, 3 tv/vla, bv	c.1680	
747	In Nomine a7	g	2 trv/vn, 3 tv/vla, 2 bv	c.1680	

B: Trio Sonatas

Z	Title	Key	Date	Comment
		all 2 vn, bv, bc (organ or harpsichord)		

Sonnata's of III Parts (London: Author, 1683); 2nd edn.: 1684; copies advertised 1699, 1707; all in PS 5

Z	Title	Key
790	Sonata 1	g
791	Sonata 2	B$\flat$
792	Sonata 3	d
793	Sonata 4	F
794	Sonata 5	a
795	Sonata 6	C
796	Sonata 7	e
797	Sonata 8	G
798	Sonata 9	c

Works

Z	Title	Key	Date	Comment
799	Sonata 10	A		
800	Sonata 11	f		
801	Sonata 12	D		

Ten Sonata's in Four Parts (London: J. Heptinstall for Frances Purcell, 1697); all in PS 7

Z	Title	Key	Date	Comment
802	Sonata 1	b	←1680	
803	Sonata 2	E^b	←1680	
804	Sonata 3	a	←1680	
805	Sonata 4	d	←1680	
806	Sonata 5	g		
807	Sonata 6	g		on a ground, from Lully's 'Scocca pur'
808	Sonata 7	C	1685→	
809	Sonata 8	g	1685→	
810	Sonata 9	F	1685→	'The Golden'
811	Sonata 10	D	?c.1688	

C: Miscellaneous Pieces (all in PS 31 except for Z631/1)

Z	Title	Key	Scoring	Date	Comment
N773A	Prelude	g	vn		pub 1705
N773B	Prelude	d	rec		pub 1708; transposition of ZN773A
	Pavan, Jig	f	?str a3 or a4	?c.1674	frag: only bs survives
	Overture	C	a4	?c.1674→	frag: only bs survives
	Prelude, Almand	b	?str a3 or a4	?c.1674→	frag: only bs survives
	Pavan	f	?str a3 or a4	?c.1674→	frag: only bs survives
	Overture, Minuet	C	?str a3 or a4	?c.1674→	frag: only bs survives
	Chaconne	d	?str a4	?c.1674→	frag: bs only; rev as *The Gordian Knot Unty'd*, Z597/6
N774	Jig	A	?str a4	←1687	frag: vn 1 only; pub *Apollo's Banquet* (1687)
	Air	g	vn, bs	1693–4	pub John Lenton, *The Gentleman's Diversion*
	Minuet	g	vn, bs	1693–4	pub Lenton, *The Gentleman's Diversion*
670	The Queen's Dolour	a	?outer parts of lost consort piece; recon PS 31 for str a4		?memorial to Mary II (d. 28/12/1694)

Z	Title	Key	Scoring	Date	Comment
751	Pavan	g	2 vn/trv, bs/bc	c.1677–8	
749	Pavan	a	2 vn/trv, bs/bc	c.1677–8	
748	Pavan	A	2 vn/trv, bs/bc	c.1677–8	
750	Pavan	B♭	2 vn/trv, bs/bc	c.1677–8	
780	Sonata	g	vn, bv, bc	?c.1688	frag: bv missing in sole source; recon in PS 31
	Two in One upon a Ground	a	2 vn, bs	←1690	variant of *Dioclesian*, Z627/16
	The Staircase Overture	B♭	str a4, bc	?1675	frag: vla missing; recon in PS 31
752	Pavan	g	3 vn, bs	c.1678	
731A	Three Parts upon a Ground	D	3 vn, bv, bc	c.1678	alternative version of Z731B
731B	Three Parts upon a Ground	F	3 rec, bv, bc	c.1678	alternative version of Z731A
730	Chacony	g	str a4, [bc]	←c.1680	
770	Suite	G	str a4	c.1682	frag and inc: recon in PS 31
771	Overture	d	str a4, bc	c.1682	?for lost vocal work
	Overture	G	str a4, bc	c.1682	variant of 'Swifter, Isis, swifter flow' Z336/1
631/1	Overture	g	str a4, bc	?←1688	in PS 21; 'Overture in Mr P Opera', possibly from the lost prologue of *Dido and Aeneas*
860	March, Canzona	c	5/3/1695	4 flat tpt	Mary II's funeral; March reused in *The Libertine* Z600/2a
772	Overture	g	str a5	c.1682	
	Suite	g	?str a5	?c.1682	frag: only b part survives; follows Z772
850	Sonata	D	tpt, str a4, bc	c.1690–5	?for lost vocal work
	Cibell	C	tpt, str a4, bc	c.1690–5	consort version of ZT678

9 Keyboard music

Z	Title	Key	Comment

§: probable keyboard setting by Purcell of his own ensemble piece
¶: probable keyboard setting by Purcell of an ensemble piece by another composer
all edited in PS 6; see it for details of alternative versions and groupings

A: Domestic Keyboard Music

The Second Part of Musick's Hand–Maid (London: Henry Playford, 1689), 'carefully Revised and Corrected' by Purcell; 2nd edn. (1690); 3rd edn. (1705)

Z	Title	Key	Comment
	Air	C	¶: ?popular tune
T694	Song Tune	C	§: 'Ah! how pleasant 'tis to love', Z353
647	March	C	
T695	Song Tune	C	§: 'Sylvia, now your scorn give over', Z420
648	March	C	
T689	New Minuet	d	§: 'Who can resist such mighty charms', Z/632/15
649	Minuet	a	
650	Minuet	a	
655	A New Scotch Tune	C	¶: 'Peggy I must love you', in *Apollo's Banquet*
T682	A New Ground	e	§: 'Here the deities approve', Z339/3
	[Ground]	c	¶: J.B. Lully, 'Scocca pur'
646	A New Irish Tune	G	¶: 'Lilliburlero'
653	Rigadoon	C	¶: French dance tune, ?by Jean Favier
656	Sefauchi's Farewell	d	departure of the castrato Siface (G.F. Grossi) from London (19/6/1687); §: probable lost consort piece; recon PS 31 as str a4
	Old Simon the King	C	¶: popular ground, in *The Division-Violin* (1685)
T688	Minuet	d	§: 'Raise, raise the voice', Z334/6
	Motley's Maggot	a	¶: 'The Emperor of the Moon', ?by Richard Motley
665	Suite	C	

GB–Lbl, MS Mus. 1: autograph portion, copied c.1693–4 for teaching:

	Prelude	C	
	Minuet	C	
	Air	C	

Z	Title	Key	Comment	
	Minuet	d	§: *The Double Dealer*, Z592/7	*Works*
	Jig	C	§: 'Thus Happy and Free', Z629/44a	*243*
	Hornpipe	e	§: *The Old Batchelor*, Z607/4	
	Air	C	§: *The Double Dealer*, Z592/9	
	Hornpipe	g	§: *The Fairy Queen*, Z629/1b	
	Hornpipe	A	¶: attrib. John Eccles	
	Minuet	D	§: *The Virtuous Wife*, Z611/8	
	Air	g	§: *The Virtuous Wife*, Z611/9	
	Minuet	d	§: *The Virtuous Wife*, Z611/7	
	Suite	a	related to Z663, with jig instead of saraband; jig ?by Blow	
	Suite	C	related to Z666, Prelude ¶: metrical version of French unmeasured prelude	

A Choice Collection of Lessons (London: for Frances Purcell, 1696), ?from lost autograph; lost 2nd edn. (1697); 3rd edn. (1699)

660	Suite 1	C	
661	Suite 2	g	
662	Suite 3	G	
663	Suite 4	a	
666	Suite 5	C	
667	Suite 6	D	
668	Suite 7	d	Almand labelled 'Bell Barr'; Hornpipe §: *The Married Beau*, Z603/3
669	Suite 8	F	Minuet §: *The Double Dealer*, Z592/3

other keyboard pieces (for unauthenticated keyboard settings of Purcell's ensemble music, see PS 6):

641	Air	G	
642/1, 2	Almand – Corant	a	
645	Ground in Gamut	G	
651	Minuet	G	
652	Prelude	a	
654	Saraband with Division	a	
T681	Ground	c	§: 'With him he brings the partner', Z344/11
T696/2	Minuet	d	
D218	Almand	a	
D222	Ground	d	§: 'Crown the altar', Z321/7
	Ground	b	§: 'Crown the year', Z323/3
	Prelude	g	alternative to Z661/1

Z	Title	Key	Comment
	Prelude	a	alternative to Z663/1
	Prelude	C	alternative to Z665/1
	Prelude for the fingering	C	*The Harpsicord Master* (1697)
T678	Trumpet Tune called the Cibell	C	

B: Organ Music

Z	Title	Key	Comment
716	Verse	F	
717	Voluntary	C	
718	Voluntary	d	related to Z719; for single organ
719	Voluntary for Double Organ	d	related to Z718
720	Voluntary	G	
721	Voluntary on the Old 100th	A	also attrib. Blow
	A Verse to Play after Prayer	d	anon. in source; ?by Purcell or Blow

10 Theoretical works

'A Brief Introduction to the Art of Descant, or Composing Musick in Parts', in J. Playford: *An Introduction to the Skill of Musick* (London, 12/1694); partly rev from earlier works by T. Campion, C. Simpson, J. Playford and others

'Plaine & easy Instructions for Learners on ye Spinnet or Harpsicord', 'Rules for Graces' by 'the late famous Mr: Hen Purcell', in *The Harpsicord Master* (London: John Walsh, 1697); reprinted in *A Choice Collection of Lessons*, 3rd edn. (1699)

Bibliography

<@> means that at the time of publication a digital copy was freely available on the internet.

AdaDub	Martin Adams, 'Purcell's "curiously poor and perfunctory piece of work": Critical Reflections on Purcell via his Music for the Centenary of Trinity College, Dublin', *Music, Ireland and the Seventeenth Century*, ed. Barra Boydell and Kerry Houston, Irish Musical Studies 10 (Dublin: Four Courts Press, 2009), 181–202.
AdaLau	Martin Adams, 'Purcell's "Laudate Ceciliam": An Essay in Stylistic Experimentation', *Irish Musical Studies* 1 (1990), 227–47; repr. HolBar, 307–27.
AdaOde	Martin Adams, 'Purcell, Blow and the English Court Ode', *PurStu*, 172–91.
AdaPoe	Martin Adams, 'Poetry for Reading and Singing? Purcell, Dryden, Dramatic Opera and the Musicality of the Iambic Pentameter' (2014) <@>.
AdaPur	Martin Adams, *Henry Purcell: The Origins and Development of his Musical Style* (Cambridge: Cambridge University Press, 1995).
AllCor	Peter Allsop, *Arcangelo Corelli, 'New Orpheus of our Times'* (Oxford: Oxford University Press, 1999).
AllSon	Peter Allsop, *The Italian 'Trio' Sonata from its Origins until Corelli* (Oxford: Clarendon Press, 1992).
AndRim	Richard Andrewes, 'Edward Francis Rimbault, 1816–1876', *Fontes Artis Musicae* 30 (1983), 30–4.
ARCHP	*The Ashgate Research Companion to Henry Purcell*, ed. Rebecca Herissone (Farnham: Ashgate, 2012).
ArkGen	[G.E.P. Arkwright], 'Index to the Songs and Musical Allusions in The Gentleman's Journal, 1692–4', *The Musical Antiquary* 2 (July 1911), 225–34.
ArnAcc	F.T. Arnold, *The Art of Accompaniment from a Thorough-Bass as Practised in the XVIIth & XVIIIth Centuries*, 2 vols. (Oxford: Oxford University Press, 1931; repr. New York: Dover, 1965).
BaiTal	Anthony Baines, 'James Talbot's Manuscript (Christ Church, Music MS 1187). I: Wind Instruments', *GSJ* 1 (1948), 9–26.
BalBir	Olive Baldwin and Thelma Wilson, 'Music in the Birthday Celebrations at Court in the Reign of Queen Anne: A Documentary Calendar', *HSECEM* 19 (2008), 1–24.
BalBro	Olive Baldwin and Thelma Wilson, 'Henry and Daniel Purcell: Brothers or Cousins?', *HSECEM* 25 (2021), 52–63.
BalCou	Olive Baldwin and Thelma Wilson, 'Henry Purcell's Countertenors and Tenors', *Der Countertenor: die männliche Falsettstimme vom*

		Mittelalter zur Gegenwart, ed. Corinna Herr, Arnold Jacobshagen and Kai Wessel (Mainz: Schott, 2012), 79–95.
	BalDel	Olive Baldwin and Thelma Wilson, 'Alfred Deller, John Freeman and Mr Pate', *M&L* 50 (1969), 103–10.
	BalHon	Olive Baldwin and Thelma Wilson, '"Honest Jo. Priest" and his School in Chelsea', *EMPR* 53 (Spring 2024), 3–10.
	BalKno	Olive Baldwin and Thelma Wilson, 'Purcell's Knotting Song', *MT* 128 (1987), 379–81.
	BalLev	Olive Baldwin and Thelma Wilson, 'Richard Leveridge, 1670–1758', *MT* 111 (1970), 592–4, 891–3, 988–90.
	BalMad	Olive Baldwin and Thelma Wilson, 'Purcell's Mad Songs in the Theatre and Concert Rooms in the Eighteenth Century', *British Music, Musicians and Institutions c.1630–1800: Essays in Honour of Harry Diack Johnstone*, ed. Peter Lynan and Julian Ruston (Woodbridge: Boydell Press, 2021), 91–105.
	BalSin	Olive Baldwin and Thelma Wilson, 'The Singers of *The Judgment of Paris*', *The Lively Arts of the London Stage, 1675–1725*, ed. Kathryn Lowerre (Farnham: Ashgate, 2014), 11–26.
	BalSop	Olive Baldwin and Thelma Wilson, 'Purcell's Sopranos', *MT* 123 (1982), 602–9.
	BalSta	Olive Baldwin and Thelma Wilson, 'Purcell's Stage Singers', *PMHP*, 105–29, 275–81; repr. *HolBar*, 59–90.
	BalWho	Olive Baldwin and Thelma Wilson, 'Who Can from Joy Refraine? Purcell's Birthday Song for the Duke of Gloucester', *MT* 122 (1981), 596–9.
	BamBar	Daniel John Bamford, 'John Barnard's *First Book of Selected Church Musick*: Genesis, Production and Influence', 3 vols., Ph.D. diss. (University of York, 2009) <@>.
	BaxToc	Jonathan Baxendale, 'An Anonymous Toccata: Figure This', *MT* 141 (2000), 40–51.
	BDA	*A Biographical Dictionary of Actors, Actresses, Musicians, Dancers, Managers, and other Stage Personnel in London, 1660–1800*, ed. P.H. Highfill jr. *et al.*, 16 vols. (Carbondale and Edwardsville IL, 1973–93).
	BDECM	*A Biographical Dictionary of English Court Musicians 1485–1714*, comp. Andrew Ashbee and David Lasocki, assisted by Peter Holman and Fiona Kisby, 2 vols. (Aldershot: Ashgate, 1998).
	BicOrg	Stephen Bicknell, *The History of the English Organ* (Cambridge: Cambridge University Press, 1996).
	BloMot	John Blow, *Latin Motets*, ed. Jonathan P. Wainwright (York: York Early Music Press, 2006) <@>.
	BloVen	John Blow, *Venus and Adonis*, ed. Bruce Wood, PSCS 2 (London: Stainer & Bell, 2008).

BoaClo	Ellen Te Selle Boal, 'Purcell's Clock Tempos and the Fantasias', *Journal of the Viola da Gamba Society of America* 20 (1983), 24–39.
BoaMou	*Boalch-Mould Online: A Research Database of Harpsichords and Clavichords and their Makers, 1440–1925* <@>.
BoyBin	Sarah Boyer and Jonathan Wainwright, 'From Barnard to Purcell: The Copying Activities of Stephen Bing', *EM* 23 (1995), 620–48.
BoyChr	*Music at Christ Church before 1800: Documents and Selected Anthems*, ed. Barra Boydell, A History of Christ Church 5 (Dublin: Four Courts Press, 1999).
BoyLen	Malcolm Boyd and John Rayson, 'John Lenton and the First Violin Tutor', *EM* 10 (1982), 329–32.
BroFac	Clare Brown and Peter Holman, 'Thomas Busby and his "FAC SIMILES OF CELEBRATED COMPOSERS"', *EMP* 12 (August 2003), 3–12.
BroSta	Alan Browning, 'Purcell's "Stairre Case Overture"', *MT* 121 (1980), 768–9.
BulWel	Stephen D. Bullamore, 'The Sacred Music of John Weldon (1676–1736), 2 vols., Ph.D. thesis (University of Bangor, 2015) <@>.
BurArt	Michael Burden, '*King Arthur* in the 1730s', *Restoration* 34 (Spring–Fall 2010), 117–38.
BurBan	Michael Burden, 'Where did Purcell keep his Theatre Band?', *EM* 37 (2009), 429–44.
BurCav	Michael Burden, '"He had the Honour to be Your Master": Lady Rhoda Cavendish's Music Lessons with Henry Purcell', *M&L* 76 (1995), 532–9; repr. *HolBar*, 91–8.
BurCha	Donald Burrows, *Handel and the English Chapel Royal* (Oxford: Oxford University Press, 2005).
BurCra	Michael Burden, 'Purcell's Operas on Craig's Stage: The Productions of the Purcell Operatic Society', *EM* 32 (2004), 442–58.
BurDeb	Michael Burden, 'Purcell Debauch'd: The Dramatick Operas in Performance', *PMHP*, 145–62; repr. *HolBar*, 513–30.
BurElg	Michael Burden, 'Purcell and Elgar', *EM* 24 (1996), 181–2.
BurFai	Michael Burden, 'Casting Issues in the Original Production of Purcell's Opera *The Fairy Queen*', *M&L* 84 (2003), 596–607.
BurGal	Michael Burden, '"Gallimaufry" at Covent Garden: *The Fairy-Queen* in 1946', *EM* 23 (1995), 268–84.
BurHis	Charles Burney, *A General History of Music*, 4 vols. (London, 1776, 1789) <@>.
BurLet	*The Letters of Charles Burney*, vol. 1: *1751–1784*, ed. S.J. Alvaro Ribeiro (Oxford: Clarendon Press, 1991).
BurRee	Charles Burney, 'Henry Purcell', *The Cyclopaedia, or Universal Dictionary of Arts, Sciences and Literature*, ed. Abraham Rees, 39 vols. (London: Longman, Hurst, Rees, Orme & Brown: 1802–20), xxix <@>.

BurRem		Michael Burden, *Purcell Remembered* (London: Faber and Faber, 1995).
ByrMar		Maurice Byrne, 'The English March and Early Drum Notation', *GSJ* 50 (1997), 43–80.
CamDol		Margaret Campbell, *Dolmetsch: The Man and his Work* (London: Hamilton, 1975).
CarMac		Stephanie Carter, 'Thomas Mace and Music in Seventeenth-Century Cambridge', *Journal of Seventeenth-Century Music* 28 (2022) <@>.
CarPla		Stephanie Carter, 'Published Musical Variants and Creativity: An Overview of John Playford's Role as Editor', *Concepts of Creativity in Seventeenth-Century England*, ed. Rebecca Herissone and Alan Howard (Woodbridge: Boydell Press, 2013), 87–104.
CarPub		Stephanie Carter, 'Music Publishing and Compositional Activity in England, 1650–1700', Ph.D. thesis (University of Manchester, 2010) <@>.
CBCR		*The Cheque Books of the Chapel Royal*, ed. Andrew Ashbee and John Harley, 2 vols. (Aldershot: Ashgate, 2000).
CCED		*Clergy of the Church of England Database* <@>.
CCLMC		*Christ Church Library Music Catalogue*, comp. John Milsom <@>.
ChaEnd		Mary Chan, 'The Witch of Endor and Seventeenth-Century Propaganda', *Musica Disciplina* 34 (1980), 205–14.
ChaJig		Terence Charlston, 'A Discourse of Styles: Contrasting Gigue Types in the A minor Jig from the Purcell Partial Autograph, GB-Lbl, MS Mus. 1', *Interpreting Historical Keyboard Music: Sources, Contexts and Performance*, ed. Andrew Woolley and John Kitchen (Abingdon: Routledge, 2016), 96–110.
ChaMee		Mary Chan, 'A Mid-Seventeenth-Century Music Meeting and Playford's Publishing', *The Well Enchanting Skill: Music, Poetry and Drama in the Culture of the Renaissance: Essays in Honour of F.W. Sternfeld*, ed. John Caldwell, Edward Olleson and Susan Wollenberg (Oxford: Clarendon Press, 1990), 231–44.
CHE		*The Cambridge Handel Encyclopedia*, ed. Annette Landgraf and David Vickers (Cambridge: Cambridge University Press, 2009).
CheChu		Ian Cheverton, 'English Church Music of the Early Restoration Period, 1660–c.1676', 4 vols., Ph.D. diss. (University of Wales, Cardiff, 1984) <@>.
ChoSha		Irena Bozena Cholij, 'Music in Eighteenth-Century London Shakespeare Productions', Ph.D. thesis (King's College, University of London, 1995) <@>.
ClaDel		Nicholas Clapton, 'The Singularity of Alfred Deller (1912–1979)', *EM* 40 (2012), 291–6.
CloEng		Nicole Cloarec, 'In Search of Purcell's Legacy: Tony Palmer's *England, My England*', *Women Activists and Civil Rights Leaders in Auto/Biographical Literature and Films*, ed. Delphine Letort and Benaouda Lebdai (Cham: Palgrave Macmillan, 2018), 207–20.

ColMor	Suzanne Cole, '"Musical trail-blazing and general daring": Michael Tippett, Morley College and Early Music', *Michael Tippett: Music and Literature*, ed. Suzanne Robinson (Aldershot: Ashgate, 2002), 151–73.
ColTip	Suzanne Cole, '"Things that chiefly interest ME": Tippett and Early Music', *The Cambridge Companion to Michael Tippett*, ed. Kenneth Gloag and Nicholas Jones (Cambridge: Cambridge University Press, 2013), 48–67.
ConLet	William Congreve, *Letters and Documents*, ed. John C. Hodges (London: Macmillan, 1964).
CooKey	Barry Cooper, 'Keyboard Music', *The Seventeenth Century*, ed. Ian Spink, Music in Britain 3 (Oxford: Blackwell, 1992), 341–66.
CorJam	Edward T. Corp, 'The Exiled Court of James II and James III: A Centre of Italian Music in France, 1689–1712', *JRMA* 120 (1995), 216–31.
CoxOrg	Geoffrey Cox, *Organ Music in Restoration England: A Study of Sources, Styles and Influences*, 2 vols. (New York and London, 1989).
CroOde	William Croft, *Three Odes with Orchestra*, ed. Alan Howard, *MB* 108 (London: Stainer & Bell, 2023).
CruClu	Margaret Crum, 'An Oxford Music Club, 1690–1719', *Bodleian Library Record* 9 (1972), 83–99.
CudVol	Charles Cudworth and Franklin B. Zimmerman, 'The Trumpet Voluntary', *Music & Letters* 41 (1960), 342–8.
CumPur	William H. Cummings, *Henry Purcell 1658–1695* (London: Sampson Low, Marston, Searle and Rivington, 1881).
CunSon	John Cunningham, '"Faint Copies" and "Excellent Originalls": Composition and Consumption of Trio Sonatas in England, c.1695–1714', *Eine Geographie der Triosonate: Beiträge zur Gattungsgeschichte im Europäischen Raum*, ed. Matteo Giuggioli and Inga Mai Groote (Bern: Peter Lang, 2018), 111–38.
CyrTem	Mary Cyr, 'Tempo Gradations in Purcell's Sonatas', *Performance Practice Review* 7 (1994), 182–98 <@>.
DarBul	Thurston Dart, 'Purcell and Bull', *MT* 104 (1963), 30–1.
DarCha	Thurston Dart, 'Purcell's Chamber Music', *PRMA* 85 (1958–9), 81–93.
DarCib	Thurston Dart, 'The Cibell', *Revue belge de musicologie/Belgisch Tijdschrift voor Muziekwetenschap* 6 (1952), 24–30.
DarHar	Thurston Dart, 'Purcell's Harpsichord Music', *MT* 100 (1959), 324–5.
DarInt	Thurston Dart, *The Interpretation of Music* (London: Hutchinson, 4/1967).
DarMus	*The Second Part of Musick's Hand-Maid, Revised and Corrected by Henry Purcell*, ed. Thurston Dart (London: Stainer & Bell, 2/1962).
DawMor	Frank Dawes, 'A Jig of Morgan's', *MT* 91 (1950), 92–4.

DayDur		*The Songs of Thomas D'Urfey*, ed. Cyrus Lawrence Day (Cambridge MA: Harvard University Press, 1933).
DaySon		Cyrus Lawrence Day and Eleanore Boswell Murrie, *English Song-Books 1651–1702, a Bibliography* (London: Oxford University Press, 1940).
DenHum		Peter Dennison, *Pelham Humfrey* (Oxford: Oxford University Press, 1986).
DexQui		Kerri Dexter, *'A good quire of voices': The Provision of Choral Music at St George's Chapel, Windsor Castle and Eton College, c.1640–1733* (Aldershot: Ashgate, 2002).
DibSta		Charles Dibdin, *A Complete History of the Stage*, 5 vols. (London: Author, 1800).
DibTou		Charles Dibdin, *The Musical Tour* (Sheffield: Author, 1788).
DilVio		John Dilworth, 'Violin Making in England in the Age of Purcell', *PMHP*, 39–48, 272–4.
DixIta		Graham Dixon, 'Purcell's Italianate Circle', *PC*, 38–51.
DolInt		Arnold Dolmetsch, *The Interpretation of the Music of the XVIIth and XVIIIth Centuries* (London: Novello, 1915; repr. 1946).
DowExo		Peter Downey, 'Performing Mr Purcell's "Exotick" Trumpet Notes', *PMHP*, 49–60.
DowRos		John Downes, *Roscius Anglicanus*, ed. Judith Milhous and Robert D. Hume (London: Society for Theatre Research, 1987).
DraCec		Giovanni Battista Draghi, *From Harmony, from Heav'nly Harmony: A Song for St Cecilia's Day, 1687*, ed. Bryan White, PSCS 3 (London: Stainer & Bell, 2010).
DraHar		Giovanni Battista Draghi, *Harpsichord Music*, ed. Robert Klakowich, Recent Researches in the Music of the Baroque Era 56 (Madison WI: A-R Editions, 1986).
DufPur		Maureen Duffy, *Henry Purcell* (London: Fourth Estate, 1994).
DufTem		Ross Duffin, *How Equal Temperament Ruined Harmony (and Why You Should Care)* (New York: Norton, 2007).
DunNew		Cheryll Duncan, 'New Purcell Documents from the Court of King's Bench', *RMARC* 47 (2016), 1–23.
DunSmi		Cheryll Duncan, 'New Light on "Father" Smith and the Organ of Christ Church, Dublin, *Journal for the Society for Musicology in Ireland* 10 (2014–15), 23–45.
DunSon		Cheryll Duncan, 'Henry Purcell and the Construction of Identity: Iconography, Heraldry and the *Sonnata's of III Parts* (1683)', *EM* 44 (2016), 271–88.
EM		*Early Music*.
EMP		*Early Music Performer*.
EMPR		*Early Music Performance and Research*.

EveDia	*The Diary of John Evelyn*, ed. E.S. De Beer, 6 vols. (Oxford: Clarendon Press, 1955).
FerPur	Howard Ferguson, 'Purcell's Harpsichord Music', *PRMA* 91 (1964–5), 1–9.
FinSon	Gottfried Finger, *Sonata in C for Oboe/Trumpet in C, Violin and Continuo*, ed. Peter Holman (London: Nova Music, 1979).
FisSco	Roger Fiske, *Scotland in Music, A European Enthusiasm* (Cambridge: Cambridge University Press, 1983).
ForAut	Nigel Fortune and Franklin B. Zimmerman, 'Purcell's Autographs', *HPEM*, 106–21.
ForCan	Robert Ford, 'Minor Canons at Canterbury Cathedral: The Gostlings and their Colleagues', Ph.D. diss. (University of California, Berkeley, 1984).
ForDom	Nigel Fortune, 'Two Studies of Purcell's Sacred Music: (b): The Domestic Sacred Music', *Essays on Opera and English Music in Honour of Sir Jack Westrup*, ed. F.W. Sternfeld, Nigel Fortune and Edward Olleson (Oxford: Blackwell, 1975), 62–78.
ForFil	Robert Ford, 'The Filmer Manuscripts: A Handlist', *Notes* 34 (1978), 814–25.
ForFun	Robert Ford, 'Purcell as his own Editor: The Funeral Sentences', *Journal of Musicological Research* 7 (1986), 47–67.
ForOsb	Robert Ford, 'Osborn MS 515, a Guardbook of Restoration Instrumental Music', *Fontes Artis Musicae* 30 (1983), 174–84.
ForSou	Nigel Fortune, 'A New Purcell Source', *Music Review* 25 (1964), 109–13.
FreSmi	Andrew Freeman, rev. John Rowntree, *Father Smith, otherwise Bernard Schmidt, being an Account of a Seventeenth-Century Organ Maker* (Oxford: Positif Press, 1977).
GilArn	Todd Gilman, *The Theatre Career of Thomas Arne* (Lanham MD: University of Delaware Press, 2014).
GilBet	Charles Gildon, *The Life of Mr. Thomas Betterton, the Late Eminent Tragedian* (London: Robert Gosling, 1710) <@>.
GilGar	Todd Gilman, 'David Garrick's Masque of King Arthur with Thomas Arne's Score (1770)', *Restoration* 34 (Spring–Fall 2010), 139–62.
GoeHar	Thérèse de Goede, 'The Harmonic Language of English "Continued Bass" in the Seventeenth Century, *MEBE*, 229–51.
GofGoh	Moira Goff, 'The Testament and last Will of Jerome Francis Gohory', *EM* 38 (2010), 537–42.
GreArt	M.J. Greenhalgh, 'Arthurian Legend?', *MT* 112 (1971), 1168–70.
GriMan	David Griffiths, *A Catalogue of the Music Manuscripts in York Minster Library* (York: York Minster Library, 1981).
GriMin	David Griffiths, 'Music in the Minster Close: Edward Finch, Valentine Nalson and William Knight in Early Eighteenth-Century

	York', *Music in the British Provinces, 1690–1914*, ed. Rachel Cowgill and Peter Holman (Aldershot: Ashgate, 2007), 45–59.
GroPur	'The Purcell Club', 'The Purcell Commemoration', 'The Purcell Society', *A Dictionary of Music and Musicians*, ed. George Grove, 4 vols. (London: Macmillan, 1879–93), iii. 52–3.
GSJ	*The Galpin Society Journal.*
GwyPur	Dominic Gwynn, 'The English Organ in Purcell's Lifetime', *PMHP*, 20–38.
GwyWes	Dominic Gwynn, 'Purcell's Organ at Westminster Abbey: A Note on the Cover Illustration', *EM* 23 (1995), 550.
HalPri	Monica Hall, '*Princess An's Lute Book* and Related English Sources of Music for the Five-Course Guitar', *The Consort* 66 (2010), 18–34.
HamDry	Roswell G. Ham, 'Dryden's Dedication for *The Music of the Prophetess*, 1691', *Proceedings of the Modern Language Association* 50 (1935), 1065–75.
HarArt	Ellen T. Harris, 'King Arthur's Voyage into the Eighteenth Century', *PurStu*, 257–89.
HarChi	Myles Hartley and Jonathan Wainwright, 'Bodleian Library, MSS Music School C.32–37: Musical Networks, Motet Texts and Royalist Resonances', *VdGSJ* 17b (2023), 6–28 <@>.
HarDel	Michael and Mollie Hardwick, *Alfred Deller: A Singularity of Voice* (London: Cassell, 1968).
HarDid	Ellen T. Harris, *Purcell's Dido and Aeneas* (New York: Oxford University Press, 2/2017).
HarPla	Douglas Ross Harvey, 'Henry Playford, a Bibliographical Survey', 3 vols., Ph.D. thesis (Victoria University, Wellington NZ, 1985) <@>.
HawHis	Sir John Hawkins, *A General History of the Science and Practice of Music*, 5 vols. (London: T. Payne, 1776); repr. in 2 vols. (London: Novello, 2/1853; repr. New York: Dover, 1963) <@>.
HayHau	Bruce Haynes, *The Eloquent Oboe: A History of the Hautboy from 1640 to 1760* (Oxford: Oxford University Press, 2001).
HayPit	Bruce Haynes, *A History of Performing Pitch: The Story of 'A'* (Lanham MD: Scarecrow Press, 2002).
HefAlt	Stephen Hefling, *Rhythmic Alteration in Seventeenth- and Eighteenth-Century Music: Notes Inégales and Overdotting* (New York: Schirmer, 1993).
HeiHay	Simon Heighes, *The Lives and Works of William and Philip Hayes* (New York: Garland, 1995).
HelPre	Wendy Heller, '"A Present for the Ladies": Ovid, Montaigne and the Redemption of Purcell's Dido', *M&L* 84 (2003), 189–208.
HerCat	Rebecca Herissone, *Musical Creativity in Restoration England. Appendix: Catalogue of Restoration Music Manuscripts* <@>.
HerCre	Rebecca Herissone, *Musical Creativity in Restoration England* (Cambridge: Cambridge University Press, 2013).

HerCro	Rebecca Herissone, '"Exactly engrav'd by Thomas Cross"? The Role of Single-Sheet prints in Preserving Performing Practices from the Restoration Stage', *Journal of Musicology* 37 (2020), 305–48.
HerFow	Rebecca Herissone, '"Fowle Originalls" and "Fayre Writeing": Reconsidering Purcell's Compositional Process', *Journal of Musicology* 23 (2006), 569–619.
HerHay	Rebecca Herissone, '"[T]ranscribed from the author[']s original manuscript": Philip Hayes and the Preservation of the Music of Henry Purcell', *MEBE*, 399–448.
HerHen	Rebecca Herissone, 'Daniel Henstridge and the Aural Transmission of Music in Restoration England', *Beyond Boundaries: Rethinking the Circulation of Music in Early Modern England*, ed. Linda Phyllis Austern, Candace Bailey and Amanda Eubanks Winkler (Bloomington IN: Indiana University Press, 2017), 165–84.
HerMag	Rebecca Herissone, 'The Origins and Contents of the Magdalene College Partbooks', *Royal Musical Association Research Chronicle* 29 (1996), 47–95.
HerOrg	Rebecca Herissone, *'To fill, forbear or adorne': The Organ Accompaniment of Restoration Sacred Music* (Aldershot: Royal Musical Association and Ashgate, 2006).
HerPin	Rebecca Herissone, 'Robert Pindar, Thomas Busby and the Mysterious Scoring of Purcell's "Come ye Sons of Art"', *M&L* 88 (2007), 1–48; repr. *HolBar*, 235–82.
HerPla	Rebecca Herissone, 'Playford, Purcell and the Functions of Music Publishing in Restoration England', *Journal of the American Musicological Society* 63 (2010), 243–90.
HerRec	Rebecca Herissone, 'Performance History and Reception', *ARCHP*, 303–51.
HerRev	Rebecca Herissone, 'Purcell's Revisions of his own Works', *PurStu*, 51–86.
HerScr	Rebecca Herissone, '"A complete and correct score"? Scribal Annotations and the Notion of Textual Fixity in Late Seventeenth-Century English Music Publications', *The Musical Quarterly* 101 (2018), 244–311.
HerThe	Rebecca Herissone, *Music Theory in Seventeenth-Century England* (Oxford: Oxford University Press, 2000).
HigRec	John J. Higney, 'Henry Purcell: A Reception/Dissemination Study, 1695–1771', Ph.D. thesis (University of Western Ontario, 2008).
HofGam	Bettina Hoffmann, *The Viola da Gamba*, trans. Paul Ferguson (Abingdon: Routledge, 2018).
HogCor	Christopher Hogwood, 'Creating the Corpus: The "Complete Keyboard Music" of Henry Purcell', *The Keyboard in Baroque Europe*, ed. Christopher Hogwood (Cambridge: Cambridge University Press, 2003), 67–89; repr. *HolBar*, 127–49.
HogMan	Christopher Hogwood, 'A New English Keyboard Manuscript of

		the Seventeenth Century: Autograph Music by Purcell and Draghi', *British Library Journal* 21 (1995), 161–75 <@>.
	HogTri	Christopher Hogwood, *The Trio Sonata* (London: BBC, 1979).
	HogTud	Christopher Hogwood, 'Thomas Tudway's History of Music', *Music in Eighteenth-Century England: Essays in Memory of Charles Cudworth*, ed. Christopher Hogwood and Richard Luckett (Cambridge: Cambridge University Press, 1983), 19–47.
	HolBar	*Purcell*, The Baroque Composers, ed. Peter Holman (Farnham: Ashgate, 2010).
	HolBat	Peter Holman, *Before the Baton: Musical Direction and Conducting in Stuart and Georgian Britain* (Woodbridge: Boydell Press, 2020).
	HolCla	Peter Holman, 'Inexperience or Boldness? The Orchestral Writing of Jeremiah Clarke's Early Concerted Works', *EMP* 48 (Spring 2021), 1–24.
	HolCom	Peter Holman, 'Compositional Choices in Henry Purcell's "Three Parts upon a Ground"', *EM* 29 (2001), 250–61; repr. *HolBar*, 340–51.
	HolCon	Peter Holman, 'Continuity and Change in English Bass Viol Music: The Case of Fitzwilliam Mu. MS 647', *VdGSJ* 1 (2007), 20–50 <@>.
	HolDra	Peter Holman, 'The Italian Connection: Giovanni Battista Draghi and Henry Purcell', *EMP* 22 (2008), 4–19; repr. *HolBar*, 43–58.
	HolEcc	Peter Holman, 'Six Generations of Music and Scandal: New Light on the Eccles Family of String Players', *VdGSJ* 15 (2021), 33–58 <@>.
	HolFid	Peter Holman, *Four and Twenty Fiddlers: The Violin at the English Court 1540–1690* (Oxford: Clarendon Press, 2/1995).
	HolFin	Peter Holman, 'The Sale Catalogue of Gottfried Finger's Music Library: New Light on London Concert Life in the 1690s', *RMARC* 43 (2010), 23–38.
	HolGib	Peter Holman, 'Henry Purcell and Joseph Gibbs: A New Source of the Three-Part Fantasias', *Chelys* 25 (1996–7), 97–100.
	HolHar	Peter Holman, 'The Harpsichord in Nineteenth-Century Britain', *Harpsichord & Fortepiano* 24, no. 2 (spring 2020), 4–14.
	HolLif	Peter Holman, *Life after Death: The Viola da Gamba in Britain from Purcell to Dolmetsch* (Woodbridge: Boydell Press, 2010).
	HolMan	Peter Holman, 'A Purcell Manuscript Lost and Found', *EM* 40 (2012), 469–87.
	HolNot	Peter Holman, 'Notation and Interpretation', *A Performer's Guide to Music of the Baroque Period*, ed. Anthony Burton (London: Associated Board, 2002), 21–48.
	HolOrg	Peter Holman, '"Evenly, Softly and Sweetly Acchording to All": The Organ Accompaniment of English Consort Music', *John Jenkins and his Time: Studies in English Consort Music*, ed. Andrew Ashbee and Peter Holman (Oxford: Clarendon Press, 1996), 353–82.

HolPar	Peter Holman, 'Original Sets of Parts for Restoration Concerted Music at Oxford', *PMHP*, 9–19, 265–71.
HolPor	C.J. Holmes, 'The Portraits of Arne and Purcell', *The Burlington Magazine* 27 (1915), 182–9.
HolPur	Peter Holman, *Henry Purcell* (Oxford: Oxford University Press, 1994).
HolRos	Peter Holman, 'Purcell and Roseingrave: a New Autograph', *PurStu*, 94–105.
HolThe	*Restoration Theatre Airs*, ed. Peter Holman and Andrew Woolley, MB 110 (London: Stainer & Bell, 2025).
HolTri	*Restoration Trio Sonatas*, ed. Peter Holman and John Cunningham, PSCS 4 (London: Stainer & Bell, 2012).
HolVio	*Restoration Music for Three Violins, Bass Viol and Continuo*, ed. Peter Holman and John Cunningham, MB 103 (London: Stainer & Bell, 2018).
HolWes	Peter Holman, 'Samuel Wesley as an Antiquarian Composer', *Music and the Wesleys*, ed. Nicholas Temperley and Stephen Banfield (Urbana IL: University of Illinois Press, 2010), 183–99.
HowArt	Alan Howard, *Compositional Artifice in the Music of Henry Purcell* (Cambridge: Cambridge University Press, 2019).
HowCre	Alan Howard, 'Understanding Creativity', *ARCHP*, 65–113.
HowMou	Alan Howard, 'Eroticized Mourning in Henry Purcell's Elegy for Mary II, "O dive custos"', *Eroticism in Early Modern Music*, ed. Bonnie J. Blackburn and Laurie Stras (Farnham: Ashgate, 2015), 261–98.
HowOde	Alan Howard (ed.), *Odes on the Death of Henry Purcell*, PSCS 5 (London: Stainer & Bell, 2013).
HowPoe	Alan Howard, 'Purcell and the Poetics of Artifice: Compositional Strategies in the Fantasias and Sonatas', Ph.D. thesis (King's College, London, 2006).
HowSin	Alan Howard, 'Composition as an Act of Performance: Artifice and Expression in Purcell's Sacred Partsong "Since God so tender a regard"', *JRMA* 132 (2007), 32–59.
HPEM	*Henry Purcell 1659–1695: Essays on his Music*, ed. Imogen Holst (London: Oxford University Press, 1959).
HSECEM	*A Handbook for Studies in Eighteenth-Century English Music*.
HumPol	Robert Hume, 'The Politics of Opera in Late Seventeenth-Century London', *Cambridge Opera Journal* 10 (1998), 15–48.
HumPub	Charles Humphries and William C. Smith, *Music Publishing in the British Isles, from the Beginning until the Nineteenth Century* (Oxford: Blackwell, 2/1970).
HunPat	David Hunter, 'Bridging the Gap: The Patrons-in-Common of Purcell and Handel', *EM* 37 (2009), 621–32.

HunPri		David Hunter, 'The Printing of Opera and Song Books in England, 1703–1726', *Notes* 46 (1989), 328–51.
JohAca		H. Diack Johnstone, 'The Academy of Ancient Music (1726–1802): Its History, Repertoire and Surviving Programmes', *RMARC* 51 (2020), 1–136.
JohOrn		H. Diack Johnstone, 'Ornamentation in the Keyboard Music of Henry Purcell and his Contemporaries', *PMHP*, 82–104.
JohSon		H. Diack Johnstone, 'Ayres and Arias: A hitherto Unknown Seventeenth-Century English Songbook', *Early Music History* 16 (1997), 167–201.
JonMat		Simon Jones, 'The "Stupendious" Nicola Matteis: An Exploration of his Life, his Works for the Violin and his Performing Style', 3 vols., Ph.D. thesis (University of York, 2003) <@>.
JonPub		Erik Reid Jones, 'The Victorian Revival of Purcell's Music: Publications and Publishers', *The Choral Journal* 36, no. 1 (August 1995), 19–23.
JonSon		Edward Huws Jones, *The Performance of English Song, 1610–1670* (New York: Garland Publishing, 1989).
JRMA		*Journal of the Royal Musical Association.*
KanCor		Min-Jung Kang, 'The Fashion for Corelli in England', *MEBE*, 91–107.
KanTri		Min-Jung Kang, 'The Trio Sonata in Restoration England (1660–1714)', Ph.D. thesis (University of Leeds, 2008) <@>.
KinGoo		A.H. King, 'Benjamin Goodison's Complete Edition of Purcell', *Monthly Musical Record* 81 (1951), 81–9.
KlaSco		Robert Klakowich, '"Scocca pur": Genesis of an English Ground', *JRMA* 116 (1991), 63–77.
KniBat		David Knight, 'The Battle of the Organs, the Smith Organ at the Temple and its Organist', *BIOS Journal* 21 (1997), 76–99.
KniHar		David Knight, 'Renatus Harris, Organ Builder', 2 vols., M.Mus. thesis (University of Reading, 1994).
KniWes		David Knight, 'The Organs of Westminster Abbey and their Music, 1240–1908', 2 vols., Ph.D. thesis (King's College, University of London, 2001) <@>.
KosHar		John Koster, 'History and Construction of the Harpsichord', *The Cambridge Companion to the Harpsichord*, ed. Mark Kroll (Cambridge: Cambridge University Press, 2019), 2–30.
KruPri		D.W. Krummel, *English Music Printing, 1553–1700* (London: Bibliographical Society, 1971).
LamBal		Roy Lamson jr, 'Henry Purcell's Dramatic Songs and the English Broadside Ballad', *Proceedings of the Modern Language Association* 53 (1938), 148–61.
LanHay		H.C. Robbins Landon, *Haydn: Chronicle and Works*, iii: *Haydn in England, 1791–1795* (London: Thames and Hudson, 1976).

LasBab	David Lasocki, 'Charles Babel's Manuscripts for the Recorder: Light on Repertoire and the Art of Preluding (c.1700)', *EMP* 38 (April 2016), 4–21.
LasHau	David Lasocki, 'The French Hautboy in London, 1673–1730', *EM* 16 (1988), 339–57.
LasRec	David Lasocki, 'Professional Recorder Playing in England 1500–1740', *EM* 10 (1982), 22–9, 183–91.
LauCam	Margaret Laurie, 'The "Cambury" Purcell Manuscript', *Irish Musical Studies* 5 (1996), 262–71.
LauCon	Margaret Laurie, 'Continuity and Tempo in Purcell's Vocal Works', *PurStu*, 192–206.
LauSon	Margaret Laurie, 'Purcell's Extended Solo Songs', *MT* 125 (1984), 19–25; repr. *HolBar*, 299–305.
LauTem	Margaret Laurie, 'Did Purcell Set *The Tempest*?', *PRMA* 90 (1963–4), 43–57.
LebAlb	Ester Lebedinski, '"Obtained by peculiar favour, & much difficulty": Vincenzo Albrici and the Function of Charles II's Italian Ensemble at the English Restoration Court', *JRMA* 143 (2018), 325–59.
LebRom	Ester Lebedinski, 'Roman Vocal Music in England, 1660–1719: Court, Connoisseurs and the Culture of Collecting', Ph.D. thesis (Royal Holloway, University of London, 2014) <@>.
LebTra	Ester Lebedinski, 'The Travels of a Tune: Purcell's "If love's a sweet passion" and the Cultural Translation of Seventeenth-Century English Music', *EM* 48 (2020), 75–89.
LedSty	David Ledbetter, 'Stylistic Change in English Lute and Keyboard Sources in the Time of Orlando Gibbons', *Aspects of Early English Keyboard Music before c.1630*, ed. David J. Smith (Abingdon: Routledge, 2019), 207–39.
LeeCat	Peter Leech, 'Music and Musicians in the Catholic Chapel of James II at Whitehall, 1686–1688', *EM* 39 (2011), 379–400.
LocDra	Matthew Locke, *Dramatic Music*, ed. Michael Tilmouth, *MB* 51 (London: Stainer & Bell, 1986).
LowSta	Kathryn Lowerre, *Music and Musicians on the London Stage, 1695–1705* (Farnham: Ashgate, 2009).
LS	*The London Stage 1660–1800*, ed. William Van Lennep et al., 5 parts (Carbondale IL: Southern Illinois University Press, 1960–8) <@>.
LSNV	*The London Stage 1660–1800, ii: 1700–1729, a New Version*, comp. Judith Milhous and Robert D. Hume, in: *Eighteenth Century Drama: Censorship, Society and the Stage* <https://www.eighteenthcenturydrama.amdigital.co.uk/>
LucExo	Richard Luckett, 'Exotick but Rational Entertainments: The English Dramatick Operas', *English Drama: Forms and Development*, ed. Marie Axton and Raymond Williams (Cambridge: Cambridge University Press, 1977), 123–41, 232–4.

LucPla	Richard Luckett, 'The Playfords and the Purcells', *Music in the Book Trade: From the Sixteenth to the Twentieth Century*, ed. Robin Myers, Michael Harris and Giles Mendelbrote (New Castle DE: Oak Knoll Press; London: The British Library, 2008), 45–67.
LucSha	Richard Luckett, '"Or rather our musical Shakespeare": Charles Burney's Purcell', *Music in Eighteenth-Century England: Essays in Memory of Charles Cudworth*, ed. Christopher Hogwood and Richard Luckett (Cambridge: Cambridge University Press, 1983), 59–77; repr. *HolBar*, 493–511.
MabIta	Margaret Mabbett, 'Italian Musicians in Restoration England (1660–90)', *M&L* 67 (1986), 237–47.
MacBes	Dolly MacKinnon, '"Poor Senseless Bess, Clothed in her Rags and Folly": Early Modern Women, Madness and Song in Seventeenth-Century England', *Parergon* 18 (2001), 119–51 <@>.
MacMus	Thomas Mace, *Musick's Monument* (London: Author, 1676) <@>.
MaiMor	Alana Mailes, 'Teaching in Exile: Cesare Morelli's Transcriptions in Pepys Library, MSS 2803–4, *EM* 45 (2017), 267–82.
M&L	*Music & Letters*.
ManNew	Sandra Mangsen, 'New Sources for Odes by Purcell and Handel from a Collection in London, Ontario', *M&L* 81 (2000), 13–40.
ManRev	Robert Manning, 'Revisions and Reworkings in Purcell's Anthems', *Soundings* 9 (1982), 29–37.
MarBer	Anne Martin, *Musician for a While: A Biography of Walter Bergmann* (Hebden Bridge: Peacock Press, 2002).
MarVir	Darryl Martin, 'The English Virginal', 2 vols., Ph.D. thesis (University of Edinburgh, 2003) <@>.
MB	*Musica Britannica*.
McGGro	Rosamond McGuinness, 'The Ground Bass in the English Court Ode', *M&L* 51 (1970), 118–40, 265–78.
McVCal	Simon McVeigh, *Calendar of London Concerts 1750–1800*, Goldsmiths, University of London <@>.
MEBE	*Musical Exchange Between Britain and Europe, 1500–1800: Essays in Honour of Peter Holman*, ed. John Cunningham and Bryan White (Woodbridge: Boydell Press, 2020).
MefTem	John Meffen, 'A Question of Temperament: Purcell and Croft', *MT* 119 (1978), 504–6.
MesAlb	Matteo Messori and Anna Katarzyna Zaręba, 'Vincenzo Albrici (1631–1687) und sein Bruder Bartolomeo: Neue biographische und musikalische Funde', *Schütz-Jahrbuch* 39 (2017), 54–70 <@>.
MLE	Music for London Entertainment, 1660–1800.
MolPur	Peter Mole, 'On the Trail of Purcell's Spinet', *EM* 36 (2008), 409–14.

MolSpi	Peter Mole, 'The English Spinet with particular reference to the Schools of Keene and Hitchcock', Ph.D. diss. (University of Edinburgh, 2009) <@>.
MorDar	Davitt Moroney and William Oxenbury, 'Robert Thurston Dart: Bibliography of Publications', *Source Materials and the Interpretation of Music: A Memorial Volume to Thurston Dart*, ed. Ian Bent (London: Stainer & Bell, 1981), 431–52.
MorLov	Thomas Morgan, *Suite: Love and Honour*, ed. Richard Platt, Musica da Camera 19 (London: Oxford University Press, 1974).
MorVoi	Timothy Morris, 'Voice Ranges, Voice Types and Pitch in Purcell's Concerted Works', *PMHP*, 130–42.
MPP	*Music Publishing and Printing*, ed. D.W. Krummel and Stanley Sadie, The New Grove Handbooks in Musicology (Basingstoke: Macmillan, 1990).
MT	*The Musical Times*.
MulDio	Julia and Frans Muller, 'Purcell's *Dioclesian* on the Dorset Garden Stage', *PMHP*, 232–42.
MulWor	Julia Muller, *Words and Music in Henry Purcell's First Semi-Opera, Dioclesian: An Approach to Early Music Through Early Theatre* (Lewiston NY; Lampeter: Mellen, 1990).
MunPla	Peter Alan Munsted, 'John Playford, Music Publisher: A Bibliographical Catalogue', Ph.D. diss. (University of Kentucky, 1983).
MurOde	Estelle Murphy, 'The Fashioning of a Nation: The Court Ode in the Late Stuart Period', 2 vols., Ph.D. thesis (National University of Ireland, Cork, 2012).
NieGui	Friederich Erhardt Niedt, *The Musical Guide*, trans. Pamela L. Poulin and Irmgard C. Taylor (Oxford: Clarendon Press, 1989).
NorCur	Roger North, *Cursory Notes of Musicke (c.1698–1703)*, ed. Mary Chan and Jamie C. Kassler (Kensington NSW: Unisearch, 1986).
NorMus	*Roger North on Music*, ed. John Wilson (London: Novello, 1959).
OllWes	Philip Olleson, *Samuel Wesley, the Man and his Music* (Woodbridge: Boydell Press, 2003).
OweObo	Samantha Owens, '"Seven young Men on Hautboys": The Oboe Band in England, *c.*1680–1740', *MEBE*, 282–93.
PagGui	Christopher Page, *The Guitar in Stuart England: A Social and Musical History* (Cambridge: Cambridge University Press, 2017).
PalNov	Fiona M. Palmer, *Vincent Novello (1781–1861): Music for the Masses* (Aldershot: Ashgate, 2006).
ParPer	Andrew Parrott, 'Performing Purcell', *PC*, 387–444.
PC	*The Purcell Companion*, ed. Michael Burden (London: Faber and Faber, 1995).
PepDia	*The Diary of Samuel Pepys*, ed. Robert Latham and William Matthews, 11 vols. (London: Bell & Hyman, 1970–83).

PerDar		Allen Percival, 'Robert Thurston Dart', *Source Materials and the Interpretation of Music: A Memorial Volume to Thurston Dart*, ed. Ian Bent (London: Stainer & Bell, 1981), 21–6.
PicHal		Oliver Pickering, 'Henry Hall of Hereford's Poetical Tributes to Henry Purcell', *The Library*, 6th series, 16 (1994), 18–29.
PicPos		Oliver Pickering, 'Henry Hall of Hereford and Henry Purcell A Postscript', *The Library*, 7th series, 2 (2002), 194–8.
PikRej		Lionel Pike, 'Purcell's "Rejoice in the Lord", all Ways', *M&L* 82 (2001), 391–420; repr. *HolBar*, 205–34.
PinArt		Andrew Pinnock, '*King Arthur* Expos'd: A Lesson in Anatomy', *PurStu*, 243–56.
PinDeu		Andrew Pinnock, '*Deus ex machina*: A Royal Witness to the Court Origin of Purcell's *Dido and Aeneas*', *EM* 40 (2012), 265–78.
PinDou		Andrew Pinnock, 'A Double Vision of Albion: Allegorical Re-alignments in the Dryden-Purcell Semi-Opera *King Arthur*', *Restoration* 34 (spring–fall 2010), 55–81.
PinInd		Andrew Pinnock, 'Play into Opera: Purcell's *The Indian Queen*', *EM* 18 (1990), 3–21.
PinMan		Andrew Pinnock and Bruce Wood, 'A Mangled Chime: The Accidental Death of the Opera Libretto in Civil War England', *EM* 36 (2008), 265–84.
PinNom		David Pinto, 'Purcell's In Nomines: A Tale of Two Manuscripts (Perhaps Three)', *Chelys* 25 (1996), 101–6.
PinPhe		Andrew Pinnock, 'The Purcell Phenomenon', *PC*, 3–17.
PinTru		Andrew Pinnock, 'A Wider Role for the Flat Trumpet', *GSJ* 42 (1989), 105–12.
PinWhi		Andrew Pinnock, 'Which Genial Day? More on the Court Origin of Purcell's *Dido and Aeneas*', *EM* 43 (2015), 199–212.
PlaDan		*The Complete Country Dance Tunes from Playford's Dancing Master (1651–c.1728)*, ed. Jeremy Barlow (London: Faber Music, 1985).
PlaInt		John Playford, *An Introduction to the Skill of Musick ... Corrected and Amended by Mr. Henry Purcell* (London: Henry Playford, 12/1694) <@>.
PMHP		*Performing the Music of Henry Purcell*, ed. Michael Burden (Oxford: Clarendon Press, 1996).
PooPor		Rachael Poole, *Catalogue of Portraits in the Possession of the University, Colleges, City and County of Oxford*, 2 vols., i: *The Portraits in the University Collections and in the Town and County Halls* (Oxford: Clarendon Press, 1912).
PorCha		Stephen Porter, 'Henry Purcell and the Charterhouse: Composer in Residence', *MT* 139 (1998), 14–17.
PriAut		Curtis Price, 'Newly Discovered Autograph Keyboard Music of Purcell and Draghi', *JRMA* 120 (1995), 77–111; repr. *HolBar*, 169–203.

PriDon	Curtis Price, intro. to *Don Quixote: The Music in the Three Plays of Thomas D'Urfey*, MLE, series A, vol. 2 (Tunbridge Wells: Richard Macnutt, 1984).
PriFid	Curtis Price, 'Restoration Stage Fiddlers and their Music', *EM* 7 (1979), 315–22.
PriIns	Curtis Price, intro. to *Instrumental Music for London Theatres, 1690–1699: Royal College of Music, London, MS 1172*, MLE, series A, vol. 3 (Withyham: Richard Macnutt, 1987).
PriIsl	Curtis Price and Robert D. Hume, intro. to *The Island Princess, British Library, Add. MS 15318, a Semi-Opera*, MLE, series C, vol. 2 (Tunbridge Wells: Richard Macnutt, 1985).
PriPur	Curtis Price, *Henry Purcell and the London Stage* (Cambridge: Cambridge University Press, 1984).
PriThe	Curtis Price, *Music in the Restoration Theatre* ([Ann Arbor MI]: UMI Research Press, 1979).
PRMA	*Proceedings of the Royal Musical Association.*
PS	*The Works of Henry Purcell*, rev. 2nd edition (London and Sevenoaks: Novello; London: Stainer & Bell).
PSCS	Purcell Society Edition Companion Series (London: Stainer & Bell).
PurCat	Henry Purcell, *Come Let us Drink: Catches Compleat, Pleasant and Diversive*, ed. Michael Nyman (Great Yarmouth: Galliard, 1972).
PurCom	'The Purcell Bi-Centenary Commemoration', *MT* 36 (1895), 811–13.
PurCon	*Eight Concerts of Henry Purcell's Music, Commemorative Book of Programmes, Notes and Texts*, ed. Watkins Shaw ([London]: Arts Council, 1951).
PurDid	Henry Purcell, *Dido and Aeneas*, ed. Robert Shay (Kassel: Bärenreiter, 2023).
PurExh	'The Purcell Exhibits at the British Museum', *MT* 36 (1895), 797–9.
PurGla	Henry Purcell, *I was glad*, ed. Bruce Wood (Borough Green: Novello, 1977).
PurGre	Henry Purcell, *The Gresham Autograph, Facsimile*, intro. Margaret Laurie and Robert Thompson (London: Novello, 1995).
PurGro	Henry Purcell, *Fantasia: Three Parts upon a Ground*, ed. Denis Stevens and Thurston Dart (London: Hinrichsen, 1953).
PurHan	*Henry Purcell 1659(?)–1695, George Frideric Handel, 1685–1759, Catalogue of a Commemorative Exhibition, May–August 1959* (London: British Museum, 1959).
PurJus	Henry Purcell, *Fantasien für Streichinstrumente*, ed. Herbert Just, 2 vols. (Hanover: Nagel, 1930, 1935).
PurMar	Henry Purcell, *March and Canzona*, ed. Thurston Dart (London: Oxford University Press, 1958).
PurMis	Henry Purcell, *Miscellaneous Keyboard Pieces*, ed. Howard Ferguson (London: Stainer & Bell: 1964).

PurOrg		Henry Purcell, *Organ Works*, ed. Hugh McLean (London: Novello, 2/1967).
PurSon		Henry Purcell, *Ten Sonatas in Four Parts*, ed. Christopher Hogwood, 2 vols. (London: Eulenburg, 1978).
PurStu		*Purcell Studies*, ed. Curtis Price (Cambridge: Cambridge University Press, 1995).
PurSui		Henry Purcell, *Eight Suites*, ed. Howard Ferguson (London: Stainer & Bell, 1964).
PurTwe		Henry Purcell, *Twenty Keyboard Pieces (and one by Orlando Gibbons) from Purcell's Manuscript in the British Library*, ed. Davitt Moroney ([London]: Associated Board, 1999).
PurWar		Henry Purcell, *Three-, Four- and Five-Part Fantasias for Strings*, ed. Peter Warlock and André Mangeot (London: J. Curwen, 1927).
RadGen		Mark A. Radice, 'Henry Purcell's Contributions to *The Gentleman's Journal*', *Bach* 9, no. 4 (October 1978), 25–30; 10, no. 1 (January 1979), 26–31.
RanCor		Matthias Range, *Music and Ceremonial at British Coronations from James I to Elizabeth II* (Cambridge: Cambridge University Press, 2012).
RanGla		Matthias Range, 'The 1685 Coronation Anthem "I was glad"', *EM* 36 (2008), 397–408.
RanPig		Matthias Range, 'Francis Pigott's "I was glad" and its Performance at Three Coronations', *HSECEM* 19 (2008), 47–57.
RasRog		Rudolf Rasch, *The Music Publishing House of Estienne Roger and Michel-Charles Le Cène*, part 2: *Catalogues*, Utrecht University <@>.
RawFin		Robert G. Rawson, 'From Olomouc to London: The Early Music of Gottfried Finger (c.1655–1730)', Ph.D. diss. (Royal Holloway, University of London, 2002) <@>.
RayGib		Clare G. Rayner and Sheila Finch Rayner, 'Christopher Gibbons: "That Famous Musitian"', *Musica Disciplina* 24 (1970), 151–71.
RECM		*Records of English Court Music*, ed. Andrew Ashbee, 9 vols. (Snodland and Aldershot: Author and Scolar Press, 1986–96).
RimBon		Edward F. Rimbault, 'An Historical Sketch of Early English Dramatic Music', in Henry Purcell, *Bonduca, a Tragedy*, Musical Antiquarian Society (London: Chappell, 1842) <@>.
RMARC		*Royal Musical Association Research Chronicle*.
RobBow		Matthew A. Roberson, 'Of Priests, Fiends, Fops and Fools: John Bowman's Song Performances on the London Stage, 1677–1701', Ph.D. diss. (Florida State University, 2006).
RobCat		Brian Robins, *Catch and Glee Culture in Eighteenth-Century England* (Woodbridge: Boydell Press, 2006).
RobLey		John H. Robinson, 'John Leyden's Lyra Viol Manuscript in Newcastle University Library and George Farquhar Graham's Copy in the National Library of Scotland', *VdGSJ* 2, part 1 (2008), 17–57 <@>.

RobMad Thirteen Mad Songs by Purcell and his Contemporaries, ed. Timothy Roberts, 2 vols. (Teddington: Fretwork, 1999).

RogClo Malcolm Rogers, 'John and John Baptist Closterman: A Catalogue of their Works', *The Volume of the Walpole Society* 49 (1983), 224–79.

RohPoe Katherine T. Rohrer, 'Poetic Metre, Musical Metre and the Dance in Purcell's Songs', *PurStu*, 207–42.

RosPer Stephen Rose, 'Performance Practices', *ARCHP*, 115–64.

RosTet Ellen Rosand, 'The Descending Tetrachord: An Emblem of Lament', *The Musical Quarterly* 65 (1979), 346–59.

RycTru David Rycroft, 'Flat Trumpets Facts and Figures', *GSJ* 42 (1989), 134–42.

RylTem George Rylands and Anthony Lewis, '*The Tempest, or The Enchanted Island*', *MT* 100 (1959), 320–2.

SanCor Francis Sandford, *The History of the Coronation of ... James II ... and ... Queen Mary* (London: Thomas Newcomb, 1687) <@>.

SavFai Roger Savage, 'The Shakespeare-Purcell *Fairy Queen*: A Defence and a Recommendation', *EM* 1 (1973), 200–21; repr. *HolBar*, 435–54.

SavGen Roger Savage, 'Calling-Up Genius: Purcell, Roger North and Charlotte Butler', *PMHP*, 212–31.

SavScu Roger Savage, 'Purcell's "Scurvy" Poets', *Music in the London Theatre from Purcell to Handel*, ed. Colin Timms and Bruce Wood (Cambridge: Cambridge University Press, 2017), 7–24.

SawRic Paul Sawyer, *Christopher Rich of Drury Lane: The Biography of the Theatre Manager* (Lanham MD: University Press of America, 1986).

SawTre Lionel Sawkins, '*Trembleurs* and Cold People: How Should They Shiver?', *PMHP*, 243–64.

SayLut Lynda Sayce, 'Continuo Lutes in Seventeenth- and Eighteenth-Century England', *EM* 23 (1995), 666–84.

SchAyr Alon Schab, 'Distress'd Sources? A Critical Consideration of the Authority of Purcell's *Ayres for the Theatre*', *EM* 37 (2009), 633–45.

SchCha Alon Schab, 'On the Ground and Off: A Comparative Study of Two Purcell Chaconnes', *MT* 151 (2010), 47–57.

SchCon Alon Schab, 'Compositional Technique in Henry Purcell's Consort Music', 2 vols. Ph.D. thesis (Trinity College, Dublin, 2011) <@>.

SchDio Alon Schab, 'Revisiting the Known and Unknown Misprints in Purcell's *Dioclesian*', *M&L* 91 (2010), 343–56.

SchGro Stephan Schönlau, 'Creative Approaches to Ground-Bass Composition in England, c.1675–c.1705', Ph.D. thesis (University of Manchester, 2019) <@>.

SchLul Stephan Schönlau, 'Emulating Lully? Generic Features and Personal Traits in the Passacaglia from Henry Purcell's *King Arthur* (1691), *Rivisti di Analisi e Teoria Musicale* 20, nos. 1–2 (2014), 119–46 <@>.

SchSon	Alon Schab, *The Sonatas of Henry Purcell: Rhetoric and Reversal* (Rochester NY: University of Rochester Press, 2018).
ScoCon	Hugh Arthur Scott, 'London's First Concert Room', *M&L* 18 (1937), 379–90.
SemDan	Richard Semmens, 'Dancing and Dance Music in Purcell's Operas', *PMHP*, 180–96, 282–5.
SemFur	Richard Semmens, '"La Furstemberg" and "St Martin's Lane": Purcell's French Odyssey', *M&L* 78 (1997), 337–48.
ShaAnc	Robert Shay, 'Henry Purcell and "Ancient Music" in Restoration England', Ph.D. diss. (University of North Carolina at Chapel Hill, 1991).
ShaArt	Robert Shay, 'Dryden and Purcell's *King Arthur*: Legend and Politics on the Restoration Stage', *King Arthur in Music*, ed. Richard Barber (Cambridge: D.S. Brewer, 2002), 9–22.
ShaBas	Robert Shay, 'Bass Parts to an Unknown Purcell Suite at Yale', *Notes*, 2nd series 57 (2001), 819–33.
ShaBin	Watkins Shaw, *The Bing-Gostling Part-Books at York Minster: A Catalogue with Introduction* (Croydon: Church Music Society for The Royal School of Church Music, 1986).
ShaCol	Robert Shay, 'Purcell as Collector of "Ancient" Music: Fitzwilliam MS 88', *PurStu*, 35–50.
ShaFun	Robert Shay, 'Purcell's Revisions to the Funeral Sentences Revisited', *EM* 26 (1998), 457–67.
ShaMan	Robert Shay and Robert Thompson, *Purcell Manuscripts: The Principal Musical Sources* (Cambridge: Cambridge University Press, 2000).
ShaMus	*Shaw's Music: The Complete Musical Criticism of Bernard Shaw*, ed. Dan H. Laurence, 3 vols. (London: Bodley Head, 1981).
ShaPor	William A. Shaw, 'Three Unpublished Portraits of Henry Purcell', *MT* 61 (1920), 588–90.
ShaSuc	Watkins Shaw, *The Succession of Organists of the Chapel Royal and the Cathedrals of England and Wales from c.1538* (Oxford: Clarendon Press, 1991).
SilFre	Alexander Silbiger, 'On Frescobaldi's Recreation of the Chaconne and Passacaglia', *The Keyboard in Baroque Europe*, ed. Christopher Hogwood (Cambridge: Cambridge University Press, 2003), 3–18 <@>.
SilPas	Alexander Silbiger, 'Passacaglia and Ciaccona: Genre Pairing and Ambiguity from Frescobaldi to Couperin', *Journal of Seventeenth-Century Music* 2 (1996), no. 1 <@>.
SimBal	Claude M. Simpson, *The British Broadside Ballad and its Music* (Rutgers NJ: Rutgers University Press, 1966).
SimRec	Adrienne Simpson, 'The Orchestral Recorder', *The Cambridge*

Companion to the Recorder, ed. John Mansfield Thomson and Anthony Rowland Jones (Cambridge, 1995), 91–106.

SmaEnd   Basil Smallman, 'Endor Revisited: English Biblical Dialogues of the Seventeenth Century', *M&L* 46 (1965), 137–45.

SmiPer   Fiona Eila Joyce Smith, 'Original Performing Material for Concerted Music in England, c.1660–1800', Ph.D. thesis (University of Leeds, 2014) <@>.

SmiTru   Don L. Smithers, *The Music and History of the Baroque Trumpet before 1721* (Carbondale IL: Southern Illinois University Press, 2/1988).

SmiSed   Hannah Smith, 'Court Culture and Godly Monarchy: Henry Purcell and Charles Sedley's 1692 Birthday Ode for Mary II', *Politics, Religion and Ideas in Seventeenth- and Eighteenth-Century Britain: Essays in Honour of Mark Goldie*, ed. Justin Champion, John Coffey, Tim Harris and John Marshall (Woodbridge: Boydell Press, 2019), 219–38.

SmiWal   William C. Smith, *A Bibliography of the Musical Works Published by John Walsh during the Years 1695–1720* (London: Bibliographical Society, 2/1968).

SnoPor   Janet Snowman, 'A Portrait of Henry Purcell', *PurStu*, 290–5.

SpeChi   Robert Spencer, 'Chitarrone, Theorbo and Archlute', *EM* 4 (1976), 407–23.

SpiCat   Ian Spink, *Restoration Cathedral Music 1660–1714* (Oxford: Clarendon Press, 1995).

SpiLib   Ian Spink, 'Purcell's Music for *The Libertine*', *M&L* 81 (2000), 520–31.

SpiOde   Ian Spink, 'Purcell's Odes: Propaganda and Panegyric', *PurStu*, 106–71.

SpiPau   Ian Spink, 'Music, 1660–1800', *St Paul's: The Cathedral Church of London 1604–2004*, ed. Derek Keene, Arthur Burns and Andrew Saint (New Haven CT and London: Yale University Press, 2004), 392–8.

SpiSoc   Ian Spink, 'The Old Jewry "Musick-Society"': A Seventeenth-Century Catch Club', *Musicology* 2 (1965–7), 35–41.

SpiSon   Ian Spink, *English Song, Dowland to Purcell* (London: Batsford, 2/1986).

SprLut   Matthew Spring, *The Lute in Britain: A History of the Instrument and its Music* (Oxford: Oxford University Press, 2001).

SquFai   William Barclay Squire, 'Purcell's *Fairy Queen*', *MT* 61 (1920), 25–9.

SquThe   William Barclay Squire, 'Purcell as Theorist', *Sammelbände der Internationalen Musikgesellschaft* 6 (1905), 521–67.

SteDru   Crispian Steele-Perkins, 'Dart's Dated Drums Dropped', *Historic Brass Society Journal* 6 (1994), 338–42 <@>.

SteKey   Rita Steblin, *A History of Key Characteristics in the Eighteenth and*

		Early Nineteenth Centuries (Rochester NY: University of Rochester Press, 3/1996).
	SteTru	Crispian Steele-Perkins, 'Practical Observations on Natural, Slide and Flat Trumpets', *GSJ* 42 (1989), 122–7.
	StrDic	Graham Strahle, *An Early Music Dictionary: Musical Terms from British Sources, 1500–1700* (Cambridge: Cambridge University Press, 1995).
	StuGib	Paul Michael Stubbings, '"This day did the Organs begin to play at White-hall before the King": The Work and Influence of Christopher Gibbons (1615–76), Ph.D. thesis (Canterbury: Christ Church University, 2022) <@>.
	TalFug	Michael Talbot, *Vivaldi and Fugue* (Florence: Olschki, 2009).
	TalPin	Michael Talbot, 'Robert Pindar', *M&L* 95 (2014), 148–9.
	TayCla	Thomas F. Taylor, *Thematic Catalog of the Works of Jeremiah Clarke* (Detroit: Information Coordinators, 1977).
	TemPar	Nicholas Temperley, *The Music of the English Parish Church*, 2 vols. (Cambridge: Cambridge University Press, 1979).
	TemPla	Nicholas Temperley, 'John Playford and the Metrical Psalms', *Journal of the American Musicological Society* 25 (1972), 331–78.
	ThoCha	Robert Thompson, 'Travelling Incognito: The Chaconne from *Dioclesian*', *VdGSJ* 18b (2024), 75–81 <@>.
	ThoDan	Jennifer Thorp, '"Borrowed Grandeur and Affected Grace": Perceptions of the Dancing Master in Early Eighteenth-Century England', *Music in Art* 36, no. 1/2 (2011), 9–27.
	ThoFan	Robert Thompson, 'Revealing Errors: Purcell's Fantasia Sources Revisited', *VdGSJ* 18a (2024), 152–62 <@>.
	ThoGlo	Robert Thompson, *The Glory of the Temple and the Stage: Henry Purcell 1659–1695* (London: British Library, 1995).
	ThoHow	Robert Thompson, '"A Particular Friendship": Bell Barr, Annabella Howard and Sarah Churchill', *EM* 43 (2015), 213–23.
	ThoIsa	Jennifer Thorp, *The Gentleman Dancing-Master: Mr Isaac and the English Royal Court from Charles II to Queen Anne* (Clemson SC: Clemson University Press, 2024).
	ThoJen	Robert Thompson, 'Some Late Sources of Music by John Jenkins', *John Jenkins and his Time: Studies in English Consort Music*, ed. Andrew Ashbee and Peter Holman (Oxford: Clarendon Press: 1996), 271–307.
	ThoMan	Robert Thompson, 'Manuscript Music in Purcell's London', *EM* 23 (1995), 605–18; repr. *HolBar*, 113–25.
	ThoOpe	Jennifer Thorp, 'Dance in Opera in London, 1673–1685', *Dance Research* 33 (winter 2015), 93–123.
	ThoPla	Robert Thompson, 'The Elusive Identity of John Playford', *MEBE*, 344–56.

ThoPri	Jennifer Thorp, 'Dance in Late Seventeenth-Century London: Priestly Muddles', *EM* 26 (1998), 198–210.
ThoSou	Robert Thompson, 'Sources and Transmission', *ARCHP*, 13–63.
ThoWit	Robert Thompson, '"Francis Withie of Oxon" and his Commonplace Book, Christ Church, Oxford, MS 337', *Chelys* 20 (1991), 3–27 <@>.
ThuWhi	Simon Thurley, *Whitehall Palace: The Official Illustrated History* (London: Merrell, 2008).
TilCha	Michael Tilmouth, 'Chamber Music in England, 1675–1720', Ph.D. diss. (University. of Cambridge, 1960).
TilTec	Michael Tilmouth, 'The Technique and Forms of Purcell's Sonatas', *M&L* 40 (1959), 109–21; repr. *HolBar*, 285–97.
TipBlu	Michael Tippett, *Those Twentieth-Century Blues: An Autobiography* (London: Hutchinson, 1991; repr. Pimlico, 1994).
TipCon	Michael Tippett, 'Our Sense of Continuity in English Drama and Music', *HPEM*, 42–51.
TipMus	Michael Tippett, *Tippett on Music*, ed. Meirion Bowen (Oxford: Clarendon Press, 1995).
TupEig	Sandra Tuppen, 'Purcell in the Eighteenth Century: Music for the "Quality, Gentry and others"', *EM* 43 (2015), 233–45.
TupTri	Sandra Tuppen, '"Triumph, victorious Love": *Le Triomphe de l'Amour* (1681) and English Dramatic Opera', *EM* 51 (2023), 179–202.
TylGui	James Tyler and Paul Sparks, *The Guitar and its Music, from the Renaissance to the Classical Era* (Oxford: Oxford University Press, 2002).
UnwTal	Robert Unwin, 'An English Writer on Music: James Talbot, 1664–1708', *GSJ* 40 (1987), 53–72.
VanBri	Martha Vandrei, '"Britons, Strike Home": Politics, Patriotism and Popular Song in British Culture, c.1695–1900', *Historical Research* 87, no. 238 (November 2014), 579–702 <@>.
VanChu	Eric Van Tassel, 'Music for the Church', *PC*, 101–99.
VdGSJ	*The Viola da Gamba Society Journal* <@>.
WaiPat	Jonathan Wainwright, *Musical Patronage in Seventeenth-Century England: Christopher, First Baron Hatton 1605–1670* (Aldershot: Scolar Press, 1997).
WalAct	Andrew R. Walkling, 'The Masque of Actaeon and the Antimasque of Mercury: Dance, Dramatic Structure and Tragic Exposition in *Dido and Aeneas*', *Journal of the American Musicological Society* 63 (2010), 191–242.
WalAll	Andrew R. Walkling, 'Performance and Political Allegory in Restoration England: What to Interpret and When', *PMHP*, 163–79
WalDra	Andrew R. Walkling, *English Dramatick Opera, 1661–1706* (Abingdon: Routledge, 2019).

WalGra		Andrew R. Walkling, 'The Ups and Downs of Louis Grabu', *RMARC* 48 (2017), 1–64.
WalMas		Andrew R. Walkling, *Masque and Opera in England, 1656–1688* (Abingdon: Routledge, 2017).
WalPol		Andrew R. Walkling, 'Politics, Occasions and Texts', *ARCHP*, 201–67.
WalSon		Andrew R. Walkling, 'Unique Songsheet Collection at the Clark Sheds New Light on Henry Purcell and his Contemporaries', *The Center & Clark Newsletter* (fall 2012), 8–10 <@>.
WeaDan		John Weaver, *An Essay towards a History of Dancing* (London: Jacob Tonson, 1712) <@>.
WebCla		William Weber, *The Rise of Musical Classics in Eighteenth-Century England: A Study in Canon, Ritual and Ideology* (Oxford: Clarendon Press, 1992).
WebTru		John Webb, 'The Flat Trumpet in Perspective', *GSJ* 46 (1993), 154–60.
WelSui		John Weldon, *Suite in D minor*, ed. Peter Holman (London: Nova Music, 1981).
WesPur		J.A. Westrup, *Purcell*, The Master Musicians (London: J.M. Dent, 1937); repr. with intro. by Curtis Price (Oxford: Oxford University Press, 1995).
WhiAle		Bryan White, 'Letter from Aleppo: Dating the Chelsea School Performance of *Dido and Aeneas*', *EM* 37 (2009), 417–28; repr. *HolBar*, 99–110.
WhiCec		Bryan White, *Music for St Cecilia's Day from Purcell to Handel* (Woodbridge: Boydell Press, 2019).
WhiCla		Bryan White and Andrew Woolley, 'Jeremiah Clarke (c.1674–1707): A Tercentenary Tribute', *EMP* 21 (November 2007), 25–36.
WhiFer		Bryan White, '"A Pretty Knot of Music Friends": The Ferrar Brothers and a Stamford Music Club in the 1690s', *Music in the British Provinces, 1690–1914*, ed. Rachel Cowgill and Peter Holman (Aldershot: Ashgate, 2007), 9–44.
WhiGra		Bryan White, 'Grabu's *Albion and Albanius* and the Operas of Lully: "… acquainted with all the performances of the French opera's"', *EM* 30 (2002), 410–27.
WhiLos		Bryan White, 'Lost in Translation? Louis Grabu and John Dryden's *Albion and Albanius*', *MEBE*, 187–206.
WhiMer		Bryan White, 'Music and Merchants in Restoration London', *Beyond Boundaries: Rethinking Music Circulation in Early Modern England*, ed. Linda Phyllis Austern, Candace Bailey and Amanda Eubanks Winkler (Bloomington and Indianapolis: Indiana University Press, 2017), 150–64.
WhiNoi		Bryan White, 'Music for a "brave livlylike boy": The Duke of Gloucester, Purcell and "The noise of foreign wars"', *MT* 148 (2007), 75–83.

WhiPol	Bryan White, 'Anthems and Politics in the Restoration Chapel Royal', *M&L* 102 (2021), 442–81.
WhiPre	Bryan White. 'Previously Unknown Purcell Autograph at Auction', *EMP* 12 (August 2003), 30.
WhiShe	Bryan White, '"Brothers of the String": Henry Purcell and the Letter-books of Rowland Sherman', *M&L* 92 (2011), 519–81.
WhiStu	Bryan White, '"Studying a Little of the French Air": Louis Grabu's *Albion and Albanius* and the Dramatic Operas of Henry Purcell', *Art and Ideology in European Opera: Essays in Honour of Julian Rushton*, ed. Clive Brown, David Cooper and Rachel Cowgill (Woodbridge: Boydell Press, 2010), 12–39.
WilCha	Ruth M. Wilson, *Anglican Chant and Chanting in England, Scotland and America, 1660–1820* (Oxford: Clarendon Press, 1996).
WinAnn	James Anderson Winn, *Queen Anne, Patroness of Arts* (Oxford: Oxford University Press, 2014).
WinArt	James Anderson Winn, '"Confronting Art with Art": The Dryden-Purcell Collaboration in *King Arthur*', *Restoration* 34 (spring–fall 2010), 33–53.
WinHow	Amanda Eubanks Winkler, *O Let Us Howle Some Heavy Note: Music for Witches, the Melancholic and the Mad on the Seventeenth-Century English Stage* (Bloomington IN: Indiana University Press, 2006).
WinRed	Lewis Winstock, *Songs and Music of the Redcoats* (London: Leo Cooper, 1970).
WinSoc	Amanda Eubanks Winkler, 'Society and Disorder', *ARCHP*, 269–302.
WolOve	Silas Wollston, 'New Light on Purcell's Early Overtures', *EM* 37 (2009), 647–55.
WolVio	Silas Wollston, 'The Instrumentation of English Violin Band Music, 1660–1685', Ph.D. thesis (Open University, 2010).
WolOxf	Susan Wollenberg, *Music at Oxford in the Eighteenth and Nineteenth Centuries* (Oxford: Oxford University Press, 2001).
WooAut	Bruce Wood, 'A Newly Identified Purcell Autograph', *M&L* 59 (1978), 329–32.
WooBab	Andrew Woolley, 'Charles Babel's "Concerts a deux" (1702)', *Les copistes en musique en France aux xviie et xviiie siècles: travaux, ateliers et institutions*, ed. Pascal Denécheau and Laurent Guillo (Turnhout: Brepols, forthcoming).
WooCor	Bruce Wood, 'Two Purcell Discoveries 2: A Coronation Anthem Lost and Found', *MT* 118 (1977), 466–8.
WooDid	Bruce Wood and Andrew Pinnock, '"Unscarr'd by turning times"?: The Dating of Purcell's *Dido and Aeneas*', *EM* 20 (1992), 372–90.
WooEqu	Bruce Wood, 'Only Purcell e're shall Equal Blow', *PurStu*, 106–44; repr. *HolBar*, 3–41.

WooFai	Bruce Wood and Andrew Pinnock, '*The Fairy Queen*: A Fresh Look at the Issues', *EM* 21 (1993), 44–62; repr. *HolBar*, 151–67.
WooFun	Bruce Wood, 'The First Performance of Purcell's Funeral Music for Queen Mary', *PMHP*, 61–81.
WooKey	Andrew Woolley, 'English Keyboard Sources and their Contexts, c.1660–1720', Ph.D. thesis (University of Leeds, 2008) <@>.
WooOde	Bruce Wood, 'Purcell's Odes: A Reappraisal', *PC*, 200–53.
WooPer	*English Keyboard Music, 1650–1695: Perspectives on Purcell*, ed. Andrew Woolley, *PSCS* 6 (London: Stainer & Bell, 2018).
WooPoe	Bruce Wood, 'Purcell and his Poets', *EM* 43 (2015), 225–31.
WooPur	Bruce Wood, *Purcell: An Extraordinary Life* (London: Associated Board, 2009).
WooSco	Andrew Woolley, 'Purcell and the Reception of Lully's "Scocca pur" (LWV 76/3) in England', *JRMA* 138 (2013), 229–73.
ZimCat	Franklin B. Zimmerman, *Henry Purcell, 1659–1695: An Analytical Catalogue of his Music* (London: Macmillan, 1963).
ZimGos	Franklin B. Zimmerman, 'Anthems of Purcell and his Contemporaries in a newly Discovered "Gostling Manuscript"', *Acta musicologica* 41 (1969), 55–70.
ZimHan	Franklin B. Zimmerman, 'Purcell's Handwriting', *HPEM*, 103–5.
ZimPas	Franklin B. Zimmerman, 'Purcellian Passages in the Compositions of G.F. Handel', *Music in Eighteenth-Century England: Essays in Memory of Charles Cudworth*, ed. Christopher Hogwood and Richard Luckett (Cambridge: Cambridge University Press, 1983), 49–58.
ZimMon	Franklin B. Zimmerman, 'Purcell and Monteverdi', *MT* 99 (1958), 368–9.
ZimPoe	Franklin B. Zimmerman, 'Poets in Praise of Purcell', *MT* 100 (1959), 526–8.
ZimPur	Franklin B. Zimmerman, *Henry Purcell, 1659–1695, his Life and Times* (London: Macmillan, 1967, Philadelphia PA: University of Philadelphia Press, 2/1983).
ZimSer	Franklin B. Zimmerman, 'Purcell's "Service Anthem" "O God, thou art my God" and the B-Flat Major Service', *The Musical Quarterly* 50 (1964), 207–14.

Printed in the United States
by Baker & Taylor Publisher Services